CHRISTIANITY IN LATIN AMERICA

From the arrival of the conquistadores in the fifteenth century to the spread of the Pentecostal movement today, Christianity has molded, coerced, refashioned, and enriched Latin America. Likewise, Christianity has been changed, challenged, and renewed as it crossed the Atlantic. These changes now affect its practice and under-standing, not only in South and Central America and the Caribbean, but also – through immigration and global communication – around the world. Focusing on this mutually constitutive relationship, *Christianity in Latin America* presents the important encounters between people, ideas, and events of this large, hetero-geneous subject. In doing so, it takes readers on a fascinating journey of explorers, missionaries, farmers, mystics, charlatans, evangelists, dictators, and martyrs. This book offers an accessible and engaging review of the history of Christianity in Latin America with a widely ecumenical focus to foster understanding of the various forces shaping both Christianity and the region.

Ondina E. González is an independent scholar who has been a visiting professor at Agnes Scott College and Emory University. She is co-editor of *Raising an Empire: Children in Early Modern Iberia and Colonial Latin America.*

Justo L. González has taught historical theology at various institutions, including the Evangelical Seminary of Puerto Rico, Candler School of Theology at Emory University, and Columbia Theological Seminary. For the past thirty years, he has developed programs for the theological education of Hispanics. His numerous books on church history have been translated into several languages and are widely used throughout the world.

Christianity in Latin America

A History

ONDINA E. GONZÁLEZ

JUSTO L. GONZÁLEZ

CAMBRIDGE
UNIVERSITY PRESS

CAMBRIDGE UNIVERSITY PRESS

Cambridge, New York, Melbourne, Madrid, Cape Town, Singapore, São Paulo, Delhi

Cambridge University Press
32 Avenue of the Americas, New York, NY 10013-2473, USA

www.cambridge.org
Information on this title: www.cambridge.org/9780521863292

First published 2008

Printed in the United States of America

A catalog record for this publication is available from the British Library.

Library of Congress Cataloging in Publication Data

González, Ondina E., 1958–
Christianity in Latin America : a history / Ondina E. González, Justo L. González.
p.   cm.
Includes bibliographical references and index.
ISBN 978-0-521-86329-2 (hardback) – ISBN 978-0-521-68192-6 (pbk.)
1. Latin America – Church history.   I. González, Justo L.   II. Title.
BR600.G67   2007
278–dc22   2007016971

ISBN   978-0-521-86329-2 hardback
ISBN   978-0-521-68192-6 paperback

To Karl and Catherine

Contents

Preface

To write an introduction to Christianity in Latin America is no simple task, nor is it one we have undertaken lightly. As throughout the world, and in some cases more so, Christianity in Latin America is rich, varied, and complex. Its history includes hundreds of individuals who have been the object of careful monographs. Among such figures are devoted missionaries, fortune seekers, mystics, martyrs, charlatans, evangelists, dictators, visionaries, and many others. In the course of writing this book, we have often been tempted to delve more deeply and in more detail into the lives of many of these; however, we have constantly reminded ourselves that this is only an introduction to the subject. When we have singled out certain individuals or events for more detailed discussion, it often is because they illustrate a particular point that needs to be made and not necessarily because they are more important than others.

For similar reasons, we have refrained from giving bibliographical references to support every statement made in the book. When there is a direct quotation, the narrative and the information provided in the accompanying note should give the reader enough guidance to identify and find the source of the quotation. If a scholar's work is mentioned in the narrative without a corresponding note, full bibliographical information may be found at the end of the book in "Sources Referenced." Additionally, among the numerous materials that deal with various subjects discussed in this book, we have singled out some that may be particularly useful to the reader. These may be found in the section "Some Suggestions for Further Reading."

For us, writing this book together has provided an opportunity to work across generational lines – uncle and niece. Our PhDs are exactly forty years apart. Therefore, in general, one of us has brought to the table the more classical readings and concerns in the field and the other has brought the most recent scholarship. Thus, in our list of acknowledgments we must begin by expressing gratitude to each other. It has been an enjoyable experience!

As is always the case in a survey such as this, we owe much to scholars and researchers who have gone before us and on whose work we draw. To list them would be impossible. But we should always remind ourselves, particularly as historians, that each generation builds on the work of earlier ones.

Finally, our dedicating this book to our spouses is an insufficient acknowledgment of their support both in this project and in the entire business of living. Thank you again!

Introduction

It is said that Charles V, annoyed when someone blocked his carriage, asked who dared stand in the way of the Holy Roman Emperor, the King of Castile, Leon, Aragon, and the Two Sicilies – and a dozen other titles of lesser importance. The man impeding the king's progress – Hernán Cortés by name – responded, "One who gave thee more lands than did thy father!"

The story may not be absolutely true, but the point it makes certainly is. The "discovery" and conquest of the "New World" forever changed the "Old." As a result, the Irish would eventually become known for their potatoes, the Italian for their polenta and tomato sauces, and the Swiss for their chocolate. Such dietary changes are but a sign of the profound impact of the Americas on Europe. Even traditional religion and theology were challenged, forcing theologians to rethink much that they had considered settled. According to ancient traditions, before leaving Jerusalem the apostles divided the world among themselves, so that the Gospel would be preached "to every creature." But now there were millions of people in lands where apparently no apostle had set foot. Were they excluded from the grace of God? Were they actually human? Did they have souls? Were they rightful owners of their land? As we will see in Chapter 2, these debates – with far-reaching economic and political consequences – soon raged in Europe.

As we know, the Americas would never be the same after that fateful 12th of October, 1492, when Columbus first set foot on these lands. But Europe as well would never be the same after Columbus returned on the equally fateful but less known March 15, 1493. Hernán Cortés not only destroyed the Aztec empire, but he also disrupted traditional economic and political patterns in Europe. He not only gave Charles V more lands than did his father but also provided him with gold to pay the enormous debt he had contracted in

1

order to become Holy Roman Emperor. American gold and silver also made it possible for Spain to imagine that it was economically prosperous while in fact providing capital for the rapidly developing industrialization in other European nations from which Spain found it easy and convenient to purchase goods rather than producing them itself.

While the changes in Europe were momentous, those in the Americas were cataclysmic and may still be felt. Entire civilizations were destroyed in a matter of years. European diseases, forced labor, and social upheaval destroyed much of the population. Besides their diseases, Europeans brought with them animals and crops that would eventually change the entire landscape of the hemisphere. The buffalo practically disappeared, and their place was taken by cattle, horses, sheep, and hogs. Early in the sixteenth century, sugar cane came to the West Indies, and the ancient hardwood forests rapidly receded before the cane fields. Then came coffee, and the remaining forests were thinned in order to plant it under their shade. In the vast plains of North America, buffalo grass was supplanted by another grass – wheat. If it is true that Mexican and Peruvian wealth contributed to Spain's underdevelopment as compared to northern Europe, it is also true that the riches of the southern sections of the western hemisphere prevented their industrial development, while its northern reaches, originally much poorer, would develop their industry to the point of becoming the richest area of the world.

AN OLD WORLD RELIGION IN A NEW WORLD

Europeans did not bring only their diseases, crops, and livestock; they also brought their religion. They could not do otherwise, since for them, religion permeated all of life, to the point that there was no practical distinction between religion and politics or religion and economics. In the lands now known as Latin America, it was the Spanish and the Portuguese who settled first and most permanently. The form of Christianity they brought with them was Roman Catholicism. But this was a particular brand of Catholicism – one forged in the Iberian Peninsula over the centuries. Toward the end of the Middle Ages, Spanish nationalism had been on the rise and was blended with religion in the myth of the *Reconquista*. This myth claimed that ever since the Moors invaded the Peninsula in 711, Christian Spaniards had been resisting them and regaining lost territory. It was out of this myth of the Reconquista that Spain was born as a nation convinced that God had entrusted it with the defense of the Catholic faith against all Muslims, Jews, heretics, and other unbelievers. Thus, when the New World was "discovered," and then as it was explored, invaded, and exploited, Spaniards were convinced that this was a sacred trust so that they could bring their religion to the benighted people in these lands.

And they brought their religion and its institutions. The latter were patterned after what had developed in the Old World as new territories were conquered. The invaders brought their religion in much the same way as they had earlier brought it to southern Spain during the Reconquista and to the Canary Islands – by force of arms. The conquistadores were not only men in armor riding horses and carrying firearms. They were also men in clerical garb riding mules and carrying crosses. And it was not only the men in armor who became rich; there were also clerics who invested in various enterprises of conquest and thus became wealthy.

It is important to realize that these men – soldiers as well as clerics – were not hypocrites. They truly believed that they were serving God. They became incensed when the inhabitants of the land could not perceive the superiority of Christianity. They had masses constantly said for the salvation of their souls. As he lay dying, a victim of a conspiracy among his fellow conquistadores, Francisco Pizarro, the cruel conqueror of the Inca empire, drew a cross with his own blood so he could die contemplating the cross. Hernán Cortés, the conqueror of Mexico, kissed the hem of the robes of the first Franciscan missionaries arriving at the newly conquered land. Obviously, to say that they were sincere does not mean that they were good – and even less that what they did was good. It does mean that they were convinced that in their deeds they were serving not only their greed and lust for violence but also God.

THE TWO FACES OF THE CHURCH IN LATIN AMERICA

It was not difficult for many to become convinced that they were indeed doing good, not only for themselves but also for those whom they called "Indians."[1] They were certain that the ultimate goal of all life is the salvation of one's soul, and therefore as they saw people flocking to church – even though often under coercion – they were prone to believe that this justified the violence, oppression, and destruction that had led to such results. Furthermore, after

---

[1] The term "Indians" was given to the indigenous populations of the Americas by Columbus, who believed he had landed in the Indies. Although recognizing that this is a misnomer and implies a cultural uniformity that did not exist, for the sake of simplicity we will follow standard usage.

the very first encounters, most of the original inhabitants of these lands whom the colonizers met were people already severed from their ancient way of life, broken by abuse and oppression, trying to adjust to a new way of life, and floundering in that attempt.

However, there were those – mostly friars – who had opportunity to see the original inhabitants in their own setting, to observe their family life, and to understand the enormity of what had been done to these people. Many of them became staunch defenders of the Indians and their rights. And soon they found support among the faculty in the most prestigious university in Spain – the University of Salamanca – where a number of Dominican theologians defended the right of the Indians to their property and their freedom.

Thus, almost from its very outset, the church in Latin America had two faces. The dominant face was the one that justified what was being done in the name of evangelization. In the chapters that follow, we will see frequent examples of unleashed greed, wanton destruction, and outright exploitation – all of them justified by ecclesiastical authorities. Conversely, we will also encounter those who protested against injustice – and particularly against injustice in the name of Christianity. This is the other face of Latin American Christianity. While it is true that for a number of reasons – demographic, political, economic, and religious – the initial British colonization of North America was generally accomplished with less cruelty to the native population than its Spanish and Portuguese counterparts, it is also true that there have always been in Latin American Catholicism voices of prophetic protest that were seldom matched in the British colonies.

As we will see, these two faces of Christianity in Latin America have persisted through the centuries. When Spain's American colonies began their quest for independence, most leaders in the institutional church opposed that quest. Yet there were also priests – such as Hidalgo and Morelos in Mexico – who became leaders of the movement. In the late twentieth century, when the entire region was convulsed by the struggle between those who defended the status quo and those who sought radical change, most of the Catholic hierarchy defended the existing order, but there were others who became ardent supporters of change. Some did this through theological reflection, resulting in a 'liberation theology' that had an impact on Christian theology throughout the world. Others did it through denunciation even to the point of death – as was the case of Archbishop Romero in El Salvador.

Even the coming of Protestantism, and the explosive growth of Pentecostalism in the second half of the twentieth century and early in the twenty-first, did not immediately change this situation, for by the early twenty-first century there were Protestants – Pentecostals as well as others – who were convinced that the struggles for social justice and national identity were central to their Christian convictions. There were those who took the opposite tack, insisting that Christianity had nothing to do with such struggles – and even in some cases, that since their faith came from the United States, they should be faithful to the goals and systems established by that nation.

Thus, as we study the history of the church in Latin America, we must be careful, lest we see only one of these faces and forget the other. Latin American organized religion has much of which to be ashamed, but it also has much of which to be proud.

RELIGION IN DAILY LIFE

The story of the institutional church – and even of struggles within it – is only one element in the history of Christianity in Latin America. While the institutional church has always played, and continues to play, a pivotal role in Latin American Christianity, the history of that Christianity must also take into account the manner in which ordinary believers lived out their faith in their daily lives. Too often we confuse the institutional church with Christianity and thus tend to think that when we study the history of the former we have also studied the history of the latter. But that is not the case. Official ecclesiastical documents tell us when a monastery was founded or when a particular bishop arrived at a diocese. They also tell us of the theology of the organized church and how it conceived of its mission. But they say little about the actual religion of the masses. How was religion reflected in daily life? What did people do in quest of their own salvation? What did they do on behalf of others, as acts of Christian charity? Did Christian teaching actually influence their morality? What concrete forms did devotion take in particular areas? How did the ancestral customs and beliefs of the original inhabitants of these lands affect the way they understood and practiced Christianity?

In this context, one must look at society at large and try to assess how and to what degree Christian teachings were expressed in everyday life. How did this society deal with orphaned children? What role did women play in the religious life of the family and the community? What impact did Christianity have on how society was organized?

Therefore, in each of the following chapters, rather than limiting ourselves to the institutional history of the church, we will also take a look "behind the scenes" and try to discover some of the flavor of Christianity as it was lived and practiced in actuality – and not only in the institutional plans and decisions of the church.

POPULAR AND OFFICIAL RELIGION

As we study the actual religious life of people, we soon discover that it does not always match or express official church teaching. Until relatively recent times, saints were acclaimed by popular decision rather than by any official decision of an ecclesiastical body. In Latin America, as elsewhere, people have always received and interpreted Christianity within the framework of their own world view – much as in northern European lands, where the celebration of the resurrection of Jesus came to be combined with ancient fertility rites involving eggs and bunnies, and the Nativity was associated with Christmas trees and mistletoe.

Catholic missionaries to the New World had to face all the difficulties usually connected with any cross-cultural missionary enterprise, augmented by the enormity of the task before them. Even though, beginning in 1516, it was expected that every ship leaving for the "Indies" carry at least one priest, there were never enough priests or other religious workers in the New World. Although a few men with horses, gunpowder, and Indian allies sufficed to conquer mighty empires such as the Aztec and the Inca, this was not the case when it came to the evangelization of the native population. Even more difficult were the conquest and the evangelization of less centralized civilizations, such as those of the Mayas, Chichimecas, and various nomadic peoples. Over the objections of Dominicans and others, Franciscans in Mexico were known to baptize millions, often requiring only that their "converts" know the Lord's Prayer.

Unavoidably, many of these converts came to identify some of the saints of the church with their own gods and brought to their worship and piety some of the practices they had learned from their ancestors. At first some of the stricter bishops, priests, and inquisitors objected to such practices – some to the point of torturing, maiming, or even executing those considered deviant in their faith. But eventually the ecclesiastical leadership became reconciled with much of the popular belief and practice, arguing that these were means of evangelization and that the natives would slowly learn a purer form of Christianity.

Something similar happened when slaves were brought from Africa. They too brought their world view, gods, and traditions. The task of evangelizing them and teaching them the rudiments of the Catholic faith was usually left in the hands of their masters, who were legally mandated to take this responsibility but often paid little attention to the matter. Once again, while most slaves and their descendants became Christians and were baptized, ancestral customs and beliefs survived and were combined with the faith taught by the church. Ancient gods were identified with the Virgin and the saints, and ancient forms of worship were now directed toward these specific saints.

Furthermore, many of the descendants of the original inhabitants, as well as many of African descent, resisted Christianity and continued practicing their ancient rites and religions – usually in secret. Thus, these ancient beliefs persisted for much longer than the authorities of the church thought – even into the twenty-first century.

When Protestant missionaries first arrived, mostly in the nineteenth century, they condemned all these practices and beliefs as "paganism" and accused the Roman Catholic Church of promoting syncretism and even pagan superstition. And yet, as time went by, it became increasingly clear that at least some forms of Latin American Protestantism reflected and continued ancient worship practices.

In relatively recent times, it has become customary to refer to the religious practices of the masses, sometimes encouraged by the church and sometimes not, as "popular religion" – which in itself is a change from the former name of "popular religiosity." While not strictly orthodox and often little informed by theology and doctrine, much of Latin American Catholicism has actually consisted of this popular religion – a religion that accepts the dogmas and rites of the church but in actual practice assigns them a secondary role.

Partly as a response to Protestant criticism, partly as a result of increased biblical and historical studies, and partly in response to the Second Vatican Council, in the second half of the twentieth century efforts were made in some Catholic circles to eradicate such practices and beliefs. However, after a number of failed attempts to do this, and after some theological and sociological criticism of such attempts, by the late twentieth century many had become convinced that most popular religion does not contradict the Catholic faith but is actually an expression of it.

In any case, it is clear that as Christianity established itself in Latin America, it was not limited to the official church and its teachings or even to the religious practices and devotions recommended to the laity by the clergy but actually combined in a variety of ways with other religious practices and beliefs. Many of these were accepted by the church as popular expressions of the faith, while others were rejected as deviant or heretical.

Thus, in most of the chapters that follow we will look not only at the institutional history of the church and at expressions of the Christian faith in everyday life but also at what could be called "variant" forms of religion – some of them accepted, or at least allowed by the institutional church, and some rejected as heretical.

THE MAIN TURNING POINTS

Although life is not really divided into periods, we find it convenient and even necessary to speak of childhood, adolescence, early adulthood, maturity, and so on as if the lines separating them were clearly defined. Likewise, any history has to be divided into segments or periods, even though the historian knows quite well that the story being told is most often a continuum and that the dates set for the end of one period and the beginning of another are seldom as clear-cut as one may be led to imagine. The chapters in this book will follow a chronological outline, beginning with Chapter 1, which deals very briefly with pre-Columbian American and Iberian societies and their religions, thus setting the stage for the cataclysmic encounter between the two, and also with the cultural and religious background of those who were brought as slaves from Africa. In Chapter 2 we will discuss the actual arrival and the first steps of Christianity in this New World – what steps were taken for the Christianization of the indigenous population; how patterns, institutions, and expectations brought from Iberia influenced the nascent American church; and other similar subjects. Then Chapter 3 will look at Christianity during the formative period of the Spanish and Portuguese empires, as the church and its institutions were consolidated and Christianity in its various forms took a firmer hold among the population. Chapter 4 will deal with a series of movements of reform and of outside influences that had an impact on Latin American Christianity in the late colonial period and eventually brought about the independence of most former colonies – roughly, the eighteenth century and early nineteenth century.

Chapter 5 will look at the momentous changes that took place in the life of the church, and in religion at large, as a result of the breakdown of the Spanish and Portuguese empires and the birth of new nations early in the nineteenth century. Here again, the two faces of the church in Latin America, and even their clashes, will become apparent. The result of these clashes, as well as of an unprecedented political situation, led to a period of turmoil and of reshaping both in the life of the church and in the actual religiosity of the people. Just as in Chapters 2 and 3, in which we consider first the new situation after the conquest and the resulting religious life and then how the church and religion adjusted to their new setting, in Chapters 5 and 6 we will discuss first the immediate impact of independence on religion and then how the church and its institutions – as well as various religious practices – responded to the new situation in the nineteenth century and during most of the twentieth century – until Vatican II.

Chapters 7 and 8 will deal with the coming of Protestantism, first through Protestant immigration promoted by governments seeking to counterbalance the political conservatism of traditional Catholicism and then by missionaries from Europe and the United States – sometimes invited by governments with the same political anticonservative agenda. In these chapters we will discuss how Protestant Christianity adapted to Latin America and how it impacted the region.

In Chapter 9 we will pick up the history of Roman Catholicism after Vatican II and its follow-up in the regional meeting of bishops in Medellin in 1968. We will discuss the new forms that Catholic life and thought took, particularly in 'base ecclesial communities,' liberation theology, and the "preferential option for the poor." We will also consider some of the attempts on the part of more conservative elements to counteract the more radical consequences of Vatican II and Medellin – liberation theology in particular

Chapter 10 will deal with the most remarkable phenomenon in Latin American Christianity in the twentieth and twenty-first centuries: the growth of Pentecostalism and of autochthonous churches. Although Pentecostalism has its roots elsewhere, in Latin America it has taken its own shape, often influenced – both positively and negatively – by the dominant presence of Roman Catholicism, as well as by religious practices that have deep roots in Latin American and African religious history. Autochthonous churches – some arising out of traditional Protestantism, others out of Pentecostalism, and even some out of renewal movements within Roman Catholicism – have come to be an important presence in the Latin American religious scene.

Finally, Chapter 11 will summarize some of the main threads woven throughout Latin American religious history and make it clear that the impact of this history is no longer confined to the geographical boundaries of Latin America. We will discuss the influence that Latin American theology is having in the entire theological enterprise throughout the world. We will see Latin American missionaries leaving their native lands to go to various parts of the world. And we will try to discern what this may mean for the ongoing religious life in Latin America and elsewhere.

LOOKING AT HISTORY OUT OF BOTH THE PRESENT AND THE FUTURE

History is much more than the mere narrative of past events. It is that narrative told from the perspective of the present in which the historian lives and of the future for which the historian hopes – or fears. The reason North American schoolchildren are taught about the Declaration of Independence is not mere antiquarian curiosity. It is rather that those who teach it believe that this document and the events surrounding it are important for the present life of the nation and will hopefully be important also for the next generation. Likewise, the reason we study Latin American religious history is not merely to know how Roman Catholicism was established in Mexico or who the first Protestant missionaries to Guatemala were. It is rather that those who research and tell the story are convinced that it is relevant for today – that it is shaping and will continue to shape our world in ways we should understand.

What has been said previously regarding the content of Chapter 11 is much more than a way to wrap up the story. It is rather the central clue as to why the authors – as well as countless others – are convinced that Latin American religious history is important. Latin American culture and religion are no longer confined to the lands south of the Río Grande. Latin American theology is now being studied and discussed by theologians in the United States, Germany, and South Africa. This is one of many signs of the impact of Latin American religion on the rest of the world. So is the presence of Latin American missionaries and teachers in various regions of the world. And – most particularly for our purposes here – so is the presence of millions of Latin Americans in the United States.

Both through immigration and through the heritage of people conquered in the Mexican-American and the Spanish-American wars, the United States now includes millions of Latinos – people of Latin American origin or descent. In fact, in terms of the size of its Spanish-speaking population, the United States ranks fourth, and perhaps even third, in the entire western hemisphere – after Mexico, Argentina, and perhaps Colombia. Roughly half of all Roman Catholics in the United States are Latinos. And the process continues, for Hispanics are now one of the fastest growing segments of the population in the nation – in terms of percentage, rivaled only by Asian-Americans. While most of them are and remain Catholic, large numbers are joining existing Protestant churches – and some are creating their own churches.

What this means for the religious history of the nation is obvious. A few decades ago, it was possible to tell the religious story of the United States with very little reference to Latin America and its religion. This is no longer the case. How can one speak of North American Catholicism while ignoring the religious and cultural background of half its membership? How can one study the history of the Seventh Day Adventists, the Church of God, the Southern Baptists, or the Christian Church (Disciples of Christ) without taking into account the leadership that Hispanics are providing for these denominations, and in many cases the explosive growth of the denominations themselves among Hispanics? How can one understand the religious life of New York without reference to the religious life of Puerto Rico or the religious life of Southern California without reference to its counterpart in Mexico and Central America?

It is out of this present, and in the hope of a future in which the various cultural and religious strands coming into North America may be woven into a multicolored cloth, that the authors look at the history of Christianity in Latin America. And it is out of the same present and the same hope that we invite our readers to join us as we explore the many dimensions and the rich variety of Latin American Christianity.

1

~

Foundations

On Friday, October 12, 1492, Christopher Columbus wrote in his log:

At dawn we saw naked people, and I went ashore in the ship's boat, armed, followed by Martín Alonso Pinzón, captain of the *Pinta*, and his brother, Vincente Yáñez, captain of the *Niña*. I unfurled the royal banner and the captains brought the flags which displayed a large green cross with the letters F [Ferdinand] and Y [Isabella] at the left and right side of the cross. Over each letter was the appropriate crown of that Sovereign. . . . After a prayer of thanksgiving I ordered the captains of the Pinta and Niña, together with Rodrigo de Escobedo (secretary of the fleet), Rodrigo Sánchez of Segovia (comptroller of the fleet) to bear faith and witness that I was taking possession of this island for the King and Queen. I made all the necessary declarations and had these testimonies carefully written down by the secretary. . . . To this island I gave the name *San Salvador*, in honor of our Blessed Lord.[1]

Thus began an encounter that would change the world forever. Columbus's assumptions that he could lay claim to the lands he encountered by simply unfurling some flags, making some declarations, and offering prayers may seem strange to us today. But this attitude reflected deeply held European views on how the world was ordered, the place of Europe in the world, and its responsibility to Christianize all whom it encountered. Columbus's arrival to these lands would ultimately challenge and reshape the preconceptions that undergirded his actions and the world view of many, if not most, Europeans. The "discovery" of a new continent and its inhabitants rattled European thinkers' complacent attitude that they knew the world and how it was ordered. Clearly, the encounter with the New World transformed Europe, particularly the Iberian Peninsula. But its impact was felt no more strongly

---

[1] Christopher Columbus, *The Log of Christopher Columbus*, trans. Robert H. Fuson (Camden, ME: International Marine Publishing, 1992), 75–76.

by anyone than by the original inhabitants of the Americas; so it is with them that we begin.

If there is one thing, above all others, that one must remember when studying the pre-Columbian peoples of Latin America, it is that there was not one single civilization. Rather, there was an astounding multiplicity of civilizations and cultures (anthropologists estimate more than 350 major tribal groups), ranging from the nomadic peoples of the southern pampas and the North American plains to the high civilizations of the Andes (the Incas) and the central valley of Mexico (the Aztecs). It is about the latter two groups that we know the most, precisely because of their advanced civilizations and the ease and rapidity with which the Spanish conquered them.

There is one principal, overarching similarity between these two great empires that concerns a student of Latin American religion: Both the Aztecs and the Incas had "great religious traditions." In 1967, Robert Redfield coined the phrase "great tradition" to explain complex state-level religious traditions. According to Redfield, great traditions were those religious practices and ideologies that came from the ruling elite and priestly classes within a theocracy. Furthermore, these groups used that ideology to control millions of people from various ethnic and linguistic origins who were nevertheless economically and politically subservient to the urban centers in which the ruling classes resided. Such was the case in central Mexico and in the Andean highlands. In these two highly developed civilizations, religion served the needs of the state, and the state itself was theocratic. (Interestingly, the pattern of a "great tradition" was clearly evident in Spain as well.) We gain access to Aztec and Inca pre-Columbian religious world views through such sources as oral traditions recorded by the Spaniards, art, architecture, and pictographic and hieroglyphic accounts, as the Aztecs and the Incas did not have a written language. Archaeological evidence also supports much of what the other sources have revealed.

In this chapter, we will discuss first some of the original inhabitants of these lands, *the Aztecs* and *the Incas*. This will be followed by a section on *the Spaniards* and a discussion of *the encounter* between Indians and Europeans. Finally, we will consider *the Africans* who were brought to the western hemisphere as slaves.

THE AZTECS

At the time of their first contact with Europeans, the Aztecs from central Mexico were relative newcomers to the region, having consolidated their power over rivals in the area only in the early fifteenth century. In fact, the Aztecs were really an alliance among three major groups in the central valley, chief among which were the Mexicas. The Mexicas themselves had come to the valley as mercenaries in the thirteenth century, fighting for any city-state that would pay. In the late 1300s, the Mexicas were organized into their own city-state, distributing land and collecting tribute payments. By 1325, they had begun construction on a capital, Tenochtitlan (built on an island in the middle of Lake Texcoco). The Mexicas evolved politically and continued to amass power. Eventually their skill as warriors made them a force in their own right in Mexico's central valley. By the early fifteenth century, the Mexicas allied with two other powerful city-states to rule in the Valley of Mexico. However, being part of a tripartite structure was not enough for the Mexicas. They came to dominate their allies and began pushing beyond the valley, bringing under their control much of central Mexico. By 1502, when Moctezuma II ascended to the throne, the Aztec empire encompassed more than eighty thousand square miles, reached from the Pacific Ocean to the Gulf of Mexico, stretched down into present-day Guatemala, and its capital city had at least a quarter of a million inhabitants.

Undoubtedly the highly militaristic background of the Aztecs influenced their religion and their cosmology, for we find in both a profound sense of struggle and sacrifice. With a creation myth embracing a central theme of sacrifice, the Aztecs' "great tradition" revolved around an understanding of humanity's relationship with the gods. It also included a notion of sacred time with different ages, each one ending cataclysmically.

After the violent destruction of the first four ages, the ancient gods gathered in Teotihuacan ("city of the gods") to determine the best way to bring light and life back into the world once again. To warm themselves, they built a divine fire and sat around it discussing what they were to do. It soon became clear that a sacrifice was necessary. After four days of hemming and hawing, one of the lesser gods threw himself into the fire, followed quickly by another lesser god. From the fire came forth the spotted eagle and the jaguar – symbols of two of the mightiest warrior units among the Aztecs. Slowly, with all the remaining gods facing east, the sun began to rise. Just after it got above the horizon, it stopped and began to wobble. More sacrifices were needed to ensure that the sun and the moon would continue to move through the sky. But human life was still missing. Since the blood of *all* the gods was required to bring life back to the earth, they sacrificed themselves. Being gods, however, they did not die. One god, Quetzalcoatl, the Plumed Serpent and God of Wisdom, even after throwing himself in the fire, was able to bring human life back to the newly restored world by gathering ancient bones of previous ages from the Place of the Dead and infusing them with life. Though now fully restored, the gods needed to recreate the world every day to ensure that the sun and moon still moved through the heavens and that human beings could continue to thrive.

Miguel León-Portilla, a leading scholar in Nahuatl (the language of the Aztecs) studies, reminds us that the ancient gods had to do "penance" (sacrifice), in order to reach, or deserve, their goal – the restoration of the world. This pattern of sacrifice and worthiness was also part of the relationship between humanity and the gods, whose secrets were known only to the Aztec priests. Because the creation of the world was an ongoing process, it required constant penance by the gods; thus religious celebrations involving prayers, songs, and reenactment of the primordial sacrifices were essential in maintaining the proper relationship with the gods. If the gods sacrificed their blood for the re-creation of the world, then in reenacting the gods' actions, humans had to give blood too. Blood, "the precious liquid that fosters the flow of life," was the very sustenance the gods needed. As part of the sacrificial rituals, beating hearts were excised from the chests of hapless victims (usually captured in war), human blood was smeared on the effigies of the gods, and bits of flesh of the sacrificial victims were eaten in victory ceremonies.

When the Spaniards reached Tenochtitlan in 1519, human sacrifice had reached enormous proportions. The Aztecs' principal god, Huitzilopochtli, was a bloodthirsty deity who had attained a place of prominence in the pantheon as the power of the Mexica spread. It was primarily to him that the thousands of captives were sacrificed. In fact, one of Moctezuma II's predecessors is said to have sacrificed more than twenty thousand people at the dedication of a new temple to Huitzilopochtli. The need for so many victims, also known as "the divine dead," drove warfare and created a perpetual state of conflict between the Aztecs and their neighbors. Tlaxcala, an independent city-state surrounded by the Aztec empire, for example, was constantly at war with the Aztecs, even though the latter could have easily defeated them. The Aztecs needed the captives that only war could bring. (Is it any surprise that the Spaniards made quick allies of the Tlaxcaltecas in their conquest of the Aztecs?) The link between warfare and religion was further strengthened through the ritual that preceded any battle: The Aztecs would send to their foes items that symbolized war – shields, arrows, and cloaks – and declare that they were about to attack in order to secure sacrificial victims. Often the response to this advanced warning was the sending of tribute – in the form of humans – as a way of avoiding the onslaught of the Aztec army.

As important as finding victims was the taking captive of foreign deities by bringing their effigies back to Tenochtitlan. For two key reasons this step was crucial to the Aztecs: First, it was a powerful symbol of a community's defeat; second, it demonstrated the Aztecs' willingness to absorb the conquered gods into their pantheon, smoothing the merger of new subjects into Aztec culture by allowing them to keep their gods. This accommodation only went so far, however. Huitzilopochtli always remained supreme over the gods of the conquered.

One needs to be careful in judging the place of sacrifice and death in the Aztec mindset. Efforts at understanding – and not only reacting to – human sacrifice are not limited to modern-day scholars. Some sixteenth-century Spaniards explained ritualistic sacrifice among the Indians as a misguided means by which they gave that which was most precious – life – to their gods. Perhaps the Spaniards understood the power of sacrifice, which also had a place in their own religion. In any case, for the Aztecs, death clearly was crucial to the maintenance of life, and the life they struggled so valiantly to ensure they also saw as preordained by the gods.

Despite the predestined nature of one's existence, scholars believe that from the Aztec perspective, a good life still had to be earned through a lifelong series of acts of penance and sacrifice, precisely because the gods had done likewise to bring humanity back to the earth. Furthermore, only through public and private acts of devotion could one become deserving of one's predetermined life. It was through domestic rituals that an individual could most consistently prove worthy of the gods' benevolence.

Such lessons were inculcated from the very beginning of life. Children were taught the concepts of penance, sacrifice, and merit from their earliest years. The words pronounced at the birth of a child, from the *Florentine Codex*, reveal much about what that child would be taught:

> You have arrived on earth, my youngest one, my beloved one, my beloved youth. . . . Perhaps you will live for a little while? Are you the one we deserved? Perhaps you will know your grandfathers, your grandmothers, those of your lineage. . . .
>
> In what manner have Your Mother, Your Father, the Lord of Duality endowed you?
>
> Perhaps Our Lord Tloqueh, Nahuaqueh, the One Who Is Near, the One Who Is Close, will offer you something, will favor you? Or it may be that you were born without merit, that which can be deserved? You have suffered fatigue, strain, my youngest one, my beloved one, precious necklace, precious feather.
>
> You have arrived, rest now, find repose. Here are gathered your beloved grandfathers, your beloved grandmothers who awaited you. Here into their hands you have come, you have arrived. Sigh not! Be not sad!
>
> Indeed you will endure, you will suffer fatigue, strain. For verily Our Lord has ordered, has disposed that there will be pain, affliction, need, work,

labor for daily sustenance. There is sweat, weariness, and labor if there is to be eating, drinking, and the wearing of raiment. . . .

My beloved child, wait for the word of Our Lord![2]

Indeed, the Aztecs, believing they were living at the end of the fifth age, were waiting for the word of their lord as the conquest by the Spaniards began.

THE INCAS

Politically and administratively the Inca empire was the most sophisticated state in pre-Columbian America. (Originally the term "Inca" referred only to the emperor, also known as the Sapa Inca. Over time the term "Inca" has come to mean the entire empire and its people.) As with the Aztecs, there was a multitude of different cultures and languages within the empire. Geographically, its expansion was astounding. Tawantinsuyu, or the "Four Corners of the World," as the Inca empire was known before the conquest, encompassed huge swaths of South America. From its capital in modern-day Peru, the empire stretched northward through Ecuador to parts of Colombia, eastward into the Bolivian highlands, and southward into Chile and Argentina. It had an extensive network of roads and runners (more than twenty-five thousand kilometers of roads), a supremely well-organized military, and a system of tribute payment and distribution – including state-run regional warehouses of clothing, food, and weapons – that held the empire together. The Incas lacked a written language with which to keep track of their empire; however, they did use a memory aid known as *quipus*. With this multicolored, multi-knotted system of strings, Inca officials recorded how much each individual and community had contributed to the forced labor system, how much the community had produced, and how much had been distributed. Additionally, the Incas had no animal of traction. They did have the llama, which certainly provided them with food and was used as a beast of burden. But while these sure-footed camelids will usually carry around 100 pounds or so, they will not pull loads. Clearly human power ran Tawantinsuyu, for the Incas also lacked the wheel and hard-metal tools.

The expansion of Inca territorial holdings began in earnest in the mid-fifteenth century under the leadership of Pachacuti. In his great battle against the Incas' longtime foes, the Chanca Indians, in 1438, Pachacuti and his

---

[2]   Miguel León-Portilla, "Those Made Worthy by Divine Sacrifice: The Faith of Ancient Mexico" in *South and Meso-American Native Spirituality: From the Cult of the Feathered Serpent to Theology of Liberation*, edited by Gary H. Gossen in collaboration with Miguel León-Portilla (New York: Crossroads Publishing Company, 1993), 53.

followers seized the Chanca's sacred idol that led them into battle. The Chanca forces fell into complete disarray, and what might have been a fairly evenly matched battle turned into a complete rout. The Inca gods had defeated the Chanca gods. To the Incas, the pattern of their gods reigning supreme over other gods repeated itself for almost one hundred years – until the arrival of the Spaniards. To the Incas, their gods were nearly invincible.

What we know of pre-Columbian Andean religion comes largely from oral traditions repeated to Father Bernabé Cobo, a Jesuit priest who came with the Spaniards, studied Quechua – the language of the Incas – and in 1633, in his *Historia del Nuevo Mundo*, published much of what he had learned. Because of the enormous diversity of local religion within the Inca empire, Cobo wrote of the official religion, or the "great tradition." His descriptions may not be as distant from the experience of the common Inca as one might at first believe, for there is evidence that by the late fifteenth century, local religions had been significantly altered by the imposition of the Inca state religion.

The Inca pantheon included the creator god Viracocha. Like the Christian Bible, Inca mythology has two creation stories. Unlike the Christian Bible, the Inca stories describe two distinct creations. Viracocha's first attempt at creating humanity failed, largely because humans sinned against him and he destroyed them. His second effort was more successful. After fashioning stones in his own image, Viracocha used these models to create men and women. He sent them forth from caves and springs and trees and rivers to the four corners of the world, teaching each group different customs and languages. Then he walked among his creation, disguising himself as an old man in tattered clothing, to test humanity. It failed him yet again. At a community festival, Viracocha – as the old man – was stoned by the people. Only one old woman showed him any kindness by offering him something to drink. She and her family were the only ones spared when Viracocha destroyed the town with yellow and red hail. He then left humanity to its own devices, walked across the waters of the Pacific Ocean, and promised to return in times of crisis.

Of even more importance than Viracocha within the Inca state were the Gods of the Heaven, which included Ilyapa, God of Thunder, who brought the rains; Quilla, Goddess of the Moon; and Inti, the Sun God. It was through Inti that the Sapa Inca's own semi-divine nature was derived. At least in part, this accounts for the extreme devotion lavished on Inti by the Sapa Inca. In fact, Pachacuti had the capital of the Inca empire, Cuzco, rebuilt as a ceremonial center with its great temple to Inti. According to Cobo, the temple in Cuzco housed an effigy of Inti made entirely of gold and inlaid with exquisite jewels.

(Sights of such quantities of gold would tempt the Spaniards into astonishing acts of greed and cruelty.)

Although the Gods of the Heaven and Viracocha himself were distant, the Andean religion of the Incas was also "a religion of the earth" – hence the importance of the Gods of the Earth. More closely tied to the people than the great state gods were the ancestor gods. Among these were the mummified remains of local leaders and of the deceased Sapa Incas, whose bodies were brought out for major festivals. Ancestor worship long pre-dated the supremacy of the Incas, but with the rise of his power, Pachacuti introduced state-wide royal ancestor worship. Under this system, a new Sapa Inca did not inherit the wealth of the deceased Sapa Inca; rather, he had to generate his own wealth, largely through new conquests. The riches of the deceased emperor were used to support the newly created cult with his mummified remains as the tangible link to other Andean gods such as Inti.

Also among the Gods of the Earth were the *wakas*, or *huacas*, who existed throughout Tawantinsuyu. These were anything and everything else the Incas held as sacred: a huaca might be a particular location, an unusually formed tree, a very large boulder, or even the place from which an Inca clan believed it originated. These gods grounded the Andean people in the ancient past, in nature, and in the very soil that gave them life. And because the huacas could be anywhere, they later proved to be the bane of the Spanish priest concerned with idolatrous practices among the indigenous neophyte Christians.

All of these gods and ancestors required worship and praise, often in the form of public ritual, sometimes in the form of offerings, and occasionally in the form of human sacrifice. Not all sources agree that human sacrifice occurred among the Incas, but Cobo commented that sacrifice was rare and only for very special occasions, with sacrificial victims largely limited to children and adolescents, who were considered the most worthy of gifts to bring the gods. Whatever the case, unlike the Aztec gods, who required human blood in order to keep the world going, Inca gods viewed sacrifice and offerings as forms of thanksgiving. Such offerings could also be fruits of a harvest, precious metals, beautiful feathers, or foods especially prepared for the gods. Additionally, while offerings to huacas could occur even in a domestic setting, festivals and larger rituals required the participation of priests.

This priestly class was as much an arm of the Inca state as was the military. Like the Aztec religion, after conquering a people, the state religion of the Incas absorbed the gods of the newly dominated culture. These groups could continue worshiping their traditional gods, but the priests of Inti superimposed the official Inca religion upon local practices. Interestingly, it is at the provincial level that women priests were most prevalent, sharing many responsibilities with male counterparts. Fray José de Arriaga, a Spanish priest writing in the mid-seventeenth century, left a description of how he understood those responsibilities:

> *Wakapvillas,* which is to say "he who talks to the *waka*," is the greatest [of the provincial priests], having in his charge the custody and care of the *waka* as well as the responsibility for talking to it and repeating back to the people that which he pretends the *waka* tells him, although sometimes the devil speaks to them through the rock. And they also receive the offerings and make the sacrifices and carry out the fasts and order the preparation of *chicha* [a fermented corn drink] for the festivals of the *wakas* and teach their idolatry and tell their fables and reprimand those who are careless in the worship and veneration of their wakas.[3]

Women also had important religious roles in the major urban centers or wherever there was a temple to the sun. There women would enter convents where they would dedicate themselves to important Inca gods. As a form of tribute, girls aged ten to twelve from the provinces would be sent to these religious houses to consecrate themselves and their virginity to the appropriate god. Children of the provincial nobility were also brought to Cuzco to learn the Incas' ways – including the worship of Inti and other powerful Inca gods – then sent home to instruct their communities. This cultural conquest of a tribe was coupled with the ready presence of the Inca military, which was able to stay nearby because the state-owned warehouses provided them with food and clothing. Additionally, once an area was conquered, the new Inca rulers would shift the population, moving native speakers of Quecha, the principal language of the Incas, into newly conquered lands. And conversely, they would move peoples from those lands into territory that had long been part of Tawantinsuyu.

There was also an economic aspect of Andean religion that was instrumental in helping the Incas maintain control of their empire. Land was divided into three parts, and while records are unclear as to the percentage of each division, the purpose of each is known: One part was for the religious cults, with its harvest dedicated to the gods as offerings or used to support those professionally involved in the cults. Another portion of the land was given over

---

[3] José de Arriaga, "La extirpación de la idolatría en el Perú," in *Crónicas peruanas de interés indígena,* edited by Francisco Esteve Barba (Madrid: Ediciones Altgas, 1968), 206–207, as quoted in Manuel M. Marzal, "Andean Religion at the Time of the Conquest," in *South and Meso-American Native Spirituality: From the Cult of the Feathered Serpent to Theology of Liberation,* ed. Gary H. Gossen in collaboration with Miguel León-Portilla (New York: Crossroads Publishing Company, 1993), 109–110.

to the Sapa Inca to support the royal mummy cult and to sustain the military. And the last portion belonged to the local community, where there had long existed patterns of communal cultivation and reciprocity and obligation.

The Inca world was structured much like a pyramid, with the Sapa Inca as the principal contact with the world of the gods. Then came the priests, whose main responsibility was to ensure that rituals were carried out correctly and the desires of the gods were made known to the people. And supporting this pyramid were the people who believed that everything they had, from their children to the harvests, belonged to the gods. It was this pyramidal social structure that would ultimately prove a fatal flaw in the Incas' efforts to withstand Spanish conquest and domination.

THE SPANIARDS

At the dawn of the encounter, in Europe there were a variety of religions and ways of expressing faith – even before the Protestant Reformation. In Spain, Isabella and Ferdinand felt that the presence of Judaism and Islam not only challenged their power but also imperiled their subjects' very souls. It was a problem the monarchs set out to solve. Although religious diversity neither ended nor began with the ascension of Ferdinand and Isabella to the thrones of Aragon and Castile, respectively, they saw themselves as the protectors of Catholic Spain. In controlling and even suppressing the faith of Jews and Muslims, they achieved a spiritual order that allowed them to turn their attention to other matters.

The beginning of Jewish presence on the Iberian peninsula is difficult to pinpoint. Gravestones, the earliest evidence of Jews among Iberian Christians, date from the third century. Early in Visigothic Spain (CE 409–711), Jews were well integrated into Iberian society. Nevertheless it was during this time that the Jews faced one of their many great challenges on the peninsula. The Visigothic rulers were followers of Arian Christianity, which Catholics considered a heresy. By the end of the sixth century, however, being at odds with Catholic Europe proved too much, and in 589 the Visigothic king converted to Catholic Christianity, declaring it the religion of all of Spain. Since the Roman Church tended to be less tolerant of Judaism than Arianism was, it is no surprise that anti-Jewish legislation began to appear. At first these laws targeted mixed marriages and public office holding and in 613 culminated in requiring the forced conversion of Jews to Christianity. That was the legislation; the reality was that over the years the Jewish community continued in the Spanish holdings, often protected by later monarchs who held that the Jews were their "property" and under their special protection – an attitude toward subjects that would reappear in the royal attitude toward the American Indians encountered almost a millennium later. Nevertheless, within a century of the first conversion edict in Spain, the Spanish Christians would face an external challenge they could not defeat: the invasion of the Muslims from North Africa.

The Muslim invasion of Spain began in 711 and within a decade the Moors, as Spanish Muslims are called, controlled almost the entire peninsula, with stronger power in the south than in the north. The first great caliphate of Spain was in Cordoba, where stands to this day one of Europe's most magnificent mosques, constructed in the eighth century. (Unfortunately, during the reign of Charles V in the first half of the sixteenth century, a cathedral was built inside the mosque. In the very center of the mosque, in the midst of its low-vaulted ceilings and numerous double arches, one finds a Gothic chapel in an uncomfortable architectural juxtaposition with the Moorish structure.[4]) Another great center of Islamic power in Al-Andalus, modern-day Andalucia, was the city of Granada. It would be there that the Moors would finally lose their last stronghold in Spain in 1492.

The religious history of medieval Spain is checkered. There were times of religious intolerance on the part of both Christians and Muslims. But on the whole, when compared with the rest of Europe, medieval Spain – Christian, Jewish, and Muslim – was known for its religious tolerance. But toward the end of the Middle Ages, tolerance was not what Spanish Christians rulers wanted most; they wanted a Christian Spain. They sought to justify their claim on Spain by rewriting history, making it appear that beginning almost immediately after the Muslim conquest Christian Spain engaged in a constant struggle to retake the lost lands. In truth, the "reconquest" often pitted Christians against one another as well as against Muslims, with Islamic and Christian soldiers frequently changing sides. While it is unclear exactly when the recasting of history that created the reconquista myth actually began, it is clear that by the time Ferdinand and Isabella assumed their respective thrones, the conviction that the Christians had been fighting a centuries-long war for God's glory was firmly entrenched in the Spanish psyche. What we do know is that Christian rulers were helped by a series of internal conflicts among the Moors and between the Moors and their uneasy allies, the Berbers. Additionally, as the Christians pushed south into lands controlled by the Moors, they began organizing themselves into kingdoms, creating political

---

[4]   The original sixteenth-century plan was to raze the mosque and build the Cordoban cathedral, but there was a great outcry from the community. The result was the chapel in the middle of the mosque. Legend tells that when Charles V saw what it was that he had approved, he said, "You have destroyed something unique and built something commonplace."

entities that would rule the Iberian peninsula once the Muslims were defeated. (Indeed, Portugal dates its independence from 1139 after a decisive victory over the Muslims at Ourique.) With the marriage of Ferdinand and Isabella, the two most powerful Spanish kingdoms would be jointly ruled.

Spain was not the only European country involved in battles against Islam. Across Europe the Middle Ages were marked with the fervor of the crusades, which certainly reached into Spain. But the Spanish Christians did not need to go to Jerusalem in order to fight the Muslims; they had the infidels dwelling among them. The myth that saw Christian Spaniards as united in their struggle for the very soul of the region resulted in the development of a profound militaristic tone within Spanish Catholicism. The military might of the state became involved in religious matters in ways that were not typical of other European countries. Church, state, and military unity became a matter of course for Spain. As Christians conquered Muslims, it became ingrained in the Spanish Christians' mindset that God's work was done with the sword as well as with the cross. In 1492, when Ferdinand and Isabella succeeded in gaining control of the last Moorish stronghold in Spain, they believed they had done so being led by the militant arm of God.

This militant Christianity had already led the "most Catholic Monarchs" (as they were dubbed by Pope Alexander VI), but especially Isabella, to begin a reformation within the Spanish Catholic church itself. She rightly saw the laxness within the daily existence of the Spanish clergy, the accumulation of wealth and power of the clergy, the lack of education among those charged with guiding parish life, and the all-too-common problem of concubinage. Isabella's religious zeal led her to nominate to the pope, as prospective prelates, men who met Isabella's standards of morality and education. While this right to put forth nominations for Spain was an informal arrangement with the pope (with the exception of the recently conquered Moorish land, where that right was part of a formal agreement), this royal privilege would be formalized when it came to the Americas. As will be discussed later in this chapter, the control of the Spanish crown over the Roman Catholic Church in the Americas was near complete.

Isabella sought to reform not only the episcopacy and the clergy but also the religious orders. From Isabella's perspective, the orders had moved far from their original purpose and were enjoying many of the same earthly delights that the secular clergy enjoyed. These views were shared by some within religious orders who wanted to follow a more austere, simpler life than that of their brothers and sisters who preferred the comforts to which they had become accustomed. There was bitter opposition but ultimately the crown's drive to gain control of the Catholic Church in Spain succeeded. What is clear is that the reforms brought by the Catholic Monarchs were changes in style and in religious practice rather than in substance. There was no reformation of the content, no theological reform that accompanied the imposition of control. But for Ferdinand and Isabella, there was still the perduring problem of the Jews and the Moors. Until Spain was truly united, one and all under the banner of Roman Catholicism, the monarchs would not rest. Isabella and Ferdinand turned first to the Jews.

As early as the late 1470s the Spanish monarchs had been concerned with the corrupting influence of Jews on *conversos*, or "New Christians," as recent Jewish converts to Christianity were known. To ensure orthodoxy among these Christian neophytes, the crowns successfully petitioned Rome in 1478 to establish a Holy Office in Castile, where the majority of Spanish conversos lived. Ferdinand was also able to revive the Inquisition in Aragon even though there was little support, popular or ecclesiastical, for what was seen as an attack on an economically critical sector of the Aragonese society. An economic crisis did ensue when many frightened conversos fled, taking with them their money and their financial know-how.

The Spanish Inquisition penetrated into every sector of Spanish society and was as much a unifying force in the territories as was the unification of the crowns under Ferdinand and Isabella. As J. H. Elliott, an historian of early modern Spain, writes, there were political overtones to the Spanish Inquisition that ensured that there could be no clear distinction between religious and political accomplishments. Precisely because of the interaction between church and state, every military or political success was seen as another victory for Catholicism. The double purpose of the Spanish Inquisition, to enforce both purity of religious practice and political unity, was structurally supported by having the inquisitors appointed by the crown and serving under its watchful eye – a break from the earlier pattern of bishops acting as inquisitors. This politically controlled Inquisition would ultimately be replicated in the Americas.

It was not enough for the Catholic Monarchs, however, to have a system to guarantee religious purity among Catholics; they also sought a society that was religiously homogenous. Thus, in 1492, less than three months after the fall of Granada, by royal decree all practicing Jews in Spain were to convert to Christianity or face expulsion within four months. The exact number of Jews to leave Spain is unknown, but estimates are that the Sephardim, as the exiles were known, totaled anywhere from one hundred thousand to two hundred thousand.

Jews were not the only religious minority to face persecution by the Spanish Catholics. In 1499 the Moors remaining in Spain were also ordered to convert to Roman Catholicism. Much as in the seventh-century forced conversion of

Jews, many Moors simply did not convert yet remained in the country. And even those who did convert – known as *moriscos* – were suspected by the Spanish church of not being "Christian enough." By 1609, following a severe Islamic uprising in Spain, all Muslims were forced to leave the country. It is estimated that more than 90 percent of the morisco population left between 1609 and 1614.

Official concern about orthodoxy was not brought to bear solely on those who came from other religious traditions. By the earliest years of the sixteenth century there already existed in Valladolid a printed version of a *cartilla* (primer) using traditional Christian doctrine to teach children to read. Clearly, the intent was to educate the youngest of the population, but it was also to make good Catholics, largely defined as someone who knew the commandments, the prayers, and the creed. Granted, formal education was reserved primarily for boys from families in upper social groupings, but the existence of these cartillas used in homes indicates an effort to indoctrinate females as well as males.

Spain was a country that at the "great tradition" level viewed itself as united under one faith and one god and willing to accomplish its unity through military might and coercion. It was a vision that would travel across the Atlantic to Spain's new territories.

Spain itself, just as the Inca and Aztec worlds, had its own "little traditions" – those religious customs and beliefs that are local in nature. The version of Spanish Catholicism that came to the New World was not only that of the church hierarchy and the official theologians; it was also the style of Catholicism practiced by the people who migrated to the Indies: by and large commoners, and in many cases illiterate, unskilled workers. As anthropologist Manuel M. Marzal tells us, their practice of Catholicism was unique to each locale and was a combination of local beliefs, ethical norms, organizational structures, and styles of worship. Key among these beliefs was the centrality of a god who was creator, provider, and punisher. One made deals with God primarily through the intercession of the saints, with each locality having its own "special" saint who was both honored by the community and with whom individuals bartered veneration in exchange for spiritual help. Religion as practiced – as opposed to religion as prescribed – also held that God's grace was most likely found in certain places (e.g., shrines and pilgrimage sites) and that the year needed to be marked with calendrical religious celebrations that required, among other things, the procession of statues of saints throughout the community.

While such rituals may have varied from town to town, religious diversity within Spanish Catholicism was not limited to the practices of individual localities; rather there was also a diversity among individual groups within a community. For many, devotion led to taking of religious vows; convents for men and women were popular throughout Spain. These forms of religious vocation certainly found their way to the Indies. But so did another one, that of the *beatas*. A beata was almost always a pious woman who wore the habit of a particular order and who took simple vows to follow the rules of that order but did not take the irrevocable vows of a woman becoming a nun, nor was she under the authority of the order. Rather, the beata was under the control of the secular religious hierarchy, even if she lived with other beatas in a *beaterio*. Some of these devout religious women created problems for the official church because the control the church had over them was tenuous at best – after all, these women were not safely enclosed in either convents or marriages. It was not unusual for beatas to attract a following of devoted admirers, both male and female, and even gain power over men who looked to them as religious leaders.

On occasion, such women who amassed power found themselves subject to the Spanish Inquisition, as did another religious group, the *alumbrados*, who were considered heretics by church authorities. The alumbrados, or Illuminists, believed in total submission to the divine will through purification of the soul, which required direct contact with God. For a few Illuminists, submitting to the divine will could take interesting routes, including repeated sexual encounters with a group's leader. Such activities were seen as bringing the participant nearer to God by the close physical experience with God's true disciple – the leader. For Illuminists, the inner religious life was more important than outward signs or ceremonies. Thus, they did not believe in the veneration of the images of saints or even in the efficacy of good works, two deeply held tenets of the Roman Catholic Church – which certainly made them fodder for the Inquisition.

The lack of emphasis on good works extended beyond the Illuminist heresy. Inquisitorial records and municipal constitutions of the early sixteenth century make it clear that unseemly behavior in sacred places was a problem throughout Spain. All sorts of nonreligious behavior (e.g., drinking, singing secular and risqué songs, having dramatic presentations) were all too common in shrines. Historian William Christian points out that the constitution of the city of Badajoz even instructed that men and women should remain clothed when sleeping in holy sites. The official church tried to suppress such practices, but, as is often the case when trying to enforce moral behavior, it simply did not work. Eventually, the Inquisition itself had more pressing problems with the advancement of heretical ideas from the Low Countries and the German lands: Lutheranism posed a much greater threat to the unity of Catholic Spain. As the sixteenth century dawned, Spain was bound and determined to keep all of its lands Catholic.

THE ENCOUNTER

With the reconquest of Spain nearly completed, the monarchs of Spain turned their attention, albeit divided, to the pesky Genoese sailor who had come to them with an intriguing idea: sailing west to get to the East. While Spain had been busy making the peninsula safe for Christianity, Portugal had been establishing itself as a maritime power. In 1418 Prince Henry the Navigator had created his famous navigation school at Sagres, Portugal's most south-western point. Since the overland route into the Far East had been cut off by the advances of the Ottoman Empire, Henry was dedicated to finding an alternative route by sea. By the 1480s Portugal was well on its way to achieving that goal; by the 1490s Spain could no longer ignore its neighbor's success. Columbus's idea might well do the trick of beating the Portuguese to the East. Ferdinand was none too interested in Columbus's plan, but Isabella was willing to entertain his scheme. Perhaps it was her religious fervor and the idea of spreading Christianity into the Muslim world that made the queen hear out Columbus; perhaps it was the prospect of filling the royal coffers from the wealth generated by a lucrative trade route into the spice-rich islands of Asia; perhaps it was simply the possibility of another adventure. In any case, the queen listened, bargained, and finally agreed to allow Columbus to sail under the aegis of the flag of Castile, a decision she was not to regret. In this she was continuing a Spanish Reconquista tradition in which expeditions were privately financed but undertaken always with the permission of the crown. A negotiated contract would be drawn up between the monarch and the adventurer, guaranteeing him certain rights and privileges upon the successful completion of his endeavor and ensuring that the crown received the lion's share of the generated wealth.

After two months at sea, Columbus landed somewhere in the Bahamas, and the world has never been the same. According to his own words, Columbus encountered a beautiful people with whom he wanted to develop "a friendly attitude" because, he claimed, "they are a people who can be made free and converted to our Holy Faith more by love than by force."[5] The "handsome and of good disposition" Arawaks (a description that helped create the image

---

[5] Columbus, *The Log of Christopher Columbus*, 76

of the noble savage), or Taínos, the sedentary, peaceful people of Hispaniola, would give Columbus enough gold to make his gamble pay off.

With gold and other exotic treasures in hand, Columbus set sail back to Spain. He was greeted warmly enough by Isabella, who saw in the collection that Columbus presented her the promise of future gains. But further exploration and gains would have to wait until the Catholic Monarchs had permission from Pope Alexander VI to hold title to the lands Columbus had encountered. The pope's temporal authority was a medieval tradition that allowed him to grant right of dominion over new lands in exchange for the responsibility of the grantee to Christianize any peoples living in those lands. Having close ties to Ferdinand, the pope was quick to grant the king's wishes for formal authority over the Americas through the bull *Inter caetera*. Portugal, always interested in what lay beyond the seas, was not pleased with the vagueness of the papal bull, which basically granted Spain all lands – even those as yet undiscovered by Europeans – lying beyond a line a hundred leagues west of the Cape Verde Islands. After Portugal threatened war if Spain insisted upon implementing the papal bull, the two countries renegotiated the line of demarcation at 370 leagues west of the Cape Verde Islands in the Treaty of Tordesillas in 1494.

This papal pronouncement was quickly followed in 1501 by a bull granting the Spanish crown the right to collect the tithes levied in the Americas in order to pay for its missionary activities. And by 1508, Pope Julius II granted the Spanish monarch the *patronato real*, which gave the crown the right to make nominations for all American ecclesiastical posts, from priest to bishop. Now there was virtually complete royal control of the ecclesiastical structure in the Indies, an unparalleled union between crown and cross. As we will see in Chapter 2, eventually these grants of power would unleash heated debates throughout Europe about just war and what constituted the right to conquer.

Columbus's second voyage saw the arrival of the first Christian missionaries to American soil. Foremost among these were three Franciscans, a Hieronymite, and the ex-Benedictine Fernando Boyl, who served as apostolic vicar of the new lands. Boyl soon rebelled against Columbus and returned to Spain, but others remained. They and the few who followed shortly after did little in the early years of Caribbean conquest. In fact, it may be precisely their lack of activity that led to what must have been the attitude of many indigenous folks so poignantly expressed in the story of Hatuey. As told by Bartolomé de Las Casas, the great protector of Indians whom we will discuss later in this chapter and in Chapter 2, Hatuey was an Indian leader from the island of Hispaniola who fled from the Spaniards to nearby Cuba. There he learned that the Spaniards were on their way. Gathering the people who had fled with him, Hatuey reminded them of what they knew about the Spanish: that they murdered, stole, and lied. He asked, "'[d]oes any of you know why it is that they behave this way?' And when they answered him: 'No, unless it be that they are innately cruel and evil,' he replied: 'It is not simply that.' . . . He had beside him, as he spoke, a basket filled with gold jewellery and he said: 'Here is the God of the Christians.'"[6]

Hatuey, of course, was captured by the Spaniards and condemned to death by burning at the stake. As he awaited his execution, a Franciscan priest asked the Indian leader if he wanted to go to Heaven, for in the brief time left him on the earth, the priest explained, Hatuey could be baptized and avoid the fires of Hell. Being the first he had heard of such a thing, Hatuey asked "whether Christians went to Heaven. When the reply came that good ones do, he retorted, . . . if that was the case, then he chose to go to Hell." Such, wrote Las Casas, was "the reputation and honour that our Lord and our Christian faith have earned as a result of the actions of those 'Christians' who have sailed to the Americas."[7]

Many of the people whom Las Casas condemned in his recounting of Hatuey's story were early settlers of the island who had received from the Spanish crown an *encomienda*. An old Spanish institution that rewarded the efforts of soldiers, this grant of the labor of the defeated foes was slightly altered in the Indies. In the Americas, the *encomendero*, or holder of the encomienda, was required to treat his charges well and protect and Christianize them. In exchange, Indians were to work for the encomendero in whatever capacity he chose. In the Caribbean, Indians were parceled out to settlers who could demonstrate a need for laborers in mining, farming, or any other effort they might undertake. In theory the Indians were considered free and allowed to exercise that freedom within limits; in reality, the encomienda was slavery. Encomenderos rarely, if ever, fulfilled their side of the encomienda equation, instead working "their" Indians to death, so sure were the Spaniards that their supply of laborers was unending. But they were wrong. As a result of this forced labor system and the accompanying disruption of family and community structures, diet, and their very way of life, thousands of people died. For Hispaniola, hotly debated precontact population figures range from two hundred thousand to 1.2 million or more. While the number of inhabitants on the island before the arrival of the Spaniards is unclear, what

---

[6] Bartolomé de Las Casas, *A Short Account of the Destruction of the Indies*, ed. and trans. Nigel Griffin (London: Penguin Group, 1992), 27–28.

[7] Ibid., 29.

is clear is that, by 1509, there were only around sixty-two thousand (a decline of just under 95% on the high end to 69% on the low end). By 1540, there were a few hundred Indians left on the island. Certainly, perhaps even more than the devastation wrought by disease, the introduction of the encomienda signaled the beginning of the destruction of indigenous civilizations in the Caribbean.

However, not all Christians who came to the Caribbean were of the same ilk as those whom Hatuey encountered. There was, for example, Antonio de Montesinos, a Dominican priest on Hispaniola who, on the Sunday before Christmas, 1511, preached a sermon coauthored with his fellow Dominicans. His words enraged some of his fellow clergy and the Spanish colonists to the point that they protested directly to the Spanish crown. The same sermon, however, would eventually galvanize Bartolomé de Las Casas into action on behalf of the Indians. In his *Historia de las Indias*, Las Casas quoted Montesinos as saying:

> I am the voice of one crying in the wilderness. In order to make your sins known to you I have mounted this pulpit. . . .
>
> This voice declares that you are in mortal sin, and live and die therein by reason of the cruelty and tyranny that you practice on these innocent people. Tell me, by what right or justice do you hold these Indians in such cruel and horrible slavery? By what right do you wage such detestable wars on these people who lived mildly and peacefully in their own lands, where you have consumed infinite numbers of them with unheard of murders and desolations? Why do you so greatly oppress and fatigue them, not giving them enough to eat or caring for them when they fall ill from excessive labors, so that they die or rather are slain by you, so that you may extract and acquire gold every day? . . . Are they not men? Do they not have rational souls? Are you not bound to love them as you love yourselves? . . . Be sure that in your present state you can no more be saved than the Moors or Turks who do not have and do not want the faith of Jesus Christ.[8]

Montesinos's charges and those of some of his fellow Dominicans as well as the concerns of the crown over the harshness of the encomenderos resulted in the creation of the Laws of Burgos of 1512. These laws sought a way to combine an existing labor system with evangelization and to codify a more benevolent treatment of the Indians. After all, the indigenous peoples were considered the vassals of the Spanish crown, and it would have its subjects well treated. For Spanish authorities, benevolence meant removing the Indians from their

---

[8]   Benjamin Keen, trans. and ed., *Latin American Civilization: History and Society, 1492 – the Present* (Boulder, CO: Westview Press, 1991), 71–72.

villages and gathering them into *congregaciones* – newly created communities overseen by clergy for easy evangelization. It also meant restricting to a few months per year the period of required labor for each individual before a forty-day break was given and ensuring that pre- and post-partum women were assigned tasks less strenuous than working in mines. By the terms of the Laws of Burgos the encomendero was once again reminded that he was responsible to ensure that the Indians received instruction in the Christian faith, that they were given a modest wage, and that his male indigenous charges were limited to one wife per man. Needless to say, efforts by the crown to guarantee a minimum standard of treatment for the laborers and to control the worst abuses of the encomenderos were largely ineffective. The colonists applied the age-old tradition of *obedezco pero no cumplo* (I obey but I do not comply), which basically meant that they disregarded any provisions within the Laws of Burgos that did not suit them, and they continued to use Indian labor as they saw fit. But their lack of response to the new laws did not silence their critics.

Chief among the advocates for the Indians was Bartolomé de Las Casas. It was 1514 when Las Casas was "transform[ed] ... from a self-marginalized agitator for reform into something greater and, for the Spanish colonist, far more menacing: the 'Defender of the Indians,'" a role he continued until his death in 1576 at eighty-two years of age.[9]

Las Casas had come to the Indies as a colonist in the early years of the sixteenth century (1502). He was given an encomienda on the island of Hispaniola, ordained into the secular priesthood in 1507, and granted another encomienda in Cuba in 1511 for his efforts in the subjugation of that island. He always described himself as a gentler, kinder encomendero who did not follow the practices of his fellow colonists although he did not, yet, condemn their treatment of the Indians. By 1515, however, Las Casas had renounced his past life and was making his case against the settlers directly to King Ferdinand, describing the atrocities that he – Las Casas – had witnessed in the conquest of Cuba and that were of such a nature that "[m]en and women hanged themselves and even strung up their own children [in order to escape the horrors of enslavement to the encomenderos]. As a direct result of the barbarity of one Spaniard ... more than two hundred locals committed suicide, countless thousands in all dying in this way."[10] In 1522 Las Casas finally succumbed to the entreaties of a Dominican and joined the order, taking his advocacy for the Indians of America to new levels, as we will see in Chapter 2.

---

[9] Anthony Pagden, introduction to *A Short Account of the Destruction of the Indies*, by Bartolomé de Las Casas, ed. and trans. Nigel Griffin (London: Penguin Group, 1992), xix–xx.
[10] Las Casas, *A Short Account*, 30.

The hue and cry raised by some of the orders had little success in preventing the abuse of native peoples, but the religious did not give up their campaign to improve the lives of the indigenous peoples of the Indies. Their initial efforts focused on the Caribbean, but as the conquest of the mainland began, they would turn their efforts there as well. It was, however, in the midst of the horrific experiences of the Caribbean that we begin to see the two faces of the church in Latin America: the one, an arm of the state that served the needs of the settlers, and the other that sought to be the conscience of the conquest and colonization.

By the time the conquistadores reached the mainland, landing on the coast of Mexico in 1519 under the leadership of Hernán Cortés, their goals for conquest had shifted slightly from those of the original settlers in the Caribbean. The early settlers wanted to get rich quick and return to Spain, hence the sheer barbarity of their treatment of the labor force in the Caribbean. In New Spain, as Mexico was known, the goal was not only to get rich quick but also to create a life in the Indies that would resemble one that the lowly born conquistadores could never attain in Spain, one that included landed estates. So, while they certainly treated the Indians with terrible cruelty, the mainland settlers refrained from some of the worst abuses witnessed by Las Casas in the islands. But the Spaniards had first to conquer the Indians they encountered in Mexico, a surprisingly easy task for the five hundred men and sixteen horses that landed at Veracruz in eleven ships on April 12, 1519.

The efforts of the conquistadores were aided by the indecisiveness of the Aztec ruler, Moctezuma II. According to the Aztecs' own account of their defeat – rendered primarily in the *Florentine Codex* and years after the fact – there were omens, as many as ten years before the Spaniards arrived, that clearly indicated that a cataclysmic disaster would occur. The Aztecs' concept of the order of the universe and the role of destruction in that order predisposed them to view the arrival of the Spaniards as part of the long-coming catastrophe. The documents reveal that after initial contact on the coast of Mexico was made with the invaders, Moctezuma came to believe that the Spaniards very likely were Quetzalcoatl and other deities returned to earth. After all, did not these strange-looking men have fire sticks (guns)? Did they not have huge "deer" (horses), which they rode? Surely, these were the tools of gods, or at the very least great magicians. Since Moctezuma's own magicians could do nothing to stop the conquistadores' march toward Tenochtitlan and since the human sacrifices performed in the presence of the newcomers did nothing to placate the Spaniards, Moctezuma waited fatalistically for his defeat. Translations from the *Florentine Codex* recount Moctezuma's response to the Spaniards this way: "Motecuhzoma ordered the sacrifice because he took the Spaniards to be gods; he believed in them and worshiped them as deities. That is why they were called 'Gods who have come from heaven.'" It was precisely Moctezuma's inability to determine the true nature of the white men that led to his inaction. If they were gods, then he must not offend them. If they were humans, then he must defend his people against them. Too unsure and frightened to make a decision, he left his people without a leader.

The Spaniards themselves experienced no such uncertainty in their march to the Aztec capital. From their perspective, the events that led inexorably toward their ultimate victory were part and parcel of their role in God's great plan, which included conversion of the natives, by force if necessary. Bernal Díaz del Castillo, the chronicler of the conquest of Mexico, tells us that the Spaniards also tried to convert the Aztecs through example. After arriving in Tenochtitlan, where they were welcomed as guests by the hesitant Moctezuma, the conquistadores constructed a church within the walls of a palace given over for their use:

> In two days we had our church finished and the holy cross set up in front of our apartments, and Mass was said there every day until the wine gave out.... [B]ut after it was all finished we still went to the church daily and prayed on our knees before the altar and images, for one reason, because we were obliged to do so as Christians and it was a good habit, and for another reason, in order that Montezuma and all his Captains should observe it, and should witness our adoration and see us on our knees before the Cross, especially when we intoned the Ave Maria, so that it might incline them towards it.[11]

But such examples were lost on the Aztecs, who simply saw the Spaniards desecrating the images of the gods and expressing revulsion at the most sacred of rituals.

Ultimately, the defeat of the Aztecs and the control of their empire would take the Spaniards a little more than two years, facilitated by the assistance of the indigenous enemies of the Aztecs, superior military weaponry, and the devastation of the Indians brought by diseases to which they had no immunity. The Aztecs desperately needed to understand, within the framework of their cosmology, the disaster that had befallen them; the only explanation that made any sense was that their gods had been defeated by a more powerful Christian god. From that point on, the formerly powerful warriors of Central Mexico posed little if any threat to the conquerors. The Indians of the Yucatan Peninsula and the Andes, however, would prove to be different stories altogether.

---

[11] Bernal Díaz del Castillo, *Discovery and Conquest of Mexico, 1517–1521*, ed. Genaro García, trans. A. P. Maudslay (New York: Farrar, Straus and Cudahy, 1956), 225.

The Mayas of the Yucatan were far more difficult to conquer than were the Aztecs, initially because the Mayas had received word of the Spaniards from Caribbean Indians and were prepared to fight, but in the long run because the Maya civilization was less centralized than the Aztec. By the time the Spaniards arrived on the peninsula, the principal political organizations within the region were local chiefdoms. The Spanish tactic of severing the head in order to control the body (or perhaps a more benign metaphor would be of a chess game in which the goal is to capture the king as opposed to a checkers game in which the goal is to capture the most pieces) would not work, precisely because there was no single leader, no great ruler. Nor would religious conquest be easy, as the Spaniards were to find out.

The military conquest of the Mayas, which began in 1527, took more than a decade, and even then the Mayas continued a hit-and-run strategy that kept the Spaniards off kilter until 1545. In fact, the final conquest of the Mayas would not be until 1697. Nevertheless, as the soldiers were battling the Indians, in 1544 Franciscan missionaries began their own struggles with the Mayas and with the Spanish settlers. In a pattern that was repeated throughout the Indies, the mendicant orders in the Yucatan, specifically the Franciscans, tried to limit contact between the settlers and the Indians in order to prevent the exploitation and corruption of the latter. In fact, as historians have pointed out, the friars did not want to teach the Indians the Spanish language for fear that the friars' role as mediators between the Spaniards and the Indian would cease. Yet in an interesting reversal of roles, in 1562 a chance discovery of Indian idols hidden in a cave led church officials in the Yucatan to begin an extirpation campaign in which the use of torture was so horrific and widespread that even the Spanish settlers complained to Spanish officials. Over a three-month period, under the leadership of Franciscan Diego de Landa, more than 4,500 Indians were subjected to the *garrucha*. In this form of torture, people were hanged from their wrists, previously tied behind the victims' back. If the individual did not confess as the friars thought appropriate, stones would be attached to the feet of the hapless victim and that person was left suspended from the wrists. If this was not enough, flogging and burning by hot wax were often next, ultimately followed by a formal punishment: years in forced labor, fines, more flogging. The crippling garrucha was used indiscriminately, maiming thousands and resulting in the death of at least 150. Is it any wonder that the settlers complained? Their labor force was being rendered useless.

For the Mayas, all the suffering and violence they experienced at the hand of the friars was a signal that their old gods had been defeated. The new god had won. Indeed, in *The Book of Chilam Balam of Chumayel* (an indigenous

Yucatecan town), which is a Mayan account of the Spanish conquest along with indigenous religious information, the writer wails: "the descendants of the former rulers are brought to misery; we are christianised, while they treat us like animals." Yet, as historian Inga Clendinnen points out, even Christianity imposed with such a heavy hand did not succeed in "killing off" the old gods nor in giving the Spaniards the sole right to the interpretation and implementation of Catholicism. As we will see in Chapter 2, Indian communities throughout the Indies created and claimed their own brand of Christianity, a unique mixture of indigenous ways and Spanish ways – from both the little and great traditions. In spite of enormous efforts by the Spaniards to create religious homogeneity or at least hegemony, there was in the New World the birth of a new religious reality just as there was also the birth of new racial and cultural realities.

In many ways the spiritual and physical conquest of the Andes and the Inca empire mirrored elements of the Aztec and Maya conquests. As in the case of the Aztecs, the Spaniards used the tactic of gaining control of the ruler in order to gain control of the people; the Spaniards were aided by disease, which killed thousands of Indians and weakened thousands more; and it was a small band of Spaniards helped by indigenous enemies of the Incas who ultimately prevailed. As in the case of the Mayas, the Andean religious culture would not surrender easily to Christianity, leading to ugly and protracted extirpation campaigns by the church.

The conquest of the Inca empire was led by Francisco Pizarro, the illegitimate son of a minor Spanish noble. He was a proven conquistador long before he set his sights on South America, having been granted an encomienda in Panama for his efforts in its early settlement. After some failed expeditions and after securing royal permission for his campaign, Pizarro began the climb up the Andes from the Pacific in September 1532 with 168 men, 63 of whom were horsemen. By November of that year Pizarro's contingent was in Cajamarca, a town in the Andes. But on that spring evening, Cajamarca was no ordinary town; Atahualpa, the Sapa Inca, was there. The Inca ruler was in the midst of an internecine struggle that erupted after the preceding Sapa Inca's death from a smallpox epidemic in the 1520s. (The disease had traveled south along trade routes, reaching the Inca empire long before the Spaniards did.) At the time of the Spaniards' arrival, Atahualpa had the upper hand in the civil war. Early intelligence had informed Pizarro that the Sapa Inca was in the town, so he arranged a meeting with Atahualpa. Pizarro's men hid near Cajamarca's central plaza, the arranged meeting place. The Sapa Inca, not suspecting any treachery on the part of the Spaniards and more concerned with his fraternal enemy than with the invaders, came to the plaza with very lightly armed body guards. At a predetermined signal, the hidden Spaniards fired into the crowd enclosed by the plaza. Panic ensued; thousands were crushed to death by the stampede to leave the confines of the square, and the Sapa Inca was captured. Amazingly, even in hindsight, Atahualpa did not comprehend the significance of his capture. He still continued to be more preoccupied with the war with his brother than with his own fate at the hands of the Spaniards, ordering his brother's execution while he, Atahualpa, was a prisoner. Eventually, even after literally getting as ransom a room full of gold, the Spaniards garroted the Sapa Inca. Now with the ruler gone, the Indians' numerical advantage over the Spaniards became totally irrelevant. They were paralyzed. Pizarro with his few men and native allies easily took control of the Inca empire.

Once again the Spaniards viewed the inexorable march toward ultimate victory as a sure sign that they were part of God's great scheme to Christianize the Americas. In spite of the acts of atrocity committed by the Spaniards in their battles with the indigenous peoples, the conquistadores always understood themselves to be good Christian men. In a civil war among the conquistadores that followed the defeat of the Incas, Francisco Pizarro was killed. As he lay dying, this perpetrator of untold inhumanities against the Indians made the sign of the cross with his own blood on the floor so that it would be the last thing upon which he gazed in this world. The militant arm of Spanish Christianity that had developed after the centuries-long struggle to reconquer the peninsula had been replicated in the Americas.

THE AFRICANS

In addition to indigenous American groups and the Europeans, there were other people who had profound impact on Latin America; those, of course, were the Africans. While they do not appear in the Americas in great numbers until well after the conquest (although some Blacks did come with the conquistadores), it is important that we include them in a chapter on the foundations of the Christian church in the Latin world, for their contributions to its present character are immeasurable, particularly in the Caribbean and Brazil.

The Africans who came to the New World rarely came willingly or as free people. In overwhelming numbers they came as slaves, cut off from their lands and loosened from the moorings that provided the anchors of life. But the fact that they came as slaves in no way meant that they did not bring with them their traditions and cultures, including religions. Nor did being enslaved mean that these men, women, and children had no influence on the culture beyond the walls of their quarters. Such influence was most greatly felt in

Brazil and the Caribbean, where black slavery was most prominent, although it would be wrong to assume that black slaves did not exist in other regions of Latin America. However, the impact of African life and culture on the broader culture is perhaps more visible today in Latin America than during colonial times, for today that influence is often embraced as a part of national identity.

What of the roots of the African influence on Latin American Christianity and religious life? The majority of slaves to come into Latin America came from West Africa primarily because of its proximity to the Americas but also because it was along the Atlantic coast of Africa that Portugal established its factories, or fortified trading posts, during the heyday of its sea explorations. These outposts were created to facilitate trade – including trade in slaves – with the indigenous peoples along the coast, making Portugal the first great powerhouse to sail the Middle Passage, bringing to the Americas many and varied cultures and religions of West Africa.

Perhaps most famous of these imported religions is that of the Yorubas, which when melded with Catholicism would create Santería, as we will see in Chapter 6. Yoruba cosmology held that there was only one world – the here and now – but within that one world there was a visible part, that which humans occupied, and an invisible part that was occupied by the *orisha* and the ancestors. The orisha were spirits that gave humans access to the knowable part of the great creative force of the universe by inhabiting a person and sending him or her into a trance as part of rituals that included dance, music, and food. The orisha could be seen in trees or rocks, be present in lightning or the ocean; the orisha could be anywhere. The interaction with these spirits was, in part, an effort to understand the existence of evil and suffering in the world. To help followers comprehend the communication from the spirits and to lead the community, most African traditional religions had (and have) religious leaders – priests and priestesses. But the preeminent position of religious leaders was not limited to times of worship; these men and women were key in the structure of the community and in all its activities, such as planting, farming, hunting, healing, and raising children. It was precisely the involvement of religion in everyday life and actions that proved most threatening to New World slaveholders. The practice of traditional African religions by slaves was a way to maintain cultural identity, to define power within the slave population, and to provide a basis of resistance far beyond the reach of the slave master. As we will see in later chapters, just as the indigenous populations did, black slaves – both those brought directly from Africa and those born into slavery in the Americas – and freed Blacks would find ways to disguise their traditional religious practices by wrapping them in the cloak of Roman Catholicism. First, however, would come the encounter, the conquests, and the wars of the Americas at the hands of a relatively few Spaniards.

CONCLUSION

The conquistadores who wrought such destruction viewed themselves not only as military men but also as soldiers of the cross, bringing the one true religion to those they defeated and defiled, saving the pagans from a fate worse than death. Without a doubt they and those they conquered were forever changed by the encounter, but they were not the only ones. The Roman Catholic Church was itself altered. The European missionaries who came with the conquistadores brought with them their ideas of what humanity was, who could be a Christian, and how the world was structured. What they found in the Americas did not fit those ideas. They saw horrors heretofore unimagined as they witnessed thousands of humans sacrificed, as they encountered polygyny among the elite indigenous males, and as they found mummified remains of ancestors worshiped as links to another world. But what must have surely confounded them even more was that many of these horrors were practiced by people who also lived in highly stratified societies, as did the Europeans. Some of them lived in beautiful cities said to rival anything in Europe. And some had extensive trade networks that brought every needed item to enormous marketplaces. The missionaries were mystified by how these European-like traits could coexist with every evidence that the Americans were barbarians at best and probably subhuman. Theological scholars in Spain struggled to find answers by debating and discussing the very nature of the New World peoples, to which we will return in Chapter 2. And perhaps most challenging to the Catholic Church was the questioning of religious authority. After all, the church had taught that God's world was ordered in a way that conformed to the doctrine of the Trinity: There were three continents, and this was a vestige of the Trinity that had created the world – Father, Son, and Holy Spirit. Now, there was at least one more continent. The whole understanding of the physical world's relation to the spiritual world needed to be rethought. How did revealed truth (the tripartite structure of the world and the Trinity) relate to observed truth (the existence of more than three continents)? How could the church fathers be so wrong about how the world was put together? If they were wrong about one point, could they not be wrong about others, too?

We cannot overestimate the long-term impact the encounter with the Americas had on European religious thought. It was far more profound than would be for us the discovery of people much like ourselves inhabiting another planet. Yet challenges to church teachings were not the only changes brought to Europe on the ships that sailed from the New World; there were also political changes that resulted from Spain's conquest of the Indies. Ships that crossed the Atlantic returned to Spain loaded with some gold and a great deal of silver, filling the royal coffers of Spain (and enriching merchants, many of whom were not Spanish). With the massive influx of wealth, Charles I of Spain was able to cover the debt he had incurred in 1519 in order to purchase the votes that made him Holy Roman Emperor Charles V. It was he who underestimated, then had to face, the early threat posed by that pesky German priest Martin Luther. It was he who ultimately had to surrender some power to the German princes in the religious struggles between Lutherans and Roman Catholics. And it was Charles V who waged war upon war in regions all over Europe to keep his extensive empire together, wasting the wealth brought from the Indies – a pattern his son Philip II followed.

Columbus's first steps in the western hemisphere began a journey that is not over yet. The exotica he found ultimately came at a price for all involved. Chapter 2 will examine some of those early costs: the evolving role of the Roman Catholic Church in the conquest itself, the efforts by the indigenous peoples to retain their traditional religious identity even in the face of the imposition of Catholicism, and the scholarly debates that swirled around Europe in an effort to make sense of what Columbus had found.

∾

The Arrival of Christianity

As we have seen in Chapter 1, in the process of bringing Christianity to the Indies, the Spanish conquistadores laid waste to the high civilizations of the Americas in the name of Christianity. They carried the sword and the cross, transporting across the Atlantic the militant arm of the faith. In their wake came the missionaries who also largely represented the same aggressive church. Yet, as we have also seen, the church was not necessarily of one accord.

Just as with Columbus, whose deep piety and eagerness to bring the love of Christ to heathen prompted him, at least in part, to cross the Atlantic, a ceaseless, deep-felt love for Christ brought many missionaries to the New World: love of a Christ who suffered, endured ridicule, and sacrificed. That Christ would also be the role model for others who also migrated across the Atlantic to bring their faith to the newly encountered lands. Unfortunately, we cannot categorize all action by church representatives in the Americas as selfless and other-serving. For every missionary who treated the Indians with the gentle hand of persuasion, there were others who used the brutal hand of coercion. As we will see, some of the varied responses to the indigenous populations came from the missionaries' own understanding of their role vis-à-vis the conversion of pagans to Christianity, but some came out of frustration and confusion over expectations that were not easily met.

The conflicting behavior of the missionaries was also reflected in the theological and political debates that filled the rarefied halls of Spanish universities and the royal courts of the peninsula. Churchmen and schoolmen debated, in medieval style, on what was the exact nature of the Indian. Some theologians drew upon Aristotle, the consummate cataloger, to assess where in God's great universal order these strange beings belonged, while others challenged the very premises on which his writings were based. Civil lawyers scrutinized human law to find justification for the conquest. And canon lawyers turned to their understanding of God's laws to sanctify the actions of the crown and the pope. Though often contentious, the debates rarely, if ever, produced any sort of conclusion. In the final analysis, the debates, writings, and discussions of Spain's brightest minds had little bearing on the lives of the Indians. In fact, it would perhaps be more accurate to state that it was the encounter with the Indians and their subsequent treatment at the hands of the conquistadores that had an impact on the intellectual life of Spain and the rest of Europe.

Theologians and missionaries were not the only ones unable to respond consistently to the encounter between Europeans and New World inhabitants. Amerindian reactions to the efforts of the Spanish friars and priests were also varied, reflecting accommodation and resistance. Some indigenous communities found ways of weaving into the fabric of Roman Catholic rituals the thread of indigenous religious practices. For example, in the Andes, huacas were sometimes hidden under Catholic altars. Conversely, some Indian leaders spurred outright rebellions, calling for indigenous gods to overthrow the Spaniards' god. And some Indians, undoubtedly, were sincere converts to Christianity yet found ways to make its practice uniquely American.

Who can blame the people who felt the force of the encounter between European and indigenous cultures and peoples for being inconsistent in their reactions? It would be no easy feat to fit the square peg of European religious reality and theology into the round hole of New World experiences and cultures. While we certainly cannot ignore the impact of power relations and conquest on the process of accommodation, each group did follow a similar pattern of engaging the new worlds in which it found itself. First, there was an effort to squeeze the new reality into old preconceptions of the universe. Second, there was a disquieting realization that traditional concepts of how the world was put together no longer made sense. And third, there was an acquiescence to the transformations resulting from the intermixing of things European and things American.

In our efforts to make sense of the impact of the encounter in the Americas on the Christian church, we will begin with the *theological and intellectual struggles* that emerged in Spain as word of the events across the Atlantic reached scholars and churchmen in universities throughout the kingdom. Erudite debate, however, had little impact on methods employed by evangelists in the Indies. We will explore institutions created by the missionaries and the ways in which they tried to reach the indigenous population in their *efforts at conversion*. And just who were the evangelists? Who came as missionaries to the Americas? In the section on *the friars*, we will discuss some of the orders that sent their brothers and the particular perspective each had about the Christianizing process. But try as they might, the missionaries could not ensure that the Catholicism that emerged in the Indies was a replica of that in Europe. In fact, *faith in the Americas* was decidedly different from that on the Iberian peninsula. And certainly one of the factors that altered the church was the *continuation of old ways* of the Indians. In the early colonial years, the meeting of two worlds had profound results for all involved as people in the Americas and in Europe dealt with the implications of a world suddenly expanded. Thus, the present chapter examines how many of those affected by the encounter coped with new realities of the church.

THEOLOGICAL AND INTELLECTUAL STRUGGLES

Almost immediately upon Columbus's return, the Catholic Monarchs turned to the pope for legitimization of and permission to continue their endeavors in the Indies, as we have seen in Chapter 1. The granting of such rights assumed the pope had temporal as well as spiritual authority, but such assumptions were problematic when it came to the Americas. There was a tradition that held that the pontiff had earthly authority over lands of pagans, but only certain pagans: those who lived in territories formerly part of the Roman Empire or who could legitimately be considered under the rule of a Christian prince. Clearly, the inhabitants of the Americas did not fall into either of these two categories. Thus, when apologists for the Spanish crown's project in the New World wanted to justify its right to conquer and rule in the Americas on grounds stronger than the papal donation, they turned increasingly to the writings of the Scottish theologian John Mair, who held that the natives of the Americas were "natural slaves." Mair drew on Aristotle's description of human beings as "natural slaves" or "natural masters": "As the Philosopher [Aristotle] says in the third and fourth chapters of the first book of the *Politics*, it is clear that some men are by nature slaves, others by nature free. . . . it is fitting that one man should rule and another obey."[1] Now some Spanish thinkers had a novel answer to the dilemma of what gave the crown the right to govern in the Americas: It was the nature of the natives themselves; they needed to be governed by an enlightened, Christian ruler. Following this line of reasoning, the Amerindians appeared to act like barbarians, live like barbarians, and have all the Aristotelian-defined characteristics of barbarians, and, because barbarians are slaves and slaves are barbarians, the Spaniards had a moral obligation to rule in the Americas – an obligation that superceded any judicial rights of conquest the crown might also have.

[1] John Mair, *In secundum librum sententiarum* (Paris, 1519), f. clxxxvij^r, as quoted in Anthony Pagden, *The Fall of Natural Man: The American Indian and the Origins of Comparative Ethnology* (Cambridge: Cambridge University Press, 1982), 38.

But not all Spanish churchmen and scholars found Aristotle's classifications to be compelling justification for the brutal conquest of the Americas. Chief among those who argued against the pope's right of donation and the interpretation of Aristotle's philosophy that led to the justification of conquest was Francisco de Vitoria, the dean of the "school of Salamanca." The University of Salamanca, in northern Spain, was the country's premier university and could boast some of the top theologians and philosophers of Europe. Led by Vitoria, the school of Salamanca, as Vitoria and his students became known, pushed beyond the bounds of strict theological inquiry and applied theological principles to ethical questions, including the conquest of the Americas. For them, the "Indian problem" was at its core a theological issue and a question about relations among different groups of people that went further than Amerindians and Spaniards.[2]

Rejecting Aristotle's concepts outright as not adequately describing God's creation, Vitoria argued that the Indians – and here he meant the high-culture Indians of central Mexico and the Andes about whom he knew the most – had all the characteristics of civilization and the use of reason; therefore, they could not be justly deprived of their possessions, including their land and their labor. By such definitions, he considered the Indians fully human and not a subspecies that could be conquered with impunity. But Vitoria was then left with the question of what to do with the cannibals and practitioners of human sacrifice whom the conquistadores encountered. Surely these people who existed so far out of the bounds of goodness, decency, and natural law had to be governed in some manner. But on what grounds? It is in response to the contradiction of a civilized people acting in uncivilized ways that Vitoria and his followers made an interesting contribution to the debate about the nature of the Indians: they were like children, having the potential for use of true reason but not there yet. Unlike European children, however, even as the Indians grew older, their environment and customs did not bring about complete realization of that potential. Consequently, until such time as the Indians had "grown," they had to "remain in just tutelage under the king of Spain, his [the Indian's] status now slave-like, but not slavish."[3]

While the musings of Vitoria and his pupils were theoretical in nature, the rarified discussions of the university of Salamanca came into contact with the real world in Valladolid in 1550–1551 in the well-known debate between

---

[2] Francisco de Vitoria is often considered the "father" of international law since his thoughts about just war and state sovereignty laid the groundwork for the way in which nations relate to one another.

[3] Pagden, *The Fall of Natural Man*, 104.

Juan Ginés de Sepúlveda and Bartolomé de Las Casas. Sepúlveda was a royal chaplain and an unrepentant advocate for the idea of Indian inferiority, but he was no theologian, which may have contributed to the cold reception he received from the churchmen at the universities of Salamanca and Alcala. They believed this mere priest was delving into questions for which he was not trained, questions beyond his ability to tackle. So, the academics blocked the publication of Sepúlveda's treatise on the inferiority of the Americans and the justness of the wars raging against them.[4] It was not, however, only Sepúlveda's lack of credentials that caused the university scholars to reject his work; he was, more importantly, challenging the conclusions of Vitoria a decade earlier on just war and the nature of the American Indian. This humanist turned once again to Aristotle's notion of the natural slave, arguing that the Indians, "who in prudence, wisdom . . . , every virtue and human-ity are as inferior to the Spaniards as children are to adults, women are to men, the savage and ferocious to the gentle, the grossly intemperate to the continent and the temperate and finally, I shall say, [are] almost as monkeys are to men."[5] The wars against the Indians, Sepúlveda contended, were just wars because the Indians were sinful and practiced all manner of vice. Fur-thermore, they needed to be saved from themselves, which could happen only at the point of a sword. Spain needed to rule over the Indians for their own good because the natives of the Americas could never be true humans with full and complete use of reason and therefore full and complete freedom of action.

The failure to get his work published did not stop Sepúlveda from making his ideas known (and it must be said that the majority of Spaniards undoubtedly supported his point of view). As a chaplain to the king, his thoughts and opinions were familiar to the crown. Thus, when Charles V wanted to have the merits of his enterprise in the Indies debated, it was Sepúlveda who represented the "just war" side. And it should be no surprise that Bartolomé de Las Casas appeared as the advocate for the Indians.

As discussed in Chapter 1, in the Indies Las Casas underwent a transforma-tion, converting from a beneficiary of forced Indian labor as an encomendero to the life-long defender of the Indians. His efforts as protector of the indige-nous population were well known in Spain, where he traveled frequently, always arguing for more protective laws and better treatment of the Indians.

---

[4] Sepúlveda's *Democrates secundus sive de justis causis belli apud Indos* would not be published until 1892, almost 350 years after it was written, most likely in 1544.

[5] Juan Ginés de Sepúlveda, *Democrates segundo, o de las justas causas de la guerra contra los indios,* ed. Angel Losada (Madrid, 1951), as quoted in Pagden, *The Fall of Natural Man,* 117.

When in the metropolis he recruited fellow Dominicans as missionaries to the Americas, advocated in court on behalf of the Indians, and encouraged the passage of the New Laws of 1542, which will be discussed later. By 1550 his reputation was well established in court and with the Council of the Indies, which advised the king on all matters American.

Las Casas's relationship with the Spanish crown and the Council began decades before the Valladolid debates. In the late 1510s, Las Casas, in person, successfully petitioned the crown to grant him land on the coast of Venezuela to establish an utopian settlement where he hoped the goodness and peaceful persuasion of Spanish farmers and priests would entice the Indians to conversion. Alas, his efforts failed largely because of not-so-peaceful Spaniards. As a result, Las Casas withdrew to a Dominican monastery in despair where he spent several years in theological study and mediation. He did not, however, give up his role as defender of the Indians. By 1531 Las Casas had witnessed such corruption and greed by Spanish officials that he wrote to the Council of the Indies, again protesting the malevolent behavior that seemed quickly to overtake royal representatives: "Those who come here to give orders become daring and lose their fear of God and faith in their king and fidelity to him and respect for the people, and then they make a pact with the devil, to whom they give their souls so they can rob."[6] While in reality there was little the Council of the Indies could do from such a great distance, Las Casas was becoming one of the principal sources of information on what was happening to the Indians. His reappearance on the scene in 1531 launched, for him, a period of prolific writing, complaining, traveling, and advocating that would last until his death.

When Las Casas arrived in Valladolid in 1550 to debate Sepúlveda before a *junta* comprising royally appointed religious and legal experts who were to decide on the justness of the Spanish enterprise, he was ready, having spent many years arguing for the humane treatment of the indigenous Americans. The junta was called into being by Charles V, who was troubled over whether the conquest and colonization of the Americas was just. As part of its work, the junta held the now-famous debate.[7]

---

[6] Bartolomé de las Casas, 1531, as quoted in Antonio M. Fabié, *Vida y escritos de don Fray Bartolomé de Las Casas, Obispo de Chiapa*, [reprinted in *Colleción de documentos inéditos para la historia de España* (Vaduz: Kraus Reprint, 1966), 70: 482] as quoted in Luis N. Rivera, "The Theological Juridical Debate," in *The Church in Colonial Latin America*, ed. John F. Schwaller (Wilmington, DE: Scholarly Resources, 2000), 8.

[7] The junta finally disbanded in 1551 without offering an opinion to the king. But more than likely an opinion one way or the other would have had little impact on the lives and treatment of the Indians.

Chief among Las Casas's contentions before this group of churchmen and scholars was that the wars taking place in the Indies were morally just only on the Indian side. It was they who were fighting a defensive war, having been unjustly attacked by the Spaniards. The Indians had a right to defend their homes and their possessions from the onslaught of a more militarily advanced invader, especially as the Indians had posed no threat to Christianity. The Spaniards, however, had no such just cause. Additionally, Las Casas argued, in a putative effort to save potential victims of sacrifice or cannibalism (a just cause in principle), the Spaniards were killing more innocent people than would have perished otherwise. And while the church certainly had the right to deal harshly with heretics, the peoples of the Americas should not be included in such a category because they suffered from what theologians called "invincible ignorance," never having been exposed to the Gospel.

The debate lasted for days, with the opponents never in each other's presence, but both reading prepared comments, of which Las Casas's were the longer – by days – and undoubtedly the more tedious. Even though each side claimed victory, in the end the encounter between Sepúlveda and Las Casas brought no real change in Spain's actions in the New World. What is important for us here is that the two sides in this debate portray the two faces of the church's presence in the Indies: Sepúlveda, the cross and sword inextricably intertwined, each serving the purpose of the other; and Las Casas, the church's role as protector of the weak, bringing "true" conversion by example, standing against prevailing culture.

But why would the questions of justification even come up? Why was the right to conquer and colonize such a pressing issue when the fact of conquest and colonization was well under way? In Spain there was no way of separating the political from the religious, hence, "[e]very theological dispute about the New World and its inhabitants took on a political character and vice versa; every political disagreement over the relationship of Spain to the natives became a theological debate."[8] Since a foundation for Spanish presence in the Indies was Christianity, which theoretically presupposed the equality before God of all who had been baptized, the treatment of the Indians did matter. And as the historian Lewis Hanke reminds us, the Spanish conquest of the Americas was an unprecedented effort to bring Christian values to bear in Spain's relations with other peoples. Theological questions had profound impact on both policy and those who formulated it; they did not, however, have an impact on the experience of Amerindians.

[8]   Rivera, "The Theological Juridical Debate," 5.

One curious effort at ensuring that conquest in the Indies was just, at least in the minds of the Spaniards, was the *Requerimiento* (1514), a declaration read aloud (usually in Spanish and without the aid of a translator) to the Indians before they were attacked. The intention of this document was to explain to the Indians the rights of the Spaniards in the New World and the obligation of the natives. After recounting the Christian creation story and the pope's legacy from St. Peter, Pope Alexander's donation of the lands of the Indies to the Spanish monarchs was detailed with the expectation that the Indians would peacefully become passive subjects of the king. The conquerors magnanimously stated that the natives could take whatever time was necessary to understand all that had been said. The *Requerimiento* also declared, however, that if despite every effort made by the Spaniards to help the Indians comprehend what lay before them they refused to acquiesce to the authority of the Spanish crown, then the soldiers would "with the help of God" wage war against the Indians, subjecting them to "the yoke and obedience of the Church and their Highnesses." Furthermore, if the Indians resisted, the conquistadores would be within their rights to enslave men, women, and children. And lest the Indians not fully understand who would be to blame for such actions, the *Requerimiento* spelled out that the fault would lie with the Indians themselves. The *Requerimiento* relieved the conquistadores of any sin and transformed the wars of conquest into just wars whose goal was the spread of Christianity.

EFFORTS AT CONVERSION

Such justification was not sufficient for a monarch concerned about the colonists, the Indians, and the former's treatment of the latter – not to mention his own soul. Repeatedly, royal worries over actions in the Indies were not only a matter for dialogue and debate. As we discussed in Chapter 1, the Laws of Burgos were promulgated in 1512 in an effort, albeit ineffective, to curtail the worst excesses of the colonists in the Caribbean. In 1542 Charles V enacted the New Laws in a similar attempt to control the encomienda system and to protect the rapidly dwindling indigenous population in the Americas.[9] While such efforts proved disastrous in Peru – where a civil war broke out – and were never enforced in New Spain for fear of a violent response by the colonists, they reflect the Spanish government's paternalistic relationship with

---

[9] Among other provisions, the New Laws of 1542 sought to limit the encomienda to one generation, removing the right to bequeath the grant; outlawed Indian slavery; and undercut the power of a growing colonial elite comprising mostly encomenderos.

its Indian subjects. As the father king, the Spanish monarch was to treat his subjects benevolently and ensure their well-being. It was, in fact, the work of missionaries – particularly Las Casas – that brought to the attention of the crown and the Council of the Indies the brutal treatment of the natives and their need for protection. The church, or at least part of it, became the conscience of the conquest.

The missionaries themselves, however, were not above changing the Indians' social structures by, for example, banning trial marriages. They also seemed to have no compunctions about totally disrupting Indian society through relocation, in order to meet the goal of installing Christianity to the Americas. *Congregaciones*, or *reducciones* in the Andes, were religious relocation. These "congregations," as mentioned in Chapter 1, were an effort to gather the Indians in centralized, new villages – built by Indian labor supervised by friars – whose purpose was to protect the Indians from the Spaniards' greed, make extraction of labor and tribute for the crown easier, and aid in conversion. In areas of high population concentration and urbanization, such as Tenochtitlan or Cuzco, congregaciones were not necessary, but in those regions where Indian communities were far and wide apart, the gathering of various villages into one place made sense to the friars as they struggled to carry out evangelization. Ideally, a congregación would be laid out on a Spanish-style grid pattern with a central plaza that was surrounded by the church and any other major buildings the community might have. Radiating from the plaza were straight streets, which represented the order and civility the missionaries were trying to impart along with conversion. Equally important to the Spaniards in such town developments was the social status indicated by the proximity of one's house to the plaza: the closer one lived to the plaza, the higher one's social ranking. The Indians were expected to learn Spanish/Christian ways in schools and workshops. The use of Spanish agricultural methods and the planting of Spanish crops, such as wheat, were one way to ensure that the Indians were also introduced to Spanish customs. Traditional indigenous family structures were also altered, with communal living replaced by nuclear family homes. Premarital sex, a common feature in many Indian cultures, was forbidden – as was having multiple wives. By removing the Indians from their traditional homes and putting them under the watchful eye of the friars, it was thought that the link to their sinful past would be broken. Thus, the native residents of these new communities would be more easily reeducated. Needless to say, as in many things the Indians took a Spanish idea and made it their own or rejected it outright. The typical congregación had nothing but an open area for a plaza with an Indian-constructed church at one end.

The streets were not laid out in any particular order, nor were the houses. And often the priest in a congregación had to accept the fact that many of "his" Indians would simply run away, returning to their traditional homes or disappearing into the countryside. Another problem for those overseeing the congregaciones was that their creation tended to pit the Spanish colonists, who were losing the labor provided by Indians, against the friars. Sometimes, as the two sides sought control of the indigenous populations, they fought pitched battles.

The success of congregaciones varied from region to region. In what is modern-day Paraguay, for example, the Jesuits were fairly successful in maintaining Guaraní congregaciones. Together with the Indian residents, the missionaries were able to protect the communities from the Spanish colonists, even joining with Jesuits working across the border in Brazil to defeat slave raiders who threatened the villages.

The Portuguese crown, too, tried to protect the natives (primarily Tupí speakers) from the brutality of the settlers in Brazil. By the mid 1500s the Jesuits, who dominated evangelization efforts in Brazil, were doing their best to shield the Indians by congregating them in new villages, or *aldeias*. These communities, much like those in Spanish America, were to be free of European interference, and the Indians who resided there were to be off-limits to Brazilian slave raiders. Much to the chagrin of the Jesuits, Brazilian Indians did not flock to the aldeias, and by the late 1550s it was apparent that peaceful efforts at congregating the population were failing. By 1557 the Jesuits were in full support of the Portuguese crown's military operations against resistant Indian communities. The military's success in bringing Indians to the aldeias led to more than forty thousand Indians, in the Bahia region alone, living in Jesuit-controlled communities where they experienced disruptions of traditional patterns and dislocation from traditional environments. As in Spanish America, the removal of such a large number of Indians from the potential labor pool in Portuguese America resulted in conflicts with the settlers.

Such conflicts did not exist in the borderlands because often the only European settlement was the mission. The late sixteenth century saw the advent of this system in what is today the United States. In Georgia, for example, as early as the 1570s the Franciscans established missions in the principal settlements of local chiefdoms. Unlike the congregaciones, missions were built near existing Indian populations and did not force relocations. Instead, friars, of which there was often only one per mission, would travel to outlaying villages. These religious institutions operated simultaneously in Florida, South

Carolina, Texas, New Mexico, and Arizona and were the work of various religious orders.[10] While some lasted for only brief periods given the hostility of local Indians, others went on to thrive and grow into major settlements as converted Indians relocated to areas near the mission.

THE FRIARS

Who were the friars who came to the Americas? As mentioned in Chapter 1, the religious orders were represented early, arriving with Columbus on his second voyage in 1493. Among the first groups were Franciscans, who became the largest order in the New World and would play a significant role in the evangelization of the indigenous communities. Founded in 1210 by St. Francis of Assisi, the Franciscans, or Order of Friars Minor, were, and are, a mendicant order whose efforts concentrated on praying and preaching. They followed the Rule of St. Francis, which called for poverty, humility, and simplicity. Many were also skeptical about intellectual pursuits, choosing to place their trust primarily in faith. The Spanish order had been greatly affected by Queen Isabella's reforms, and by the sixteenth century it truly reflected values that were counter to the prevailing secular culture. The Franciscans also possessed a strong missionary zeal that was part and parcel of their equally strong millenarian bent. Many believed profoundly that the second coming of Christ was at hand and they needed to baptize as many people as possible in order to ensure the latter's admittance into the kingdom of God. They were ready for the missionary work in the Indies.

It was precisely this missionary zeal, combined with the vows of poverty and limited material needs, that prompted Hernán Cortés to ask King Charles V to send Franciscans to New Spain. And they came. The Franciscans took their charge to evangelize the New World seriously, sometimes portraying that seriousness symbolically. In 1524 a group of twelve arrived in the Valley of Mexico, that number not being accidental but rather in imitation of the twelve apostles. Assured that the end of the world was imminent, the friars brought a real sense of urgency to their work. Furthermore, once they arrived in the Americas they encountered unparalleled death rates among the indigenous population who were confronting European diseases. Since there was no knowledge of contagion and biological immunity, the friars understood the death of the Indians in eschatological terms and as confirming the order's central role in preparing for the coming apocalypse. For them, baptism was the

---

[10] The first Spanish mission built in the state of California was constructed in 1769 by the Franciscans in San Diego.

first and foremost duty of the day, and mass ceremonies were common with thousands of Indians baptized at one time. By 1533 the sixty or so Franciscans who were in Mexico claimed to have performed the sacrament for 1.2 million Indians. By 1536, another 3.8 million had been brought into the family of Christ through this method. Such astronomical numbers were as mind-boggling for other religious orders of the time as they are for us now.

The Dominicans, Augustinians, and Jesuits (who followed later) were troubled by the lack of religious education that preceded baptism by the Franciscans. The Dominicans, or Order of Preachers, was founded in 1216 and soon thereafter was charged by the pope with ferreting out heresy throughout the Catholic world. The primary institution at their disposal for such efforts was the Inquisition, in which the Dominicans would play a vital role for centuries to come, including in the tribunals established in the Americas. And because they were so concerned with orthodoxy, the emphasis of the order was primarily on education through preaching and teaching, hence their unusually high representation among scholars and church intellectuals. When they came to the Indies, the Dominican friars brought with them their commitment to educate before conversion. The members of this white-clad order began arriving in the Caribbean as early as 1510, and they often decried the horrific brutality they witnessed, as we have seen in Montesinos and Las Casas. Very soon they were also working on the mainland and squabbling with the Franciscans over how to proselytize correctly.

The Augustinians, too, became very active in missionary work on the mainland, building missions, preaching, teaching, and converting. But as with other orders, the Augustinians realized that preaching in Spanish would have little effect if their purpose was to educate and convert. The friars soon learned the languages of the regions in which they worked.[11] History tells us of Friar Pedro Serrano, an Augustinian in New Spain, who could as easily preach and take confession in Nahuatl as in Otomí and Totonaco. While such facility with languages clearly varied from individual to individual, most of the mendicant orders shared a commitment to preaching in the language of the natives, even going so far as to publish dictionaries to aid priests in their interactions with Indian communities.[12]

The Jesuits came relatively late to the Americas. The first group arrived in Brazil in 1548 at the behest of the king of Portugal, who wanted the order

[11] The areas of the New World were divided among the various orders so as not to have too much competition.
[12] Language was also a tool in the priests' efforts to separate the Indians from the settlers. If the Indians did not understand Spanish then it would be almost impossible for the settlers to issue them orders.

to protect and evangelize the native population – a task they undertook with some zeal, as we have already seen. The Jesuits, or Society of Jesus, was founded in 1534 in large part as a response to the Protestant Reformation. Like the other mendicant orders, the Jesuits took vows of poverty and obedience, but unlike other orders, the Jesuits also vowed obedience directly to the pope – a characteristic that would ultimately result in serious political problems for the order, as we will see in Chapter 4. However, in the sixteenth century their desire to spread Roman Catholicism took them to the New World.

In Brazil the order's dedication to the Indians' well-being is perhaps best exemplified in the person of Father António Vieira, who was raised in Bahia – eastern central Brazil – and entered the Society of Jesus as a fifteen-year-old in 1623. After being ordained in 1635, he took up the call to protect the Indians of Brazil. Father Vieira's sermons tended to anger Portuguese settlers. Particularly repugnant to them was a homily during Lent of 1653 in which he declared "All of you are in mortal sin; all of you live in a state of condemnation [for living off of the blood of enslaved Indians]; and all of you are going directly to Hell. Indeed, many are there now and you will soon join them if you do not change your life."[13] So enraged were the colonial elite and the slave raiders that by the late 1650s Father Vieira had to sail for Portugal for his own safety. Much like Las Casas, Vieira continued his work in support of the Indians at the Portuguese royal court. And, as in the case of Las Casas, such efforts finally proved futile in the face of opposition from the colonists. Eventually Vieira returned to Brazil where he spent the last half dozen years of his life continuing his fight for the natives, dying in 1697.

Vieira's fellow Jesuits did not limit themselves to Brazil and the border regions with Spanish South America. Since they arrived well after other religious orders in Spanish America, the Jesuits went to regions where other orders did not predominate, primarily in South America. In those areas and indeed throughout Latin America, as well as making a mark in its effort to protect Indians, the order was also important in the higher education of the sons of important colonists.[14] (Father Vieira himself was educated by the Jesuits in Bahia.) The first schools and seminaries in Brazil were founded by Jesuits. They also opened educational institutions in Lima and Mexico City in which the pupils were taught the fundamentals of any sound European education: philosophy, theology, languages, and humanities.

[13] E. Bradford Burns, ed., *A Documentary History of Brazil* (New York: Alfred A. Knopf, 1966), 83, as quoted in Peter Bakewell, *A History of Latin America*, 2nd ed. (Oxford: Blackwell Publishing, 2004), 353.

[14] Other orders had already opened primary educational institutions so the Jesuits turned to higher education.

In terms of education, the religious orders did not serve only the white elite. In 1536 the Franciscans opened a school in Tlatelolco, New Spain. Here, the converted sons of native nobility were Europeanized, pursuing much of what their Spanish counterparts were studying in other schools: rhetoric, philosophy, and music. The intention of the school at Tlatelolco was to create a native elite that would return to its communities and act as intermediaries for the two cultures. The Franciscans also wanted to train native priests at Tlatelolco, something the majority of colonists found untenable. After a couple of decades, the school closed its doors. No native men were ordained priests in the Indies until late in the colonial period.

While there were no native priests, there were also very few secular European priests to be found in the early years of colonial rule. Hernán Cortés intentionally requested regulars as opposed to seculars because he did not trust the worldliness of the latter. He saw them as greedy and easily tempted. His views were shared by many, including the Spanish crown. When Charles V needed to send priests to the New World, he turned to the revitalized mendicant orders. This, however, posed a dilemma for the king because he also wanted to establish an episcopal system in the Americas. Such structures relied upon bishops, archbishops, and an ecclesiastical hierarchy that typically comprised secular priests. Regular clergy, in contrast, were subject to the head of their orders, not to a particular bishop, which potentially undermined the latter's control. In Pope Adrian VI Charles found the answer to how to combine the regulars and the episcopacy. The bull *Omnimoda*, issued in 1522, allowed the mendicant orders to wield enormous ecclesiastical power in the New World. This papal bull gave permission to friars to act as diocesan priests in the absence of a member of the secular clergy; in other words, the mendicants could give absolution, perform marriages, administer other sacraments, and even carry out some duties of a bishop (such as confirmation) if there was not a bishop within two days' journey. This system worked well in the Indies since it met the need to evangelize – to which the mendicants were particularly well suited – and the need to ensure that there was someone available to perform required rites and oversee the religious development of recent converts. By the 1550s, however, a more traditional episcopacy system had developed, as we will discuss in Chapter 3, paralleling an increase in the number of secular clergy. Naturally, conflict developed between the seculars and the regulars as the former viewed the latter as usurpers of ecclesiastical rights and jurisdiction and the latter saw the former as ill-prepared for the responsibilities of ministering in the Americas.

In Spain, royal attitude toward the mendicants in America also changed. Charles V's son and heir, Philip II, was influenced by the proceedings at the

Council of Trent, which sought to strengthen ecclesiastical hierarchy over the religious orders. Furthermore, under the patronato real the Spanish crown controlled the secular clergy in the Indies while the orders retained their ecclesiastical independence, a situation that the king certainly did not want. In 1574 Philip issued the *Ordenanza del Patronazgo*, which called for the secularization of the mendicants in the Indies. Under this order, the friars were to be subordinated to the ecclesiastical authority exercised through the secular bishops appointed by the king, as was his indisputable right under the patronato real. Protest and threaten as they might, the orders were ultimately resigned to accepting the authority of the Spanish monarch over their activities in the Indies. But such hegemonic control over the church did not necessarily translate into hegemonic control over society. While what the church brought with them across the Atlantic was European-style – especially Spanish-style – Catholicism, what was being created in the Indies was uniquely American.

FAITH IN THE AMERICAS

Although the main thrust of the missionary enterprise was to change the minds and lives of the native populations, that very enterprise produced change in Catholicism itself – what we might call the *mestizaje* of the Roman Catholic Church. In order to communicate their message, missionaries needed to learn the native languages. But that was not enough; they also needed to couch their teachings in images and metaphors that the natives could understand. And by doing so, the Catholic Church in the Americans was forever transformed.

As mentioned previously, some friars realized that preaching in Spanish to non-Spanish speakers was not terribly effective. Thus, shortly after arriving in the Americas, some talented missionaries took on the task of learning native languages. Perhaps among the more famous of those men were Andrés de Olmos, who wrote the first Nahuatl grammar text (1547), and Bernardino de Sahagún, a Franciscan in New Spain who in 1569 completed a compilation of Aztec history, grammar, and language.[15] Sahagún himself tells us he undertook this task at the command of his chief prelate and for the purpose of informing his fellow missionaries. He contended that unless they understood the native

---

[15] The manuscript would not be published until the nineteenth century. Some historians argue that the delay in publication was due to several facts: an unwillingness to publicize heathen practices; the inclusion of graphic accounts of the conquest of New Spain from the native perspective; an increasing disregard for native traditions and practices, culminating in a 1577 royal ban on research into indigenous religion and history; and an effort to limit the friars' power in the colonies by curtailing their relationships with the Indians.

language, history, and culture, it would be extremely difficult for them to communicate effectively or to assure their converts' adherence to the faith.

Hand in hand with learning indigenous languages was the need to use metaphors and images familiar in the Americas. Employing "old" New World symbols as tools for introducing "new" Old World ideas was common among the evangelists. Sermon and catechism manuals of the colonial period reveal that preachers relied on images that were known to the Americans to explain alien Christian theological concepts. For example, in the Andes priests would focus on the symbol of the cross as a sign of God's "ownership" by pointing out the symbol's existence in nature: in the Southern Cross in the skies, in the shape of the condor in flight, in the seeds of various fruit. The priests would recall the destruction of the Inca empire as evidence that God punished sinful ways, and they told their parishioners that the massive demographic collapse was due to the Indians' return to worship of the huacas. Yet the very use of indigenous images in conversion efforts altered Christianity itself. It created an atmosphere in which the native population could claim Christianity as its own. As early as the sixteenth century this "ownership" was apparent when the indigenous church made itself known to the European authorities in the person of Juan Diego, or so the legend goes.

In 1474 Cuauhtlatoatzin was born into the lowest class of Aztec society. He lived some fifteen miles north of Tenochtitlan and worked most of his life weaving mats and tending crops in fields. At the age of fifty or fifty-one, Cuauhtlatoatzin converted to Christianity, was baptized by a Spanish priest, and was given the Christian name Juan Diego. According to tradition, early one Saturday morning in 1531 Juan Diego was walking into Mexico City for catechism class when he heard his name called from nearby Tepeyac Hill – a pre-Hispanic Aztec site dedicated to the virgin mother of the gods, Tonantzin. There, on the hill, beckoning her "most humble of . . . son[s]" was an apparition of the Virgin Mary dressed as an Aztec princess who asked the Indian, in his native Nahuatl, to convey her wish to the bishop. She wanted a shrine built on that site so that "I may therein exhibit and give all my love, compassion, help, and protection, because I am your merciful mother, to you, and to all the inhabitants on this land and all the rest who love me, invoke and confide in me."[16] Naturally Juan Diego obeyed the Virgin's directives and went straight to Bishop Juan de Zumárraga, the first prelate of New Spain. The Spaniard was not impressed with Juan Diego's tale and sent him on his way.

---

[16] Antonio Valeriano, *Nican Mopohua* (or *Huei Tlamahuitzoltica*), n.p., n.d., (as published by Luis Lasso de la Vega [in Nahuatl], n.p., 1649). English translation at http://www.sancta.org/nican.html.

Juan Diego returned to Tepeyac, confessed his failure, and asked the Virgin that she send someone whom the bishop would believe. This manifestation of the Virgin Mary, however, was more stubborn than Bishop Zumárraga was dismissive; she sent Juan Diego back. Once again the bishop dismissed the messenger and his tales of the Virgin; yet this time, in order to rid himself of the annoying Indian, the bishop asked for a sign that the Virgin had indeed appeared to a mere Indian. Not to be deterred, on Juan Diego's fourth visit to her, the Virgin Mary supplied the sign the bishop requested. Juan Diego was instructed to fill his cloak with all sorts of roses that he would find growing on the hill where the Virgin had first appeared to him, even though it was the depths of winter. He did as directed and took his flower-laden cloak to the bishop's palace. After much delay he was admitted into Zumárraga's presence. As Juan Diego released his mantel and the roses fell to the ground, the image that we associate with the Virgin of Guadalupe appeared on his cloak. Immediately the bishop took the cloak and placed it in his private chapel from where he eventually moved it to the main church of the city. Now the bishop complied with the wishes of the Virgin and constructed a shrine on the very hill once dedicated to the Aztec mother goddess.

For the institutional church, the Virgin's appearances in New Spain signaled her approval of evangelization efforts and of the presence of the Spaniards. Paradoxically, for the Christianized indigenous community of Mexico, her appearance indicated a commitment to them and, as we will discuss later in this chapter, legitimized their place within the colonial social order. But there were many such symbols in the early colonial period, including the Virgin of Caridad del Cobre in Cuba.

In 1600 two men, Rodrigo and Juan de Hoyos (who some traditions say were Indians), and a ten-year-old slave boy, Juan Moreno, sought shelter when a violent storm overtook them as they rowed their boat across the Bay of Nipe in eastern Cuba. Early the next morning, as they resumed their journey, they spied a white object floating in the now-still waters. When they finally reached it, they realized that it was not the seabird they had first assumed it to be; rather, it was a 16-inch-high statue of the Virgin Mary strapped to a board with the inscription "I am the Virgin of Caridad." Miraculously, the statue was completely dry. Much like the Virgin of Guadalupe for Mexico, the Virgin of Caridad del Cobre would become a national symbol of unity for Cuba – but only later, as Latin American nations struggled for unique identities. As part of this process and the accompanying politicization of religious symbols, the myth of the Virgin of Caridad del Cobre would evolve: the three men in the boat came to be described as one black, one white, and one Indian.

One cannot overestimate the importance of the Virgin Mary throughout Latin America. Our Lady of Copacabana, for example, became a patron of Bolivia. In Brazil, Our Lady Aparecida, the principal patroness of the country, appeared to a mulatto hunter in the Amazonian jungle in the early eighteenth century. And in Nicaragua, tradition holds that the image of Our Lady of the Immaculate Conception of El Viejo was brought to Central America in the sixteenth century by the brother of St. Teresa de Jesús.

But Marian cults were not the only ones of importance during the colonial period. As William Taylor's research makes clear, often images other than those of the Virgin generated significant local and regional devotion. A case in point is the *Cristo Renovado* of New Spain. By the early seventeenth century, this near-life-sized crucifix located in Mapethe, a small central Mexican mining town, had long been neglected and deteriorated to such a state that the archbishop wanted the image buried with the next adult to die in the community. But no adult died for six years, and strange things began to happen: nightly noises – groans and heavenly music – came from the chapel housing the crucifix. Then, in 1621 the image began sweating and twitching and finally levitated during a storm. When the statue came to rest once more on the cross, it had been miraculously restored. Miracles continued with the Christ figure periodically sweating, opening its eyes, spurting blood, healing local residents, and occasioning a very successful maize harvest. This Christ's reputation spread so much that by the end of the year the archbishop ordered the removal of the crucifix to Mexico City, where the chapel for the Cristo Renovado was considered one of the Valley's great shrines by century's end.

Though devotion to the Virgin of Guadalupe ultimately would overshadow that to the Cristo, the eighteenth-century dedication of Otomí Indians who lived near the original site of the crucifix tells us much about the interweaving of things Indian and things European. The ecclesiastical authorities claimed that the miraculous powers of the Cristo Renovado rested with the image itself. Colonial Otomís held the original location to be sacred as well. Clearly the latter maintained their pre-Columbian sense of sacred space. In the second quarter of the eighteenth century, Otomí leader Don Augustín Morales received license to rebuild the now totally dilapidated chapel. Perhaps because of internecine squabbling among Indian leaders and legal wrangling between Indians and local Spanish officials over who controlled the finances related to the shrine, the chapel was a long time in coming. Even during the many years of construction, there were religious processions to the site. Mapethe was not so much a pilgrimage destination for people from around central Mexico as it was a place of local devotion, for devotees tended to come from areas surrounding the small community. The Otomís successfully combined old concepts of sacredness of space with new concepts of the holiness of the crucifix in a manner that resonated with them. They made Christianity their own.

Even as Christianized Indians adopted and adapted the new faith, priests in the Americas continued to find ways of expressing the faith in simple terms. Often evangelizers turned to sacramentals – holy water, candles, and rosaries – as ways of instructing the Indians. The extra income from sales that such items generated for the priests was undoubtedly an attractive feature, but underlying the use of tangible reminders of the faith as instructive devices was the belief that the Indians were too unsophisticated to understand the abstract concepts of Christianity. Likewise, the cult of saints was deemed an easy way for the priests to tie the new faith to old patterns, thereby linking Catholicism more closely to the world of the Indians. This path, however, was reluctantly pursued by the priests whose initial goal was the complete obliteration of pre-Hispanic religions – which proved impossible. Instead, various saints gradually replaced the gods of the Americas; for example, the patron saint of pregnant women, St. Anne, replaced a goddess of fertility. However, the priests emphasized that the saints were subordinate to the Triune God of Christianity, a concept often lost on the Indians. The saints, however, were quite significant in their own right to the peoples of the Indies; in fact, the calendar of saints' days and the corresponding celebrations were more central in the yearly religious cycle of many a New World community than was the liturgical calendar. Some scholars argue that in addition to the equating of saints with bygone gods, the role of the Catholic saints in the Americas derives from two distinct European roots: First, veneration of saints had long been part of popular Catholicism in Spain and undoubtedly crossed the Atlantic Ocean with the multitude of Spanish commoners. Second, increasingly in response to the Protestant Reformation taking place in Europe, the church hierarchy, including the missionaries who came to the New World, emphasized the non-Protestant elements of Roman Catholicism, and among those was the cult of saints.

CONTINUATION OF OLD WAYS

The ease with which the cult of saints was integrated into the lives of the Indians was a two-edged sword. The veneration of saints could and did often mask the worship of pre-Hispanic gods. Once indigenous peoples made a saint their own, such as in the case of the Virgin of Guadalupe, the message understood by the Indian community was no longer solely controlled by the church. As mentioned previously, the indigenous Mexican communities around Mexico City saw the Virgin as their protector. With dark hair, brown skin, and indigenous dress, she became a symbol of God's acceptance of them, in constrast to the local Spanish religious authority. It was an Indian through whom she chose to convey her wishes to the religious powers-that-were; she spoke in an indigenous language; and she called Juan Diego "my son." She made herself Indian. One theory as to the origin of the name Guadalupe ties the apparition even more closely to the indigenous community. Some believe that Guadalupe is a Hispanization of the Nahuatl title used by the Virgin in her conversation with Juan Diego: she supposedly called herself coat-laxopeuh ("the one who crushes the serpent," perhaps the plumed serpent Quetzacoatl?), which is pronounced *"quatlasupe."* Interestingly, another theory is that the archbishop named the apparition after a shrine to Our Lady of Guadalupe in Extremadura, the region from which many settlers came. Yet, some historians claim that for many Indians she actually was the Aztec goddess Tonantzin disguised as the Virgin Mary. What we do know is that: (1) there are no records from 1531 that recount the apparition, and (2) the cult of the Virgin that clearly existed in Mexico City by the 1550s was not primarily Indian. Yet, as with the story of the Virgin of Caridad del Cobre, the myth of the Virgin of Guadalupe evolved to meet the needs of the community. The story of the Virgin of Guadalupe as it has come down to us is emblematic of how under the pretense of devotion to a new Christian image, indigenous peoples continued old religious practices.

Likewise in the Andes many people found ways to continue traditional worship. According to lore, the Andean god Pachacamac, the two-faced creator and destroyer, told his people:

> I have been angry with you because you have abandoned me and accepted the god of the Christians. But I have set aside my anger, because the god of the Christians and I have agreed that you should serve us both, and both he and I are well pleased that you should act in this way.[17]

Indeed, that may have been what was in the minds of Andean Indians when during Christian feast days they would offer to images of Catholic saints the traditional gifts of guinea pigs, coca, and chicha. Similarly, the festival of Corpus Christi became intricately linked with the Andean observance of Caruamita, or the ripening of the maize. Corpus Christi marked the time of the year when the huacas needed special attention, even sacrifices and

---

[17] Bartolomé de Las Casas, *Apologética historia* (before 1559), ed. E. O'Gorman (Mexico City: Universidad Nacional Autónoma de México, Instituto de Investigaciones Históricas, 1967), 131: 687, as quoted in Sabine MacCormack, *Religion in the Andes: Vision and Imagination in Early Colonial Peru* (Princeton, NJ: Princeton University Press, 1991), 241.

confessions, in order to ensure the crops would flourish. The intertwining of the Christian calendar with indigenous spiritual annual cycles is a hallmark of religious adaptation and accommodation.

There is also clear evidence that indigenous communities were not solely passive recipients of new religious ideas or blenders of the old and the new. Amerindians often reverted to old religious practices, not just old religious symbols. As we have seen in Chapter 1, among the Mayas, Diego de Landa went to great lengths, often brutal, to uncover and uproot non-Catholic religious practices. What he and his fellow Franciscans confronted was that their converts were still worshiping idols, which they stored in caves along with human skulls. Additionally, often under torture – and therefore, for some historians, of questionable veracity – some Mayas confessed to Spanish officials that the Indians were also crucifying victims, usually children, before removing their hearts and throwing the still-crucified bodies into *cenotes*, or sinkholes thought to be the entryway to the Underworld and the home of Chac, the Maya rain god. Two other torture-induced revelations made matters even worse: first, trusted Indians, such as schoolmasters, played key roles in performing the sacrifices; and second, some of these sacrifices occurred during Holy Week and Easter. For the Spaniards, the timing of the supposed human sacrifices was an outrage above all others.

In the Andes, the Catholic Church's efforts to extirpate all ancient indigenous religious practices are legendary. The discovery in 1564 by a local priest of a Peruvian millenarian movement known as *Taqui Onqoy*, or "dancing sickness" in Quechua, is a dramatic example of indigenous efforts to maintain ancient ways. For the more than eight thousand adherents, mostly Christianized Indians, to this Andean indigenous religious revival, the huacas were no longer limited to inhabiting geological formations or other elements of nature; now they selected human beings to possess. The chosen individual, or *taquiongo*, would enter an almost trance-like state and dance wildly about. But a few Indian dances is not what alarmed the priests most; rather it was the huacas' call to renounce the Christian faith and European ways. Through the taquiongos, the huacas made it clear that they were about to unleash an Armageddon in which the Christian god, who only cared for the Europeans, would be vanquished by the ancient gods. Furthermore, any Indian who chose the Christian god over his or her ancestral gods would perish along with the Spaniards. Church officials responded immediately, sending out the morally righteous priest Cristóbal de Albornoz to suppress and eliminate the movement. Though it took him two years, he did exactly that.

And in 1595 in New Granada (modern-day Colombia), the Muisca Indians were subjected to similar efforts by Spanish priests to eradicate any vestiges of ancient religious practices, particularly the continued existence of shrines and idols. The use of torture was again integral to the Spaniards' efforts to arrive at the "truth." Indians confessed to having shrines passed down from previous generations and to keeping idols to which they paid homage. Some shrines included small statuettes – occasionally filled with earth – or pieces of colored cloth, or bits of cotton tied together and stored in pots. Other shrines had figures of unrefined gold or bundles of ancestral bones.

Once discovered, such hidden practices by any Indian community did not go unpunished. The guilty were quickly dealt with. Initially, Indians who deviated from traditional Catholic practices were subject to the Inquisition. In fact, the first person in New Spain punished by the Holy Office was an Indian charged with concubinage in 1522. The most infamous of Indian trials before the Mexican court was that of Don Carlos Chichimecatecuhtli, a nobleman from Texcoco, who was brought before the inquisitors for challenging the church's teachings and advocating a return to pre-Hispanic religious ways. He was found guilty and "relaxed to the secular arm," in other words, put to death. By 1571 when a Tribunal of the Holy Office was officially established in Mexico, pure-blood Indians were exempt from the Inquisition. This did not, however, free Indians from the wrath of the church if they were to stray from its teachings. Rather, once the Holy Office definitively determined the transgressor's "racial" category[18] and investigated the accusations of Indian waywardness, the malefactor was turned over to the bishop's or archbishop's office for trial and punishment.[19] The justification for such a decision was that the recent converts were too simpleminded to understand fully the requirements of the faith and the Holy Office was entirely too harsh in its punishments, as the case of Don Carlos made clear.

The Inquisition did, however, have jurisdiction over all other members of society, and it is from their trial records that we can learn much about "deviant" religious behavior among otherwise silent actors on the American stage. Among the cases heard by the Tribunal were, of course, those involving heresy such as alumbradismo or crypto-Judaism – secret Judaism – but more often before the courts were trails for bigamy, witchcraft, and blasphemy. Recent research into blasphemy cases reveals what we might consider an interesting inversion of the colonial reality: African slaves sometimes used

[18] In the New World "race" was determined by a number of factors including one's phenotype as well as one's place within society and one's reputation.

[19] This arrangement never functioned very well. Both the Holy Office and the bishops' offices trespassed on the jurisdiction of the other, with the Holy Office meting out punishments and holding autos de fe and the bishops using titles such as inquisitor.

blasphemy as a way to free themselves, even if only temporarily, from the harsh conditions under which they lived. Take the example of the slave Juan Baptista who in 1598, while being cruelly tortured by his master, cried out "I renounce God." After recovering from his wounds, Juan denounced himself to the Mexican inquisitors. He asked that they remove him from his master's presence lest Juan's soul and salvation be imperiled through blasphemy brought on by excessively harsh punishment received at his master's hand. This tactic did not always work since usually the inquisitors and slave owners were both Spaniards. But occasionally slaves were successful in having themselves transferred to a new master. Of Juan Baptista's fate we know nothing.[20]

For some of the New World's residents, the Inquisition could be a tool to make life miserable for an unwelcomed neighbor. Routinely the court would hear accusations of how a certain individual down the street kept a concubine; or how the spinster in the community was really a witch who would put the evil eye on children and crops; or how a local craftsmen claimed to be a widower when he married for a second time although his first wife was still living. In these types of cases, one was either a bigamist or not, had a concubine or not. But in cases of doctrinal orthodoxy or apostasy, it was not unusual for denouncements to be met with claims of ignorance: "I did not know"; "I am too poor to have received proper religious training"; "I forgot, it has been so long since I have seen a priest." The latter claim had some basis in reality, for a scarcity of priests was a problem that plagued the New World from the onset of Spanish settlement. Nevertheless, what inquisitorial records reveal is a decided division between practiced faith and orthodoxy with some defendants claiming that life simply got in the way of correct religious observances.

CONCLUSION

The early history of the encounter between Europeans and Americans is replete with much that "got in the way." Spaniards sure that God was on their side in conquest efforts had to confront challenges to their tactics from other Spaniards. Scholars positive that they knew God's universe were forced to reevaluate all that they understood of the world. Monarchs who took seriously their roles as "father" to the Indians had to reconcile brutality done in their names with the love of Christ expressed in efforts to protect indigenous populations. Religious orders turned to force, sometimes quite cruel, to bring the love of God to resistant Indian groups. And the church itself had to face

---

[20] Javier Villa-Flores, "'To Lose One's Soul': Blasphemy and Slavery in New Spain, 1596-1669," *Hispanic American Historical Review* 82, no. 3 (2002): 435-468.

the ineffectiveness of its message and its inability to exercise control in the New World.

Subjugated groups, both those already in the Americas and those forcibly brought to the Indies, were also pushed to grapple with what it meant to be Christianized. Some rebelled outright, calling on their ancient gods to preserve the old way. Others accommodated themselves to the practices of the dominant culture. Some took on habits of the conquerors merely as disguises to veil continued patterns. And still others found ways of subverting the imposed systems by claiming them as their own only to turn them on the originators of such systems.

What we see in all these efforts to impose Roman Catholicism and Catholic institutions and the responses to them is the ambivalence of the church – both benevolent and brutal, gentle and cruel. As we will see in Chapter 3, the two faces of the church remained throughout the middle colonial years. We will see the church continuing to change and becoming increasingly American. We will also see the Christian faith shaped by the experiences of the New World.

3

❧

The Shaping of the Faith

In 1613, the Christianized indigenous Andean nobleman Don Felipe Guaman Poma de Ayala completed a lengthy one thousand plus page missive, written primarily in Spanish, to King Philip III of Spain, a document the monarch most likely never read. Guaman Poma's hope was to convince the king, and any other Spanish official who might read his words, that colonial officials were destroying the Andes and its people. Toward that end, he wrote of Andean history from creation to the beginning of the seventeenth century and in the process made some interesting links between Andean mythology and Christianity.

As we discussed in Chapter 1, key to the Andean creation myth is the story of Viracocha wandering about disguised as an old beggar. Much like the stories of the Virgin of Caridad del Cobre and the Virgin of Guadalupe, the Viracocha story also underwent a transformation in light of colonial reality, as Guaman Poma's retelling of the tale clearly shows. In Guaman Poma's work, *Nueva crónica y buen gobierno* (New Chronicle and Good Government), the old, wandering beggar was revealed as the apostle Bartholomew who journeyed to the Andes and there converted pre-Inca peoples to Christianity.[1]

According to Guaman Poma, it was the Incas who had brought idolatry and paganism to the region, squashing any practice of the true faith. (Being from one of the groups conquered by the Incas, it is not at all surprising that Guaman Poma should cast aspersions on those who had robbed his family of its high social ranking.) And now, Guaman Poma told his readers, far from restoring the true faith, the Spanish clergy and officials were actually abusing the people, including sexually, as some of his more than 360 accompanying line drawings graphically portrayed. The only solution he saw that would bring

---

[1] Earlier renditions of the Viracocha story portrayed him as an unknown Spaniard. Guaman Poma's account simply takes the acculturation process one step further.

a truly Christian state into being was for the king to allow self-rule by the indigenous people.

Guaman Poma's writings have at least two interrelated but distinct goals: (1) to discredit both the past rule of the Incas and the current rule of the Spaniards, all the while elevating other Andean people in the eyes of the king, and (2) to undercut one of the principal reasons for Spanish conquest – the bringing of Christianity – thereby justifying his claim that the Andeans could govern themselves and at the same time remain loyal to the Spanish crown, under the leadership of Guaman Poma's own son. As was to be expected, he succeeded in neither goal. Nevertheless, even though more than likely his work never made it into the royal hands, there is strong evidence that it arrived safely at the court in Spain.

For us, however, Guaman Poma's story is another step in the Americanization of Catholicism. Recall that in Chapter 2 we discussed Europeans who struggled – intellectually, politically, and religiously – with the seismic implications of a continent on the other side of the Atlantic Ocean. Likewise, some Amerindians struggled to find ways of linking their world with that in Europe, as Guaman Poma's writings indicate. But Amerindians also fought to maintain their dignity in the midst of a seemingly all-consuming colonial system. And perhaps by intertwining the ancient past with the all-too-painful present, these indigenous people found some sense of place.

In this chapter we will go one step further in the evolving history of Christianity in Latin America. Here we will look at just how *the institutional church* planted its roots into American soil through the creation of hierarchical structures such as dioceses and archdioceses, the growth in the number of secular clergy, and the expansion of monastic life for both men and women. We will also examine closely the roles that the *religious orders* had within society, for these went far beyond simply providing a place of separation from the world. In fact, the religious orders were vibrant communities that actively interacted with the universe beyond their doors. The male and female monasteries became so important in the economic and social life of the colonies that their members would eventually snub attempts by the secular religious leadership to control them.

Efforts at control by the church were not exerted only on the religious orders, however. We will also look at the attempts by the Catholic Church to exercise *social control* over the population as a whole, particularly in its implementation of Tridentine rulings. Such endeavors did not squelch the place of *religion in society* as is evidenced in the lives of Martín de Porres and Rosa de Lima, both lay people who would be canonized by the Catholic Church, and Ursula de Jesús, an Afro-Peruvian mystic.

Lay religious organizations, such as confraternities (*cofradías*) and brother-hoods (*hermandades*), also became important communities for all segments of society – Blacks, mulattos, mestizos, and Whites alike. They often pro-vided social services such as dowries for poor girls, education for children, and homes for foundlings, in addition to the benefits they brought their own members.

As always, there were those who pursued their religious life on *the road less traveled*. In fact, many of these folks followed a path that brought them to the attention of church authorities, who looked none-too-kindly upon their variant forms of religious expression. We will look at the lives of some of these "deviants" and at the continued efforts by the church to extirpate idolatry and to impose orthodoxy in the Andes. Such efforts never fully succeeded.

The church also went to great lengths to eliminate *crypto-Judaism*, because such practices were deemed threatening to Spain's very hold on the Americas. Yet, as in other attempts to ensure complete hegemonic control, these efforts were doomed to failure. We will see that as the colonial project continued, the ability of the church to impose its worldview was weakened. In this chapter we will examine the myriad ways in which the Catholic Church accommo-dated itself to the New World and how it was refashioned by the realities it encountered there.

THE INSTITUTIONAL CHURCH

From the moment of its arrival in the Americas, the Catholic Church in the Indies, under the direction of the Spanish crown with its patronato real, began to build the ecclesiastical structure that would carry it through the colonial period. August 8, 1511, saw the creation of two sees on Hispaniola and one on the island of Puerto Rico. By 1517 there was a diocese in Cuba with jurisdiction over the territory that eventually became Louisiana and Florida. And the first bishopric of New Spain was founded as early as 1519. That of Mexico City was founded in 1530. All of these newly created ecclesiastical sees were suffragan dioceses of the archdiocese in Seville, which meant that the archbishop in the Spanish port city had authority over all prelates in the Americas. As we might imagine, this arrangement proved to be wholly unsatisfactory. The great distances made resolving matters of the American church rather drawn out and difficult. By 1533 the prospect of making the bishopric of Mexico City an independent and metropolitan see was raised in the Council of the Indies, a suggestion the Council approved. (A similar request was not made for the dioceses of the islands because by that time their importance had diminished as the focus of conquest and evangelization shifted to the mainland.) Despite

Council approval, advancement in status for the Mexican diocese would have to await Vatican approbation. In the meantime, the 1530s saw the creation of dioceses in Peru, Venezuela, Colombia, Nicaragua, Guatemala, and four additional ones in Mexico. Finally, in 1545 the Spanish embassador to the Vatican had in hand a letter from the pope elevating the Mexican bishopric to an independent archbishopric, with Bishop Zumárraga – of Virgin of Guadalupe fame – named the first archbishop. It would take another three years (July 1548), however, before the bull of appointment was finally on its way to New Spain. By that time Zumárraga had been dead a month.

The same papal letter also elevated Santo Domingo and Lima to the status of metropolitan sees. The church in the Americas was beginning to operate with a level of autonomy similar to churches elsewhere – within the limits of the patronato real. The other dioceses became suffragans to the newly elevated archdioceses. No longer did New World bishops need to direct their business to Seville. Instead, their decrees and rulings would reflect the realities of the Indies.

Once established on its own footing, the Catholic Church in the Indies began to draw up constitutions that governed the operations of the archdioceses and their suffragans. By 1555, under the leadership of Zumárraga's successor, the Mexican church called its first council. This gathering of bishops quickly turned its attention to matters of the Mexican church: how and when priests, clergy, and ordinaries were to perform the sacraments; qualifications for the various levels of vows and the prohibition against indigenous priests; how the clergy should behave and the lifestyle they should have; and the essentials in Christian education for the newly converted – such as being able to make the sign of the cross and recite the articles of faith. The Council also addressed issues of how to teach Christian doctrine to Indians, how to monitor public morals, and restrictions on Indian marriage. It was also at the First Mexican Council that the secular churchmen began exerting their authority over the regulars. The regulars were not permitted to perform marriages between Indians, and they would not be assigned to any new Indian parish. Nor were they allowed to build any monastery or convent without explicit permission from the king's representative in New Spain, the viceroy. As we might imagine, the regulars reacted immediately and, at least in the early stages, effectively. They solicited the help of the king in reasserting their place in the evangelization and education of Indians. In this instance, the king obliged the regulars, but as we have seen in Chapter 2, this royal endorsement of regular activities was short-lived.

The other two Mexican Councils that met during the sixteenth century dealt primarily with the Council of Trent and the implementation of its decrees.

While the Second Council (1565) declared the acceptance of the Tridentine rulings, the New World meeting was simply too close in time chronologically (the Council of Trent finished its work in 1563) for there to be even a full text of Trent's decrees available. By the Third Mexican Council (1585), reform was in the air. Presided over by Archbishop and Viceroy Pedro Moyas de Contreras, a zealous reformer in the manner of the Counter Reformation, the Third Council dealt with topics as wide ranging as Indian festivals and the evils of usury. It also dealt in detail with the ecclesiastical structure of every level of the church – from the cathedral chapter to the privileges and duties of the clergy – keeping in mind the rulings of the Council of Trent. When the Council's proceedings were sent to Rome for approval, a special commission checked them against the decrees of the Council of Trent, changing whatever they deemed contrary to Tridentine rulings. In general, the changes made to the prelates' rulings would seem to indicate that the Mexican Council tended to be fairly severe. Repeatedly, the commission in Rome required that violations of church decrees be punished less harshly than was the wont of the Mexican Council. For example, the Council ordered that anyone knowing of another person who gambled, lived with a concubine, or blasphemed was required to report the sinner under pain of ecclesiastical censure. The commission in Rome found the entire decree far too harsh and deleted it altogether. Occasionally, the commission in Rome took the ordinances coming from New Spain one step further. For instance, the Mexican bishops had decreed that bullfighting could not take place in cemeteries. The commission decided to ban bullfighting everywhere unless expressly permitted by the pope. Clearly, the Third Mexican Council dealt with all manner of issues facing the church.

Also in the Andes, the church was actively organizing itself and its parishioners. The First Council met in Cuzco in 1551, not even twenty years after the conquest. The primary focus of this meeting was doctrinal conformity within both the Indian and the Spanish communities, which were dealt with separately. The church hierarchy was concerned with the varied and erroneous interpretations of Catholic doctrine. Toward that end, the Council published a *cartilla* in Quechua with the prayers, commandments, and other essentials that any faithful person needed to know. And much like their Mexican counterparts, the Peruvian bishops also dealt with issues concerning clergy and the Spanish laity. They called for greater adherence to church teachings on matters such as performance of sacraments by the clergy. And they called on their parishioners to live morally upright lives, particularly in terms of marriage and sexual relationships. The Council also decreed that as new parishes were created throughout Peru, they were to follow the geographic division of preexisting Indian clan territories, which seems to indicate a level of understanding that acceptance of a new faith might be made easier if everything old was not cast aside.

The Second Council of Lima, meeting some fifteen years later (in 1567), divided its working into two parts: (1) the Spanish population, and (2) the Indian population. Once again the Council addressed issues of public morals and life among the Spaniards. In dealing with the indigenous community, the Council approved the ordination of mestizos although, according to historian Sabine MacCormack, this resolution was so resoundingly resisted as to be practically nonexistent. But the Council also concerned itself with who could minister to the Indians. On this topic the bishops gathered in Lima reaffirmed the increasing role of the episcopacy over the regulars in matters of the native population: it would be the bishops who would decide which clergyman was fit for such an assignment, not the orders themselves.

It is the Third Council of Lima, however, that is best known, as much for its accomplishments as for its convener, Toribio Alfonso de Mogrovejo. Archbishop Mogrovejo called the Third Council of Lima into session in 1582. For the first time in Peruvian church history, the gathering of bishops did not distinguish between the "Republic of Indians" and the "Republic of Spaniards" in its decrees, although Mogrovejo and his fellow clergymen did not seem to confuse the issues of one group with those of the other. Of primary focus was the difficulty faced by the indigenous population in adhering to Christian modes of living – such as Christian marriages – and meeting the requirements of the faith – communion, confession, and learning the catechism. The bishops worked diligently to facilitate indigenous participation in Christian life. For example, the Council decreed that parish priests could bar from communion only a person who was "unsuitable" with reference to that person's moral life. Heretofore some priests had barred those whose racial makeup they deemed problematic. With this decree the bishops hoped to ensure that "worthy" Indians could take part in the eucharist. The Third Council of Lima also had confessional manuals printed in Quechua and Aymara to aid parish priests in asking detailed questions of their Indian parishioners. In fact, a variety of religious materials was published in both languages, all made possible by the linguistic skills of the Jesuit José de Acosta, who claimed there were more than seven hundred different languages spoken in the former Tawantinsuyu. (Publishing materials in Quechua and Aymara reflected Trent's insistence that indigenous languages be used in spreading the faith.) It is critical, however, to note that creating a decree or printing materials rarely resulted in a significant change in the life of those for whom the decree was issued or the materials published. Indeed, in enforcing the Council of Trent's rulings, the Third

Council of Lima laid the groundwork for the violent extirpation campaigns of the early seventeenth century, which we will discuss later.

Some historians claim that José de Acosta – a theologian, naturalist, and participant at the Third Council of Lima – was highly influential in the theology of evangelization that developed in the Andes. Acosta is best known for his naturalist writings on the world he encountered in the Andes. He wrote of the social and economic structures, geography, religion, and history of the Inca peoples. Yet he was also the architect, if not the father, of a certain level of rigidity in attitude toward the indigenous people. Acosta held, in contrast to Las Casas, that the Andean people were too simple of mind – as reflected in the vocabulary limitations of their languages – to understand complex Christian religious concepts. Therefore, the only style of missionary endeavors that would ever bear fruit was conversion by coercion. Acosta based his assertions on his observation of Andean religious practices, which he placed in two categories: (1) those that worshiped objects derived from nature, and (2) those that worshiped objects that were the result of human imagination. In either case, Andean religions were the work of the devil, and the only way to convert a people so easily duped by the devil was with the use of force.

In sharp contrast to José de Acosta was Toribio Alfonso de Mogrovejo, who would be canonized by the Catholic Church in 1726. Upon arriving in Peru in May of 1581, St. Toribio began a twenty-four-year stint as archbishop of a diocese that extended several thousand miles. First among his many deeds was a *visita*, or ecclesiastical visit, of the area under his jurisdiction – a journey he would undertake four times during his episcopacy. In order to make such journeys worthwhile, he spent time learning some of the many languages of the people within his archdiocese. Legend tells us that he walked, often barefoot, through very difficult terrain to visit forgotten parish priests. He stayed in the homes of people and shared their meals, baptizing, saying mass, and confirming converts wherever he went. But Mogrovejo's tenure as archbishop was not without conflicts with his fellow churchmen. They felt that he was not harsh enough on the Indians – being too blind to their transgressions and heresies – and that he ignored the needs of Lima. Furthermore, he dared interfere in the work of the Jesuits in the capital.

Near the city there was a group of Indians whose spiritual needs were attended to by a secular priest assigned to them by the cathedral chapter. Also near the city was an Indian parish under the control of the Society of Jesus. As the former grew in size, the Jesuits petitioned the viceroy of Peru, who resided in Lima, to have the other group moved and incorporated into the order's parish. The Indians resisted and for their troubles had their farms burnt and were forcibly removed under orders from the viceroy. They turned to the archbishop, requesting that they be assigned their own priest, thereby making them a parish, an assignment the archbishop readily made. Push came to shove and the Jesuits turned once more to the viceroy, who this time ordered the destruction of the parish's small retreat house and the removal of the parish priest. But Mogrovejo was not done yet; he exerted his rights over the Jesuits to monitor their activities, name benefices, and conduct ecclesiastical inspections. All of this was considered an affront, especially since the archbishop himself was not a member of any religious order.

Mogrovejo proved to be a thorn in the side of the civil authorities, not only in the matter of the Jesuits, but also in many others. As part of his many ecclesiastical acts while in Lima, St. Toribio opened the first seminary in the city and placed the archbishop's coat-of-arms over the entrance, a common occurrence. The viceroy was outraged and ordered the archbishop's coat-of-arms removed and destroyed. He then ordered that no seminarian could be accepted without express viceregal approval. Not to be outdone, the archbishop simply closed the seminary altogether and informed the king of the viceroy's antics. Finally the king intervened, calling for the royal coat-of-arms to be placed next to that of the archbishopric, and decreed that Mogrovejo was the sole director of the seminary. The problems between the archbishop and the viceroy continued, with each complaining to the king and demanding justice be done. Sometimes the king agreed with one, sometimes with the other. In the midst of all the actions and counteractions by those in Lima, however, it is fairly easy to see a savvy King Philip II playing one powerful man against the other.

In the matter of who would run the church in the Indies, as in the matter of who would govern the secular realm in the monarch's name, the sixteenth-century kings proved to be politically wise. In the early years, most of the men who filled the high-ranking ecclesiastical positions in the Indies were friars, such as Zumárraga. This made sense to the crown since the primary task of the church was evangelization. But as the society of the Americas moved more toward settlement and away from initial conquest, there was a parallel shift in the work of the church, or at least an addition to the church's role. The church now became responsible not only for evangelization but also for parish work among Spaniards and Indians. This, in many ways, necessitated the rise of secular clergy who were experienced in the workings of a parish. But, as we have seen in Chapter 2, with the increased presence of parish priests and bishops who were not mendicants, tension arose over jurisdiction, privileges, and ecclesiastical authority with the friars. Archbishop Mogrovejo exercised the authority over the friars granted him, especially with the promulgation of the *Ordenanza del Patronazgo*, discussed in Chapter 2.

The *Patronazgo* was a tool used by Philip II to secularize the church and remove parochial duties from the regulars, all in an effort to strengthen his control over the American church. But he had a problem: the seculars tended to be poorly educated and had the reputation of living rather profligate lives. There was a remedy, however, included in the *Patronazgo*. The clergy would be tested, in a competition known as the *oposición*, before being assigned a benefice, which carried with it a salary and a guarantee that the priest was not likely to be removed when a new bishop came to power. In these exams each candidate would need to prove a certain level of proficiency in native languages, administration of the sacraments, moral theology, and at least one discipline declared by the candidate to be his area of expertise. Initially in Mexico, as historian John Schwaller has shown, the quality of the candidates was less than stellar. But as time passed, men who were well qualified to lead parishes began competing for the few benefices that became vacant each year – a prized position, given the guaranteed income and job security. Yet, becoming a beneficiary was fairly rare. Rather, most secular parish priests had no church-guaranteed funding and subsisted in part through the income generated by *capellanías*, or chantry funds, which required the assigned priest to say a prescribed number of masses annually for the good of the soul of the capellanía founder. In any case, any man interested in the secular priesthood had to demonstrate the ability to meet his own financial needs.

The requirements for ordination – education, source of income, and racial purity (in other words, "pure" white with no Jewish or Moorish "taint") – meant that those most likely to pursue a vocation in the priesthood were from fairly well-to-do families of European descent or European themselves. At least that describes the urban secular priest. Those priests who came from middle-group families tended to remain in the rural parishes and served in areas where an advanced education was not seen as essential for parochial duties. This is not to say that men of humble origins or even of mixed blood did not serve in the church. They did, but very rarely as priests. More often such men remained at the level of minor orders, fulfilling menial tasks in and around churches.

From the earliest days of settlement, men who pursued work as secular clergy were often creoles – people of European descent born in the colonies, also known as *criollos*. This became the case particularly with the implementation of the oposición, which was administered in the colonies. Traveling from Europe for a competition that might secure one a benefice in the countryside was not an attractive career move for many men from the continent. Thus, very quickly the secular clergy became identified with the colonists. And even those men born in Europe – known as *peninsulares* – often had strong family ties with colonists, which resulted in few conflicts between the European-born and American-born seculars. The same, however, could not be said for the friars or those in orders, as we will see.

Priests in the countryside did not suffer from rivalries because there was always a shortage of clergymen in rural settings. A rural assignment was not a secular priest's dream job. Those assigned to the countryside routinely sought a move back into the cities and tended to view their rural placement as temporary. As historian Paul Ganster points out, priests could be crafty in finding ways of (ma)lingering in a major urban center: a priest would come into the city for the oposición competition, which could take months and was always administered in the see; he would then need to tend to personal business; and afterward he would have to deal with some chronic illness that would keep him incapacitated for months. All in all, some priests managed to spend almost half of their time away from their rural parishes.

RELIGIOUS ORDERS

As with the secular priesthood, men born in the colonies began joining religious orders as soon as they were of age. However, because the orders were independent from ecclesiastical authority and routinely sent men from Europe – not only Spain – as missionaries to the Americas, there was a high percentage of European-born among the friars. Unlike the peninsulares in the secular priesthood, these European-born friars had no strong family ties with the colonists. Fairly quickly, deep rivalry developed within the regulars between creoles and foreign-born, especially when it came to high-ranking positions within a monastery. The tension between the competing groups was so fierce that only the creation by royal officials of the *alternativa* calmed friction. The alternativa was a rotation of offices among the rival factions. And even this solution was only moderately successful.

Both seculars and regulars served in rural parishes, came early with the conquistadores and thus were part of evangelization efforts, and served in *doctrinas* (Indian parishes). But certain regions, especially of South America, became the province of the regulars. An example is the role of the Jesuits in Paraguay. Eleven of the thirty-one missions – reducciones or congregaciones – under Jesuit oversight were in Paraguay. As mentioned in Chapter 2, the Jesuits' missions in this land-locked region were primarily among the semi-nomadic Guaraní Indians. By 1613, just a few years after its founding, San Ignacio Gauzú (the first mission in Paraguay) had more than six thousand Indian residents. On a daily basis the priest was engaged in prayers, teaching children and adults, monitoring the work of his charges, and conducting whatever religious rites were needed. The lives of the Indians were governed by the resident priest: from dawn to dusk the Indians labored in the fields with only a midday break for lunch. Whatever they produced was the property of the community but controlled by the priest and usually used to meet the needs of the mission and for the tribute, or head tax, that the Indians were required to pay.

Throughout colonial Latin America, as regular orders grew they became financially powerful, amassing vast landholdings and controlling large numbers of Indians. For example, historian Nicholas Cushner has determined that by the late seventeenth century in Chillos (a particularly fertile series of valleys southeast of Quito, Ecuador), more than half of all Spanish-held land was in the hands of religious orders: the Jesuits owned around thirty-nine thousand acres, the Augustinians had some thirteen thousand acres, and the Sisters of Sta. Clara controlled almost fourteen thousand acres, while the Mercedarians and the Dominicans owned land as well. Much of the land was purchased, but a goodly portion was acquired through bequests that individuals made to the orders for the benefit of the soul of the deceased.

In addition to farms and ranches, the holdings of the orders included mines and textile mills. With so much wealth to manage, the orders became business enterprises. Unlike their counterparts in Europe that leased the land they owned, in Latin America the friars themselves oversaw production and managed the assets. And much as any large landholder or mill operator, to work their estates the orders used a variety of labor, including debt peonage and black slavery. In fact, in the countryside it was often difficult to distinguish between the lay Spanish residents and the friars except for the fact that the latter were supposed to be celibate and were exempt from the tithe. There is another way in which the orders differed from the nonreligious: the orders lent money. In fact, the orders routinely made collateralized loans for mortgages and business investments (e.g., mining) while charging a standard user fee of anywhere from 3 to 5 percent per year, often in perpetuity.

While the male orders often were the money lenders of the countryside, male and female orders were the bankers of urban settings. Nunneries were located in cities largely because Spanish society, and by extension the colonies, believed that religious women needed to be protected, not just by the walls of the cloister but by the proximity of their families, access to laborers, and availability of spiritual advisors that could be found only in urban settings. But founding a convent in a city was no easy task. Such establishments required both papal and royal approval, which was granted only after the petitioner had proved that there was a need and the financial wherewithal to support the convent. Quite frequently the crown did not respond favorably and denied the colonists' request. Fearing this reaction, the colonists often acted before receiving a reply. Such was the case with the first convent established in the New World. Nuestra Señora de la Concepción was founded in Mexico City in 1540–1541 under the direction of Bishop Zumárraga with the full support of local secular authorities but without royal or papal approval. In this instance, it was not so much that the bishop feared a negative response from the king, rather it was the prelate's profound sense that the convent was sorely needed. He saw around him a large city with a growing Spanish population but no place for religious women to practice their vocation, no place to keep them safe. Furthermore, the presence of a convent provided a place for "excess" women whose marriage prospects were dim. Mexico City needed a convent. (The enclosure of most women, especially the elite, in marriage or a convent was at the heart of Spanish culture. If a woman could not or would not marry, life as a nun was an acceptable alternative.)

As cities throughout Spanish America became established, the number of convents grew. Santa Clara, Cuzco's first cloistered convent – in fact the first in Spanish South America – was founded in 1551 and is still an active convent today. In Guatemala, Franciscans requested royal permission to found a convent in 1529. By 1578, when they still had not received a reply, they established one anyway. In Havana, a Franciscan convent opened in 1574, and San Juan de Letrán, under the authority of the Dominicans, was founded in 1578.

Although convents were founded in the late sixteenth century, it was during the latter half of the seventeenth century and the first half of the eighteenth that there was a spate of convents opening throughout the colonies. (The first convent to open in Brazil was in 1677. Prior to that, Brazilian women who wanted to join convents traveled to Portugal. Neither the Portuguese crown nor Brazilian secular authorities encouraged the founding of convents in America because of the shortage of white women. They did not want the religious life to draw women from the limited pool of marriageable females.)

There were two basic types of convents: (1) the discalced, which were very strict and austere orders that followed vows of poverty and cloister closely, and (2) the calced, which were a bit more lax in lifestyle and observance of vows. Not surprisingly, discalced convents tended to be few in number and rather small, usually with no more than thirty or so nuns and often far fewer. By contrast, calced convents, precisely because of their less disciplined demands, were in the majority in Latin America. Some of these convents grew quite large. The largest were known as *conventos grandes* and could have two or three hundred professed nuns at any one time. Women in the conventos grandes came mostly from well-to-do families and brought many of the luxuries of life with them, including slaves and servants. With so many women living in one place – sometime more than a thousand – the convents had to be physically large. As the number of nuns increased, the convents acquired adjacent property, sometimes encompassing several streets and buildings within their walls. According to historian Luis Martín, in Lima La Encarnación alone occupied two and one-half city blocks and La Concepción and Santa Clara a block and one-half each.

In these grand convents guests flocked to the *locutorio* – or reception room – to visit their female relatives, conduct business, or watch the religious musical and drama productions written and performed by the nuns. Parties were held in the convents at which the nuns would wear jewels and habits adorned with fine lace and fancy ribbons. Some nuns even refused to wear the habits of their orders, usually opting instead for finery – but in the case of Doña Ana de Frías of La Encarnación in Lima, who clearly suffered from serious mental illness, only a dirty sheet. Servants and slaves tended to the needs of the wealthiest nuns in their private cells – often several rooms in size – purchased by families for their relatives' use. Some nuns even dyed their hair and wore makeup. Life changed little for the elite women who entered the conventos grandes.

So many people living together inevitably created conflict. Martín relates the events surrounding the battle between the de Merino sisters of La Encarnación in Peru and Catalina Negrón, the bellringer of the same convent. Apparently tension was already high between the sisters and Negrón when the de Merinos lured Negrón to their cell for a "friendly chat." Unbeknownst to Negrón, four of the de Merino sisters' maids were armed and waiting for her. As soon as Negrón appeared she was accosted by the maids, who savagely beat her and shaved her head. When the other nuns came running at the sound of Negrón's cries, one of the maids – a slave woman named Juana de Peralta – barred the door to the cell. A high-ranking nun tried to force her way into the cell only to be attacked by Juana and have a steaming pot of hot soup poured on her head. In the end, both injured nuns survived their wounds and all four maids were expelled from the convent. As for the de Merino sisters, we only know that a local tribunal left their punishment in the hand of the abbess.

In spite of the de Merino sisters and some of their fellow sisters in conventos grandes, many if not most women who joined convents did so out of profound religious commitment. The growth in the number of convents occurred during a period of heightened religious fervor, and many women found a convent the best place for the expression of their sincere religious devotion. Furthermore, Christianity was communal in such a manner that the faithful actions of an individual redounded to the good of the all. As historian Kathryn Burns has written, convents were key players in this "spiritual economy" in which the prayers of the nuns and their attention to spiritual matters benefitted the broader community. Furthermore, for the wealthy residents of a city, the convents served another role: they brought prestige to the city, which made the elite more than willing to invest in and contribute to such houses. Families saw sending their daughters to the nunneries as investments in the whole family's spiritual well-being.

But not all women could join religious orders. It was the elite who became the brides of Christ. Joining a calced convent was an expensive proposition. Women who wanted to take vows had to bring dowries with them, preferably in cash, as well as prove purity of lineage (*limpieza de sangre*). While the amount of the dowry varied from convent to convent and even within convents, it is safe to say that the larger the convent, the larger the city in which the convent was located, and the more prestigious the convent, the larger the dowry requirement. (Discalced convents often did not require dowries or required only very small ones. As a consequence, they tended to be poorer and often in dire financial straits.) Additionally, much like secular priests, women choosing the religious life had to prove that they had a steady source of income to meet their annual expenses. Technically, because these women took vows of poverty, the money belonged to the convent, but if the income came from a family-established endowment, it was designated for the use of a particular nun. Often convents themselves also generated income by having the nuns produce items for sale such as sweets, textiles, or pottery.

Dowries and donations made by generous benefactors allowed the religious houses to amass sizable holdings and wealth, particularly during the seventeenth century with the rise of stable, wealthy families that functioned as patrons. This money was often invested in real estate, usually urban, that generated yet more money. With all this ready wealth, the nunneries became the urban banks of the colonial period. They were as selective, however, of their borrowers as they were of their postulants, making loans to choice individuals usually at a 5-percent rate of return. And as their male counterparts did, many convents made mortgage loans that would never be repaid. The loan would pass from generation to generation as long as the convent received its 5 percent annually. The ties – social, spiritual, and economic – with the surrounding communities profoundly rooted the convents in colonial culture.

Perhaps the strongest bonds between the community and the convents were through the professed nuns. But not all nuns were equal; there were nuns of the black veil and nuns of the white veil. Nuns of the black veil were the only fully professed nuns, taking all the vows, coming from the elite families, and bringing large dowries with them. They had voting privileges within the convents and were the only ones who could hold office. Nuns of the white veil, who brought smaller dowries and came from families further down the social scale, professed as lay sisters and did much of the domestic work in the convents.

Undoubtedly the best known nun of the colonial period – and one of its best writers, male or female – was Sor (Sister) Juana Inés de la Cruz, who was a nun of the black veil in the San Gerónimo convent of Mexico City. Sor Juana, the illegitimate daughter of a Spanish captain, was by all accounts an intellectual prodigy. Raised by her grandfather, she read through his extensive library, even teaching herself Latin. At the age of sixteen she came to the attention of the viceroy's wife and became part of the viceregal household, where she pursued her intellectual interests, which ranged broadly, from mathematics to philosophy and from theology to drama. The viceroy himself tested her intellectual abilities by pitting her against the finest minds he could draw together. By all accounts, Juana acquitted herself well.

By the time she was eighteen, Juana had decided to become a nun. According to her, this was far preferable to marriage since it was the one place she could have an active life of the mind. She first tried a discalced convent, which she found far too restrictive. A year later she joined the calced convent of San Gerónimo, where she lived a life of some comfort. She had her own servants and a cell with bath, parlor, bedroom, kitchen, and, perhaps most important for her, a library. She wrote secular poetry and plays as well as religious ones, studied music and science, and exchanged ideas and views with some of the leading intellectuals of her day. Eventually Sor Juana's pursuits caused her to run afoul of church hierarchy and resulted in her silencing by the Mexican archbishop, who did not respond well to the nun's treatise on the need for women to pursue their "God-given right" to education. This woman, whose entire life had revolved around her amazing intellect, was forced to destroy her library and surrender her scientific instruments. Yet, so powerful was her draw to the intellectual life that even as a now-quiescent nun, she did experiments in the kitchen testing how long it took an egg to cook.

Sor Juana was unique by any day's standards. Her drive to learn and her keen interests in everything that crossed her path made her the intellectual equal, if not the better, of any person of her day. Her prodigious accomplishments in the seventeenth century are still surprising. Simply stated, she was amazing. Yet, at the same time, Sor Juana also represents every woman who turned to the convent as an alternative to marriage, as a way to engage her intellectual abilities, and as a safe haven from the pressures of society. Ironically, it was precisely her uniqueness – which resulted in an extensive collection of writings – that gives us access to her commonplaceness. Sor Juana's experiences give us a peek at the life and motivations of a seventeenth-century calced nun.

Life for the barefoot, or discalced, nuns was very different from that of the more relaxed convents. Las Nazarenas was such a convent in Lima. There, in addition to the required necessities of life such as eating, tending to chores, and sleeping, the nuns took part in religious ritual every day: They prayed, attended mass, made confession, listened to spiritual readings, meditated, and recreated the way of the cross. They lived a truly communal life with meals and domestic tasks shared, mostly in silence. And they adhered to their vows of poverty, bringing with them no comforts of life and seeking none once they were in the convent. While the nuns in these observant convents may have had far less contact with the secular world than did their sisters in calced convents, they nonetheless provided a service for the community: They prayed.

As much as convents might have been thought of as retreats from the world, they became involved in all manner of conflict around them, particularly the struggle between the seculars and regulars. Take the case of Santa Clara convent, founded in 1604 in Santiago, Chile. Being part of the Poor Clares, this house fell under the authority of the Franciscans. Nearly forty years after its founding, the nuns sent a secret request to the pope to transfer them to the authority of the local bishop. After waiting thirteen years for a reply from Rome, the nuns decided to take matters into their own hands. The Franciscans responded none too kindly and attacked the convent. Ecclesiastical courts became involved in an effort to adjudicate who should have authority over the convent. Eventually a ruling was issued that favored the Franciscans, but the nuns did not yield easily. The convent was surrounded by soldiers who fought the male relatives of Santa Clara's nuns. Sixty of those nuns escaped and sought refuge in a nearby Augustinian nunnery, where they remained until persuaded that they should accept the authority of the Franciscans while they waited to hear from the pope. They finally did, in 1661. By papal resolution the bishop was placed in authority over the convent.

In another convent, this time in 1574 and in Mexico City, the nuns of Santa Clara petitioned the pope to remove them from the authority of the archbishop and place them under the control of the Franciscans. As historian Jacqueline Holler recounts in her work *Escogidas Plantas*, it seems that there were several new nuns who did not want to endure a year of novitiate before taking their final vows, as the archbishop insisted they do. The Franciscans, however, were willing to let the nuns profess immediately. Under cover of darkness and their cloaks, the friars helped sneak the sisters out of the convent and into the church of an Indian barrio. When the archbishop's men arrived in the barrio to bring the women back, they encountered anywhere from two thousand to eight thousand Indians loyal to the friars. Nonetheless, the soldiers forcibly removed the nuns from the church, enduring epithets and stones hurled at them by the religious women. One of the nuns even stabbed a priest in the arm. Yet again the nuns had their way; eventually they were placed under the authority of the Franciscans.

SOCIAL CONTROL

The church did not limit itself to efforts at controlling convents or other religious institutions. It also exerted enormous control over the lives of lay people, including children. Religious leaders, among them the king, were concerned about the education that the realm's children, specifically boys, were receiving at the hands of unqualified teachers. In 1576 Philip II issued a royal decree calling for the licensing of schoolmasters. In Mexico, the result of the king's order was an October 1600 ordinance addressing those concerns. The Mexican regulations called for testing of all those, even clergy, who would teach reading, writing, mathematics, and Christian doctrine as a means of assuring that only certified individuals became teachers. Many clergy simply refused to take the exams, claiming that they were exempt from non-religious authority. But the archbishop felt differently; he ordered that clergy subject themselves to the ordinance or face major excommunication.

Among the many areas addressed by the ordinance was Christian education, which was an integral part of a school's curriculum. Specifically, in the mornings students were to learn the church's teachings. (The afternoons were devoted to math tables.) During an unspecified number of days of the week, the children were to be instructed in how to help at mass, and at least one day of the week, the students were tested on their knowledge of Christian doctrine.

In 1680 the Cuban bishop ordered compliance with the Mexican ordinance by island teachers and then took the decree even further. He ordered that every Sunday, and any other day of the week the parish priest designated, teachers were to bring their pupils to the local church to be tested by the priest. If a teacher failed either to instruct his students or bring them to the church, at the parish priest's discretion the teacher could be fined or have his license revoked. Furthermore, the bishop ordered that all who would teach Christian doctrine to children must themselves be tested on their knowledge of church doctrine, the prayers, and the principal mysteries of the Catholic faith. Additionally, they had to be persons of upstanding character and moral lifestyle. The church simply would not have its children exposed to reprobates.

The role of religion in the lives of children and the rest of society went beyond religious institutional organizations, and it was not always as banal as curricular matters or what prayers needed to be learned. In fact, the social ethos itself exerted an influence so profound that sometimes the religious zeal of youth took interesting turns. This may be seen in the story of María de San José (1656–1719), who became an Augustinian nun, a mystic, and eventually the novice mistress in an Oaxacan (Mexican) convent. While in the convent and at the direction of her confessor, María wrote her life story. In this more than two thousand page spiritual autobiography, also known as a *vida*, María wrote of a childhood replete with self-mortification, fasting, and hours upon hours of prayer. As is typical of such autobiographies, María recounted a life-changing moment. She and a few playmates were in María's family garden and happily engaged in some amusement when a confrontation between María and another girl developed. María, being something of a wilful child, cursed her playmate. All of a sudden, a bolt of lightening hit a nearby wall and struck and killed an animal on the other side. For María this was clearly the hand of God at work, admonishing her for her wicked ways. But God was not through with her yet. Upon entering her home, María recounted, she encountered the devil in the guise of a naked mulatto claiming her as his own. Such a fearful sight led to a night spent in prayer and anguish. And in the morning, a vision of the Virgin Mary holding the Christ Child reassured the frightened eleven-year-old girl and offered her son as María's bridegroom. In token of Christ's love for María, a ring – which the Christ Child had been wearing – miraculously appeared on María's finger. From that moment on, María dedicated herself to the religious life.

Raised in the countryside and without a confessor, María was largely left to her own devises in determining what constituted a life devoted to Christ. She ate sparingly most days and fasted three days a week, taking only a half-ounce piece of tortilla and a glass of water. She spent five hours a day in a small retreat house her brother built for her in the family garden. She slept on the floor with a wooden beam for a pillow and with her knees bound to her chest so tightly that she was unable to move at all. (This she accomplished without her mother's or sisters' knowledge, even though they slept in the same room.) María also wound around her waist, under her clothing, a strip of haircloth, which she never took off. She wrote of tightening the strip just a bit each day until it dug into her flesh. Eventually the ubiquitous lice began feasting in the wounds around her waist, which festered and oozed so much that in the mornings there were puddles of seepage on the floor. Finally, with the help of her two younger sisters, María removed the bits and pieces of haircloth that remained and let the foul-smelling injuries heal – only to place another similar belt around her waist.

While María's actions might seem excessive to us today, and certainly not all church authorities at the time would have considered them appropriate, it is important to remember that the manner in which María and countless others like her undertook to express their religious devotion was not totally alien to their culture. In Spain and its colonies such harsh forms of penance were viewed as acceptable within a pious life: "Spanish society . . . seemed to have passed straight from the tortured asceticism of the mediaeval to the convolutions of the baroque, without experiencing the humanizing influence of the Renaissance."[2] As we will see, María was not alone in her efforts to be "worthy" of the love of God and of being Christ's bride.

One wonders what ideas so permeated society that a child imbibed notions of the religious life that included self-torture. Perhaps it was identification with the heroes of the day. For colonial society as a whole, those heroes were the conquistadores and saints. For a female, the only heroes society sanctioned for her to imitate were the saints. Saints, of course, were both male and female, but the men who were canonized, such as Saint Martín de Porres (whom we will discuss later), often became saints because of some great service they rendered to society. Yet in a society in which gender roles were so clearly defined and rigidly adhered to, a young girl turned to female saints for her role models of a devoutly religious life. Female saints tended to be ascetics with faith expressions that we might call extreme.

Historian Kathleen Ann Myers reminds us that religious women – some nuns, some not – were "central to the building of America's Christian identity."[3] Precisely with the publication of these women's life stories, often redacted by their confessors in order to emphasize certain points or deemphasize others, the church hierarchy was making clear the lifestyles and actions it viewed as "holy." (Likewise, by determining – through the Inquisition – that the actions of certain other women were heretical, the church was establishing the outer boundaries of acceptable female behavior.) Such institutional acceptance of local holy women (e.g., María de San José and Rosa de Lima, whom we will discuss later) allowed creoles to look close to home for examples of deep religious piety. No longer did they need to look across the Atlantic. Much as the Virgin of Guadalupe's appearance to Juan Diego created the space in which indigenous communities in Mexico could claim Christianity as their own, the veneration of creole religious women localized Christianity for the American-born White.

[2] Stephen Clissold, *The Saints of South America* (London: Charles Knight and Co. Limited, 1972), 84.
[3] Kathleen Ann Myers, *Neither Saints nor Sinners: Writing the Lives of Women in Spanish America* (Oxford: Oxford University Press, 2003), 3.

These religious women, however, also had an impact overseas. By the beginning of the seventeenth century their life stories, as well as those of local religious men, were being sent to the Vatican and Spain. They were proof that the spiritual conquest was succeeding. Orthodox Roman Catholicism was being replicated in the colonies.

Although proving that orthodoxy existed and at the same time providing evidence that the church was being Americanized may seem to be contradictory results of the vidas, in fact, they were not: The institutional church used the life stories of these individuals in one way while the faithful used them in another.

The church also found ways of being more gently present in the lives of adults – far beyond the rites in which they might participate or the encounters they might have with their parish priest. One such area was in the universities, which were founded throughout the Indies by religious orders and supported by the royal treasury – at least nominally. Perhaps the two most important early educational institutions were in Mexico City and Lima. A royal decree calling for the establishment of the university in Mexico City was signed by King Philip II in 1551. In his order, the king made clear the purpose of the school: a place where the sons of the Spaniards could be instructed in matters of the holy Catholic faith along with theology, law, and medicine. In fact, in a letter thanking the king for opening the university, Viceroy Luis de Velasco stated that for some time children of Spanish descent in the Indies had been raised in "complete idleness" and without any type of proper schooling. For some, the viceroy feared, it was too late. For others, the university promised to raise the level of morality. The school, with a faculty of clerics, was the best means to control an increasingly unruly creole population.

The university in Mexico also functioned as a seminary, training priests for their work in the Indies. (By 1580, the university had established chairs in indigenous languages and required that any man seeking ordination be certified as fluent in a major Indian tongue.) The result was an increase in the number of creoles entering the priesthood. Now that they could study in the Indies, more and more young men born in the Americas were joining both the seculars and the regulars and, as a by-product, creating tension, especially within the monastic orders, as we have seen.

The story of the university in Lima (known as San Marcos) is a bit different from that of Mexico City's and perhaps more typical of the numerous universities that opened across the Indies during the seventeenth century. In 1548 and without royal permission, the Dominicans began operating a school within the confines of their convent in Lima. Its purpose was to prepare for admittance into the order the increasing number of young creole men who sought a religious vocation. By 1551, it had been granted by the monarch all the rights and privileges of the university in Salamanca; in other words, San Marcos now had university status. Yet it remained housed in the monastery until 1571 when the powerful Viceroy Francisco de Toledo forced the election of a secular rector and moved the school out of the Dominican cloister, thus severing its ties to the order. The curriculum was also expanded to include the study of law and medicine along with philosophy and theology.

Apart from whatever moral rectitude the universities might have instilled in their students, the schools both created and reinforced the prevailing social order in the colonies. By limiting their numbers to those who were male, white, and elite, these educational institutions helped preserve the dominant power structures, not only in the church but also in the governmental bureaucracy and the professions for which they trained many of the students. In fact, by 1640 in Lima, *castas* (people of mixed race) and Indians were barred from receiving any education at all, including at the elementary school level.

In addition to the Dominicans, the Jesuits were also a strong influence in the schools of the Indies. In Lima in 1582, the Society opened a school whose purpose was to educate boys in both the liberal arts and moral virtues. In Cuba, beginning in 1656, the residents and government of Havana sought royal permission to establish a Jesuit school, which finally opened in 1724. In Brazil, the presence of the Jesuits was unsurpassed by any other order, and they made their mark particularly in education. As mentioned earlier, they very quickly saw education as a way to acculturate and evangelize the indigenous population there, opening schools that took both Indians and the children of settlers. (To attend university, Brazilians traveled to Portugal until after the colonial period.) Throughout the Indies, religious orders and the church in general saw education as a means by which to control society, whether it was through the highly structured curriculum of primary schools or through their efforts to inculcate the population with what they deemed to be the virtues and attitudes necessary for a successful and orderly society.

Marriage was another institution over which the church in Latin America had control. Matrimony was more than simply a socially sanctioned union of two people. It also formed familial alliances, cemented kinship relations, and could have a significant economic impact on all parties involved. For the Catholic Church marriage also was, and is, a sacrament. In Latin America – especially before the late eighteenth century – this placed the institution squarely within the purview of the church. In fact, the power of the church to determine who could or could not marry, who could seek and be given annulments, and who could separate from a spouse was so strong that it routinely ignored secular efforts to intervene, especially after the Council of Trent.

Tridentine rulings declared there to be certain impediments to marriage, particularly degrees of consanguinity that extended even to a godparent's relationship with his or her godchild. It was the responsibility of the parish priest to ensure that no such impediment existed. After ascertaining that the couple could marry, the priest was required to post the banns. Marriage banns consisted of announcing the upcoming wedding on three consecutive Sundays for the purpose of allowing the community to inform the priest of any reason why the couple should not wed – such as the existence of a living spouse elsewhere, an all-too-common problem in the highly mobile world of Latin America. Once the banns were proclaimed and no untoward revelation came to light, the priest was required to determine if the couple entered into the marriage voluntarily. This was viewed as extremely important because cases of coercion occurred frequently in a society in which connections mattered enormously.

The story of Andrea Berrio of Lima bears witness to how far a family would go to force a child to marry. Andrea was twelve years old when in 1604 her family arranged a marriage between her and Gerónimo Ufan, described as "a certain gentleman." We can only assume Gerónimo was an adult. In any case, Andrea did not want to marry. Her family insisted, beating and insulting her, and even threatening death if the child would not relent. Eventually, she agreed and married Gerónimo, but she remained adamant about not consummating the marriage. Gerónimo insisted on his rights as a husband but could only get what he felt was his due by raping his child-bride. Andrea turned to the ecclesiastical court for help and petitioned for an annulment based on lack of freedom and consent. After hearing the horrifying stories from Andrea and having them confirmed by witnesses, the judges granted the child the freedom she sought.

The freedom to choose one's marriage partner also resulted in couples being able to marry without parental consent. Such was the case with Luisa de Avila and Pedro Hernández of Mexico City. In 1584 the couple, of unequal social standing, planned to marry. The first that Pedro's three sisters knew of the upcoming wedding was with the posting of the banns. Determined to stop the marriage, the sisters quickly wrote to their father in Acapulco. While the missive slowly found its way from Mexico City to the coast, the couple learned of the sisters' actions. Fearing that his father would object to the marriage and cause undue hardship for the couple, Luisa and Pedro pled with the priest to suspend the banns and proceed with the wedding. The priest agreed and performed a secret marriage, a routine – if not common – strategy the church employed to assure that couples who wished to marry and had no ecclesiastical impediment could do so.

Under routine circumstances, when all the formalities had been met, Tridentine decrees required that a priest, in the presence of two witnesses, perform the marriage ceremony. Once the sacrament was concluded, only the church could dissolve the marriage or grant separation of bed and table as it saw fit. In Brazil, by the beginning of the eighteenth century separation was often granted in cases of severe abuse. Catarina Vieira Velosa's "divorce," as recounted by Maria Beatriz Nizza da Silva, is a case in point. In 1720, Catarina petitioned the church in São Paulo for perpetual separation from her husband. Catarina claimed that in spite of her best efforts to be the wife the church expected of her, her husband was never satisfied and threw knives at her, slapped her, and even fired his gun at her. On one particularly brutal evening, her husband told the now-terrorized Catarina to make her final act of contrition because he was about to kill her. The shot missed Catarina, and a struggle ensued in which Catarina was choked and left bruised and covered in blood. With her father's help, the battered woman fled the house. In her petition to the church, Catarina claimed that since her husband had responded with contempt when asked by church officials to promise to behave decorously toward his wife, he clearly intended to continue the abuse. It was up to the church to decide Catarina's fate, a decision lost to the ages. Nevertheless, it is clear that the church had complete control over marriage.

RELIGION IN SOCIETY

Religious expression was manifested in a variety of ways within the culture, and perhaps we can best examine some of those by looking at the lives of people venerated for their piety. Among the most renowned of Spanish America's saints was Santa Rosa de Lima. Rosa was a beata. As discussed in Chapter 1, beatas were religious lay women who, while not becoming part of a regular order, nevertheless could take simple vows although not necessarily those of obedience, poverty, or chastity. These women often wore habits from the particular order with which they might be connected and would live very secluded lives – sometimes in their own homes, sometimes in a house with other beatas. Yet these women could also chose to move about in the world, teaching young girls, serving in the community, and occasionally becoming a problem for the secular religious authority to whom they were subject. A woman might opt to become a beata because she did not have the dowry necessary to become a nun or because she would have more freedom than a nun but be spared the confines of a marriage. And she might chose to become a beata because she believed her faith was best expressed in service.

The first of the beatas to arrive in the New World came in the mid 1520s at the behest of Bishop Zumárraga of New Spain, who needed women to teach the daughters of high-ranking Indians in the *colegio de niñas indias*. Nuns, who were cloistered, could not provide the service he needed. So he asked that holy women (beatas) come as missionaries to the Americas in order to instruct Indian women in Christian lifestyles, which included the skills necessary to run a Spanish-style household. Eventually, more beatas came to Mexico as the number of schools for Indian girls grew. Yet these schools were not long lived, flourishing only for a decade (1530–1540). Perhaps part of the reason for the demise of Zumárraga's experiment was that the women who came proved to be a bit too independent-minded to take directions from the bishop. After all, these women had been adventurous enough to cross the Atlantic on their own, without the support of family or friends, and had taken no vows of obedience. Much to the bishop's consternation, the women began wandering off or teaching the children of settlers, neither of which was what the bishop wanted of them. The initial effort at having beatas teach Indian women failed. But in fairly short order, the Americas – north and south – would produce their own beatas, as is the case with Rosa de Lima.

Rosa was born in Lima in 1586 to a Puerto Rican father and a creole mother of limited financial resources. The family was not one of the most high in Lima's society, although they were of the second rank of gentry. Such social status placed pressure on young Rosa to marry as a means of securing the family's economic well-being and its place in society. Finding a marriage partner would have proved fairly easy for Rosa given that she was considered quite a beauty. Yet marriage was not to Rosa's liking. From childhood she had chosen to devote her life to the Christ Child and his mother. For her, a life dedicated to religious expression included extreme self-mortification – what we might be tempted to call masochism. But, just as with María de San Jose's actions, we must be careful not to attach twenty-first-century definitions to sixteenth-century deeds. Two examples should suffice to convey the extent to which Rosa sought to purify herself and identify with Christ's suffering. (Rosa was greatly influenced by St. Catherine of Siena, a fourteenth-century Dominican tertiary best known for her extensive fasts and her role in European politics.) As already mentioned, Rosa was considered extremely beautiful. She often received compliments about the beauty of her hands and her face. But for Rosa, these comments represented temptations both to her and to those who made them. In order to rid herself of that devil, Rosa rubbed her face with red pepper and washed her hands in lye. Even Rosa's confessor was concerned about the extreme forms of her penance, yet she would hide from him her most ingenious means of self-torture.

As a young child, Rosa was drawn to an image of *Ecce Homo* (a depiction of Christ after being scourged and having the crown of thorns placed upon his head) that her parents kept in their home. As a young woman of twenty or so, she had a crown of thorns fashioned for herself. A local craftsman made a silver band with three rows of thirty-three sharp nails each – one for every year of Christ's life – which Rosa wore hidden under a veil. She let her hair grow long to cover the crown in the front, but on that portion of her head covered by the veil she kept her hair closely cut so as not to have it come between her scalp and the nails. In an unfortunate incident, Rosa stepped between her father and one of her brothers who were about to come to blows. Instead of hitting his son, Rosa's father hit her – on the head. Immediately blood began streaming down her face. This was the first her family knew about the crown. They and her confessor railed against the young woman, lecturing her on the evils of excessive self-mortification. Not to be deterred, however, Rosa insisted on some type of crown of thorns. The family – particularly her overbearing mother – finally relented, and Rosa was allowed to wear the crown with the nails filed down. But this was not enough for Rosa. She periodically would bash herself in the head to ensure that she felt the "thorns."

This young woman was revered by the community in Lima, not for her extreme ascetic practices but rather for her constant life of prayer, devotion to the Virgin, and saintliness. People of all social ranks sought her out. Aristocratic women came to Rosa's cell in her garden just to talk with her and purchase the fine embroidery and lace she made to support her family. Young women seeking to enter the convent came to ask advice of Rosa, and young men confused about a religious calling sought her guidance. The poor and infirm came to her house for help. Even before her death, her cell in the family's garden became something of a shrine for the people of Lima. Rosa died at the age of thirty-one in 1617. Within less than seventy years she became the first American-born saint of the Roman Catholic Church.

Within the world of seventeenth-century Lima – a time of religious flowering – castas as well as Blacks and Indians found a place within what historian Nancy van Deusen calls Lima's popular saints. These folk, usually marginalized by society, were sought out for their visions and acts of charity. They preached in the streets and shared their spiritual gifts. They were an important fixture in Lima. And it was within this context that Ursula de Jesús found her place. Ursula de Jesús was an Afro-Peruvian mystic whose spiritual life was devoted to interceding for souls trapped in Purgatory. Born into slavery in 1604, Ursula was sent to the home of a wealthy mystic and beata in 1612. For five years the young Ursula was exposed to the world of the mystics and their visions and communications with God and Christ. She believed, as did most of society, that such experiences were real and that individuals on earth could act as conduits for God.

By 1617 Ursula was a slave to a sixteen-year-old novice in the convent of Santa Clara. There she tended to all the needs of her mistress: washing, cooking, and mending. And when not working for her mistress, Ursula was working in the convent's kitchen and tending to other menial tasks within the walls of the cloister. In her autobiography Ursula describes herself as vain, lazy, and surly until a life-changing event. While in a fit of pique, Ursula took an unsafe step on a plank suspended over a well. The plank slipped and she was left literally hanging on for her life. Ursula was convinced that it was her pleas to the Virgin of Carmen that miraculously saved her. From that moment on, she gave up her vain ways and turned to a life of obedience and piety. As a result of her new dedication to the life of the spirit, Ursula began having visions in which persons from all social ranks – from nuns and priests to slaves and everyone in between – beseeched her intercession to shorten their time in Purgatory. Any good Catholic of the day knew that he or she was bound to spend time in Purgatory, for only the truly good, the saints, went straight to Heaven after death. It was not at all uncommon for people who were prone to visions to be visited by souls languishing in that intermediate stage. Helping to release souls from Purgatory was seen as a worthy and worthwhile task. And Ursula seemed to be particularly good at it.

In 1645, after forty-one years of bondage, Ursula's freedom was purchased by a nun of the black veil in Santa Clara. Finally as mistress of her own fate, Ursula decided to become a *donada*, or servant, at Santa Clara. She continued to perform menial tasks at the convent, but now she could also devote time to her spiritual life. As befitted the age, Ursula practiced self-mortification: She wore a hair shirt and straps studded with iron wrapped around her arms and waist. She wore a crown of thorns and bound a barbed cross across a bodice made of pig skin with the still-embedded bristles turned toward her skin. She also whipped herself at least twice a day and spent hours lying face down on the floor before an image of Christ. Throughout her acts of penance Ursula was under the direction of several spiritual confessors, one of whom instructed her to keep a diary – an act that she faithfully continued from 1650 until her death in 1666.

Ursula's writing reveals a life filled with joy at being chosen by God to help souls in Purgatory, as well as a life filled with despair at having to deal with the injustices she experienced as a black woman both within the convent and in her interactions with the rest of Lima. She also reveals her belief in a god who judges all, no matter of what race or social status, on the basis of their own deeds. Yet her visions of Purgatory and Heaven were of socially stratified places reflecting the realities of Lima. While Ursula de Jesús has not been canonized, nor has she ever reached the popularity of Santa Rosa, even today, in the barrio that houses Santa Clara, people still speak of the Afro-Peruvian mystic.

Ursula's reputation as a non-white who found a place of prominence within the religious world in Lima is overshadowed by San Martín de Porres. Martín was born in 1579 in Lima to a freed woman of color and an "unknown father" – so the baptismal records indicate. Yet Martín's father, don Juan de Porres, a prominent Spanish administrator in the Indies, had enough of a role in the life of his son that he gave his offspring his surname. In any case, as a mulatto, Martín's prospects were limited in the race-conscious colonial world. Eventually he was apprenticed to a surgeon/barber from whom he learned much about healing – a skill that would serve him well in later life. Thus, when his father left Lima, he was able to send the thirteen-year-old Martín to the Dominican priory with a knowledge of healing herbs.

Because he was mixed-race, Martín de Porres was probably never allowed to be more than a donado in the almost five decades that he lived in the monastery. (Some scholars hold that he eventually took simple vows, though not ones that would have made him a lay-brother; others hold that Martín became a full brother within the order.) Yet, he became known throughout Lima for his humility, devotion to the poor, gift of healing, and love of animals. San Martín's Process – the investigation performed by the Catholic Church to determine if someone is worthy of beatification – is replete with stories of his unique connection with animals. His words inspired a moribund mule to give many more years of service to the convent; he ordered rats to leave his sister's house (and they did); and he even raised a dog from the dead. For the poor of the city he truly was a godsend, supplying a dowry for a young girl of marriageable age, founding an orphanage for the street urchins of the city, and planting fruit trees and medicinal plants in public areas so the poor would have access to them. The ill and injured routinely went to the monastery seeking Martín's help. Against the orders of his prior, he welcomed them into his own cell. When challenged by his superior for disobedience, he is purported to have replied, "Charity knows no rules."

But much as his female counterparts, San Martín did not ignore arduous acts of penitence. He was known for mercilessly scourging himself every evening while repeating the invectives hurled at him by patients or people he met on the street. It seems that Martín's prowess in healing and helping were by in large appreciated by the lower ranks of Lima's society – black and Indian alike. Some among the elite and even some of the brothers within his own monastery saw Martín as a "mulatto dog" unfit for anything other than menial tasks. Like

Ursula de Jesús, he experienced the "stain" of being born black. Yet, also like Ursula, it was within the religious expressions of the time that San Martín found his place in society. Martín de Porres became the first black American saint of the Roman Catholic Church.

Among the many individuals whose personal stories moved their fellow residents in Latin America to new depths of faithfulness and service was Pedro Claver. Claver came to the New World in 1610 as a novice in the Society of Jesus. When in a few years the young man from Catalonia took his final vows of ordination, he declared himself "the slave of the slaves forever." Claver attended to this life-long task in the port city of Cartagena on the Caribbean coast of what is now Colombia. There, for almost forty years, the priest would meet the newly arrived ships with fresh water, food, and a kind word. Yet, he could not share with the bondsmen and bondswomen unless he could speak their language. Quite quickly he developed a team of translators who accompanied him to the docks. These men, including Francisco Yolofo and Andrés Sacabuch who worked with Claver for more than twenty years, were often slaves themselves, purchased by the Jesuits but, at Claver's insistence, dedicated to his work with the slaves. Together Claver and his friends – for they became his closest friends – arrived at the dock whenever a ship came into port. Almost immediately they would tend to the needs of the dying, baptizing them if there was time or laying their bodies to rest. They would then separate the new arrivals into linguistic groups and then the men from the women. Finally, they would tend to the physical needs of the slaves, giving them fresh water, fresh fruit, clothing, washing their bodies, tending to their injuries. All the while, the missionaries would talk about their faith in an effort to convert the men, women, and children, for the Jesuits' main concern was for the slaves' souls and their salvation. In fact, Fray Alonso de Sandoval, Pedro Claver's mentor in the work among slaves, clearly stated Jesuit thinking when he declared that it was far better for Africans to be brought as slaves to a place where they might be baptized into Christianity than to remain free in a land where was no chance for salvation. We must remember that what might strike us as a difficult argument to accept was the basis for actions that brought amelioration of hunger, thirst, nakedness, and fear. All told, Pedro Claver believed he baptized three hundred thousand slaves in his life's work.

However gentle and well-meaning Claver's actions were, they were some-times met with criticism from his superiors: He was spending too much time with the slaves; his cell had become a stockroom for blankets, clothes, and supplies; he was antagonizing the white elite in the city. In truth, it was not uncommon for Father Pedro to criticize the excesses of the white residents of the city and to refuse to confess them. He was routinely heard to say that there were many priests who would act as confessors for the white population while there were far too few who worked with the black population.

In spite of his sharp tongue and what many saw as an insolent manner, the priest did have followers among the elite. Men and women of consequence gave in response to Claver's pleas for funds. Doña Isabel de Urbina not only gave Claver money but she also put her own slave, Margarita, at the saint's disposal. It was Margarita's job to prepare the banquets that Claver and his assistants took to the leprosarium on feast days of the church. Other Blacks, freed and enslaved, also helped Pedro with his work. Historian Steven Clissold writes about Angela Rodríguez, who visited the sick with Claver. There was Bernardina, who for thirty years went door to door asking for alms to support the priest's work. And there were also Justina and Martina, who took it upon themselves to collect the bodies of slaves left for the mortuary cart and ensure they received Christian burial at which Father Pedro said the mass.

Pedro Claver continued his work among the slaves until the last four years of his life when, in cruel irony, the now-debilitated and largely immobile priest was left in the care of a Jesuit slave who neglected his charge, supposedly stealing what little Claver had and even failing to keep the seventy-three-year-old man clean. Days before his death, Claver's simple room became the site of pilgrimage by the city's elite, merchants, religious leaders, and Blacks – both free and enslaved. It was in 1888 – the year that black slavery was finally abolished in Latin America – that Pedro Claver was canonized.

In addition to the singular lives of saints – both popular and canonized – religion in colonial Latin American society also had a corporate expression. Chief among groups that functioned as religious outlets for people were the cofradías. In the case of both Portuguese and Spanish America, the cofradía (*confraria* in Portuguese) had medieval roots that were planted as a response to the plagues and manifold misfortunes that befell Europe during the late Middle Ages. As groups of like-minded individuals – such as the elite, folk from the same neighborhood, or followers of a particular saint – came together to provide mutual aid and support to one another and to promote the cult of a saint, the confraternity (or sodality) blossomed. (Hermandades were similar organizations whose members tended to belong to the same profession – such as cobblers or silversmiths – and were dedicated to the patron saint of that profession. In this section, what is said of the cofradías applies to the hermandades.) By the fifteenth century, these lay religious organizations were firmly established on the Iberian peninsula where, as historians tell us, they all shared two common features: (1) a focus on Christian virtues, and (2) providing for the physical well-being of members and their dependents. They also tended to concentrate their religious fervor on one particular saint, often going to great lengths to celebrate that saint's day. Additionally, confraternities built chapels or churches using funds from a common pool created by the payment of annual dues and collected alms. Like so many other Iberian institutions, cofradías were replicated in the Americas.

In the case of Brazil, perhaps the best known and certainly the most successful confraternity was the *Santa Casa da Misericórdia* (Holy House of Mercy) of Bahia. Patterned after the original association in Portugal and with numerous "branch offices" throughout Brazil, the Misericórdia drew its members mostly from the elite families of the colony. It was a mark of status to be a member of the Holy House of Mercy. Their charitable work included establishing foundling homes and hospitals, providing dowries for poor girls and homes for spinster women, ensuring that prisoners received whatever aid they needed, and providing so that those who could not afford Christian burials received them. These acts of mercy were extended to any person without prejudice in terms of social or legal standing. Additionally, the Misericórdia also sponsored lavish religious processions and festivals.

It was not only the wealthy, however, who were members of confraternities. In regions where there were large black populations – enslaved or otherwise – confraternities became key tools for their religious indoctrination. The earliest black sodality in Brazil was founded for African slaves by the Jesuits in 1552. For the Jesuits, the confraternity was a means to ensure that the newly baptized attended mass regularly and showed up for religious training. For the slaves, cofradías proved to be a cushion against the shocks of slavery. Their meetings – the only associations slaves were allowed – were places where Africans might find others who spoke a familiar language or with whom they shared cultural traditions. And since these associations held religious festivals and processions, slaves were often able to integrate traditional dances and musical instruments from their home countries. Black confraternities are seen as the principal source of Afro-Brazilian Catholicism.

The close link between church and state created for the black populations through their confraternities is evident in the petitions they routinely sent to colonial officials, often about a dispute between a master and a slave who was a member of the confraternity. In these petitions, the leaders of the associations reminded the reader that in the eyes of God black and white Christians were equal, and they demanded religious equality and its concomitant fair treatment here on earth. While such religious equality was something that the king could accept, in the colonies it remained rather elusive. Additionally, in urban settings, where sodalities were common, slave confraternities made loans to members for the purchase of their freedom and provided legal counsel in court cases against masters.

The confraternity also paid for religious services that the slaves themselves could ill afford, given the high rates exacted by the clergy. Brazilian priests in the countryside were far from the administrative arm of the single Brazilian colonial archdiocese (in Bahia, raised to a metropolitan see only in 1676). Thus, for much of the early- and mid-colonial period, the Brazilian church was administered from Portugal, where the king had *padroado real* – the Portuguese version of the Spanish patronato real. At such great distances, however, church officials had little control over their clergy. Against stated church policy, priests charged exorbitant prices for performing sacraments, including masses, baptisms, and last rites. In gold-rich Minas Gerais, priests would not say last rites without first receiving payment in gold. Individual slaves could not afford these expenses. Thus, confraternities often paid the priests, especially for burials.

As the number of black confraternities grew, particularly in the late seventeenth and in the eighteenth centuries, they assumed a ubiquitous place in Brazilian society. There was rarely a parish that did not have a black sodality attached to it.

Throughout Latin America confraternities were responsible for many of the social services available to the poor and needy. By the middle of the sixteenth century, Havana could boast at least six cofradías. In the late seventeenth century, there were an additional fourteen cofradías and another six hermandades in the city. But they were not what the island's bishop thought they should be. In 1680 Bishop García de Palacios complained that many of the confraternities were not deeply religious and "were not of God's service . . . nor good for the faithful."[4] In the seventeenth century in Lima, some of the wealthiest and most pious residents of the city were members of a confraternity dedicated to María de La O (the expectant Mary) and directed by the Jesuits at the College of San Pablo. With the immense fortune that the members raised through personal gifts as well as begging for alms, the sodality provided dowries for poor girls. This in turn gave the group significant control over who married whom. In Mexico City by the mid-eighteenth century, the cofradía attached to the Congregación de la Caridad and Señor San José would take on the responsibility of securing funding for the *Casa de Niños Expósitos* (foundling home). Throughout the Indies some confraternities supplied *mestizas* (women of mixed Indian

---

[4]   Archivo General de Indias, Santo Domingo 903, Sínodo Diocesano, Libro I, Título II, Constitución I, as quoted in Leví Marrero, *Cuba: Economía y sociedad*, vol. 5. *El siglo XVII (III)* (Madrid: Editorial Playor, SA, 1976), 94.

and Spanish blood) with dowries sufficient for admittance into convents as nuns of the white veil, but only if the young women were deemed worthy of the members' consideration.

THE ROAD LESS TRAVELED

Not all women proved to be of fine-enough character to warrant support by the community. Such was the case of Marina de San Miguel, who found herself facing the Mexican Inquisition in 1598. As explained in Chapter 2, the Inquisition in the New World typically bothered itself primarily with minor crimes against the church such as bigamy, blasphemy, and witchcraft. According to Jacqueline Holler's work on Marina, crimes as serious as major heresy – of which Marina's case is one – represented only 11 percent of those heard by the Mexican Holy Office.

As was common in the legal proceedings of the Inquisition, Marina was arrested but not told of the charges against her. During the period of investigation, while Marina was imprisoned, she was repeatedly asked to search her soul for what she had done that might result in a denunciation to the Holy Office. In fact, Marina had been denounced for the heresy of alumbradismo. As discussed in Chapter 1, this movement was viewed as heretical because it questioned some basic tenets of the church, including the need for the clergy to act as an intermediary with God. Marina, a self-described beata and mystic, was charged with being a leader in a group of alumbrados in Mexico City. In the nine confessions taken over the course of the three-month investigation (November 20, 1598, to January 28, 1599), the beata told, in progressively more graphic details, of a very interesting existence that included an active sex life, alone as well as with multiple partners of both genders. She recounted visions, which she ultimately decided were of diabolical origins, of intimacies with Jesus Christ, and of venturing into Purgatory to free souls. And she revealed that she routinely hid her multitude of sins from her confessors for fear of losing her reputation as a *doncella*, or pure maiden, who had taken a vow of chastity. Interestingly, Marina herself never confessed to being an alumbrada. Finally on February 2, 1599, and after all her testimonies, she was informed of the accusations brought against her and her trial began. In March 1601, a half-naked and gagged Marina was paraded during an *auto de fe* (a public act of contrition and remorse often required of those found guilty by the Inquisition). She was also fined and sentenced to one hundred lashes and confinement in a plague hospital for ten years. Not surprisingly, she became very ill while there. Did Marina die in the hospital? We do not know for she disappears from the records.

What is of interest in all of Marina's confessions is the way in which she and her followers used the church and its teachings to justify an unsanctioned lifestyle. For example, Marina and Juan Nuñez, one of her lovers and an accountant by trade, discussed between themselves how their intimacies over twenty years were not sinful because they went about them with pure minds. Rather, she contended at her trial, when she and Juan had been together she had believed that their actions were a form of mortification and seen as good and holy by God. Ironically, Marina clearly understood the power the church had in the community, but its control of her was almost nonexistent. For years she publicly did what she needed to do to maintain the appearance of purity while privately living a rather dissolute lifestyle: taking communion without making a full confession; tying her life to that of Gregorio López, one of Mexico's great mystics and "popular saints," while dabbling in alumbradismo; and entering into "trances" in which she helped free souls from Purgatory while faking the ecstasies. In the course of the inquisitorial investigations, Marina confessed to everything from eating meat on prohibited days to having carnal relations with the devil disguised as Christ; from being "tempted" not to believe in the existence of the Virgin Mary to believing that God would redeem someone from Hell when the church teaches that such would never happen. Although we might be inclined to think that Marina's life was unique (and indeed we know of it solely because of her trial, which certainly makes it unusual), it would be unwise to assume there were no other men or women with views as divergent from the teachings of the church as Marina's.

Consider, for instance, people who practiced magic. Church teachings presented a complex view of what constituted magic. Nevertheless, they were unequivocal in its condemnation: Magic was prohibited by church edict, it came from the devil, and it went against God's wishes. Research has revealed, however, that practitioners were not as clear about the separation between religion and magic as church officials seemed to have been. Furthermore, inquisitors tended to treat these transgressions as fairly minor infractions of religious orthodoxy. Depending upon the region of the Indies and local circumstances, punishments ranged from confiscation of all property and imprisonment to additional Christian education and penance. One is also left wondering if male inquisitors viewed witchcraft as mere superstition or ignorance because its participants – both as witches and purchasers of the service – were mostly women. Such might have been the case with Michaela de Molina, a mulatta living in Guatemala in 1696, who was accused of bewitching the Indian María de la Candelaria. After a public quarrel between the two women, María began bleeding from the mouth and nose and vomiting a variety of unusual objects: rags tied with strings, chunks of coal, locks of hair, hay, and bits of soap. Much of this occurred in front of two priests who never reported the incidents to the Inquisition nor were even called to testify. (Rumors of the ensorcellment prompted the local inquisitor to investigate.) Perhaps the priests ignored what they saw because those involved, including those who ultimately testified, were all women. Perhaps the whole incident was of little importance to the priests because those causing the trouble and those harmed by it were either Indian or black. In any case, magic had a secure place in the religious life of colonial society.

In large part, those who turned to magic did so in order to rectify what they saw as a situation gone awry. Carole Myscofski argues that people often felt short-changed by the promises of the church. For example, the sacrament of marriage promised a union of love and tenderness. But many marriages did not live up to the ideal. In fact, the single largest category of magic in the Indies was love magic: Usually women – from all social classes and racial categories – sought out love magic as a way to make a wayward spouse behave. That is what Francisca de los Angeles did when she turned to a cousin for advice. It seems that Francisca's husband was not all that she had hoped. The female cousin instructed Francisca to grind up dried earthworms and put them in her husband's food and drink. By turning to magic Francisca hoped to bring the reality of her marriage into line with what she had been promised in the exchange of vows. We do not know if Francisca's remedy was effective, but many people who confessed to or testified in front of the Inquisition truly believed that magic worked, that it brought the world into the order that God ordained.

The close tie between religion and magic existed in the minds of the practitioners and those who employed magic. In Brazil a means of securing someone's affection was to whisper into a lover's mouth – when he or she was otherwise distracted such as when asleep or after physical intimacy – the words of consecration used during mass: *hoc est enim corpus meum* (this is my body). (It is interesting to note that at least in Brazil, African and native American influences on European magic – magic that used Latin or Portuguese words – are not evident until the close of the sixteenth century.) Francisca Roiz accused Joanna Ribeiro of causing the death of Francisca's son in part by using salt from a church baptism. And María Gonçalves, a well known practitioner, had her own miter and preaching chair. Thus, magic often made use of religious symbols sanctioned and employed by the church. But it took those symbols, usually distant from the lives of the common people, and turned them into instruments to reconstruct daily life.

Daily life among central Andean Indians was exactly what concerned priests. As already stated, indigenous communities found ways of integrating traditional religious practices with Roman Catholicism. Historian Kenneth Andrien's work reveals that in the mid-seventeenth century indigenous religious leaders in Cajatambo (north of Lima) were making traditional offerings of guinea pigs, chicha, llama blood, and coca leaves to the huacas in the days leading up to the feast day for St. Peter. They were, in fact, asking permission to participate in the celebrations surrounding the saint. These rituals alarmed priests, who took decisive action in what became known as "extirpation of idolatry campaigns." And, as efforts to eradicate any vestiges of such practices demonstrates, the church left no rock unturned as it struggled – unsuccessfully – to impose orthodoxy.

Extirpation campaigns in the Andes began in earnest in the 1610s. Before then it seems that there was an unstated policy of turning a blind eye to idolatry: Overworked priests in the provinces charged with parishes numbering four to five hundred families simply could not monitor all the activities of their parishioners. Undoubtedly they knew that a certain amount of adherence to old religious practices continued, and many of them probably accepted this level of syncretism as inevitable. In 1608, however, Father Francisco de Avila, who was in jail for exploiting his Indian parishioners, denounced his accusers by charging that they were using Christian rituals to hide their worship of huacas. So effective was Avila in arousing passion among his fellow churchmen that charges against him were dropped, and he was named *juez visitador de idolatrías* (judge-inspector of idolatry) by the archbishop of Lima. There is little doubt, however, that even setting aside Avila's self-serving motives, such ancient practices among the indigenous communities truly existed.

Regardless of Avila's motivation, other deeply religious Catholic clergymen became very active in the extirpation of idolatry. We cannot reduce their motivations to simple vindictiveness. Just as there were Indian converts who whole-heartedly embraced Christianity, there were priests who engaged in efforts to impose orthodoxy out of a sincerity of faith. Nevertheless, there was not full agreement among church officials that such vigorous efforts were necessary. Some church leaders blamed lazy and poorly trained priests. Other churchmen believed the Indians were committing religious errors, not idolatry. The former required more education and acts of penance. The latter required punishment.

The first wave of extirpation campaigns ended in 1621 with the death of Avila's chief supporter, the archbishop. There was a brief revival from 1625 to 1627 with the arrival of another hard-line archbishop, who died under mysterious circumstances. After that, there was a lull, and the church seemed to return to its policy of looking the other way.

Extirpation campaigns were again given life in 1649 with the publication of a pastoral letter of the archbishop of Lima, Pedro de Villagómez, in which he exhorted the church to rise up and finally deal a death blow to the practices of idolatry in the archdiocese. It was during this second wave that the evil-doings in Cajatambo were uncovered and dealt with by the burning of the huacas. The judge-investigator sent to Cajatambo by Villagómez also found that indigenous religious leaders were encouraging parishioners to confess to the local Catholic priest sins deemed as such by the Catholic faith and to confess to local ministers sins as defined by traditional religious practices. Some historians believe that what priests and archbishops interpreted as acts of idolatry or pacts with the devil were really efforts by the indigenous community to incorporate the new, imposed religion into their old ways. For the people of the Andes, incorporating a conquering faith into a conquered one was a way of life; it simply was how things were.

In 1671 Archbishop Villagómez died and with him much of the passion for the extirpation campaigns, which had reached their apogee during his tenure. After that, even though there were sporadic revivals of persecution for idolatrous practice, it seems that there was little heart for the effort. The powers of the judge-investigators were far less sweeping than in earlier campaigns, and wayward religious activities were increasingly seen as sins of ignorance.

Interestingly there was no similar effort at extirpation in New Spain. There is no doubt that new converts to Christianity wove the threads of their former religious practices into the fabric of their existence. But the atmosphere was different in the Viceroyalty of New Spain than in Peru. According to historian James Lockhart, in Mexico the cult of saints seems to have taken root much more deeply than in the Viceroyalty of Peru. Household incense burners in the shape of male and female saints were popular items in the late sixteenth-century Mexico City marketplaces, and once in the home, pre-conquest offerings were made to the images. The Holy Office responded simply by banning the production of the incense burners. In 1593 in Mexico City, local artisans crafted an image of St. Francis riding an eagle perched on a cactus – the traditional image of the Mexica. In 1594, artists went one step further. They made a banner whose border contained images of preconquest rulers. In the middle was yet again the figure of St. Francis astride an eagle. This banner was carefully hung across the doorway of a chapel dedicated to Saint Joseph and beheld by the viceroy as well as other governmental leaders. All reports are that these gentlemen greatly admired the banner. For some reason, in Mexico Spanish officials – ecclesiastical or governmental – did not seem as threatened by the interweaving of pre-Hispanic religious practices and Christianity as did their counterparts in Peru. Perhaps the Spaniards in Mexico simply viewed such matters as the way things were.

CRYPTO-JUDAISM

In 1639, Manuel Bautista Pérez and ten other alleged crypto-Jews (New Christians who secretly practiced Judaism) were executed in Lima in the city's bloodiest auto de fe. Even after spending five years in an Inquisition jail, this very successful and powerful merchant of Portuguese descent resolutely refused to confess to heresy. Had he, his life might have been spared, but his property would have been confiscated. He might have been exiled or fined, and he would forever have been a social outcast, stained by his trial. As it was, he was relaxed to secular authorities who carried out the capital punishment, his property was taken, and his descendants were marked as having "unclean blood" because a forebear had been found guilty by the Inquisition. What happened in Lima in 1639 was truly an extraordinary event, for in the history of the Inquisition in Spanish America scarcely one hundred people were executed.

Since the earliest days of the conquest – and indeed in Spain long before that – crypto-Jews were seen as a menace to both crown and church. In Spain it was the effort to root out all vestiges of Judaism that led King Ferdinand in the fifteenth century to request a tribunal of the Holy Office in Aragon. For colonial authorities – both secular and ecclesiastical – heresy of any sort was, as historian Irene Silverblatt has written, just one step shy of treason. And crypto-Judaism was the worst of the lot. After all, New Christians who continued their old ways threatened the church's very effort to create an orthodox realm, especially with regards to the vulnerable Indian and black populations who could be so easily led astray.

By the sixteenth century the Tribunal of the Inquisition in Lima was seeking out crypto-Jews with a vengeance, and Bautista Pérez got caught in the fury. The church had reason to worry, so it thought. From 1580 to 1640 the crowns of Portugal and Spain were united, and during that period Portuguese could travel throughout the empire, as any resident of Spain could. New Christians in large numbers left Portugal for Spain where conversos were more readily welcomed. In fact, there was such a large migration that Spaniards eventually conflated New Christians with crypto-Jews and being Portuguese. After residing in Spain, sometimes for a few years and sometimes for a few generations, many New Christians moved on to the New World. As Bautista Pérez himself declared, for New Christians the New World represented the chance for a new life. In Peru, Bautista reasoned, he could distance himself from other New Christians and live the life of an Old Christian, transacting business and conversing only in Castilian. It might have worked, except for the Dutch.

The Dutch controlled portions of northeastern Brazil from 1630 to 1654. Being a nation that observed religious tolerance, Holland and its colonies were places where Jews openly practiced their religion without fear of persecution. So, Jews flocked to Dutch territories, including northeastern Brazil – far too close to Spanish America for the church's comfort. Church officials in the Viceroyalty of Peru were convinced that New Christians/Portuguese in Peru were plotting with Jews in the Dutch-held lands to overthrow the Spanish crown and to abolish Christianity. Something had to be done, and the Inquisition was just the institution to do it.

Church officials as well as many of the Old Christians in the colonies believed that crypto-Jews could communicate with potential converts – the Indians and Blacks – by means of a secret language. To Old Christians, so the witnesses at the Inquisition trial of Bautista Pérez testified, what was being said sounded "normal," but to the crypto-Jews and the indigenous and black populations, the true meaning was clear: subversion on both a political and religious level. In an equally extraordinary development – to use Silverblatt's words – witnesses and inquisitors declared that what were really traditional indigenous and African rites, such as using tobacco or drinking cola, were Jewish rituals, claiming that Bautista's participation in these activities was proof of his continued practice of Judaism. So convinced were they of the rightness of their cause that officials of the Inquisition were seemingly blind to the fallacies in the accusations.

But the Peruvian Tribunal was not alone. Just six years later, in 1649, Mexico would have its own auto de fe in which 108 suspected Jews were penanced. By this time, Portugal had successfully broken away from Spain and fears of a Portuguese-style uprising among New Christians in the Indies grew. In the meantime, many New Christians fled Peru for Mexico in the wake of the Inquisition's activities in the Andean capital. Furthermore, many of the conversos who migrated to the Indies went to New Spain, where they were actively engaged in commerce. Their presence in the capital city was very evident, especially since the viceroy himself was of Portuguese descent and brother-in-law to the leader of the successful Portuguese rebellion in Iberia. The strong link between the New Christians of New Spain and the now-independent Portuguese was too much for Philip III. He ordered harsh, restrictive measures against anyone of Portuguese descent and replaced the viceroy of New Spain. The colony was on heightened alert for possible insurrection among its increasing New Christian population. In 1642 Inquisition officials rounded up almost 100 suspected crypto-Jews/Portuguese. They would continue to arrest and try crypto-Jews until the auto de fe of 1649 brought this particular phase of anti-Jewish activity to an end.

Historian Stanley Hordes has suggested that the motivations of the inquisitors in New Spain went beyond purely religious concerns or fear of a revolt by those of Portuguese descent. Rather, he argues that it was the significant wealth the community had amassed that attracted the church's attention. Indeed, archival sources make it clear that Inquisition officials went to great lengths to trace and document the wealth of many of their victims. It is also equally clear that full and accurate financial reports were not forthcoming to the Suprema in Madrid, in spite of repeated requests, and that members of the Mexican Tribunal enriched themselves as a result of their hunt for crypto-Jews. Nevertheless, we would be unwise to dismiss concerns over religious orthodoxy as a reason for the zealousness of the inquisitors' efforts. As in all things, it was a combination of factors that led to the church's actions in Mexico and Peru. In these cases, we can see the church as having political motives (to stop a possible rebellions), financial motives (to enrich Tribunal members), and religious motives (to preserve religious hegemony and purity).

CONCLUSION

As Christianity was establishing itself in Latin America, it began a process of change and accommodation that the church itself more than likely did not recognize. The church was intent on creating Iberian institutions and society in the new colonies. Whether those institutions were in the form of ecclesiastical structures, such as dioceses and archdioceses, religious houses, or cofradías, the European church tried to impose its world order in the Americas. But what it found was that the colonies were a totally different world in which the realities of racial mixtures and geographic diversity had to be taken into account. An American church was being born with American saints and sinners in abundance both in and out of the institutional church.

In Chapter 4 we will see that the church in the Indies was challenged not only by what it found in the Americas, but also by what was happening in Europe. In Spain, the end of the seventeenth century saw the ouster of the house of Hapsburg and the rise of the Bourbons, who were certainly reform-minded. With the new rulers came new colonial policies that resulted in heightened control of colonial institutions, including the church – perhaps best exemplified by the expulsion of the Jesuits in 1767. Furthermore, the advent of the eighteenth century brought to Europe drastic changes as the influence of the

Enlightenment spread across the continent. The strong Catholic presence in Spain and Portugal mitigated the impact of the new thinking for a while. But it would be Enlightenment thought that in part emboldened Latin Americans to seek their independence. And when they did, they brought further changes to the church.

4

∾

Reform Movements

As we have seen, in the sixteenth and seventeenth centuries the Spanish church in America struggled to find its place. Positions varied from that of Don Felipe Guaman Poma de Ayala, who suggested that the king let the "true Christians" – the Indians – govern in the Indies, to that of Fray Francisco de Avila, who zealously tried to eradicate any vestiges of indigenous religions in the Andes. Indeed, even as the ecclesiastical authorities made herculean attempts to impose hegemony and homogeneity over religious practices through the expansion of monastic orders, systems to increase the number of clergy, and the establishment of institutional structures, the church itself was giving birth to something uniquely American through its cofradías, its home-grown saints, and its truly interesting characters.

In Chapter 3 we discussed the impact of the realities the church encountered in the Americas, but there were other forces exerting pressure on the church as well. The eighteenth century brought cataclysmic changes to the European continent, and the church in the Indies was not immune to those. In fact, the effect in the Americas of the transformations occurring on the continent was such that ultimately the colonies would seek their independence, severing the church's close connection with the Iberian crowns. Many of the patterns that characterized the Latin American church's relationship with the Spanish or Portuguese crown would simply be transferred to the newly minted independent states – at least initially.

In this chapter we will examine ways in which the Catholic Church continued expanding its reach into the Americas, especially with its northward *push into the borderland* along the west coast of North America. There, perhaps best personified in one person, Friar Junípero Serra, we see the two faces of the church. To this day, the friar evokes passion – both reverence and hatred – and is the subject of heated debates about the consequences of the Spanish encounter with indigenous peoples. But no matter on which side of the argument one stands, there is no doubt that Fray Serra's indelible mark is evident on the landscape of California.

Equally permanent were the changes wrought on Latin America by *forces in Europe*. At the end of the seventeenth century, Spain's monarch, Charles II – known as *el hechizado* (the bewitched) for his rather eccentric ways and manifold physical abnormalities undoubtedly caused by generations of Hapsburg inbreeding – died without issue. The subsequent War of Spanish Succession (1700–1713) brought the Bourbons of France to the throne. The Spanish crown was now under new management that brought with it an emphasis on the power of the monarch and the relationship of the colonies to the metropolis – an emphasis highly influenced by Enlightenment thought. In Portugal, likewise, there was a new attitude toward Brazil evident in the actions of the Marquis of Pombal, the minister of state and foreign policy. Among many reforms in Portugal and Spain, both Iberian countries sought to tighten their control over their respective colonies in order to increase wealth extraction. And in both cases, the political authorities in Spain and Portugal believed that the church stood in their way. Neither Charles III, the Spanish king most responsible for what have become known as the Bourbon Reforms, which we will discuss later, nor the Marquis of Pombal tolerated any interference from the church in his actions in the Indies. In fact, both would respond to what they deemed as a challenge to their power by expelling the Jesuits from all their territories.

The *expulsion of the Jesuits* was no small feat. Its ramifications in the New World were profound. As we have mentioned, the Jesuits were prominent in the educational institutions of the Indies. Furthermore, they were the single largest landowner and controlled much of the wealth of vast stretches of the Americas. Their exclusion from the Iberian empires – and ultimately most of Europe as well – drastically altered the economic and political landscape of the Indies. In some regions, such as Paraguay, their departure left the indigenous population vulnerable to the excesses of the colonists. There were few, if any, who did not feel the repercussions of the loss of the Society of Jesus.

It is true, however, that implementing change from a distance is never easy, especially when it comes to reforming an institution as powerful as the church. In the latter half of the eighteenth century, the crown turned its attention to the social impact of the church as the monarchs sought to *alter the influence* the church had over marriage, the manner in which its monasteries and convents functioned, and even the church's role in public acts of charity. In some cases, the monarch was successful in exerting his power over the church, as in the church's role in marriage and the expulsion of the Jesuits. In others, he fought a losing battle, as in his efforts to change the function of good deeds within colonial society. Regardless, for monarchs to gain dominance over their colonies they had to bring the church to heel. They seemingly spared no avenue available to them to accomplish just that.

But the situation in Europe would not remain static. The later years of the eighteenth century brought the French Revolution and very quickly thereafter the rise of Napoleon I. As the Emperor's troops moved through Europe, they took with them the "liberal" ideals of the Revolution, which led to the *rise of liberalism*, a political and economic ideology that held as key tenets certain basic civil liberties guaranteed in a written document. Among those rights were equality before the law; freedom of speech, assembly, and the press; and religious toleration. Likewise, liberalism advocated limited government involvement in economic affairs. All of these ideas would become cornerstones of many of the independent Latin American countries, but even before that time, liberalism would have an impact on how many Latin Americans, including the clergy, saw themselves and their relationship to the church.

And then there is *Brazil*. Brazil followed a pattern all its own, in terms of both how it was structured – administratively, politically, religiously, and economically – and how it gained its independence. The relationship between the Portuguese crown and the colony was rarely as well-articulated as that between Spain and its American colonies. Thus, for most of the colonial period, the relationship among Brazil, the church, and the crown tended to be one of benign neglect. The process toward separation from Portugal also differed substantially from that followed by Brazil's Spanish neighbors in their pursuit of independence from Spain. Brazil's break with the metropolis was slow and generally nonviolent, with the result that it is difficult to draw a clear demarcation and pinpoint specific events that changed the role of the church.

Nevertheless, Brazil and Spanish America shared much during the late colonial period, including an increasingly ill-defined role for the church in the colonies that made determining the *edges of life* – namely, what was acceptable and what was not within religious practices – difficult. Furthermore, there is little doubt that African religions and African and creole (born in the colonies) slaves had profound influence in what we might call fringe Christian religious expressions.

PUSH INTO THE BORDERLANDS

Missions throughout what is today the southwest of the United States existed since the sixteenth century. The first permanent mission in modern-day New Mexico was established in 1598, only to be destroyed in the Pueblo Revolt of 1680. (In 1692 the Spaniards returned to reconquer the lands lost to the Pueblo people.) In 1687, Jesuit friar Eusebio Francisco Kino traveled into the Sonora Desert region, which crosses the modern-day border between the United States (in the state of Arizona) and Mexico (in the state of Sonora), to found missions and to "civilize" the indigenous populations as well as provide a Spanish presence in the area. Father Kino's companion and fellow Jesuit, Father Juan María Salvatierra, moved on to Baja California in 1697, where he founded Misión Nuestra Señora de Loreto Conchó (Our Lady of Loreto), considered by some as the "mother" mission of all such establishments in California – Upper and Lower. The second decade of the eighteenth century (1710s) saw the successful founding of missions in Texas, first in east Texas to protect against French advances in the area and, beginning in 1718, at San Antonio. The Texas missions would become largely unimportant to Spain once Louisiana became a Spanish holding in 1762. After that, Spain's attention shifted to Louisiana in an effort to keep the English at bay.

But the English and French were not Spain's only competitors for land in North America. Russia, too, posed a problem for Spain. By the middle of the eighteenth century, the tsar was threatening to establish settlements in the part of the New World that the Spanish called Alta California. The Spanish style of claiming a region was simply to arrive, declare that it belonged to the Spanish crown, and then move on, oftentimes without developing physical settlements. This pattern left vast areas of Spanish-claimed lands vulnerable to colonization by other powers. Russia's intentions clearly imperiled Spain's claim to the west coast of North America. The only solution was to found missions, especially since settlers did not seem willing to go to the area on their own. (In fact, during the era of Spanish California, secular Spanish settlers, including soldiers, totaled only around 3,400.)

Being expelled from the Spanish empire in 1767 (a topic to be discussed in some detail later in this chapter), the Jesuits could not carry out this arduous task. Thus, Charles III designated the Franciscans to take on mission work in California. Into the fray stepped Father Junípero Serra.

Serra was born on the island of Mallorca in 1713, and by the age of seventeen he had taken religious vows and joined the Order of Friars Minor. His intellectual gifts and his oratorical abilities brought him a university professorship by the time he was thirty-one. Yet, he remained restless. Five years later he requested permission to travel to the New World, where he hoped to help Christianize the indigenous population. His request was granted by his superiors, and Serra went to New Spain. There, for the next twenty years, he worked as a missionary in the Queretaro region and as an administrator in a Franciscan college in Mexico City. In 1769, just two years after the Jesuits had left their labors, Serra was appointed as father president of the missionary efforts into the new territory of Alta California. He set out for the north, along with five other friars, one supply and two passenger ships, and two overland parties that comprised soldiers, muleteers, and Indians from the mission in Baja California. On May 15, 1769, Father Serra celebrated mass in San Diego, the first Spanish outpost in Upper California.

The arduous exploration of Alta California continued with the expedition members routinely reminding themselves that their efforts were to the greater glory of God by bringing Christianity to the "pitiful people" and to the service of the king by expanding his dominion in North America. By November, the explorers were at San Francisco Bay. It would be the fall of 1776, however, before a presidio and a mission were built in the area. In total, Serra oversaw the founding of nine missions. (Eventually, there would be twenty-one permanent Spanish missions in Alta California.) The missionary made his headquarters at Mission San Carlos of Carmel, where he died in 1784, after fifteen years of service to the Catholic Church in Alta California. Over the course of those years, he had walked hundreds of miles, in spite of suffering from scurvy and other medical problems, and was responsible for the conversion of some five thousand Indians. Even in his own day, Serra was known for his devotion to duty, obedience to superiors, and charity to his converts.

The missions themselves proved to be highly successful economically. In addition to solidifying the Spanish presence in the region, by the 1780s they were supplying most of the needs of the colonists. It was Serra and his fellow priests who introduced a variety of agricultural products (such as oranges, lemons, grapes, and olives) as well as cattle, sheep, and horses to the west coast. But the economic success of the religious enterprises came at a heavy cost, and it is this that fuels the present-day heated debate over Father Serra.

The indigenous population at the point of Spanish arrival in California is estimated to have been around three hundred thousand. By 1821, the end of the mission period, that number was down to two hundred thousand. This decline was due to many of the same factors that reduced the indigenous populations of the rest of Spanish America: disease, overwork, and destruction of traditional social supports. The missions have alternatively been described as concentration camps or as the source of civilization for the region. Likewise, Serra is portrayed as either the savior of the Indians or the perpetrator of cultural genocide. In our day, these irreconcilable viewpoints frame the debate that swirls around the canonization process he is now undergoing. (In 1986, Junípero Serra was declared venerable by the Catholic Church, and in 1988 he was beatified by Pope John Paul II.) Indeed, in correspondence with the Spanish governor of Alta California in 1780, Father Serra mentioned that "there may have been inequalities and excesses on the part of some Fathers" when applying corporal punishment to the neophytes, as the Indian converts were known. Serra clearly believed in physical punishment for Indians who did not obey the priests in the missions, but he also expressed concern that the punishment should not be too severe. He counseled restraint, yet even in Mission San Carlos, Indians were forced to provide the labor that made it an economic success, and if they resisted, they were flogged.

Spanish settlers came in the wake of the mission. And from their colonies grew many of the important cities of modern California. Undoubtedly it is for that reason as well as the introduction of certain agricultural products that a statue of the priest represents the state of California in Statuary Hall in the U.S. Capitol. But the debate still continues as to what his efforts wrought for the Indians of the west coast. Was Father Serra merely a product of his times? Did he advocate policies for the treatment of Indians that were excessive even in his day? Does he deserve the designation as "the father of California"?

FORCES IN EUROPE

Focused on transforming Alta California, Junípero Serra was in all likelihood unaware of the powerful changes that had been and were still sweeping across the European continent. The eighteenth century opened with Spain in complete turmoil. In 1700, its last Hapsburg king, Charles II, died childless. Mentally and physically enfeebled from birth, el hechizado had ascended to the throne of Spain at the age of four. His mother – who, being the niece of his father Philip IV of Spain, was also his cousin – was queen regent. Charles was clearly not suited to govern the Spanish empire, nor was he capable of deciding who should inherit the throne upon his death. However, during the last year of his life, after a nominal reign of thirty-five years, he wrote a will passing the crown to his grand-nephew Philip of Anjou, younger grandson to Louis XIV of France, and therefore a Bourbon.

In order to preserve his empire, Charles required as terms for his bequest that Philip renounce any claim he had to the French throne and that he not partition the Spanish empire. (Many other monarchs of Europe wanted to see Spain divided and Charles's move was met with discontent.) If Philip refused the stipulations of the inheritance, the crown was supposed to pass to an Austrian prince and distant relative of Charles. The unwitting Spanish king had set the stage for a European-wide conflict. And it came, after his death in 1700.

The War of Spanish Succession, which erupted after Philip took the throne, left Spain financially crippled and without some of its European holdings.

France, however, which had fought with Spain against England, Austria, Holland, and Prussia, now had tremendous influence over Spain and the direction the crown took. Almost immediately that impact was visible as the Bourbon kings of Spain set about revamping Spanish administration, taxation, and society – which, of course, included Spanish America.

As early as 1709, in the midst of the war, Philip V (the former Philip of Anjou) broke off relations with Rome over the pope's (Clement XI) support of one of Philip's rivals for the Spanish crown. Over the next forty years, tensions between Rome and Madrid were common, with the pope often acceding to demands for more power over the church by the Spanish king.

By mid-century, Ferdinand VI (r. 1746–1759) was able to achieve an astonishing coup over the pope: The concordat of 1753 gave the Spanish crown *patronato universal*, the right to nominate bishops and appointees to certain important ecclesiastical positions throughout the Spanish realms. As we know, the Spanish crown had long held such privileges in its American territories, but now, this power was extended to all Spanish possessions – with the exception of fifty-two positions that remained within the pope's purview. The Spanish church was well on its way to being fully bureaucratized and under the crown's control.

It was Ferdinand's successor, Charles III, however, who brought Spanish regalism to new heights. (Regalism, which holds that a monarch should have sovereignty in ecclesiastical matters of a temporal nature, can be a component of absolutism, a political philosophy favored by French monarchs of the time.) Strongly influenced by elements of Enlightenment thought, Charles III moved to secure control of the church throughout his empire, assuring that this once-powerful institution would be a servant of the crown rather than its partner, as it had been under the Hapsburgs.

The Enlightenment provided the philosophical underpinnings to Charles's actions, but only part of this radical new philosophy was welcomed in Spain. The writings of the early *philosophes* did not find a warm reception south of the Pyrenees. In fact, works by such writers as the Baron de Montesquieu, Voltaire, and Diderot, who were extremely critical of the Catholic Church and called for citizen participation in government, were banned from the Spanish empire by action of the Inquisition. Likewise, ideas from the latter half of the eighteenth century, particularly those of Jean-Jacques Rousseau that called for a "social contract" and the "consent of the governed," made little headway in Iberia, even among the well-educated who were the most disposed to concern themselves with French and English thought. Free-thinking was not part of Spain's Enlightenment. Nevertheless, it would be foolish to believe that the act of banning books resulted in Spain's complete isolation from the ideas of the great thinkers of the eighteenth century.

It is important to remember that the Enlightenment was not only about political philosophy or criticism of organized religion. Another important component of the Enlightenment was what we might call the social sciences. It was in the application of rational thought and the importance of experimentation that Charles and his ministers found much to value in the Enlightenment. Eighteenth-century reformers in Spain tended to view new ideas from a pragmatic point of view: What would increase income for the crown? What would make the government more efficient? What would strengthen the state? And often the answer was to control the church. It was not enough, however, to control the church in Spain alone; state power over the church needed to be exerted empire-wide, and the Americas were no exception. As an advisor to the Council of Castile, Spain's most powerful governmental council, reported in 1768, the most effective means to create a politically quiescent population in the Indies was to reform the clergy – both secular and regular – because they "have more influence over the masses." Thus, he continued, the government needed to be ever vigilant in assuring that the clergy observed the vows and rules that purportedly governed their lives as well as the "healthy principles of obedience and love to Your Majesty."[1]

Among Charles's early efforts at controlling the American church was the appointments of loyal clergymen to positions of responsibility in the ecclesiastical hierarchy. Increasingly during the Bourbon Reforms, European-born clergymen were chosen to fill the highest vacancies in the colonial church. Of the twenty-two prelates who participated in the provincial councils that met in the 1770s, eight had been appointed after Charles ascended to the throne, and only one of these was American-born. A comparison of the ages and birthplaces of the remaining fourteen shows that there had been a tendency to Americanize the church in the colonies. Thus, what had been a trend toward creole ecclesiastical leadership was reversed under Charles III.

The movement to de-Americanize the church went hand-in-hand with the king's decrees ordering that secular clergy assume control of Indian parishes while regular clergy continue their evangelization in frontier regions. (Charles III's policies echoed the ultimately failed ones of Philip II's

---

[1] Archivo General de las Indias, Indiferente General 3041. Extraordinary Consultation of the Tribunal of July 3, 1768, as quoted in Elisa Luque Alcaide, "Reformist Currents in the Spanish-American Councils of the Eighteenth Century," *The Catholic Historical Review* 91, no. 4 (October 2005): 749.

fifteenth-century attempts at curtailing the power of the regulars in the Indies.)
Zealous bureaucrats removed regulars from many of the doctrinas that their
orders had served since the sixteenth century. Secular clergy, the king reasoned, were easier to control since they were subject to the authority of
bishops who, under the patronato real, were basically royal appointees. Having in place in Latin America bishops born in Spain, many of whom were
regalist-minded, gave Charles added power over the institutional church in the
Indies.

Charles also exerted his authority over the institutional church through
other means. By 1769, he had issued the *Tomo Regio*, which ordered the convening of ecclesiastical councils in the colonies, the first since the late sixteenth century. Additionally, the royal decree dictated the topics that were to
be debated, including the founding of seminaries to ensure the educational
quality of the clergy, the promotion of indigenous clergy with scholarships to
the seminaries, a return by regular clergy to communal life, and the eradica-
tion of idolatrous practices among the indigenous peoples. The crown also
wanted to Hispanize the church by requiring that rituals previously held in
native languages be held in Spanish.

Four councils took place in the Indies: Mexico City (1771), Lima (1772),
Charcas (1774–1778), and Santa Fe de Bogota (1774). Historian Elisa Luque
Alcaide's analysis of the working of these councils indicates that many competing elements were present. Each council responded to the royal directives
differently, depending upon the individual bishop and his receptiveness to
regalist trends. Some councils turned to church documents – such as *De Syn-
odo Dioecesana* issued under Benedict XIV – which stated that no provincial
council or synod could make decrees on matters of faith and morals that the
pope had not already ruled on. For example, Charles III called for the condemning of a particular doctrine upon which the pope had not spoken; at
least one council refused to do so. These bishops were in the pope's camp,
honoring ecclesiastical authority over royal authority. The four councils also
rejected the king's call to perform their duties only in Spanish, precisely
because the Council of Trent ordered priests to explain the rites, practices,
and doctrines of the church in the language parishioners would understand.
Although some bishops, particularly those appointed by Charles, had already
begun reforms along the lines ordered by the king even before the convening of the councils, by and large the councils accomplished little. What historian William Taylor writes about late-eighteenth-century colonial culture
might well apply to the American provincial councils' response to the crown's
initiatives: It was a matter of accommodation and appropriation rather than
submission.

Reform of the church in the Indies by the state, however, would take a much more direct route than the convening of provincial councils. Such changes began with the effort to abolish clerical privileges, known as *fueros*. Fueros, part of church life for centuries, provided individual clergy with immunity from civil jurisdiction. In other words, members of the clergy could not be prosecuted or sentenced in civil court. Nor could they be subject to any form of coercion – such as torture or arrest – at the hands of civil authorities. Rather, they were subject only to ecclesiastical courts and judges, who tended to be lenient with their own. The church was also able to grant sanctuary to anyone. Charles III and his advisors viewed both of these privileges as usurping royal authority and jurisdiction and not serving the state's best interest. For many of the clergy in the Americas, the only thing they had worth having was the ecclesiastical fueros. Attacks on these privileges were met with loud protests even from regalist-prone bishops and provincial councils, which had been directed not to discuss fueros since the crown deemed questions about them as its concern alone. In the long run, the government was not able to do away with the fueros. Thus, when the American colonies gained their independence, many of them had to deal with clerical immunity.

The Spanish monarch's attempts at exerting authority over the church within the American kingdoms were not the only such efforts by a European monarch in the eighteenth century. Portugal also attempted to control church practices in its American colony.

In the late seventeenth century, prospecting efforts in Minas Gerais, in southeastern Brazil, yielded grand results with the discovery of rich gold deposits that rivaled the silver deposits of Spanish America. By the 1720s, diamonds were also found in Brazil. There appeared to be no end to the wealth accumulated by the Portuguese crown from its American colony. With this new-found wealth, King John V acted more and more like his autocratic neighbors in France. Perhaps he had good reason to do so, especially when it came to the religious orders.

With the discovery of great mineral wealth naturally came an increase in population in the region. And with the population came the church. But the friars who first attended the needs of the miners in Minas Gerais also attended to their own needs: They became deeply involved in the smuggling that plagued the area. Historians estimate that at least one-half of the gold pulled from the ground was moved out of Brazil through contraband. By 1711, King John had banned all religious orders from Minas Gerais. With the loss of friars, the area experienced a shortage of churchmen since secular priests were not interested in filling the void precisely because the state limited what they could charge for sacraments.

EXPULSION OF THE JESUITS

But the church in Brazil did not truly feel the heavy hand of the Portuguese crown until the rise of the Marquis of Pombal. The Pombaline Reforms began in 1750 when the Marquis – a title he received in 1769 – was named minister of foreign affairs and of state by the new king, Joseph I. Much like his counterparts in Spain, the Marquis sought ways of increasing the power of the state, especially in the person of the king. (It so happened, however, that Joseph I was a weak king; therefore, the real power lay with Pombal.) He turned first to economic reforms, advocating a mercantile system with Brazil, fed by an increase in the number of slaves brought to the colony. In the colonies he instigated administrative reforms as well as changes within the military and the system of taxation. The Marquis then turned his focus to the church. As historian Peter Bakewell has written, Pombal reserved a special animus for the Jesuits. He denounced those in Brazil for participating in smuggling – which they may well have been doing. He claimed that foreign spies were operating in Brazil in the guise of Jesuit priests, and he declared that they had a hand in political unrest in Portugal. Finally, in 1758, he accused the order of lèse majesté after an unsuccessful attempt on Joseph's life. By 1759, Pombal had secured a royal decree ousting Jesuits from all of Portugal's dominions. The order's assets were confiscated, including the schools they operated, their untold number of slaves, and the property they owned in Brazil, which brought a hefty influx of cash to the crown as it sold or rented the former Jesuit holdings. (The Jesuits had long used African slaves to work their extensive estates, as had other religious orders. The orders' involvement in Indian slavery often took the form of legitimizing slave raids by certifying that the Indians sold into slavery had been taken in "just wars" against rebellious natives. Needless to say, the zeal with which such legal strictures were followed varied from region to region and from expedition to expedition.) In any case, the Marquis was rid of the religious order he hated so much.

But Pombal's actions against the orders were not limited to the Jesuits. He went on to control the activities of the Mercedarians in Amazonia, confiscating their lands, including cattle ranches, and ousting them from the colony. In its efforts to amass power, the Portuguese crown was intent upon ridding itself of meddlesome orders.

In Spain, Charles III also sought to control the church by reforming religious orders. In these efforts he was more successful than in others, particularly when it came to dealing with the one order he believed plagued his empire more than any other: the Society of Jesus. And the evening of Sunday, March 23, 1766, gave him the excuse he needed. That night Madrid erupted in riot.

For some time, the price of basic staples, including bread, had been increasing, creating unstable situations as the lower rung of society was having trouble paying for the necessities of life. Then, on March 20, the hated Marquis of Esquilache, one of the many foreign-born ministers of state whom Charles brought into the Spanish government, issued an unpopular decree that prohibited men from wearing broad-brimmed slouch hats and long capes that swept the ground. The Marquis claimed that such apparel could easily hide the face of a criminal or a sword used for lawless activities. This was too much for the *madrileños*: first, this non-Spaniard had liberalized trade that partly caused the increase in bread prices, and now he was telling Spaniards how to dress. At first there was limited unrest, but by March 23, 1766, agitators succeeded in fomenting a riot. Six thousand people gathered in Madrid's Plaza Mayor and marched on Esquilache's mansion, bound and determined to see his ouster. The next morning, between twenty thousand and thirty thousand people were in the streets demanding changes in royal policies. Finally, by March 26, when the king agreed to address many of the populace's concerns, the city was again quiet.

For four days, Madrid had been ruled by the residents of the city – not a situation easily accepted by an absolutist monarch. It did not help that the riots eventually spread to another seventy towns throughout Spain, although none as serious as that in Madrid. Someone had to be blamed for the city's unrest; that turned out to be the Society of Jesus. It is true that within the Jesuits' ranks there were supporters of the rioters; it is also true that there were other groups – including some among the aristocracy – that were interested in seeing several of Charles III's reforms halted and saw the riot as a means to achieve that end. Yet, the appointments of the avowed anticlerical, Enlightenment-influenced Count of Aranda and the Count of Campomanes to determine who caused the riots surely doomed the Jesuits. After a *pesquisa secreta* (secret investigation) orchestrated by Campomanes, the order was found guilty of everything from advocating regicide to provoking the Esquilache riots, as they came to be known. The king now had the excuse he needed to deal with "that pest."

Included in Campomanes's accusations against the order were its activities in the Americas. Indeed, even before Charles came to the throne in 1759, the Spanish crown had had to deal with the recalcitrant order operating in the Indies. Chief among the problems created by members of the Society was their initial refusal, then grudging acceptance, of the 1750 Treaty of Madrid. Under the terms of this treaty between Portugal and Spain, Portugal was to give up some of the land over which it had control along the Río de la Plata. In exchange, Spain was to leave two large tracts of land that bordered Brazil. This treaty might not have posed a problem for the Jesuits except for the fact that the land near Brazil was home to seven of the thirty Guaraní missions overseen by the Society. The Jesuits were ordered to resettle in Spanish territory the more than thirty thousand Indians under their care and to do it immediately. Additionally, four other Jesuit missions lost important, economically productive lands because they were on the now-Portuguese side of the Uruguay River. (Some historians estimate that the thirty missions under Jesuit control generated almost one million dollars a year, primarily through trade, and spent one hundred thousand annually, all of which was exempt from taxation. Such enormous profits were possible because of the non-wage labor of the Guaranís and the tight-handed, paternalistic manner with which the Jesuits ran their missions. The Jesuits were accused of creating a theocratic "state within a state" in the Paraguay missions, free from civil or royal interference.)

The response to the treaty from the Jesuits in Paraguay was swift and vocal. The missionaries sent letters to their European superiors protesting the expulsion of Indians from their lands, claiming that it was against the laws of nature to do so. (Many of these letters were intercepted, and the missionaries' comments became part of Campomanes's evidence against the Society.) They wanted the boundaries stipulated by the treaty to change, and they questioned the need even to obey the decree. But in the end, they complied. It was the Guaranís themselves who resisted – with arms – their forced migration. And it was not until 1756 that a combined Portuguese and Spanish force finally subdued the Indians. In the end, however, Charles III annulled the Treaty of Madrid in 1761, believing that it ceded too much valuable land to the Portuguese. The Jesuits and the Guaranís were allowed to return to their war-damaged missions. By the time of the 1766 riots in Madrid, there was little affection between the ruling authority in Spain and the Society of Jesus in Spanish America.

There were several factors that made the Jesuits vulnerable to enmity from the state: (1) the Society had accumulated immense wealth in both the metropolis and the colonies; (2) it had control of a significant number of educational institutions in the Spanish empire and therefore considerable influence over the educated portion of the population; (3) its members' willingness to comply with royal orders was suspect, especially given their actions in Paraguay; (4) it opposed many of the reform efforts by Charles and his government; (5) the Jesuits' primary loyalty was to the pope, exercised through a vow of obedience made directly to him; and (6) the order had already been expelled from Portugal (1759) for supposed involvement in a conspiracy to murder the king, and from France (1764) for financial malfeasance. (Additionally, the head of the Jesuit order was rumored to have written that Charles III was, in fact, the illegitimate child of the Spanish queen and her Italian lover.) For Charles, the Jesuits were simply far too independent and troublesome, especially in the colonies.

When Campomanes presented his findings to the king, Charles responded by issuing a decree on February 27, 1767, expelling the Society of Jesus from all the Spanish empire in order "to uphold obedience, tranquility and justice among his people."[2] As John Lynch recounts, at midnight on the night of March 21, troops descended upon the six Jesuit houses in Madrid. They ordered the occupants to get up and to board waiting transport that would take them to the port of Cartagena and departure from Spain. The same scene was repeated throughout Spain, from where around three thousand Jesuits were eventually deported. In Asuncion, Paraguay, the military accompanied royal officials charged with secreting the priests to Buenos Aires, from where they left for Europe. In Havana, in order to ensure calm, the military began rounding up vagrants, wandering minstrels, and any others who happened to be near the Jesuit school at 10:00 in the evening. By 12:30 at night the governor and his aides were at the door of the school demanding entrance. Guards kept the clerics under watch until they were finally put aboard the ships that took them to Cadiz, Spain, and from there to Italy. From contemporary documents, it seems that at least in Havana the portion of the population to feel the loss of the Jesuits most deeply was the elite, devout women of the city, for they had lost their spiritual guides and confessors. (Under pressure from Spain and other European countries, Pope Clement XIV suppressed the entire order in 1773. It was 1813 before the Society received papal permission to reorganize.)

In the colonies, some 2,200 religious were expelled, many of them creoles. This created some of the problems the expulsion presented for royal officials in the colonies, because many of the Jesuits sent into exile were their own relatives or kinsmen of important residents of the principal cities of the Indies. Historian Jonathan Brown notes that 58 percent of Jesuits deported from Chile were American-born, as were 66 percent of those exiled from New Spain. And it was not only family members who reacted strongly. Workers in the mining regions of New Spain, many of whom were mulattoes or Blacks, rioted when they learned of the Society's fate. But by and large the expulsion of the Jesuits from the Spanish world was executed without much resistence.

Other religious orders and many individuals, as well as the state, benefitted from the king's actions against the Jesuits. In the colonies – as throughout the rest of the empire – lands, schools, and other property, including thousands of slaves, were immediately confiscated. In Peru that amounted to 203 haciendas and 5,200 slaves. In Cuba, the twenty-one Jesuits present on the island in 1767 owned – as an order – three sugar mills, farms, houses, and the slaves necessary to run all their enterprises. As we mentioned earlier, the Franciscans were given control of the missions in California. They also took control of cattle herds in Chiapas and sugar mills in Guatemala. Other orders took over schools once managed by Jesuits, thereby increasing their presence and influence in the colonies. Individuals were able to purchase or rent from the crown much of the land and slaves once owned by the Society. Many folks did not shed tears when the Jesuits were forced to leave the America, yet their departure created ruptures that took some time to heal. Education, especially at the secondary level, suffered since many of the teachers were Jesuits. Universities lost leading scholars and the funding provided by the Jesuit-owned haciendas. Many Indians under the tutelage and "protection" of the order were now susceptible to the demands of colonists. And many an individual lost his or her confessor and priest.

In Spanish America the expulsion of the Jesuits served as a warning to the other orders. This single action by Charles III went a long way toward creating the compliant and subservient church he viewed as one more tool to implement his authority. It would be wrong, however, to assume that Charles was not a devout Catholic or in any way wanted the church to lose its place of importance in the Spanish empire. Rather, he wanted the church to limit its influence to spiritual matters and leave temporal matters, including the temporal dimension of the church, in the hands of government officials. There were enough problems in the religious realm that needed attending; the church would be well advised to turn its attention there, so Charles felt.

ALTER THE INFLUENCE

Patricia Seed's study of conflicts over marriage in colonial New Spain points to a steady decline of church authority beginning in the middle of the seventeenth century, even though it would be the eighteenth century before this erosion of power was sanctioned in legislation. For example, the 1670s and 1680s saw a loss in the church's ability to assist couples who wished to marry in spite of parental disapproval. As noted in Chapter 3, parents who disagreed with a child's choice in marriage partner – or whose child refused to marry the parents' choice – often reacted by imprisoning their child. Typically the church would intervene with the support of royal police, who would respond within hours of the clergy's request. By the middle of the seventeenth century, however, such requests were greeted with "bureaucratic foot dragging":

Government officials responded slowly to ecclesiastical requests for help. It was not unusual for it to take days for the church to get the needed help; in the meantime, families could spirit away the offending child and remove him or her from the jurisdiction of the interfering clergy. With governmental help less readily available, the church turned to another weapon in its arsenal: excommunication. This technique worked occasionally, but even then, individuals found clever ways of avoiding the church's sanction while not complying with its demands. As the seventeenth century came to a close, the church had to react with less zeal when coming to the aid of couples wanting to marry, for the social pressures to accept its authority were waning.

In 1690 came more evidence that the church as a force in the molding of social mores was in decline. That year saw a clear break in the number of secret marriages the Mexican church was willing to perform. Up to that time, roughly two-thirds of couples who faced parental opposition to their marriage were able to wed because the church dispensed with the required banns and married the couples in secret, especially if there was a pregnancy. After 1690, the church used secret marriages only to protect the honor of deflowered women from the highest social class who also often had some connection to the church. Obviously this change in attitude had a profound impact on couples of lower social ranking who sought private marriages. They were on their own; the church provided no help in safeguarding a poor woman's honor. But the church's willingness to sanction secret marriages for the elite saved the reputation of Doña Tomasa de Toro, who succumbed to her "fragility" and became pregnant without the benefit of marriage. Local ecclesiastical authorities were quietly informed of the noble girl's loss of honor. The banns were dispensed with and the girl and her lover were married without the public declaration of the impending nuptials.

Likewise, in the early eighteenth century, the church lost its ability to enforce the promise to marry. Before then, as far as the church was concerned, a declaration of intention to marry was a commitment tantamount to marriage itself. Only under extreme circumstances would church authorities allow a man to withdraw his promise to marry without suffering serious repercussions. By the 1720s, the church changed its policy and now saw matters concerning a broken engagement as private, between the couple. Seed argues that this change in policy was really in response to pressure by society, which viewed such promises as a completely private matter.

The case of María Patricia exemplifies these changes. In 1727, María, the daughter of a convent washerwoman, was seduced by Matías Santa Cruz, the nephew of an Augustinian curate, after he promised to marry her. Matías's mother opposed the marriage and enlisted the help of her brother-in-law – the curate. But María and her mother, who wanted the marriage to take place, would not be moved. They insisted that Matías keep his promise and took the case to the local ecclesiastical court. Instead of enforcing the commitment, the judge declared that only the court in Mexico City could deal with such an issue. That court required María's presence before it would adjudicate the case. As María and her family were far too poor to make the trip to the viceregal capital, the court directed María's mother to figure something out with Matías's family on her own. As in the case of secret marriages, the poor – particularly women – bore the brunt of the church's change in policy.

Over the course of the eighteenth century, wealthy families increasingly saw the civil courts as the venue for solving problems of marriage conflicts with their children. In 1776, Charles III made that process official. That year he issued the *Real Pragmática* (Royal Pragmatic) that declared that civil authority rather than ecclesiastical courts would settle matters of marriage conflicts. Promulgated two years later in the Indies, the Pragmatic also ensured that parents had an even stronger voice in their children's marriage choices by declaring that they had a veto over undesirable marriages. We must remember that during the eighteenth century parents held enormous sway over whom their children chose to marry, and only a small percentage of couples found themselves in conflict with their parents. The vast majority either agreed with their parents' choice, acquiesced to that choice, or had parental blessings. Nevertheless, now parents who disagreed with their children had a strong hand in enforcing their desires. The church could no longer rule on a couple's right to marry in the face of parental opposition. Specifically, the Pragmatic stipulated that unequal marriages could be stopped by parents. And "unequal" was legally defined as being of different races, at least where Whites were concerned. (Initially Blacks, mestizos, mulattoes, and other castas were exempt from the Pragmatic. By 1803, Blacks and all the castas were brought under its jurisdiction.) However, parents determined to stop a marriage went to the civil courts with other inequality claims as well. In fact, 72 percent of marriage conflict cases heard by Mexico's highest court involved challenges related to issues other than race: economic differences, class differences, and even differences in physical appearances (the intended was not good-looking enough).

By the 1780s, parental approval was legally required before a marriage could take place. And by 1803, all pretense at limiting a parent's ground for objecting to a marriage was eliminated. A parent could stop the marriage – on any grounds – of a son younger than twenty-five or a daughter younger than twenty-three. (According to historian Susan Socolow, the greatest impact of the Pragmatic was on women, who tended to marry young. In Argentina, for example, most women married in their early twenties while most men married at an older age.) By the end of the century the church's role in marriage was simply to do the parents' will. It no longer could counter the wishes of parents, assist young couples wanting to marry, or even define the terms under which marriage could take place. That prerogative now belonged to the state. While Charles's stated intention in promulgating the Pragmatic was to limit the social disorder he believed occurred with interracial marriages, the effect was that the church lost even more legal authority. But in reality, that erosion of power began long before the legislation became a fact. Simply stated, the church was losing its relevance within society.

The deterioration of ecclesiastical authority was also obvious in efforts to reform monastic life. Church leaders as well as the crown had long been disturbed by the lax morals and loose lifestyles of monastics throughout the Spanish empire. Under Charles III, royal and church concerns merged; efforts at reforms already undertaken by bishops throughout the Indies were given the royal imprimatur. Yet, despite the union of two such powerful institutions, little really changed within monastic life.

By the seventeenth century the calced conventos grandes throughout the Indies had ceased being houses of spiritual retreat and contemplation. Instead they were places of parties and plays, festive gatherings and late night visits, numerous servants, and comings and goings. Throughout the century, bishops did their best to reform the convents through the power of their office, enjoining the nuns to turn from their worldly ways and return to their vows of poverty, obedience, and cloister. Much to the bishops' chagrin, their directives elicited great protests from the nuns and not behavior modification. Ultimately, the nuns did what they wanted to do, and life returned to normal in the conventos grandes. The church had no real power in the face of opposition from nuns and the powerful colonial families who backed them.

By the eighteenth century, if anything, the convents were even further removed from their spiritual beginnings. Many nuns of Lima's grand convents had ceased wearing the habits of their orders and taken to donning silks and jewels. They produced plays with secular actors, and in 1755, Archbishop Don Antonio de Barroeta y Angel of Lima had to remind the nuns that bulls and calves were not allowed in the convent, even if the nuns insisted upon staging their own bullfights.

The situation was no better in New Spain, where nuns were accused of having too many servants, spending far too much money on food, and having too much contact with the outside world, including with men and boys. Nuns were also admonished for wearing lavish habits and acting as foster mothers to young girls living with them in their private cells.

In Havana, bishops were concerned with the quantity of goods the nuns of Santa Clara – the city's largest convent – were selling from the door of their convent, the number of servants living at the convent, and the excessive expenses incurred by the nuns. As was the case throughout the Indies, bishops of eighteenth-century Havana were unsuccessful in their efforts to bring the nuns into observance of their vows.

Specifically, bishops in the Indies wanted to restore the *vida común* (common life) to the convents. It was here that the crown and the bishops found common ground. A vida común meant that nuns slept in dormitories rather than private cells, ate meals together that had been prepared in a common kitchen, and had only enough servants to meet the needs of the convent – not of the individual nuns – and that financial resources were pooled for the good of all. But these changes were not easily implemented, even with royal backing. Reports, appeals, and royal cédulas all dealing with conventual reform crossed the Atlantic with great regularity during the reign of Charles III. Bishops complained of the lack of compliance with royal decrees that called nuns to reform. Nuns complained of heavy-handed tactics by bishops to force compliance and appealed their superiors' decisions. And the king sought a compromise. Eventually, in the case of New Spain, the king decreed that all convents needed to return to the common life, even though they had allowed private lives for much of their history. But he provided a loophole for already-professed nuns. They had the option of choosing the common life or private life. Not surprisingly, the majority of nuns in Mexico chose to continue with life as usual. The presence of two different systems of conventual life doomed the less popular one to failure. And fail it did.

In Peru, the common life never really took root in the conventos grandes. Changing from private lives to a vida común took a great deal of money. New facilities to accommodate communal living needed to be built or old ones refurbished. But by the middle of the eighteenth century, convents in Cuzco, for example, were experiencing financial hardships that precluded expenditures on construction. In fact, times were so difficult in Cuzco that individual nuns resorted to small-scale business opportunities to raise cash needed to support themselves and the households within their private cells. (In the early 1780s Peru suffered from the Túpac Amaru rebellion, which was largely in response to the fiscal reforms of Charles III. Particularly violent and destructive, the rebellion engulfed Cuzco, thus the convents of the city, like all other institutions in the region, sustained significant financial losses.) In a very real sense, the common life was not an option for the convents of Cuzco. And in Lima, the nuns simply refused to yield.

In Havana, efforts at reforming convent life were more effective, even if painfully slow. Historian John James Clune chronicles the transformation of the Santa Clara convent in Havana. It was only through persistent royal and ecclesiastical involvement that change finally began in 1783, after almost twenty years of reform efforts and bitter opposition from the nuns. Like other nuns in the Indies, those in Havana were given the option of assuming the common life or continuing in the private life. By 1795, almost half of the nuns had chosen to live in community, and Santa Clara seemed to be on its way to becoming an "ideal" convent. But fate conspired against a relatively easy transition for the Clarisas of Havana. That year, international politics resulted in twenty-five Clarist nuns and their personal servants migrating from Santo Domingo to Havana to take up residence in Santa Clara as private-life nuns. The influx put a terrible strain on the already financially strapped convent. In 1797, the crown responded by declaring a moratorium on admissions of new novices in order to decrease the number of nuns the convent needed to support. The ban was in place for almost a decade and resulted in a house of many crippled, infirm, and blind women. Finally, in 1813 the ban was lifted and four novices entered the convent, without personal servants. The government of Spain had succeeded in bringing about the common life in Santa Clara, but at the expense of the vibrancy of the religious community.

The eighteenth century was also a time in which the Spanish government tried to enforce its power by subtly shifting the very means to salvation, albeit unsuccessfully. The crown tried to make charity a tool of the state rather than a personal act that brought eternal benefit to the individual. Royal rhetoric, especially under Charles III, held that acts of charity by individuals – specifically the giving of alms – fostered idleness on the part of the poor. By not distinguishing between the "deserving poor" and the undeserving, alms giving simply created an environment in which wayward individuals, including children, could continue their dissolute ways, ultimately becoming a burden to the government, because they would become either indigent and need help or criminals and terrorize the populace. Individual acts of charity not only did not benefit the giver; they now were portrayed as detrimental to the empire.

This royal attitude was undergirded by Enlightenment thought that viewed the social welfare of the citizen as the responsibility of the state. Yet, in the case of Latin America, the shift to government-sponsored charity was more than the workings of an enlightened mind. In its move toward absolutism, the crown wanted to control a distant and increasingly disorderly population. But between the rhetoric and the reality there was a chasm that could not be crossed.

The response of Havana's elite to the city's foundling home, Casa Joseph, is a clear example of the government's failed efforts to control the residents by controlling acts of charity. Interestingly, it also gives us a window into the changing attitudes of the city's wealthy residents toward pious works and salvation. The foundling home, opened in the early eighteenth century at the instructions of King Philip V, was never on secure financial footing. It was ignored by the local government and by the local elite. Neither felt any obligation to respond to the plight of children left in streets to die or abandoned by their mothers in the countryside. Indeed salvation through good works was not on the minds of Havana's powerful elite, as they did not give to any other charitable works in the city. The home itself was always on the brink of financial collapse. In the middle of the century so dire were its circumstances that it closed its door, but a royal decree ordered its immediate reopening. Toward the end of the century, however, *habaneros* began giving to the home, providing it a substantial yet insufficient endowment. Precisely at the time that the government rhetoric was trying to tie private acts of charity to social disorder, the residents of Havana were responding to a bishop's appeal linking gifts to the foundling home with personal salvation. The appeal itself was certainly not new. Bishops early in the century had made similar requests but to no avail. What changed the attitudes of the island's elite? Sugar.

With sugar leading the way, trade and commerce flourished in the latter half of the eighteenth century, and with them came increased capital accumulation among the elite and the elevation of Havana to one of the realm's principal and wealthiest cities. After establishing their temporal wealth, the elite of the island began worrying about their eternal souls, and only then did they see value in becoming patrons of abandoned children. Royal rhetoric about governmental responsibilities and social disorder had no impact on Havana's residents.

In Mexico City we see a similar phenomenon in the opening of its Poor House in 1774. As historian Silvia Arrom notes, the secular founding of the home reflected a shift from traditional styles of charity – usually orchestrated by the church and performed as part of one's religious convictions – to a modern style in which social welfare became the primary tool used by the state in response to the needy and as a way of containing social disorder by removing the poor from the streets. However, the creation of the Poor House changed very little. The wealthy still felt it was their obligation to give to beggars; beggars still felt it was their right to ask for alms; and the poor remained visible and unenclosed.

Even as the church was losing some ground in the colonies, as we have seen there were other areas in which it was firmly entrenched. Change had to come from the people; it could not be dictated from on-high, either by the church or by the crown. Likewise, the Spanish crown had no control over momentous events occurring in Europe that would ultimately result in the dissolution of its empire. And in the Americas, the church itself encountered radical divisions in its own ranks as the region lurched toward independence.

RISE OF LIBERALISM

Once again changes in Europe had profound impact on the church in Latin America. This time it was a war inextricably linked to the new consciousness about citizens' rights and government's responsibility. The French Revolution rocked the European continent. Not only was a monarch executed by the people of France, but the masses were claiming the right to govern themselves through elected legislative assemblies. The revolutionary *Declaration of Rights of Man and the Citizen* reverberated across Europe. Churches were attacked and priests were murdered. The old order in France was collapsing, and the Catholic Church with it. Monarchs throughout the continent sought to preserve the old way of life by going to war with the rebellious country. At the end of the eighteenth century, at one time or another, France was pitted against most major European countries. And in the middle of the fray arose a young corporal, Napoleon Bonaparte. His military prowess was such that his rise was meteoric, from fairly humble origins to the leader of the army that restored calm to a France run amok by the end of the Revolution.

France was so thankful and Bonaparte so powerful that he was able to crown himself emperor in 1804 and eventually call a truce with the Catholic Church, restoring some of its position in France while keeping it under his control. Then he began his push across Europe, including an invasion of the Iberian peninsula.

When the French occupied Spain in the early nineteenth century, Ferdinand VII was forced to abdicate, and in 1808 Joseph Bonaparte was crowned king of Spain and all its possessions. But the people of Spain largely refused to recognize the usurper. Instead, in 1810 a national parliament, or *cortes*, ultimately formed in Cadiz, a region of Spain not under French control. Similar bodies also arose in the colonies. Even though the cortes ruled in the name of the deposed king, many elements of liberalism were extended to the people of the Spanish world, including a written constitution. Relative autonomy, while avowing loyalty to Ferdinand, was a new and welcomed taste for the people of Spanish America who for some decades had been feeling increasingly alienated and unappreciated by the metropolis. The return of Ferdinand in 1814 was not greeted with much enthusiasm. And the empire shuddered as he tried – unsuccessfully – to reinstate an absolutist monarchy.

The church in the colonies was split over Ferdinand's efforts. For the hierarchy, life under an absolute monarch ensured that the church at least had
a position of power, while life under a liberal constitution meant that the
church would have no such place in the life of the state. Church authority was
clearly in favor of the reinstituted monarchy. But those in favor of a liberal
constitution and autonomy found support within the church as well, especially among the lower-level clergy. Father Miguel Hidalgo y Costilla, a creole
priest in the small town of Dolores, Mexico, called his parishioners – mostly
Indians and mestizos – to arms in the face of a conservative crackdown against
Mexican autonomy. Hidalgo undoubtedly represented the moral laxness that
troubled church officials. He openly questioned church doctrine, kept prohibited books, and lived with his mistress. Yet in his parish he was cherished
and found great loyalty. Imbued by Enlightenment ideas, he believed in the
perfectability of the human condition through the application of practical
solutions. He spent his own money and exerted his tireless energy to improve
the living conditions of his parishioners. Thus, when he issued the famous
grito de Dolores his community responded. With the ringing of the church
bells, Hidalgo began an insurrection that ultimately drew in eighty-thousand
people. They marched on Mexico City in October 1810 and carried a banner of
the Virgin of Guadalupe ahead of them. The undisciplined nature of Hidalgo's
rebellion made it impossible to control. The movement had changed from its
origins of seeking independence to class warfare, pitting mestizos and Indians
against the Whites of Mexico. Facing such a formidable and well-equipped
foe, eventually the force of the movement began to wane. The priest and his
fellow leaders were captured and executed in 1811.

But the church continued being a source of leadership for revolts in Mexico.
In Hidalgo's stead rose the mestizo priest José María Morelos y Pavón, who
served very humble Michoacan parishes in western Mexico. Morelos was a
bit savvier than Hidalgo in that he led a small, well-disciplined force and
articulated the goals of his movement. Specifically he wanted land reform,
an end to Indian tribute payments, and the abolition of slavery. But he also
promised to honor the place of the Catholic Church in Mexican society and
to respect private property. His ploy to garner creole support failed, as did his
attempt to bring reform to Mexico. In 1815, after more than four years as the
leader of a revolutionary movement, Morelos was captured, tried for heresy
and treason, defrocked, and executed.

It is not surprising that leaders for independence movements came from
among parish priests. By this point the majority of the church hierarchy was
peninsular-born and loyal to Spain while lower-level clergy were creoles. Furthermore, when faced with a financial crisis in 1804, the Spanish government

had seized American church funds normally used for charitable works and to provide financial support for the lower-level priests. These income supplements were essential to the well-being of parish priests, who could barely survive on the salary paid by the church. The very efforts by the Spanish government to control the church put it at odds with the creole clergy. At the same time, fearing the consequences of radical movements such as those led by Hidalgo and Morelos, the creole elite looked outside of the church for leadership in its struggle for independence.

BRAZIL

The clergy in Brazil had a wholly different relationship with the state than did its counterpart in Spanish America, even though the Brazilian clergy was also subject to royal patronage, through the padroado real. By and large members of the clergy in Brazil operated more independently than did those in Spanish territories, particularly because the ecclesiastical structure to support strong oversight did not begin to develop until the late seventeenth and early eighteenth centuries. In fact, the directives from the Council of Trent were not implemented in Brazil until the nineteenth century. The minimal administrative apparatus also meant fewer conflicts between the regulars and the seculars as the two groups staked out different realms of influence and quarrels about jurisdiction arose only infrequently. Regular missionaries were also fairly independent from the colonial system in that they did not rely on state finances to support them. Rather, they had developed extensive systems of cattle and sugar estates and farms and used black slave labor to generate the income necessary to support their missions, schools, and other activities. (In this they were similar to the Jesuits of Spanish America.) The Catholic Church in Brazil was in full support of black slavery and it made no effort to interact with slaves as parishioners. There was no real missionary effort directed at Blacks because the church considered them property and part of a white patriarchal system. In other words, black slavery was not the business of the church, except when it came to owning slaves themselves. Occasionally there would be an individual priest who fought for the rights of slaves, but as a whole, the church supported the racial status quo in colonial Brazil. Being left to run itself – with the notable exception of the Pombaline Reforms – what the Brazilian church ran most efficiently by the end of the eighteenth century was its vast financial enterprises.

The early nineteenth century was also a period of stability for the Brazilian church, which is somewhat surprising given that when Napoleon captured Lisbon in 1807, he found an empty royal house. Just one week earlier, Prince John (who ruled as regent in place of his mentally ill mother until 1816 when he became king) and his royal household, totaling some ten thousand to fifteen thousand persons, had sailed for Brazil. Even with the presence of the royal family and its entourage, the church experienced no significant alteration in its place in Brazilian society. Likewise, when the king finally returned to Europe in 1821 under political pressure from a newly formed Portuguese parliament, he left the Brazilian church much as he had found it. Even when Brazil finally declared independence from Portugal in 1822, the process was so peaceful that the church never experienced the divisions created by similar movements in Spanish America. The institutional presence of the Catholic Church in Brazil left a far less profound imprint than did the church in Spanish America. However, in terms of its impact on popular religious practices, there is certainly parity between Brazilian Catholicism and its Spanish counterpart.

EDGES OF LIFE

Quilombos, or *macambos*, were communities of runaway black slaves in Brazil, which, interestingly, also included white and Indian residents. There were untold numbers of these communities throughout the frontier lands of the colony, but the most famous and most successful of these was Palmares in northeastern Brazil. Probably beginning sometime in the 1590s, Palmares evolved into an alliance of eleven different communities with between twenty thousand and thirty thousand inhabitants who effectively repelled Portuguese efforts to eradicate the confederation for more than one hundred years, until they were finally defeated in 1694. The life of its most famous leader, Zumbi, allows us a glimpse into the spread of Catholicism by individuals often considered to be on the margins of life.

Zumbi was born in Palmares in 1655, but as a newborn he was captured by Brazilian troops in a raid on the quilombo. As historian Mary Karasch recounts, the infant, baptized by the Portuguese as Francisco, was given to a priest who raised and educated him, although it is unclear if the relationship was that of an adopted son or of a servant. In any case, Francisco even assisted the priest in his ecclesiastical duties, often acting as an altar boy. At the age of fifteen, however, for unknown reasons Francisco ran away and returned to Palmares. Eventually there he became chief of the quilombo and took the name Zumbi. What interests us here is that while at Palmares, Zumbi maintained a relationship with the priest, visiting him until the cleric returned to Portugal. From him Zumbi had learned Portuguese and Latin as well as Catholic teachings. And even though it is difficult to state with any assurance, more than likely Zumbi's Catholic background fit into the religious life of Palmares.

Historians speculate that the religious practices that evolved in the quilombos were a combination of several different African traditional religions and Catholicism. In 1645, for example, some Palmarinos had statues of Jesus, the Virgin, and saints in the "church." And there are documentary references to priests in the communities. But there were also African shamans and religious leaders as well as African-born slave runaways who brought with them their own traditional religious practices. Expressions of religious beliefs in Palmares were anything but traditional Catholic observances.

In Spanish America, communities of runaway slaves were known as *palenques*. These undoubtedly mirrored the religious practices of the quilombos. Like their Brazilian counterparts, life in the palenques, by necessity, was closely guarded and kept secret from the outside world. In contrast, the religious practices among slaves still in bondage are much less shrouded in mystery. While adopting several traditional Catholic practices such as godparentage and baptism of infants, Afro-American slave religion was much like that of the quilombos: a mixture of African, Indian, and European. Within the slave communities, particularly those in rural areas, the practice of traditional African religions could often be "hidden" within Catholicism or simply practiced in secret. Many African deities made the Middle Passage, surviving the crossing and being incorporated into the experience of bondage. Historian Elizabeth Kuznesof tells us that that was the case most often with gods directly related to family and to life and death. Understandably, the gods of agriculture, warfare, and kinship, for example, simply could not make the transition into slavery. Yet we must not forget that many black Americans, enslaved and free, embraced Catholicism through the confraternities and other Catholic lay organizations, as we discussed in Chapter 3.

Interestingly, much of what we know about non-orthodox black religious expression in the late colonial period does not come from Inquisition records, but rather it is through the work of anthropologists that we have recovered slaves' past. In the terms of the Inquisition, by the late seventeenth there was a clear drop off in the number of cases involving slaves. Among the likely reasons for this change, two stand out: (1) Slavery was increasingly a rural experience, especially with the rise of the plantation system, while the Inquisition was largely urban. It is in the rural areas where we might expect less acculturation by slaves and therefore more non-Catholic religious expressions. But it was also in the countryside that the Inquisition was least active. (2) As the colonial period progressed, inquisitors identified more and more with the slave owners, viewing slave tactics of using the Inquisition as a means to escape brutal treatment as a nuisance. By the eighteenth century, tribunal officials were less inclined to cause wealthy Whites any financial strain by putting their slaves on trial.

But there is at least one other factor that may have made non-orthodox practices more prevalent in the late colonial period. The church's position in society was shifting. It no longer was the sole arbiter of what was right and wrong. Societal pressures were coming to bear on the church in a way they had not when the church was a partner with the crown in the colonial enterprise. As a servant of the state, the church had lost much of its power to determine what was correct behavior and what was not. Much like today, the definitions of "acceptable" were murky.

CONCLUSION

The eighteenth century was one of paradox for the church: Precisely as it was expanding into the northern reaches of Alta California, its power in Latin American society was contracting. The Iberian crowns were exerting new-found power over the church, curtailing its activities in Europe as well as in the colonies. Religious orders were being brought to heel, and those that would not yield were being summarily dealt with. Recalcitrant prelates were replaced with those more amenable to the state's wishes. Simply stated, monarchs broached no resistance from the church in their drive to amass power. Events in Europe forced changes in the church's place in the Americas, as new thinking and political upheaval took center stage on the continent. Even American society itself viewed the church with less deference, relying more on its own understanding of what was morally right and wrong and less on the church's definitions. The practice of Catholicism also continued to change, being molded by those whose hands worked the soil and brought the church its enormous wealth.

In Chapter 5, "The Church in Turmoil," we will see that the church in Latin America faced new levels of chaos as independence came to the Americas. It was caught in a tug-of-war between the world of the past and the world that was emerging in the new states. It found itself facing enormous resentment from those at the lower levels of society on the one hand and enormous expectations from those at the upper echelons of society on the other. The new realities of nineteenth-century Latin America required that the church re-examine its role in both the political and social spheres and readjust yet again to the world around it.

5

ℭℯ

The Church in Turmoil

As we recall from Chapter 4, the eighteenth century opened with the church firmly established in Latin America, its place unassailable, its importance undeniable. It was, after all, a partner with the state in the conquest and colonization of the Indies. And it was the voice of God on the earth. At least, that is what the church thought. As the century progressed, it would be proved wrong again and again.

The ascension of the House of Bourbon to the throne of Spain in 1700 changed much for the Americas. Even from the beginning of the century there was clear antagonism between the church and the new ruling house of Spain, as French ideas of monarchical rights held sway. Slowly and surely over the course of the century, the state began exerting authority over the church until the reign of Charles III (1759–1788), when the Bourbon Reforms accelerated the rate of change. Charles altered the relationship between the church and state by making the former the servant of the latter. He used whatever powers were at his disposal – as an absolutist monarch with the patronato real those powers were rather substantial – to mold the church into his instrument. And in many ways he succeeded.

As we move on, we also recall that in Portugal and its colonies, it was the rise to power of the Marquis of Pombal in mid-century that resulted in that crown's tightening its authority over the church. His long tenure (1750–1777) as one of the principal ministers of the country meant that Pombal was able to exercise enormous influence over the course of state. Yet, unlike the case in Spain, the relationship between the church and the state in Brazil remained fairly loose throughout the century, with only the religious orders – especially the Society of Jesus – experiencing the full brunt of the Marquis's disfavor. By the end of the century, the Jesuits had been expelled from both Portuguese and Spanish territories (as well as most European countries) and ultimately dissolved by the pope.

In Spanish America, regalism was a way of life for the late-century bishops, and the church had become much more compliant and responsive to the demands of the state. It was not just the state, however, that was imposing its view of the world on the church. As we have already mentioned, increasingly throughout the century, parishioners themselves turned with less frequency to the church for help in ordering their lives, in effect forcing the church to alter its responses to the myriad circumstances that confronted the colonists. Nevertheless, there seems to have been little intent on the part of the residents of the Americas to turn their backs on the church. In fact, even in the runaway slave communities throughout the region, Catholicism was intertwined with traditional faith practices from Africa. Yet, in spite of apparent permanence, the transformation of the church that Europeans had brought to the Americas continued.

In this chapter, we will examine the century that followed independence for the majority of Latin American states, roughly from the 1820s to the 1920s. The majority of the colonies gained their freedom from Spain or Portugal during the first two decades of the nineteenth century. (Cuba, the last Spanish American colony to secure independence, did so in 1902, only then to become a United States colony, by another name.) While the struggles for freedom are not the topic of this chapter, we must outline briefly the course of events that surrounded the *successful separation* from the European kingdoms.

The church itself survived the upheaval of independence fairly intact, given the considerable dislocation created by the wars. But it survived in the pared-down version left by the Bourbons. During the post-independence period, the church in Mexico particularly suffered great vicissitudes. Thus, it is the Mexican church that will receive much of our attention in this chapter. That is not to imply, however, that the church in other areas of Latin America remained static. During the nineteenth and early twentieth centuries, there were radical changes in how the church made its presence felt in society. Even so, it remained a powerful symbol of tradition and authority – so much so that the new states sought to maintain the patronato real in order to establish their control over the church. Inevitably, this led the now-independent nations into *struggles with Rome* about which entity would have authority over the ecclesiastical hierarchy in the Americas. Eventually both sides had to yield.

The chaos of the first decades of independence also brought to life the *caudillos* – such as Juan Manuel de Rosas of Argentina, Antonio López de Santa Anna of Mexico, and José Gaspar Rodríguez de Francia of Paraguay – who filled the power vacuums created by the independence movements. These "strong men" seized control of the unstable republics and consolidated their power, sometimes appealing to the masses by claiming humble origins and, more frequently and often simultaneously, appealing to the upper classes by promising to maintain social order. They also curried the favor of the church and of the army. In the end, what the caudillos delivered were autocratic governments that soon provoked reaction. The power then shifted into the hands of those seeking a different style of government, what in the nineteenth century was called liberalism.

But the liberals found that governing the new republics was not an easy undertaking. They encountered much opposition from conservatives who were intent upon maintaining colonial structures – both political and social. We might see the battle between the liberals and conservatives as *plowing new fields versus preserving old ones*. And the field most fought over was the church and its position within society. Conventional wisdom tells us that the battle was over curtailing church privileges and prerogatives (liberalism) on the one hand and ensuring that the church continued in its role as a means of social control and traditional values (conservativism) on the other. In fact, the circumstances surrounding the church in Latin America during the nineteenth century were far more nuanced than such simple reductions might lead us to believe.

The *cristero* rebellion in Mexico is a prime example of how both sides – conservatives and liberals – found support from those whom we might have placed exclusively in one camp or another. Traditionally, we think of liberalism as supported by young intellectuals and the poor masses seeking equality before the law and within society. We tend to think of conservatives as members of the elite. Yet the cristero rebellion, whose battle cry was *¡Viva Cristo Rey!*, was largely an uprising of the populace in support of traditional church practices.

As the Catholic Church sought to redefine itself in light of changing attitudes toward its social role, women – both lay and religious – became important, particularly in missions, which took on a decidedly female cast. But even in the midst of dramatic changes, there was a level of continuity within daily expressions of faith. We will examine that continuity primarily through the eyes of women. This is possible largely because the nineteenth century was a time of extensive travel by wealthy Europeans and North Americans, often as part of scientific expeditions, and women were well represented in the groups that came to Latin America. Most frequently they came in the role of companion to a husband, brother, or father, but that did not prevent them from being keen observers of the world around them. Fortunately, many wandering women published their travel accounts, which tend to focus on the women whom they encountered on their journeys. It is from these sources that we can glimpse the continued traditional role of women within the religious life of the community. Thus, in the end, the nineteenth and early twentieth centuries proved to be a time of both change and continuity in terms of the *place of women*.

Women travelers also wrote accounts of *slave life* in both urban and rural settings. One such record relates a forced prayer service – which seemingly occurred at least on a weekly basis – on a plantation in the province of Rio de Janeiro. The discomfort we might feel at reading the story was shared by the woman who witnessed the event, yet her tale provides us with a first-hand look into religious practice on a plantation.

Another, less personal source also gives us insight into the place of the church in the life of the slave community in the nineteenth century, particularly in Cuba. Still a part of the Spanish world, Cuba was subject to Spanish rules and regulations, including those that pertained to the treatment of slaves. These slave codes were explicit on the expected role of Christian religious practice in the life of a plantation slave. We will look specifically at the slave code of 1842 to understand what steps slaveholders were legally obliged to take in order to ensure the Christianization of their slaves. It is important, however, to remember that laws are not always indicative of reality, especially of a reality isolated in rural areas with limited accessibility.

In spite of laws that tried to govern the lives of those in bondage, or patterns of devotion that continued into the republic period, and even in spite of rapid changes severely limiting the role of the clergy, Christianity continued to manifest itself in some very *unique styles*. Among those who expressed their faith in interesting ways were the folk healers of nineteenth-century Latin America. One of these was Miguel Perdomo Neira, who traveled the Andes in the latter half of the century, ultimately being the cause of a riot in Bogota in 1872. Another was "el niño Fidencio," a folk saint of northern Mexico whose curative skills were sought by the president of the country in 1928 and yet was arrested by state authorities the following year. Also in northern Mexico there was Teresa Urrea, known as "la santa de Cabora," whose spiritual healing took on an apocalyptical slant and mixed with a new philosophy cum religion, Spiritism. And then there was the Frenchman Allan Kardec, the "founder" of Spiritism, a movement with very tenuous ties to Christianity that exploded on the scene, particularly in Brazil, in the middle of the century. Truly, the journey offered by Kardecism – reincarnation, communication with spirits, and elements of Christian ethic – would be transformed into what historian Peter Winn has termed a mystical religion attractive to the Brazilian middle class.

SUCCESSFUL SEPARATION

Throughout Spanish America, independence was the work of creoles. As the abortive beginnings to Mexican independence under Hildalgo and Morelos demonstrate, efforts, without the support of the creole elite, to establish self-rule ended as failed insurrections. But between 1810 and 1825, with the exceptions of Cuba and Puerto Rico, all of Spain's American dominions successfully left the empire and established independent states. Different regions had different reasons for splitting from Spain. Areas of the Americas that experienced growth primarily in the eighteenth century – such as Buenos Aires and Caracas – did not have the centuries of ties to Iberia that areas such as Mexico or Peru did. Thus, the former were quick to take offense at the renewed efforts of Ferdinand VII to exert his authority over them after his restoration as king of Spain. Caracas rebelled first, then Buenos Aires, both in early 1810. For the *porteños* – the people of Buenos Aires – that year marked the final break with Spain. For Caracas, the struggle with Spanish troops continued until 1821 when, under the leadership of Simón Bolívar, the region was at last able to declare self-rule. By 1820, even Mexico had had enough of Spain's attempts at re-establishing imperial rule over the colony. New Spain began its successful effort at independence in that year, ultimately prevailing in 1821 as creoles raised their voices and their swords against royalist troops. In Spanish South America, it was the combined efforts of Bolívar and José de San Martín that brought freedom to the region between 1818 and late 1824, with Peru being the last of the area to achieve a permanent break with Spain. At the beginning of 1825, most of Spanish America was independent from its former colonizer.

Brazil, of course, was different. As mentioned in Chapter 4, Brazil declared its independence in 1822. Unlike the case of many of its Spanish neighbors, the declaration of independence was, in reality, independence itself. In 1808, King John had moved his court to Brazil, fleeing Napoleon's conquests. When he returned to Portugal in 1821, his son, Prince Peter, remained in Brazil – some speculate at his father's instructions. The prince and his fellow Brazilians were not amenable to the Portuguese parliament's efforts to return Brazil to colonial status. (When King John was in Brazil he had declared it a kingdom, on a par with Portugal.) In 1822, after much irritation with the new Portuguese parliament and in response to orders from that governing body to return to Portugal, the prince proclaimed Brazil's independence. He was crowned Emperor Peter I in December of that year.

STRUGGLES WITH ROME

Independence did not bring tranquility. In truth, power struggles ensued across most of Latin America as war heroes proved to be inadequate political leaders. For decades after independence, many countries experienced one regime change after another. Many of those sought to legitimize their power by gaining temporal authority over the church. Repeatedly, national governments declared that they were the heirs to the Spanish crown's patronato over the church, creating what the states termed *patronato nacional.* Rome could not have disagreed more. In fact, in the midst of the wars for independence (1816), Pope Pius VII issued an encyclical calling the bishops and archbishops of Latin America to encourage their parishioners' loyalty to Spain. But after 1820, when the loss of the American colonies was evident, the pope found himself in an untenable situation: His failure to recognize the new states could lead to a profound schism with the church in the Americas; his recognition of the new nations could lead to an equally profound schism with Spain. In 1822, the pope declared his neutrality: He would neither grant Spain's request to recognize its authority over the Americas nor would he grant political recognition to the new nation-states. Yet, that very year he sent an apostolic vicar – without diplomatic credentials – to appoint titular bishops in those areas where such were needed. Since titular bishops lacked much of the jurisdiction and authority of proprietary bishops and were not subject to the patronato, the pope avoided a conflict with Madrid. By this time, however, Latin Americans were rather suspicious of Rome and its motives. When the papal delegation refused to recognize patronato nacional, it was passed from country to country and eventually sent packing back to Rome. Tensions between Rome and Latin America increased, and they only increased further when the new pope, Leo XII, issued another encyclical in 1824, once again calling for Spanish Americans to obey and remain loyal to Ferdinand VII, who continued resolute in his efforts to reestablish his authority over what he termed the rebellious colonies.

By now, after years of conflict with Rome and Spain, there were a number of vacancies in American episcopal sees. The vacancies were caused by several reasons, among them were that: (1) some prelates left the colonies in support of the monarchy; (2) some of those who remained were later expelled by the new governments for their continued support of the monarchy; and (3) some bishops died, and the conflicts surrounding who nominated new candidates was such that no one was appointed. In any case, from the church's perspective, the absence of bishops was problematic because it was precisely during these tumultuous years that the church needed an ecclesiastical authority to advocate for its rights in the face of the new governments. Finally, in 1827, Leo XII recognized candidates for six proprietary vacancies presented to him by the government of Colombia, in direct violation of Spain's patronato real. The predictable split with Spain followed. The pope claimed that his actions were based on his concern about the spiritual well-being of Christians in America, yet historians suggest that the pope was also concerned about the proximity of and in-roads made by Protestants. The pope was none too interested in leaving fertile ground for the work of those he considered heretics.

Two popes later, Rome was ready to deal with the question of recognition of the Latin American republics. Gregory XVI refused to deal with Spanish intransigence when it came to the naming of bishops for the Indies. In 1831 he declared his intentions to reassert papal rights and fulfill his spiritual functions with regard to the church in the Americas. He also expressed his intention of recognizing the governments of those states once their stability was ensured. In 1835, following the death of Ferdinand, Gregory began recognizing the independence of Latin American countries. He made the action, however, a purely political one, disconnecting it from the matter of national patronage over the church. That conflict would continue.

CAUDILLOS

At about the same time that Rome was struggling with whether to recognize the new nations of Latin America, the region itself was struggling with chaos unparalleled since the conquest. Areas previously united under the umbrella of one viceroyalty began splitting apart as geographic boundaries, impenetrable regions that made transportation and communication painfully slow, and old rivalries defied any efforts at unity. (What had been four viceroyalties during colonial times, by the twentieth century, would splinter into eighteen different nations.) Political chaos ensued with one faction trying to gain the upper hand over the other. In Mexico alone, between 1822 and 1855 there were thirty-five regime changes. Wars between nations erupted, and social unrest followed. What the elite and the church hierarchy wanted was order, and that is what the strong men known as caudillos delivered, often with a great deal of repression and violence. Such regimes existed in one form or another and at one time or another in almost every Latin American country.

In Mexico, the best known of the caudillos was Antonio López de Santa Anna. He began his public career as a soldier in the royalist army, fighting against the insurgents of Mexico. By 1821 he, like others of his fellow soldiers, had transferred his loyalty and fought for Mexican independence. He moved up the political ladder and by 1833 was elected president. Having the title "president" and actually undertaking the activities associated with the job were two different things for Santa Anna. He left the running of the state to his vice president, Valentín Gómez Farías, an uncompromising liberal. Gómez Farías moved immediately to curtail the powers of the church by instituting many typical anticlerical reforms. He secularized mission property in Upper and Lower California. He abolished the compulsory tithe. He allowed monks and nuns to renounce their vows. He took the control of schools out of the hands of various religious orders. He also banned priests from participating in politics, either by discussing it from the pulpit or serving in political office – something many priests had done in the years immediately following independence. And perhaps most daringly, he abolished the clergy's fueros.

Santa Anna responded to the cries of outrage from the church. In 1834, he orchestrated a *coup d'état* against his own government, ousted Gómez Farías, and overturned the offending reforms.

At the same time that Santa Anna was cutting a swath through Mexico (incidentally losing much of it to the United States), Juan Manuel de Rosas was making his presence known in Argentina. Perhaps the quintessential caudillo, Rosas, ostensibly only the governor of Buenos Aires but in truth the dictator of all of Argentina, was a ruthless man who held power off and on from 1829 to 1852 and who tolerated no disagreement with his personal agenda, be that political, economic, or moral. In his rise to power and his fierce hold on authority, the church was more than a willing ally. Portraits of Rosas were placed on church altars. His enemies were depicted by clergy as enemies of Jesus Christ. The bishop of Buenos Aires wore vestments embellished with the colors of the regime. And parish priests cried out for vengeance – dispensed by Rosas's hand – against those liberals who, before Rosas's rise to power, had dared curtail the activities of the church. Rosas reversed reforms that diminished either the place of the church in society or its wealth, giving it back control over both its property and the tithe. He even invited the Jesuits back in 1836, only to expel them again in 1843 to 1844 because they refused to allow their schools to become sites of political indoctrination and still vowed obedience to the pope and not Rosas.

The relationship between the church and Rosas was not all good for the church. As much as he supported it, he also manipulated it. Rosas viewed the clergy as simply another group of bureaucrats there to do his bidding. He exercised patronage – appointing only clergy who supported him – even when Rome did not recognize his right to do so. And in 1837 he decreed that all ecclesiastical appointments from Rome and all papal bulls after 1810 were to be considered null and void in Argentina. Rosas insisted upon running the church just as he ran the country: with a firm hand.

The complicity of the church with a regime that was by any standards brutally violent is perhaps most clearly seen in the story of Camila O'Gorman and Ladislao Gutiérrez. As told by historian John Lynch, the young couple met and fell in love in Buenos Aires. In and of itself, that would not have posed a problem except that Gutiérrez was a priest. Eventually they decided to elope and left Buenos Aires in late 1847. The scandalized church and the furious Rosas responded immediately. The caudillo had the couple tracked down and brought back to Buenos Aires. The highest ecclesiastical authorities of the country encouraged Rosas to deal severely with both Gutiérrez and O'Gorman. But he did not need their urging to sentence the couple to death, a punishment he generally dispensed with a free hand. On August 18, 1848, the priest and the now eight-months-pregnant O'Gorman were executed together by a firing squad. Legend has it that O'Gorman was given a drink of holy water before she was executed so that her unborn baby would go to Heaven.

Rosas's reputation as a man predisposed to use terror grew as a result of the couple's execution. People began wondering, "Am I next?" Discontent with Rosas continued to grow. By 1852 he was forced into exile in England, where he lived for another twenty-five years.

Argentina's neighbor, Paraguay, produced a caudillo cut from a cloth wholly different from that of either Rosas or Santa Anna. Dr. José Gaspar Rodríguez de Francia ruled Paraguay first as a member of a junta in 1814, then, from 1816 until his death in 1840, as "El Supremo" (the supreme dictator). Unlike his Mexican or Argentinian counterparts, Francia had no interest in courting the elite or the church. In fact, his distaste for both institutions resulted in harsh measure to suppress both. Francia was an extreme nationalist, and as such he resented what he saw as the church's support of the royalist movement in the years of struggle against Spain. He was also a fierce adherent to the principles of the Enlightenment, including its anticlerical stances, which naturally put him at odds with a church that he believed represented the interests of the upper class and opposed any form of participation in society by the lower classes.

As a caudillo, Francia ruled Paraguay single-handedly. His beliefs, his concerns, and his idiosyncrasies governed the nation. His first step against the clergy was to deny its members the right to participate in politics. By 1815 he demanded that all members of religious orders – whom he seemed particularly to dislike – swear allegiance to the state. He also forbade any non-Paraguayan from having a position of authority within any given order and required governmental approval of all individuals elected to fill posts within the orders. Francia effectively severed contact between orders within Paraguay and any outside the country – what historian Jerry Cooney terms the separation decree. El Supremo also did to his country what he did to the orders: He isolated it from any outside contact, to the point of putting to death any who tried to leave Paraguay and suspending most of Paraguay's international trade. He did, however, foster internal development and encouraged intranational trade.

By 1824, Francia declared that religious orders were useless and only served to protect friars whose loose moral behavior was an affront to the residents of Paraguay. He confiscated the orders' lands and decreed the secularization of all friars (their work within the church would have to be as secular priests).

Many applied for secularization and were allowed to remain in Paraguay, but others, especially non-Paraguayans, were expelled. Francia also abolished ecclesiastical fueros and took control of church finances. But unlike the anticlerical reforms in Mexico in the early decades of century, Francia's reforms in Paraguay elicited very little public outcry.

Francia notwithstanding, the relationship of the church with the caudillos set a pattern that would dominate – even plague – many Latin American countries for much of their history. As these dictators sought to legitimize their power, they often turned to the church for its overt support – as they also looked to armies for military backing. We will see the repeated collusion, often with horrific consequences, among these three powerful entities. But in the nineteenth century, the power of the caudillos was not entirely limitless; they were often overthrown when they simply went too far. And many times in the 1800s their nemesis took the name of liberalism.

PLOWING NEW FIELDS VERSUS PRESERVING OLD ONES

We must be careful not to apply our twenty-first century political definitions of liberal and conservative to the nineteenth-century terms "liberalism" and "conservatism." As discussed in Chapter 4, in the nineteenth century liberalism – whose roots were in Enlightenment thought – included belief in a written constitution, an emphasis on certain basic human liberties, and a strong sense of individualism. It advocated a governmental structure with checks and balances and a federalized system as opposed to one that was highly centralized. It held that *laissez-faire* economics, which meant limited government involvement in economic affairs, was the best route to success. But in the case of Latin America, it would also come to include the belief in progress brought on by material advancement – much like European positivism. If that necessitated government intervention in economic matters, such as in infrastructure or protective tariffs, so be it. Liberalism also insisted upon maintaining public order to facilitate progress. Again, if government intervention was required, liberals – when in power – saw to it that governments intervened.

Another key component of liberalism from the beginning was anticlericalism. In an attitude that reflected the Bourbon era, liberals believed that the church was to focus its attention on spiritual matters, leaving all temporal matters in the hands of duly elected representatives. Furthermore, the continuation of fueros was anathema to the principle of equality before the law. And most galling of all was the enormous entailed wealth owned by the church. Not only did the church's ownership of property keep it out of the hands of the masses, but just at the point when governments were struggling under financial burdens, the church's vast holdings, the obligatory tithe, and the income it received from rents were simply too much.

The opponents of liberals, the conservatives, were primarily, but not exclusively, from the upper classes and often wanted strong, centralized governments. They sought to maintain the social, economic, and political structures of the colonial era – with the poor and lower classes kept in their place and the upper class in its. Key for conservatives was the central role of the church as a moderating and controlling social power and as a symbol of the continuation of social and cultural traditions. For conservatives, the church represented all that was worth fighting for. And it was around the place of the church that the fiercest battles between conservatives and liberals took place.

In the case of Mexico in the mid 1820s, those who succeeded the first wave of war-heroes-turned-ineffective-political leaders were liberals, who tried to implement many of their reform ideas. In the person of Antonio López de Santa Anna, however, the conservatives came to power in Mexico in 1834. They would rule, in one form or another, for twenty years. During those years the church was protected and its privileges continued. But it was not immune from governmental demands. As historian Asunción Lavrin makes clear, the church suffered at the hands of the conservatives, particularly through demands for loans.

Santa Anna's ill-fated wars with Texas (1835–1836) and the United States (1846–1848) and a more successful effort against French troops that invaded Mexico in 1838 at Veracruz put a severe financial strain on the Mexican treasury, which was already in bad shape following the country's own war of independence. In order to finance its continued military struggles, the government forced loans from the church, including its schools, nunneries, convents, and confraternities. In some cases, these groups had to sell land or real property or call in loans they had made to local residents in order to fund the government's "requests." In other instances, some church organizations had to borrow money from wealthier ones to meet the quota set by the ecclesiastical hierarchy at the behest of the government. In any case, the years under conservative rule were not necessarily easy ones for the church. But they were better than those that followed under a liberal regime.

By 1854, a new wave of liberals was coming of age, and they planned Santa Anna's ouster. They succeeded, and by 1855 the liberals were in power. One of the leaders, Benito Juárez, a full-blooded Indian who would later become president of the republic, became minister of justice. Under his leadership, Ley Juárez was passed. This law was a direct attack on the church: It abolished the fueros, thereby eliminating ecclesiastical jurisdiction in civil matters concerning the clergy. The clergy were now subject to the same legal proceedings as was everyone else. By 1856, Ley Lerdo was passed. It, too, was an assault on the church. This time the church was to divest itself of all its land and property not directly and immediately related to its spiritual functions. Any proceeds from the sale of the land were then taxed by the state. (Ley Lerdo also extended to any property owned by civil groups, such as Indian lands communally held. Its supporters claimed the law was an effort to put unused land into circulation, thereby creating a class of small land owners. It did not happen that way. Instead, large landowners with money bought up the church's and the Indians' property, often paying a fraction of its worth. In reality, Ley Lerdo strengthened the hand of the large landowners and impoverished Indian communities.) In 1857, the responsibility to register major life events such as birth, marriage, and death was removed from the church and made a civil function. And later that year, Ley Iglesias was enacted, which limited the amount that clergy could charge for performing sacraments. Finally, the liberal 1857 Constitution incorporated all these anticlerical laws as well as provisions secularizing education and allowing renouncement of religious vows.

The church's response was most definitely not quiet acceptance. Anyone who took advantage of land put up for public auction as a result of the implementation of Ley Lerdo was threatened with excommunication. Priests were instructed to withhold absolution, marriage, and burial rites from those who supported the Constitution of 1857, and clergy who performed the religious acts anyway were suspended and the rites nullified by the bishop. Church officials also sought ways of evading the laws through sham sales of property and other ingenious manipulations. As historian Robert Knowlton writes, it was a response of nonrecognition and noncooperation.

The church's reaction added fire to the outrage of the conservatives. By 1858, Mexico was in the middle of a very bloody civil war, the War of Reform (1858–1861). Initially the conservative movement gained the upper hand and the capital. They quickly annulled the offending laws and returned church property, all the while squeezing the church for more loans. Meanwhile, the liberal government – with its capital in Veracruz and Juárez as president – was passing even more stringent anticlerical laws than before: Church property was nationalized, ostensibly to deprive the church of funds used to support the conservative side; cemeteries were secularized; monasteries were suppressed; separation of church and state was declared, which meant that the Roman Catholic Church was no longer the national church; the tithe was abolished; marriage was made a civil contract; and the government instituted a ban against new novices in nunneries.

By 1861, the liberals were back in power. The conservatives reacted with an unusual plan, the restoration of the monarchy. They turned to French Emperor Napoleon III for help. He agreed to send French troops to Mexico in order to impose Maximillian of Austria as king of Mexico in exchange for the repayment of extensive debt owed to France. In 1864, Napoleon sent his troops, Maximillian was crowned king, and another civil war ensued. In June of 1867, Maximillian was captured and executed by liberal forces led by Benito Juárez. Liberals once again had undeniable control of Mexico.

Their tenure was marked with corruption, greed, and grabs for power. Perhaps the most blatant – and successful – hold on power was that of Porfirio Díaz, who championed liberal causes in his rise to power and then championed his own causes, including civil stability brought about by brutal violence. He did, however, view conflict with the church as not in his – or the country's – best interest. He strove to improve relations with the church and did not enforce the anticlerical provisions within the Constitution. For its part, during the *Porfiriato* – as Díaz's thirty-four-year regime is known – the church was able to expand its press and its system of educational institutions. It built hospitals and opened new seminaries. The laity began taking a lead in the role of the church in the life of its people. Trade unions formed with the blessing of the church, and religious orders played an important role in the revitalization of the church. Church congresses openly discussed social problems and ways in which the church could participate in alleviating them. By 1911, the *Partido Católico Nacional* (National Catholic Party) was formed. This party's agenda included bringing Catholic moral and social principles into the public life of the state. In all this, the church was reflecting and implementing the directives of Pope Leo XIII's encyclical *Rerum novarum*.

But the Mexican Revolution intervened. It arose out of discontent with the Díaz regime and succeeded in his ouster by 1911. Yet the war continued, pitting liberals against conservatives once more. Revolutionaries turned their ire on the church and charged it with opposing progress and seeking intervention by the United States – which may indeed have been the case. One of the revolution's leaders, Pancho Villa, had a particularly strong dislike of priests. In an interview he gave a reporter from the United States, Villa made his views clear:

> "They [the priests] may be the teachers of the doctrines of Christ, but that does not mean that because they are teachers of what is good they should themselves be permitted to break nearly all of the commandments. . . . The priests, such as I have found in the small villages . . . are paupers in mind

and body. . . . They live like lice – on others. . . . Have I not seen that a priest makes no move unless it means money to him?"[1]

The liberals prevailed, and by 1913, the Partido Católico Nacional ceased to exist. In 1917, a new constitution was written with several very key anticlerical provisions: Freedom of religion was enshrined; all education was secularized (no religious organization, Catholic or Protestant, could run a primary or secondary educational institution); public religious observances could occur only in public places of worship, which were under government supervision; and religious institutions, of any ilk, were prohibited from owning real property or holding mortgages. Furthermore, any monastery, convent, or religious school, seminary, rectory, or any other building in which religious instruction took place immediately became the property of the state – including any new churches built after the ratification of the Constitution. The church was also prohibited from running public charities. Priests were not allowed to hold public office or criticize the government in any way, and only Mexicans by birth were allowed to practice ministry in the country. New churches could be constructed only with government approval, and clergy were required to register with the state since the state limited the number of clergy allowed in any particular location. The Constitution was proclaimed in February of 1917.

Perhaps "The Creed of the Liberals" best embodies the feeling of the liberal movement in Mexico.

> I believe in one free and powerful country, cradle of a noble and eminent people, and in Juárez, its great son, our Lord who was conceived by the Virgin of America, suffered under the power of Roman clergy, was excommunicated, died, and buried; on the second day he rose again from the dead, ascended into heaven, and is seated at the right hand of Sublime Right, from there he will come to judge the bigoted and the rich; I believe in Liberal Thought, Holy Universal Peace, the communion of heros, the shame of traitors, the redemption of the people, [and] the happiness of the poor. Amen.[2]

By 1926, Mexico was engulfed in its second religious war, the cristero rebellion discussed later.

In our concentration on the changes brought upon the church by the liberal movement in Mexico, we do not intend to shortchange other regions of Latin America, which also experienced the rise of liberalism with its accompanying

---

[1] *New York American*, July 19, 1914, interview with Villa by John Roberts, as quoted in Friedrich Katz, *The Life and Times of Pancho Villa* (Stanford: Stanford University Press, 1998), 447.

[2] Jean-Pierre Bastian, *Los disidentes: Sociedades protestantes y revolución en México, 1872–1911* (Mexico City: Fondo de Cultura Económica, 1989), 266.

anticlerical legislation. For example, the Colombian Constitution of 1863 embraced many of the anticlerical provisions in the Mexican Constitution of 1857. In fact, Knowlton believes that events in Mexico influenced the course of events in Colombia. Like the constitution in Mexico, that in Colombia banned clergy from taking public office and prohibited the church from owning property not related specifically to its spiritual role. Both abolished special church privileges, and both confiscated church property – although in Mexico the church was taxed on the income generated by the sale of property while in Colombia the property was nationalized immediately.

The church in Colombia reacted to the reforms in much the same way as the church in Mexico did. Ecclesiastical officials called for resistance to the laws of expropriation and for punishment of those who did not resist. As a result, there were few people who actually took advantage of the sale of church property. In the long run, the expropriation of land in Colombia was no more effective in creating a class of land owners – its stated purpose – than was the Ley Lerdo in Mexico. Instead, those people who tended to buy the property were foreigners with money and without fear of ecclesiastical sanctions. When one of the key proponents of the Colombia plan, Rafael Nuñez, became president of Colombia in the 1880s, he drafted a conservative constitution and sought a concordat with Rome, a reversal he deemed necessary to gain the support of the church.

¡VIVA CRISTO REY!

In 1924, General Plutarco Elías Calles was elected president of Mexico. It was not a good day for the church or, some would argue, for Mexico itself. Over the decade that Calles held power, he became increasingly dictatorial and ruthless in ridding himself of those he considered political enemies. Archbishop José Mora y del Río was to become one of those enemies. Unlike his immediate predecessors in the office of president, Calles enforced the anticlerical provisions of the 1917 Constitution. In early 1926, the archbishop responded by giving an interview to a journalist in which he stated that good Roman Catholics should not accept the document. Then Calles reacted by closing religious houses and schools, deporting foreign-born priests, and prohibiting religious processions. In Mora y del Río, however, the president was not facing a weak-minded opponent. On July 31, 1926, the archbishop proclaimed an interdict instructing all priests in Mexico City to go on strike. Other prelates throughout Mexico followed the same policy. No public masses were to be said, no public marriages or baptisms performed. Mexico was without its church, and the strike would last for three years.

While Calles was in office, priests and monastics were forced into hiding. Nunneries were closed as groups of nuns went into exile in order not to relinquish the common life, which the state had ordered them to do. Those who remained in Mexico often fled to small, rural communities where they found support and help. Some priests went underground and performed mass in the dark of night for small, private groups. Some had the support of municipal leaders who resented state involvement in their regions and thus openly defied government orders to suppress religious activity. Still other priests called for an armed rebellion. Local Catholic leaders organized mostly peasants to resist the antireligious onslaught of the government. (The rebellion had very limited episcopal support. The majority of prelates endorsed more passive forms of resistance.)

The cristeros, as the rebels were known, soon numbered in the tens of thousands of soldiers, including some twenty-five thousand members of "feminine brigades." They burned down government buildings, killed teachers who were state employees, and blew up trains. The government responded by inciting its partisans to murder a priest for every teacher killed and to loot churches and use them as stables. The fighting was fierce and bloody. Yet, as historian Matthew Butler's study of Michoacan reveals, religious life did go on, which Butler sees as a form of passive resistance against the state.

The persecution of the church and the intensity of the response varied according to many factors – including the time and place as well as the relationship between local political figures and the national government. For example, priests in one particular region might have a fairly easy time of it with the support of local officials only to experience renewed repression with the election of a pro-government politico. In another region, the presence of pro-government peasants (*agraristas*) could make the life of a clergyman very difficult. In Jungapeo, a town in Michoacan, the agraristas actively looked for evidence of Catholic worship in order to implicate the local landowning class and the clergy in sedition.

Nevertheless, in the midst of what was without a doubt a political struggle, we must not forget that the church strike represented a profound spiritual loss for many Catholics. As a whole, Catholicism bound people one to another and functioned as a unifying element within Mexican society. But being a cohesive social factor was not the church's sole purpose. For Catholics it was also the means for expressing deeply held religious beliefs.

At least in the fairly rural state of Michoacan, church hierarchy – namely Bishop Leopoldo Ruiz y Flores – facilitated the church's efforts to maintain its ties with the spiritual life of its parishioners while responding to the government's attempts to control the church. Specifically, in March 1926, the bishop suspended public worship. He then sent petitions signed by thousands of the faithful to the Mexican government calling for the repeal of anticlerical laws. And finally, when it became apparent that peaceful methods would yield no result, he began a process of decentralizing church functions to ensure that the spiritual needs of his people were met during a time of persecution. Ruiz y Flores instructed the priests who remained in his diocese to continue providing religious education and to insist that parishioners continue a life of prayer and penance. Lay activity, by both men and women, also increased within the church in Michoacan, with laity leading devotions and nonsacerdotal acts. By 1927, the church was producing pamphlets that instructed lay persons how to perform sacramental functions – such as baptism, marriage, and extreme unction – whenever a priest was not available. (Mass was always reserved for the clergy.) Women became increasingly active as leaders within the church. For example, Sarah Rábago, of Huajumbaro in Michoacan, read non-sacramental masses on Sundays and led the rosary and prayers other days of the week, thereby providing some priestly functions when no priest was available. In order for the church to meet the spiritual needs of its followers, the traditional relationship between clergy and laity had to be inverted; the church had to "lease out" some of its power. This situation was only temporary, however, for as soon as peace was restored, the clergy resumed its hierarchical position vis-à-vis parishioners.

The rebels could not force the state to change the constitution, and the state could not suppress the rebellion. A stalemate ensued. By June 1929, it was clear that the standstill had to come to an end; more than thirty thousand cristeros and almost fifty-seven thousand federal troops had died. Bishop Ruiz y Flores, now in exile in the United States, was part of a delegation to negotiate with the Mexican government. The resulting compromise, known as the *arreglos* (arrangements), granted three concessions to the church: (1) not all priests had to register with the government, (2) churches could once again provide religious instruction, but only in churches, and not at schools, and (3) members of the clergy were allowed to petition the state for reform. Provisions were not removed from the constitution; property was not returned to the church. However, it was enough for the bishops to call for the cristeros to return to their homes and for church bells to ring once again.

The story of the cristeros does not end with the arreglos. In 2000, Pope John Paul II beatified twenty-five cristero martyrs who died in the rebellion, including the Jesuit priest Miguel Pro, who spread his arms forming the cross and yelled "¡Viva Cristo Rey!" as he was executed. On November 20, 2005, another thirteen cristero martyrs were beatified by the Roman Catholic Church.

THE PLACE OF WOMEN

It is quite clear that women participated in the cristero rebellion in a number of ways: in supportive roles such as nursing, collecting money to purchase arms, and assuming leadership in the religious life of the community and in more active roles as soldiers and spies. They were involved in all aspects of the Mexican reaction to repression of the church in the early twentieth century. In other countries in the Americas, women found different means of responding to the changing role of the church, often with the blessing of both the church and the state.

Such was the case with Chile. There, the liberal government that came to power after independence quickly discovered that providing social services was far more complicated than it had anticipated. There were few trained professionals to take on those responsibilities that had been the church's prior to the government taking control. Thus, there was no one to run the foundling homes or hospitals, or to visit the poor and those in prisons, and the state needed help. Additionally the Chilean government was concerned with how it appeared in the eyes of the world. Those in power came to believe that the role of women in society was a direct reflection of the country's modernization. By the 1850s, the government had hit upon an idea: if it could hire religious women as caretakers of the various social service institutions, this would provide the necessary workers. Perhaps more important, it would pave the way for secular women to become involved in the public sphere by demonstrating that respectable women – such as nuns – could function beyond the confining walls of convents.

For the church, the idea of having noncloistered nuns was nothing new. In the seventeenth century, St. Vincent de Paul had founded the first order of noncloistered nuns, the Sisters of Charity, specifically trained to work with the poor. The work of these women, and of those in other orders that were soon founded, coincided with the church's efforts to redefine its role in society in light of attacks from Enlightenment thinkers as well as the rise of liberalism. In Latin America after independence, the public charity aspect of missions took on much more importance than it had had in colonial times, and women were particularly well suited for such endeavors. Certainly preconceptions about women and their innate caregiving skills fit with the tasks that charity work required, but perhaps of equal importance was that during the nineteenth century men were leaving the church. If the church was to maintain its presence in society, it would have to use women as its soldiers. From the church's perspective, these women did indeed form the front lines in the battle to preserve the Catholic family and the faith of other women and children.

By 1854, the Chilean government had signed contracts with four different groups of nuns – mostly coming from France and including the Sisters of Charity. What both the government and the church wanted was achieved by the work of the female apostolates, as the tasks of these nuns were known. Historian Gertrude Yeager points out that the arrival of nuns who pursued the active life was an essential step in the Chilean government's efforts to modernize because the nuns legitimized and added dignity to professions that would become increasingly female – professions such as nursing, teaching, and charity work. Furthermore, lay women, mostly upper- and middle-class, throughout the country – in both large cities and small towns – became active in the work of the nuns almost from the beginning by raising funds and acting as administrators, thus becoming participants in the public sphere. This pattern of secular women's involvement in charity work was one that would continue even as public welfare was increasingly secularized in the late nineteenth and early twentieth centuries. But in the intervening years – between the beginning of the female apostolates and the secularization of public charity – the church had created a parallel network of private Catholic charities largely administered by lay women. This helped cement the church's place in society as well as giving elite and middle-class women of Chile an established means of expressing their faith in action and providing the church with workers for its missionary efforts.

Similar developments occurred in Argentina in the nineteenth century. By 1823, a liberal government created the female-run *Sociedad de Beneficencia* to oversee charitable efforts in support of women and children. The popularity of the Beneficent Society among elite women spurred the growth in the 1880s of other female associations created to meet the ever-growing needs of the poor – particularly in Buenos Aires, where the poor were mostly recent immigrants unable to weather the hardships brought on by economic downturns. Among the organizations responding to the poor were the *Conferencias de Señoras de San Vicente de Paúl* (Conferences of the Ladies of St. Vincent de Paul), first founded in Buenos Aires in 1889. These Conferences represented collective efforts at ameliorating the conditions of the poor throughout Argentina. Unashamedly Catholic, the Conferences, which – according to historian Karen Mead – by 1891 numbered fifty-three with more than 7,800 members, spread throughout the country and included women from all levels of society. The groups raised money and channeled funds to the needy. They visited poor households, taking with them new notions of hygiene, vouchers for foodstuffs, clothing, and Catholic teachings. These women were particularly concerned that couples living together be married by the Catholic Church and that children be legitimized and baptized. Following papal directives, in the early part of the twentieth century the Conferences took on matters such as low-income housing and issues of concern to female wage laborers, particularly in the capital city. The church had declared these as key factors in ensuring peaceful workers and thus social peace. And the members of the Conferences took to their new tasks with zeal. The women of the Conferences were the most visible manifestation of the Catholic Church in the lives of the poor. Eventually, in the 1910s, the work undertaken by the Sociedad de Conferencias de San Vicente de Paúl was taken over by the Catholic clergy. The men became involved in organizing marches of Catholic workers, unionizing female laborers, and providing housing. They also directed the Conferences to limit their sphere of activity. By 1916, the Conferences as leaders in public Catholic charities were a thing of the past.

However, for women in the church, the nineteenth century was not solely a time of upheaval and change. Their roles within the religious life often remained fairly traditional. Traveling through Mexico in the late 1830s, Fanny Calderón de la Barca had the opportunity to observe much of the woman's traditional role. In her travelogue, *Life in Mexico*, Calderón vividly describes ceremonies surrounding young women's admission as novices to the grand convents of Mexico City. Her position as the wife of Spain's first envoy to Mexico put her in contact with the highest level of society and afforded her preferential seating in the crowded religious ceremonies that accompanied young women's reception into convents. She painted the scene of one such ceremony for her readers: The church, ablaze with candles, was crowded to the point that Calderón described herself, upon entering the church, as being carried off between two rather large, bejeweled women – much like being carried off between two movable featherbeds, she tells us – as musicians played a Strauss waltz. Once safely ensconced in the church, she awaited the beginning of the ceremony, announced by a volley of fireworks outside the church. The altar, which Calderón could see through the grill that separated it from the congregants, was draped with lavish paraments, and the nuns, who lay prostrate, held long tapers in their hands. The young woman – only eighteen years old – was dressed in a gown of purple velvet and adorned with diamonds and pearls as well as a crown of flowers. She entered with her overwrought mother, walked past the nuns, and knelt at the feet of the bishop, who was equally resplendent in purple robes and amethysts. After answering his questions, the young woman was escorted away by the nuns, somber in their black habits. When Calderón next saw the young woman, she was wearing the habit of a nun, prostrate in front of the bishop, and covered with a black cloth, signifying her death to the world. After receiving the prelate's blessing, she arose and was embraced by the nuns, now her new family. According to Calderón, the mother was so overcome with grief that she had to be carried from the church. Apparently the young woman's wish to enter the convent had been blessed by her father but not her mother, who had no choice but to accept her husband's decision.

Calderón also described an educational system for girls that prepared them for lives of religious devotion and little else – lives in which the mass book was the primary reading for any female older than fourteen whether she be destined for the convent or marriage. For these women, attending religious ceremonies and confession was the highlights of their lives. She did note, however, that as long as an elite woman gave the appearance of religiosity and caused no scandal she could "do pretty much as she wishes." In an interesting paradox, then, religious life for elite women in Mexico was both confining and freeing.

Another traveler, this time to Brazil, found religious life less freeing than did Calderón. Elizabeth Cabot Cary Agassiz, who would go on to become the first president of Radcliff College, had long valued women's education when she sailed for Brazil with her naturalist husband in 1866. In Rio de Janeiro, she found little to her liking in terms of educational opportunities for women. Agassiz described one particular incident at the home of a comfortable family. Bored with her surroundings she wandered into a room where she espied a book – a rare sight – on the piano. She picked it up and began leafing through it, curious as to its contents. At that point, the master of the house entered the room and was scandalized to see that a woman was reading. He took the book from Agassiz and placed another one in her hands. This one, he explained, was appropriate for a woman. It was a book of moral platitudes to guide a woman's religious life rather than one to satisfy her intellectual curiosity.

SLAVE LIFE

Also sailing to Brazil with her husband was Adèle Toussaint-Samson. Arriving in the early 1850s, she too was troubled by what she observed. But in her case, it was slavery. In *A Parisian in Brazil* she described her stay on a plantation and a religious ceremony she found very disturbing. On one particular Saturday evening – and perhaps every Saturday – the master called the slaves to evening prayers. One by one the rag-clothed men, women, and children made their way across the field and into the house where a make-shift altar behind cupboard doors was revealed. Two overseers – both slaves – stood on either side of the altar. Because they had learned a little Latin from a chaplain, no longer on the plantation, it was they who led the service. First came the *Kyrie eleison*, then prayers to the Virgin Mary and every saint they deemed appropriate. At the end of the service, all the slaves cried together *miserere nobis* (have mercy on us), then prostrated themselves with their faces on the ground. Finally, every slave filed by all the Whites, including Toussaint-Samson and her husband, asking each one's blessings. She, with tears in her eyes, declared, "I bless thee" as the slaves walked past her and all her companions.

Well into the nineteenth century, the life of slaves, including religious education and practices, was prescribed by law codes. On the island of Cuba – still a Spanish colony – for example, the code of 1842 proved to be a feeble and largely ineffective attempt by the crown to regulate the relationship between master and slave, largely in response to growing international pressure to end slavery – something that would not happen in Cuba until 1886. Nevertheless, we can use the code to help us understand the expected place of Christian religious practice in the life of slaves.

The first five statutes of the 1842 code are devoted to religion, legislating when and for how long religious education was required and the obligation of masters to provide such training to slaves. Specifically, statute one indicates that it was the responsibility of the slaveholder to ensure that the slaves were properly instructed in "the principles of the Holy Roman Catholic Apostolic Religion" and were baptized as soon as possible, even by the master's own hand if the death of the slave was imminent. The requirement that masters themselves oversee the Christian education of their slaves was a departure from an earlier slave code (1789) that obliged slaveholders to pay a priest to say mass and provide religious instruction. Because masters claimed that hiring a priest was too expensive and because they simply ignored the earlier statute, subsequent slave codes removed religious education for plantation slaves from the control of the church and placed it in the hands of the masters, who frequently placed it in the hands of the overseers. This removal of authority from the clergy created an untenable situation for the Cuban church. Bishop Francisco Fleix y Solans of Havana was greatly concerned about the number of suicides among rural slaves. He felt that if the slaves had received proper religious instruction they would not destroy themselves; therefore, he reasoned, the only solution was to send Franciscan monks to the countryside to educate the slaves. The chief opponent to the bishop's endeavors was a high-ranking government official – himself a slaveowner – who complained that the monks were totally unsuited for missionary work among slaves because they were ignorant of the ways and customs of slaves and would not understand the need for total subjugation of those in bondage. Furthermore, he argued, there might be some abolitionists among the friars. Although the queen of Spain, Isabel II, was positively disposed to the bishop's request, her Council of Ministers ultimately decided against sending the Franciscans to the island. The religious education of the slaves was left in the hands of the slaveholders.

Statutes two, three, and four of the 1842 code tried to guarantee that slaves would have the time necessary to acquire the basics of their new faith as well as time to practice it. Owners were to provide religious instruction at night – after the day's labors were completed – then to require that the slaves say the rosary and participate in prayers, perhaps much like those that Adèle Toussaint-Samson witnessed in Brazil. Sundays and feast days were to be set aside – with the exception of two hours spent cleaning the house and workshops – for religious observances. Yet, in one more concession to slaveholders, the drafters of the code did allow that the annual harvest represented a unique time of year that necessitated slaves working through Sundays and other holy days. Owners were also legally obligated to guarantee that baptized slaves would be given the opportunity to fulfill the sacramental requirements of Catholicism. Finally, statue five speaks to the temporal goals of Christian education.

> [Slaveholders] shall put forth the greatest attention and diligence possible in making them [the slaves] understand the obedience that they owe to the constituted authorities, the obligation to show reverence to the clergy, to respect white persons, to behave well with the people of color, and to live harmoniously with their companions.[3]

But life for the slaves was anything but tranquil with time for religious observances. Records make it clear that work continued seven days a week, with no break for a Sabbath or religious holidays. In fact, Sunday mornings on sugar plantations were typically used for cleaning the grinding equipment, gathering firewood needed in the mills, and in general gearing up for the week's labors, which sometimes began Sunday evening. In contradiction to the slave code, planters refused to ensure that Sundays would be primarily devoted to the slaves' religious life. The owners protested that if they were forced to comply with the code, they would have to close their mills. In the face of economic claims on all of the slaves' time and strenuous objections from the powerful planter class, Cuban officials turned a blind eye to the slave code's provisions.

UNIQUE STYLES

While the religious life of slaves was easy to ignore, officials could not as easily turn a blind eye to those individuals and groups whose religious expressions were unusual. Among those were faith healers who often traveled through the

---

[3] Translation by Robert L. Paquette in Robert L. Paquette, *Sugar is Made with Blood: The Conspiracy of La Escalera and the Conflict between Empires over Slavery in Cuba* (Middletown, CT: Wesleyan University Press, 1988), 267.

new republics practicing their brand of healing just at the point that medicine was being professionalized – and standardized – by men (women were not allowed to practice "professional" medicine) who often studied in Europe and brought back the latest scientific methods of healing.

The trend to professionalize medicine stood in stark contrast to centuries of tradition that placed healing squarely within the purview of the church, with Christ himself as "the Great Physician." Before the advent of a scientific approach to diseases and treatments (which was accelerated during the Enlightenment), illness was largely viewed as a problem that required divine action – action often brought on through the intercession of saints (or an occasional bleeding). Healing, as an act of Christian charity, was valued by the community and the church. In fact, practitioners of faith healing often become popular saints, and cults quite commonly developed around a particular healer.

However, with the rise in confidence in science and a rational approach as the best way to remedy ills, healing through faith lost favor with many intellectuals and with those advocating for the modernization of the new republics. The struggle between faith healing and scientific healing very quickly became subsumed in the struggles between liberals and conservatives. The riot occasioned by Miguel Perdomo Neira's visit to Bogota in 1872 was precisely a result of "professional" men questioning Perdomo's approach to healing.

Nineteenth-century Colombia was far too familiar with internal strife frequently caused by struggles over political control. Any shift in power was often accompanied by riots and tensions that spilled out into the streets, making violence a seemingly acceptable form of expression. When the medical doctors of Bogota questioned Perdomo's healing abilities and then challenged the faith healer to prove himself, his followers – who comprised much of the populace – reacted violently. Historian David Sowell writes that Perdomo was truly "of the people." He did not charge for his services, although he did accept donations and payments for prescriptions. He used herbs and medicinal plants – a skill he acquired during his time among an Indian group – with which the people were comfortable. And perhaps most important, he operated within the familiar framework of Christian charity, keeping an image of the Sacred Heart of Jesus on the table behind which he worked – which some of his detractors saw as evidence of his ignorance. For many people of the Andes, through which Perdomo traveled extensively, the healer brought hope against illness precisely because he combined religious faith and traditional methods of healing. When their *curandero* (healer) was threatened in Bogota by professional doctors who tended to hold themselves aloof and who were highly skeptical of anything that smacked of the church, the Perdomists rioted in the streets, attacking Perdomo's challengers and damaging their homes and workplaces. So intense was devotion to the healer that after he died in late 1874 there were rumors that his grave was found opened and that Perdomo had been seen walking on the road to town – clearly allusions to his messianic appeal.

The intimate link between healing and faith was evident in the testimonials about Perdomo's healings. Repeatedly, witnesses gave thanks to God for the cures performed by Perdomo, even in cases deemed hopeless by professional doctors. They spoke of his charity and goodness, claiming – as did he – that his skills were God-given, although he did not claim to heal through special powers. That claim belonged to other cuanderos, including el niño Fidencio of Mexico.

José Fidencio Sintora Constantino was born in 1898 in central Mexico and by his mid-twenties had made his way to the small town of Espinazo in north-eastern Mexico, where he spent the rest of his life. In a pattern fairly typical of other curanderos and curanderas, Fidencio had a vision in which a bearded holy man appeared to him and endowed him with special curative powers. For almost fifteen years, el niño Fidencio – as he was called – cured any who came to see him, including the president of Mexico in 1928. Within months of the president's trip to Espinazo, thirty thousand people poured into the little town to be cured by the wonder-working healer. According to anthropologists June Macklin and Ross Crumrine, Fidencio's appeal was so widespread that he had to develop a method of generating a "general cure," suitable for most any ailment. To administer his cure to the masses, Fidencio would climb upon some high structure, such as his house, and fling fruits, tortillas, and eggs at the folk gathered below. Whoever was touched by the flying debris was cured.

People flocked to this man of God, for that is how they saw him. Much like other healers, he regularly communicated with Jesus, and, as Macklin states, his followers believed that the healer's cures were manifestations of God's presence in the world and his skills were a divine gift. Fidencio himself believed that faith had a powerful role to play in healing: He asked each patient, "Do you believe you will be cured?" For the people of Espinazo, the curandero became Christ-like. His patients would kiss his hands and feet and touch the hem of his gown in the belief that to do so would cure them. They treasured as relics wax imprints of his hard palate, which was said to have the form of the crucifix. He oversaw religious rites and even baptized residents of the community. His followers reciprocated by showering him with food, clothing, and money – which he in turn distributed to the poor, for he, like Perdomo and many other healers, accepted no payment for his services. The cult that surrounded el niño Fidencio was powerful indeed, and perhaps it was the strength of his popularity that prevented the Mexican state of Nuevo Leon, where he lived, from finally resolving its case against the healer for practicing medicine without a license.

Even today, individuals make pilgrimages to Espinazo to drink water stored on top of Fidencio's tomb and "to channel" his spirit. And in Texas, a group of Catholics have founded a church dedicated to the folk saint. For his followers, the spirit of the healer quite literally lives on, much to the discomfort of the official church establishment.

Another healer also causing unease among church hierarchy was "la santa de Cabora," Teresa Urrea. Born the illegitimate child of a wealthy landowner and an Indian in his employ in 1873, Teresa began life among her mother's people where she learned much from a curandera about the medicinal properties of various plants as well as the practice of mixing saliva with dirt to create a healing poultice. By the age of sixteen, Teresa had experienced a revelation that she was to be a healer, a path she followed zealously. In 1892, when she was nineteen, Teresa and her father would be exiled from Mexico by Porfirio Díaz, the president of the country.

In the intervening years Teresa became a threat to both the church and the government. She viewed her healing as a process that needed to go beyond the curing of individuals' various illnesses. Rather, she saw healing as necessary also for society's ills caused by officials – religious and secular. She had a strident anticlerical message that also questioned the clergy's role as mediator between a parishioner and the divine, particularly since she had direct contact with God and other spirits such as the Virgin Mary – usually as the Virgin of Guadalupe – and the archangel Gabriel. Indeed, she was so convinced that each person had a calling that she routinely performed sacraments (at least baptisms, confirmations, and marriages) – undoubtedly a habit that did not endear her to the ecclesiastical powers-that-be.

As she healed the multitudes that came to Cabora with mud and spit or oil, divined secrets from her patients – for she claimed no one could withhold anything from her – and punished nonbelievers, she also spoke of the need to love one another, regardless of one's racial make-up or social standing. As Alex Nava writes, Teresa's followers, mostly the poor and Indians from regions of northern Mexico, developed a view of the here-and-now that was both politicized and egalitarian based on their understanding of the biblical heritage. Teresita, as she was also known, became the rallying point for many Indians dealing with the injustices of the Díaz regime – particularly those measures seeking to turn over Indian lands to large landowners in the name of progress. There is some disagreement as to the level of Teresita's involvement with the Indian rebellions against the Mexican government. Some historians believe that she was directly involved and incited the Indians in their rebellion – as was claimed by the Mexican government. Others argue that her involvement was less direct, and that while she may have supported the efforts of the Indians to resist government action, she did not encourage them to revolt. In any case, the Mexican government ultimately exiled her and her father – who had become something of a profiteer and manager of the fiesta-type atmosphere that surrounded the healer.

In the same year that she began her healing ministry, Teresita became an object of interest for a growing movement in Mexico. A group of Spiritists, discussed in more detail later, came to Cabora to find out just who this saint of Cabora was. The investigating team decided that she was an elevated spirit and a great medium, able to communicate with spirit guides. The Spiritists even claimed success in convincing Teresa that Jesus was not divine, though she always maintained that she was a Catholic and admonished people to worship God, not her.

The cult of the "saint of Cabora" continued even after her move to the United States. The Mexican government contended that she persisted in inciting rebellions from across the border and sought her extradition. The U.S. government replied by suggesting that she move further into the United States for her personal safety. People from the United States and Mexico, as well as from around the world, flocked to Arizona, where she lived until her death in 1906, to kneel as she walked by and ask that she cure them of their ailments. People burdened with illnesses of all sorts sought the help of this young woman who frequently spoke with God.

Communication with spirits, such as that which Teresa declared she routinely had, is a crucial element in Spiritism, which the Catholic Church has condemned as incompatible with church teaching. Spiritism finds its roots in the belief in the possibility of progression toward perfection. But for Spiritists, that progression was achieved through reincarnation, which ultimately led to union with God. As articulated by its founder, the nineteenth-century Frenchman Allan Kardec (1803–1869), there was a hierarchy of human incarnations – though not of souls – with Blacks, particularly Africans, on the lower rungs. As one was reincarnated, one would move through increasingly whiter earthly manifestations until reaching final perfection. And all the while, one was guided by mediums who were in contact with spirits – previously incarnated souls – who had progressed to other spiritual planes. Depending upon their level of perfection, these spirits could be helpful or not – but never harmful, as there was no such thing as regression.

In the hands of its early adherents, Spiritism was viewed as scientific because communication with the spirit guides could be sensed – through their tappings on tables and walls or through mediums in trances – and therefore proven. These believers often saw this new spiritual system as a path toward modernization and away from the traditional, superstitious-laden Catholic Church. In Puerto Rico, according to historian Reinaldo Román, Spiritism was initially embraced by those who considered themselves forward-thinking and educated, though it ultimately was, by and large, taken over by lower-class folk. For the true, elite believer this usurpation was difficult to take given that the lower classes were often people of color and illiterate – both seen as signs of backward souls. Furthermore, purists argued, these new followers of Spiritism brought with them folk Catholicism, imbuing Spiritism with their superstitions and rituals. In the hands of the people, Spiritism ceased to be a philosophy and an approach to life and became a religion.

Embodying this bridge between Catholicism and Spiritism in Puerto Rico was la Samaritana (the Samaritan Woman), Julia Vázquez. Of uncertain racial origins – some claimed she was black, others claimed she was mulatta – Julia became a healer in the early 1920s and ultimately drew thousands to the farm her family rented in the mountain town of San Lorenzo. She claimed no special powers but rather cured by using spring water (a medium believed by Spiritists as being able to transfer magnetic healing powers from spirits to humans). This water had supposedly been magnetized by Vázquez's spirit guide, Father Joaquín Saras, the deceased parish priest of San Lorenzo, with whom she routinely consulted.

La Samaritana, a sobriquet originally intended to discredit Vázquez, was hailed as a miracle worker by her followers. Her visitors used the water she dispensed as they would holy water: drinking it, washing with it, or using it in whatever manner best suited their particular ailments. They made arduous pilgrimages to her homestead and suffered in order to be worthy of divine curing. For many, their devotion to and belief in Vázquez represented no contradiction with Catholicism. As one could guess, the church hierarchy saw it differently. Church leaders rejected Spiritism – and anything that resembled it – because of its denial of basic Christian teachings, such as the Trinity, the divine nature of Christ (although he is considered the principal spiritual leader of humankind), and the existence of Heaven and Hell.

In Brazil, the link between Spiritism and Christianity was clearly evident in the publication *Reformador*, whose masthead reads *Mensario Religioso de Espiritismo Cristão* (Religious Monthly of Christian Spiritism) and which began publication in 1883, continuing to this day. The monthly was intended to reach the Spiritist community in Brazil, which historian Peter Winn claims was the most important center of Spiritism in the world by the 1880s. Eventually, classical Spiritism proved not to the liking of everyone. For some, its tenets of progression toward perfection (and whiteness) did not fit within the reality they encountered every day. But the presence of and communication with spirits in Spiritism did resonate with many practitioners of Afro-Brazilian Catholicism, which we will discuss in Chapter 6.

CONCLUSION

After having survived the crisis of independence relatively unscathed, the church in Latin America found itself under assault in the nineteenth century by governments of the new republics that sought to transform the place of the church in society and challenged its traditional ways. Yet the church also found support for a continuation of its traditional values and mores as well as its centrality in society. What ensued was a period of confusion as the church tried to fit into a changing society while at the same time seeking to hold back the tide of change.

Even as the institutional church struggled between change and continuity, folk Catholicism continued to be shaped in such a way as to meet needs that neither "sophisticated" society nor the church could. As we will see in Chapter 6, however, in the mid-twentieth century the Catholic Church also increasingly responded to the everyday realities of its followers. Lay organizations, including some political parties, took up the banner of Catholic values and mores. And priests and bishops began expressing publicly their concern for the situations of their parishioners. But in some regions, the church felt imperiled enough that it supported dictatorial regimes – which became rather prolific in Latin America during the twentieth century – simply as a matter of survival. Likewise, it turned to persecution of Protestants, whom it saw as a threat to its religious hegemony in Latin America. But as always, in the face of competing interests Christianity would not remain static or be held exclusively by the Catholic Church.

In the next chapter, we will also examine how Catholicism continued to evolve in the hands of the marginalized with the rise of Umbanda in Brazil and Santería in Cuba. Just as the populace molded and changed the practice of Catholicism to meet their needs in the nineteenth century, so they would continue to do in the twentieth century. Much of this remolding laid the groundwork for the response of the Latin American church to the Second Vatican Council – to be discussed in Chapter 7.

6

~

The Church's New Place

As we recall from Chapter 5, the wars of independence were by no means the greatest test the church in Latin America would face during the nineteenth century. After suffering the dislocation brought about by independence, the church had to deal with a cultural ethos that no longer saw it as the bastion of truth and right, the guide of morals and ethics, and the powerful protector of the weak. Rather, by the fourth decade of the nineteenth century, many powerful interest groups saw the church throughout Latin America as the chief stumbling block to progress, rife with superstition and greed, and a threat to the future well-being of both state and citizen. As the church struggled to maintain some semblance of its past power and glory, it was caught up in the political struggles between conservatives and liberals, who were vying for control of the new republics.

Even when the church's "friends" (the conservatives) had the upper hand, the church suffered. The penury of the new states was such that they routinely forced loans from religious institutions, including orders, which often could ill afford to provide money to the government. When the church's "foes" (the liberals) had the upper hand, the church's influence and prestige quickly deteriorated. Not only did the church lose land, the responsibility to administer public charity, and legal privileges that its clergy had enjoyed for centuries, but in the case of Mexico, for example, it also became illegal to hold religious services anywhere outside of the church building proper. The church's response to an attack it believed to be undeserved was sometimes violent – as in the cristero rebellion – or what we might call passive aggressive – as in the declaration of interdicts throughout Mexico. In any case, it was a significant struggle for the church simply to maintain an institutional presence.

Yet the church was alive and well, often because of individuals it had traditionally relegated to secondary roles: women, the free masses, and even the enslaved. As we have seen in the previous chapter, each of these groups found unique ways of expressing Christian faith. Some women, especially – but not exclusively – among the elite, turned to social action and became a bulwark against the erosion of Catholic values in the home and among those to whom they extended Christian charity. Other women held fast to traditional rituals and attitudes that firmly placed them within a church-centered world, thereby also helping to maintain Catholicism's place within the family and society. The masses of individuals, both urban and rural, found meaning and comfort in folk Catholicism and created their own saints and healers, thus making the practice of Christianity meet their needs, often in the face of an institutional church that could not or would not respond to popular religiosity. And those in bondage, forced both in labor and religious practice, nevertheless took elements of Christianity and incorporated them into religious systems, forming new styles of faith expression that functioned within their harsh realities.

The nineteenth and early twentieth centuries were a time when the institutional church stumbled and perhaps nearly fell. Yet it managed to keep its footing precisely because those years were also ones of great turmoil when the future was not well defined for either the states or the church. In some instances, they both floundered about blindly, often blaming the other for the ills each encountered. In other instances, they found ways of accommodating one another. In the end, for the church the years after independence were a paradox of continuity and change. But ultimately, the church and state in Latin America would reach an unsteady compromise punctuated with periods of sheer antagonism.

As we move on we will find that the years between the 1930s and the 1960s – the period covered by this chapter – were hardly more stable, though the causes of the instability were different than in earlier years. Economic changes – some positive, most not – had become the primary concern within the increasingly secularized Latin American countries. Since these challenges formed the environment in which the church operated, we will take a brief look at issues usually, and perhaps erroneously, considered beyond the church's realm. *Rapid changes* wrought by efforts at integrating the economies of Latin America into the world, particularly Western Europe and then North America (primarily the United States), resulted in far-reaching consequences, such as massive urban migration. Countries pursued what turned out to be ill-conceived economic policies that led to landlessness and extreme rural poverty. In turn, campesinos moved to major urban centers in an effort to find jobs created by industrialization. With more job seekers than jobs, laborers found urban poverty with little chance of self-sufficiency.

Economic and social instability and the rise of urban masses created a fertile environment for charismatic, often despotic leaders. Known as "populists," these national leaders – the most famous of whom are probably Juan Domingo Perón of Argentina and Getúlio Vargas of Brazil – rallied workers and the industrial elite into coalitions that kept them in office for decades. Perón was in power from 1946 until 1955 and again in the early 1970s until his death in 1974. Getúlio Vargas ruled Brazil with an iron fist from 1930 until 1945 and again from 1951 to 1954, when he committed suicide. These men, and others like them all over Latin America, often used the church as a means to forestall unrest and add legitimacy to their regimes. In the hands of powerful national leaders, the church became largely ceremonial, with bishops and prelates appearing on stage with government officials, blessing government endeavors, and being a calming presence. It had been pushed *off center stage* and relegated to a supporting role. Increasingly, in many areas of Latin America, the church became irrelevant in the face of competing interests for governments and for a citizenry looking more toward secular clues than to religion for guidance in this life. However, with governments less concerned with the church's role in politics and society, it was easier for the church to reform itself without arousing too much suspicion. In some areas, such as Colombia, the Catholic Church succeeded in reclaiming a powerful voice after being suppressed by a liberal government. Yet, more and more, the church also found itself reacting to what it perceived as threats. Its reactions to the "isms" – nationalism, Liberalism, Communism, and Protestantism – consumed much of the church's attention. Occasionally, the Catholic response to apparent threats took a violent turn, as in the persecution of Protestants in Colombia. There, Protestants were murdered, their schools closed, and their buildings destroyed, all in the name of faith.

Paradoxically, just at the time that the church was becoming ever less powerful in much of Latin America, Rome was beginning to recognize that the Latin American church was a potential *source of strength*, if for no other reason than its sheer size. Simultaneously, the church was redefining itself within individual countries as well as across national boundaries. The first cardinal from Latin America, Sebastião Leme of Brazil, was named by Pius XI in 1930. It was probably no coincidence that Leme was a staunch supporter of the supranational church and its responsibilities to guide a nation, as we will see later. Churches in Latin America also developed national Bishops' Conferences, and pan-American councils met in an effort to centralize responses to the changing needs of the church. By the 1950s, the Catholic Church in many countries of Latin America had changed so much that it looked more like a "servant church" and less like one fighting to maintain its position of power.

Even before the institutional church found a way to respond to the changing social, political, and economic circumstances in Latin America, there were individual Catholics, both lay and religious, who felt a *call to action* on behalf of the church. Their concerns led to the birth of *Acción Católica* (Catholic Action) in the 1920s. This organization, which was structured along national boundaries, sought to create apolitical avenues that provided loyal Catholics the means to respond to conditions within their society – be they political, social, or economic – as well as defending and spreading Catholic principles. Militant Catholics flocked to Catholic Action as they sought effective ways to reject what they viewed as encroachments on the Catholic faith, such as the prohibition against religious education in state schools or North American (mainly U.S.) imperialism. At times, some Catholic Action organizations even became bedfellows with fascists and Nazis, particularly embracing those political systems' virulent anti-Communist rhetoric. By the 1940s, however, Catholic Action was largely supplanted by the overtly political Christian Democratic parties as Catholics sought ways to put their faith into action in the political sphere and as the reality of World War II distanced the Latin American church from European political systems.

Yet, what we will term *private Catholicism*, seemingly far removed from the work of Catholic Action or the institutional church, remained a powerful force in the lives of millions throughout Latin America. For some, it was the only presence the Catholic Church had in their lives, especially given the scarcity of priests in rural areas. For others, it was a meaningful expression of Christianity, given the circumstances in which they existed. As Catholics had to find their own way without the guidance – and restraints – provided by official representatives of the church, they often turned to symbols and rituals that grounded them in the familiar past. *Cursillos de cristiandad* were intense religious retreats seeking to deepen personal piety and resulting in groups with the same purpose. *Retablos, ex-votos*, and *milagros* are forms of folk art that expressed religious devotion and thanksgiving to patron saints. Drawing on colonial traditions, Catholics in the twentieth century continued to use these icons in their daily devotions and veneration of the saints.

There were those, however, who found little comfort in these practices. Some people simply felt abandoned by the church. The life story of Carolina Maria de Jesus, who as an adult lived in one of São Paulo's notorious *favelas*, reveals the sense of betrayal of – or perhaps better stated, the sense of irrelevance the church held for – one of Latin America's *forgotten*.

Unlike Carolina Maria de Jesus, there were some folks who, instead of rejecting the faith, found solace in Christianity by combining it with other religions practices. These *new faiths*, such as Umbanda in Brazil and Santería in the Caribbean, were the result of a miscegenation process, if you will, between folk Catholicism and traditional African religions. As we will see, turning to these religions for practical answers to life's everyday problems presented no contradiction for many Catholics.

RAPID CHANGES

In the second half of the nineteenth century and the opening of the twentieth, it became apparent to many Latin American governments that the fastest and easiest way to bring prosperity to their nations was to exploit their comparative advantage by exporting raw materials. Quickly Latin economies became export-based, often focusing most of their efforts on a single commodity. Argentina was a supplier of beef, and much of Central America became a plantation for the United Fruit Company and the production of bananas. Cuba, which had gained its independence by 1902, focused on sugar production spurred on largely by significant investments from U.S. corporations. Chile exported very large quantities of copper and nitrates. And Brazil turned its attention to rubber and coffee while Bolivia's single largest export was tin, comprising more than 72 percent of its foreign sales in 1913. As regions of Western Europe and North America industrialized, their demand for the agricultural goods and raw materials of Latin America seemed insatiable. World War I brought even more demands for strategic exports, such as tin, oil, and nitrate. All over Latin America, countries came to depend upon the foreign exchange generated by massive exports to purchase finished and manufactured goods from their principal trading partners – initially Western Europe and, beginning in the 1920s, the United States.

The key short-term economic effects were two: (1) a limited national prosperity, enjoyed primarily by the ruling oligarchies (mostly large landowners), and (2) neocolonialism, which resulted as the economies of Latin American rose or fell with the fortunes of their trading partners. If the economy of the United States suffered a downturn, then its need for raw materials declined. If, for example, Chile could not sell its copper to the United States, it could not secure the foreign exchange necessary to purchase train engines or finished goods. Latin American countries relied on the health of foreign markets for their own economic well-being.

Accompanying the growth in the export-oriented market were three key social developments that some, though not all, Latin American countries experienced: (1) a growth in the number of professionals and well-educated managers, or the middle sector, (2) the emergence of an urban working class, and (3) an increase in the size and number of major urban centers. Although Latin America remained predominately agrarian because most of its exports were agricultural in nature, there was a need for people to work in the industries that facilitated the exports. Thus, several Latin American countries began encouraging immigration from Europe. Between 1871 and 1915, Argentina, which received the most immigrants, saw the population of its capital increase by 2.5 million new arrivals, four-fifths of them from Spain and Italy. The new arrivals were a mix of skilled and unskilled laborers, who brought with them a sense of labor activism. As the immigrants' influence spread among workers – both urban and rural – labor movements became a hallmark of early twentieth-century Latin America. And, as we discussed in Chapter 5, labor activism was occasionally fostered by various Catholic organizations, both lay and religious. According to historian Lars Schoultz, the Jesuits were particularly influential in workers' movements in Colombia. As early as the 1840s, that order helped establish *Congregaciones de Obreros* (workers' societies) to advocate for economic and political change. In 1909, clergy organized the *Sociedad de Artesanos de Sonsón* (Society of Artisans of Sonson), the first trade union officially recognized by the Colombian government. Unlike early labor unions in the Unites States, however, its purpose was not to urge economic or social reform; rather the Sociedad – and other similar labor groups – tended to focus on the moral improvement of its members. By the 1920s and 1930s, efforts by the church to organize urban labor groups were largely ignored because most laborers subscribed to the principles of liberalism. However, rural laborers in regions of Colombia where conservativism held sway still looked to the church as the key organizer and leader.

The system of an export-based economy functioned until the world market crash of 1929/1930. The Great Depression had devastating effects on Latin America, with consequences that varied from country to county. In the political sphere, some countries experienced military coups; in others, the military lost power. The conservative government in Colombia fell to the liberal party. And in Cuba, the collapse of the economy, which rested heavily on sugar, resulted in massive labor unrest and agitation. By November 1930, in the face of growing unrest throughout the island, President Gerardo Machado suspended constitutional guarantees, and repression became commonplace.

By the 1930s, Latin American countries were ready for change. Within economic policy the change took the form of Import-Substitute Industrialization (ISI) – a name officially used only after World War II to the process of domestically producing goods previously imported. Import substitution was in part a nationalistic response to the realization of just how dependent economies were on those of trading partners and in part a recognition that old patterns could not continue. It moved many Latin American countries down the road to industrialization. Governments became very active in encouraging domestic manufacture of nondurable consumer goods typically imported from developed nations. Tariffs were instituted against foreign products. Land previously used primarily for export production began producing foodstuffs for domestic consumption.

After World War II, real economic growth was achieved in much of Latin America, even though it still largely relied on agricultural exports. Some countries, however, particularly in Central America, lagged far behind in economic growth. Argentina, Brazil, and Mexico experienced the greatest growth as a result of industrialization, generating some 80 percent of the region's industrial production by the end of the 1960s. But growth came at a high price.

As World War II and its aftermath closed off European markets, Latin American economies became increasingly dependent on the United States. In order to industrialize, Latin countries needed foreign capital to buy the machinery used in factories and to import the technology that would help diversify their economies. Additionally they needed technical expertise to manage new industries. The experts mostly came from the United States, as did the loans. Investments from the United States flooded Latin America between 1950 and 1965 and, as a result, investors extracted significant amounts of money in profits.

There was a price to pay both politically and socially. Socially, new-found wealth concentrated in the hands of the industrial elite, thus creating a new powerful class within Latin America. And with the limited distribution of wealth, a large urban underclass was created. This new elite sometimes vied with and other times worked in concert with the old-moneyed interests – the landed elite. During the early years of economic prosperity, the latter group accumulated large tracts of land, thereby creating a new level of rural poverty. In Brazil, for example, 22 percent of rural property owners controlled only 0.5 percent of the land in the 1950s, while 80 percent of the land remained unused or underused.

At the same time, in the cities, workers and unions gained political power as industrial magnates needed them in order to sustain production. And as these heretofore ignored groups became more powerful, they became of more interest to politicians, particularly populist leaders. By fashioning a coalition between the industrial elite and the trade unions, leaders such as Perón and Vargas were able to amass an enormous political base and push through their agendas and policies.

OFF CENTER STAGE

The church in Argentina was an early supporter of Perón and his military colleagues because it saw the armed forces as the best protection against the spread of Communism with its avowed atheistic principles. The military and Perón's quasifascist rhetoric about national identity, social order, and respect for hierarchy resonated with the Argentine church, as did Perón's positions against divorce and the separation of church and state. Furthermore, from the church's perspective, Perón's support of obligatory religious education in public schools and his social policies that so closely reflected the wording in certain papal encyclicals were further evidence that he was worthy of the church's endorsement. The church also aligned itself with the ever more powerful Argentine labor movement – particularly in Buenos Aires – which represented a significant portion of Perón's power base. When the 1943 military coup put Perón in power, it had the explicit support of the Argentine church. As historian Fortunato Mallimaci has pointed out, the temptation of having military support to make Argentina "more Catholic" was too much for the church to resist. Being an Argentine-style Catholic, which meant supporting both workers' rights and Perón, became part of the Argentine national identity: For the masses of workers, the belief was that "true Catholicism is Peronism."

By the early 1950s, however, the relationship between the church and the Perón government became strained as each tried to direct the other. The church was not willing to accept the strictly ceremonial and calming role that Perón wanted it to have. Nor was it pleased with Perón's suggestions that his late wife, Eva, be canonized. Leaders of a 1954 rebellion against Perón included priests and bishops who felt the dictator's efforts to determine what it meant to be Catholic in Argentina had gone too far. Sectors of the armed forces involved in the rebellion took as their battle cry "in the name of the Virgin, freedom, and traditional Catholicism." These rebels flew planes with crosses painted on them. Once, intending to bomb the presidential palace, the rebels instead bombed hundreds of Peron's supporters gathered in a plaza. The Peronistas responded by burning Catholic churches and colleges as well as killing priests. The love affair between the populist government of Juan Domingo Perón and the Catholic Church was over. The military coup that finally overthrew him in 1955 had the support of the institutional church in Argentina. The marriage between the military and the church would plague Argentina for decades with the church again playing a supporting role to governmental oppression.

In Brazil, many Catholics, especially among the elite, felt much the same way about their country as did many Argentine Catholics about Argentina: Brazil had drifted too far from its original Catholic roots and something had to be done. But unlike in Argentina, Brazilian church officials sought a multipronged approach to regaining their lost power.

The Brazilian church had suffered much with the rise of liberalism in the nineteenth century. The Constitution of 1891 codified the church's inferior position to the state, secularized education, and ended state funding for the church. But by the 1920s, the church had found its own leader in the person of Dom Sebastião Leme, who would direct the official course of the Brazilian Catholic Church until his death in 1942. His approach was to work with the government whenever necessary, often exerting pressure, while simultaneously creating parallel Catholic associations – mostly lay, such as schools, youth groups, and charity institutions – that would defend Catholicism. Yet, as historian Margaret Todaro Williams makes clear, Leme founded organizations, such as Catholic Action (which we will discuss later), that tended to be apolitical, or as he stated, "above and apart" from politics, precisely because, as the official church held, the church was supranational – above any nation – and thus its activities needed to be nonpartisan. Nevertheless, Leme was not above unofficially encouraging the work of other organizations that overtly supported political candidates with Catholic leanings. He also wanted to maintain a relationship with the state, especially after 1930 when the Vargas government came to power. By skillfully using his influence, Leme succeeded in getting some "pro-Catholic" legislation passed. Divorce was outlawed as were movies the church deemed immoral, clergy and monastics were given the right to vote, and marriages performed by the church were given the legal equivalence of civil marriages. (Some historians would argue that the church hierarchy was so intent upon maintaining its influence with the state that it neglected its parishioners.)

One of the "non-Catholic" organizations Leme supported was *Ação Integralista Brasileira* (Brazilian Integralist Action, or AIB), a political association that sought to combine political action with the Catholic faith. While Leme was careful never to establish official ties with the AIB, documents reveal his close affinity to the group's goals and even many of its tactics. In the five years of its existence (1932–1937, when it and all other political parties were suppressed), AIB mobilized Catholics, both lay and religious, to participate in the political process. Unlike similar organizations throughout Latin America that also appealed to the middle sector disillusioned by democracy (which gave the "unwashed masses" far too much power in the nation), the AIB took on much of the ideology of the extreme right – in other words, fascism. However, the AIB distinguished itself from the Italian and German versions of fascism by emphasizing its strong links to the Catholic Church, even taking as its motto "God, Country, and Family" and placing inherent value on the individual as a creation of God.

For Leme, the AIB was one tool among many he could use in his efforts to regain power for the church. The church's emphasis on social tranquility, obedience to authority, and respect for hierarchy melded nicely with the AIB's support of a corporatist state – a structure in which each social group or class knows its place and submits harmoniously to the authority of the group above it and ultimately to a ruling authority. Furthermore, corporativism as a useful method for combating many of society's ills had been advocated by several popes – including Pius XI in his encyclical *Quadragesimo anno* (1931), which also reaffirmed the Catholic Church's commitment to the social principles in the earlier *Rerum novarum*.

Many regular and secular clergy became deeply involved in the AIB, even assuming places of leadership in the organization, often in direct contradiction to their orders' strictures or their superiors' directions. Hélder Câmara is perhaps the best known of the priests to be active in the organization, a move that required him to disregard Leme's objections to political activism. (It was an affiliation Câmara would later find embarrassing.) Câmara and hundreds of other priests, including those in the interior of the nation, opened their pulpits in the 1930s to AIB speakers and made their congregations available for recruiting efforts. The Integralists (or AIB) made their party palatable to devout Catholics in a variety of ways, such as calling on biblical imagery, couching their struggles in messianic terms, and identifying the organization with the work of the Catholic Church.

The vast majority of Brazilian bishops ignored those areas in which Integralism crossed the line into church territory – such as the creation of its own rituals for baptism, marriage, and burial and the claim by some that the AIB was the means to salvation – because many believed that it was the best weapon against the twin threats of liberalism and Communism. The AIB's rabid anti-Communist rhetoric appealed to many members of the church hierarchy.

The AIB's downfall may not have been so much of their own making. In November 1937, Vargas declared the *Estado Novo* (New State) in response to a putative Communist rebellion. He suspended the constitution and ruled by decree. By December of that year, all political parties, including the Ação Integralista Brasileira, were suppressed. Nevertheless, Vargas understood that if he practiced what he called "preemptive cooptation" with the institutional church, he would forestall opposition from it and secure the success of the Estado Novo. This is exactly what he did, for a time.

Overthrown by a coup in 1945, Vargas succeeded in getting reelected as president in 1950. (In the same election, Presbyterian João Café Filho ran for vice president, a position he won in spite of opposition from Catholic groups and threats of excommunication for those who voted for him.) At his reelection, Vargas took a decided turn to the left and began distancing himself from the church. Catholic organizations – including the episcopacy – began refashioning themselves in the light of events in Brazil. Under the leadership of Hélder Câmara, the National Conference of Bishops (discussed later) would become the collective voice of the Catholic faithful in Brazil.

The experience of the Catholic Church in Colombia during the first half of the twentieth century exemplifies how a church can be buffeted about by circumstances. Like the church in many of its neighboring countries, Colombia's was suppressed by a liberal government during the nineteenth century. But the Constitution of 1886 reinstated much of the church's lost privileges and prestige, even declaring that Roman Catholicism was the religion of the country and a necessary tool for social order. By 1888, the government made further concessions, guaranteeing the Catholic Church that there would be no state interference and it could freely exercise its spiritual and ecclesiastical authority according to its own rules. Furthermore, the church was given a strong hand in education, its rites were recognized by civil authority, and it was allowed once again to keep civil registries. In other words, by the beginning of the twentieth century the Colombian church experienced a resurgence of its former power and authority with the support of the state.

The presidential election of 1930 once again brought a liberal government into power. It pursued many of the anticlerical reforms of earlier liberal governments: curtailing the church's influence in education and in politics, limiting its role in civil record keeping, and overseeing its nomination of bishops. The church's response was to ally itself even more closely with the conservatives, an especially fruitful relationship when, in 1946, the conservatives were back in power. Yet for the country, the ascendancy of the conservative party led to almost twenty years of warfare (1946–1964) and more than two hundred thousand deaths as conservatives sought reprisals in what became known as *la violencia*. In the face of such devastating destruction that approached anarchy, the church hierarchy tried to become a nonpartisan voice – even while some clergy participated actively in denouncing liberals.

Unlike violence in urban settings, violence in the Colombian countryside took on a decidedly religious bent. In conservative strongholds, Protestants, who were often labeled as liberals (and certainly many had those leanings), became targets. Between 1948 and 1955, more than 165 Protestant schools were closed, 42 churches destroyed, and 112 people murdered – 4 of whom were children. As late as 1955, Colombian Protestants and foreign Protestant missionaries were being evicted from their homes and farms, often with the help of the police. The difference between political violence and religious persecution was difficult to determine in the rural areas. The fighting in the countryside could as easily be called Protestant versus Catholic as it could be liberal versus conservative.

The fortunes of the church in Colombia continued to fluctuate. Its staunchest supporter, President Laureano Gómez, known as "more Catholic than the pope," was ousted in 1953, in part because of his strong hand in the rising violence throughout the country. With his ouster the church faced new, but fairly mild, opposition from the new president. But by the end of 1958, the Colombian church was back at the top of the heap. A plebiscite held on December 1 reaffirmed the church's privileges and its role in maintaining social order. Today, the Colombian Catholic Church is viewed as one of the most powerful churches in Latin America.

SOURCE OF STRENGTH

At the end of the nineteenth century, the Roman church began recognizing that power also lay in the cooperation of ecclesiastical officials across regional lines. In late 1898, Pope Leo XIII called for the first Latin American Plenary Council to meet in Rome the following year with the express purpose of revitalizing the Latin American clergy. The Latin American church was suffering from a crisis of relevance, attacks by liberals, and a loss of prestige, as well as an extreme shortage of priests. Leo XIII hoped that by convening the Council he could begin to address the issues so drastically affecting the church in Latin America. Among the many decrees to emanate from the Council was a call for bishops' conferences and the renewal of the provincial councils, so prevalent in the early colonial period. In spite of the urgency evident in the pope's call for the Council, the church in Latin America had difficulty in redirecting its efforts. Historian Hans-Jürgen Prien comments that the institutional church continued to focus on ways to recoup its lost power and privileges and to maintain a colonial ecclesiastical structure rather than on finding new ways of understanding the reality of Latin America. In the case of Brazil, these conferences, largely guided by Leme, dealt with issues such as paganism, superstition, lack of religious education, socialism, Freemasonry, and the Index of Banned Books. They tended to be defensive and protective of the faith rather than outwardly focused. Yet, from the work of the provincial councils throughout Brazil came the founding of several seminaries as well as the Catholic University of Rio de Janeiro.

According to historian Jesús Hortal, it was the work of the lay organization Catholic Action (discussed later) – not the provincial councils – that very likely spurred the Brazilian bishops to form the *Conferência Nacional dos Bispos do Brasil* (National Conference of Brazilian Bishops, or CNBB) in 1952. Over the years, the CNBB moved away from focusing solely on the preservation or restoration of the church's lost privileges. Led by Hélder Câmara, in its biennial meetings the CNBB began talking more about land reform and social justice and less about the creation of new clergy and how to battle Spiritism.

While the attention of the CNBB increasingly turned to matters beyond church function and survival, the Vatican remained very concerned about what it saw as the "religious problem" in Latin America, namely the scarcity of priests. The lack of clergy – caused largely by the effects of liberalism, poor pay, and the impression in some areas that the church was a functionary of the state – meant that the Catholic Church had few priests to act as deterrents to the work of Protestant missionaries who, now closed out of China as a mission field, had turned to Latin America as the next great area to evangelize. In 1955, Rome approved the formation of the *Consejo Episcopal Latinamericano* (Council of Latin American Bishops, or CELAM). From this point on, the bishops of Latin America could act in concert when it came to addressing region-wide issues such as ways to evangelize and stop the spread of Protestantism, how to increase the number of priests, and the preaching of justice based on the social doctrine of the church.

CELAM not only worked at a pan-American level but also sponsored regional meetings in which the members of the episcopacy tried to familiarize local priests and lay persons with issues that were unique to their regions. The bishops were becoming the leaders of a changing church. By 1961, CELAM took on perhaps its most difficult task: a critical analysis of the Catholic Church in the Latin American context. This sociological approach to the state of the church and society in Latin America would shape the actions of the episcopacy for years to come. We will discuss some of its consequences in Chapter 9.

CALL TO ACTION

It was not only the church hierarchy that took an active role in dealing with the changing church of Latin America. In the late nineteenth-century, long before the hierarchy looked beyond it own preservation, and often in response to the encyclical *Rerum novarum*, Catholic lay organizations sprang up across Latin America, particularly among workers. As already mentioned, the Jesuits helped found workers' unions in Colombia, and the Argentine Conferences of the Ladies of St. Vincent de Paul also dealt with issues confronted by workers. In Peru in 1896, the Catholic Worker's Circle of Arequipa was founded.

By the beginning of the twentieth century, lay Catholic organizations had begun to widen their work beyond the support and moral education of their individual members. In later decades of the century, they turned their attention to society as a whole, even while the church hierarchy was struggling to reclaim its lost prestige. They focused particularly on young people, resulting in new groups that drew most of their members from university students. Some of these youth groups, such as one that met regularly at the Catholic Center of

Miraflores, Peru, taught free evening classes to workers. Others used sports as a means to attract attendees, following the model of the Young Men's Christian Association (YMCA). The latter endeavor proved less than successful since often those who came to the centers were more interested in sports than in religious education.

The youth who worked diligently to bring their faith to others, the members of other lay Catholic organizations, and all the faithful who, with great determination, took their faith into the streets and became "soldiers" of the Catholic Church were known as "militant Catholics." An interesting convergence of an official show of power and the rising Catholic militancy is the Eucharistic Congresses, which took place throughout Latin America. (International Eucharistic Congresses, after which the national ones were patterned, began in France in reaction to the vitriolic anticlericalism of the French Revolution. In 1881 in Lille, France, the first International Eucharistic Congress met; from there such gatherings spread throughout the world.) The purpose was to acknowledge publicly the centrality of the Eucharist and for faithful Catholics to share communion. Masses were held across Latin America with tens of thousands in attendance. In 1935, two hundred thousand people participated in the Eucharistic Congress in Lima, a city with a population of some five hundred thousand. The church's ability to bring together so many people must have made an impression on the Peruvian government. National Congresses were held in Mexico, Bolivia, Nicaragua, and Cuba with similar results. Brazil was chosen as the site of the 1955 International Eucharistic Congress. With money bequeathed by Getúlio Vargas, who had committed suicide the year before, Brazil hosted more than a million Catholics.

Predating the flurry of Eucharistic Congresses was the creation of Acción Católica (Catholic Action, or AC), which received papal support from Pius XI in the 1920s. According to historian Jeffery Klaiber, at the end of the nineteenth century a "Catholic Action-like" group began in Italy largely in response to the anticlericalism of liberalism. Creation of similar organizations throughout the world was sporadic until Pius XI's endorsement in 1922. The pope's goal – and that of the organization – was to create an avenue for militant lay Catholics to defend the faith, evangelize in an increasingly secular world, and influence the political process without being a political party. Unlike other socially active lay Catholic organizations, AC was held in tight check by bishops and participating clergy.

Catholic Action met with varying amounts of success. In Chile, for example, AC was not founded until the 1940s and saw as its mission to "awaken" Catholics to their social responsibilities. Furthermore, it sought to defend papal encyclicals against objections by aristocrats and certain portions of the clergy who felt that the policies were not applicable to Chile. As in many other AC organizations throughout Latin America, Chile's group comprised mostly middle-sector Catholics, precisely because the goals of AC reflected much of what the middle sector had already been doing. This "new" emphasis on social action as part of the practice of one's faith was not to the liking of the ruling oligarchies. They preferred the "old" emphasis on patronage and power. Militant Catholics in Peru simply did not identify with the oligarchy. (This lack of identification with the upper echelons of society is part of the reason, Klaiber argues, that the institutional church was able to move away from the rich and powerful and lay claim to its role with the marginalized of society in the 1950s and 1960s.) Militant Catholics were, however, comfortable supporting Augusto Leguía, the ruthless dictator of Peru from 1919 to 1930, who used AC to help maintain social order by extending paternalistic aid through it to the poor of the country.

In Venezuela, Archbishop Felipe Rincón y González had to be pressured by the Vatican nuncio into forming branches of Acción Católica, which he finally did in the 1940s. In Uruguay, Catholic Action, founded in 1935, had little if any impact on the government, primarily because of the constitutional separation of church and state. Mexico was so torn apart by the cristero rebellion and its aftermath that Catholic Action never really had a chance to develop. Yet, some historians would argue that Catholic Action's greatest impact was not on the state; rather, it was the church that was changed. Specifically, active laity became involved in society and the church both in positions of leadership and as stalwart soldiers. In Peru, for example, one of the key transformative elements of AC was that it gave respectability to men who were devout Catholics. It pushed the church away from the image of being composed primarily of women and children. By requiring that its members, male and female, publicly display their faith by attending mass together and wearing badges, Catholic Action helped unify militant Catholics.

Throughout it all, Acción Católica remained "above and apart" from the political process. For some Catholics, the lack of political involvement was a shortcoming of AC. Thus, in the late 1940s and in the 1950s, it became a less prominent social/religious force and was replaced by more overtly political Catholic groups, primarily the Christian Democratic parties. After World War II and the subsequent disillusionment with fascism as a means of fighting both Communism and capitalism, all across Latin America Christian Democrats looked for what they called the "third way," somewhere between capitalism and socialism.

Rerum novarum and *Quadrageismo anno* had both criticized capitalism as well as Communism: capitalism for its extreme individualism and

Communism for its antireligious ideology. For many Catholics, the quasifascist groups (such as the Brazilian Integralists and the Chilean Falange party, named after Francisco Franco's fascist party in Spain) appeared to be the answer to the twin political evils of Communism and capitalism. World War II and the violence of the fascist parties in Germany and Italy disabused many of that notion. As a response to the global war and the revelations about fascism, Christian Democratic parties began emerging in Europe. Their popularity among Catholics was largely based on their commitment to democracy coupled with the critique of capitalism and socialism, both perceived as threats to Catholicism.

When Christian Democratic parties began appearing in Latin America, they seemed to be the answer to the ills of the region. According to political scientist Paul Sigmund, many, already radicalized by AC, turned to the Christian Democrats as a means of dealing with the iniquities of both capitalism and socialism – the basic inequities and imperialism of the former and the totalitarian consequences of the latter as well as its association with Communism. The "third way" between the extremes of capitalism and socialism generally advocated worker-run factories, cooperatives within agriculture, and organizations of those typically marginalized – women and urban and rural poor – to ensure that they had a political voice. With the rise of the Christian Democratic parties, lay Catholicism's close ties with right-wing movements began to fade as young Catholics looked increasingly to the political parties imbued with Catholic principles.

PRIVATE CATHOLICISM

Not all Catholics found participation in the political process a natural offshoot of their faith. At about the same time that Acción Católica was beginning to fade from the scene, another, less political group that focused much more on the spiritual development of its individual members began to emerge. The *cursillos de cristiandad* (CCs, intensive courses on Christianity) first appeared as a distinct movement in the late 1940s in Mallorca, Spain. Its roots, however, are unclear: Some historians claim that the CCs began as part of Opus Dei while others argue that the organization's beginnings were independent. In any case, the movement – which continues strong today – was one of intense religious fervor. Each *cursillista*, as its members are known, was selected secretly on the basis of such criteria as sex (men were preferred), job, physical health, marital status, and mental health. Once selected, the new cursillista attended a three-day retreat, or course, in which he or she participated in a program that included masses, special music, acts of piety, and lectures, all with the intention of "converting" the new member to a deeper form of Catholicism. After finishing the course, the participant went on to take part in an active Christian life filled with weekly small group meetings, as well as regional and international gatherings known as *ultreyas*. (A 1966 ultreya was celebrated in Rome and was welcomed by the pope.)

There continues to be debate about the CCs. Some critics charge that the organization is regressive in that it tends toward Marianism, its members make petitions for the dead, and the organization is deeply devoted to the eucharist and other "old-fashioned" means of personal piety. Interestingly, other critics of the CCs interpret these elements differently. They find that the intense devotion of the cursillistas is a form of free-thinking and that the movement's members reject the authority and control of the religious hierarchy. Still other critics claim that the CCs are repressive, bordering on totalitarian in the demands for conformity and adherence to prescribed thought that it places on its members. The one thing that is clear is that the CCs did not involve themselves with the social problems of their day, instead choosing to develop their members' personal spirituality. For many Catholics, the deeply personal and internally focused cursillos de cristiandad clearly filled a void. By 1972, in Brazil alone there were more than one hundred thousand cursillistas.

For many other individuals in Latin America, religious devotion took on seemingly more personal expressions yet with public overtones largely absent from the CCs. Two such public manifestations of private piety were the *retablos* and the *ex-votos*. Retablos are paintings of saints or particular religious themes for use in home shrines or placement at church altars. Ex-votos are also paintings that express personal piety. In this case, however, the art work is commissioned in gratitude for a saintly intercession or answered prayers. An important element of the ex-voto is public display in a church or shrine. For the church, these displays of gratitude had the effect of reinforcing the sense of the power of the faith to work miracles. For the supplicant, the ex-votos were the fulfillment of a promise.

Both ex-votos and retablos have a colonial heritage. In their earliest Latin American form, the retablos were standardized pictorial renderings of religious images, such as of saints, the Virgin Mary, or Christ. These painting were used as instructional tools by the friars in their evangelization of the indigenous peoples, much as similar objects had been used throughout Europe. According to theologian Ana María Pineda, retablos were a way of making visible what was considered sacred. These images were typically displayed behind church altars. Eventually, wealthy patrons commissioned local artists to paint retablos of patron saints on canvas for personal use, placing the art work in their home shrines as a means of ensuring saintly good will for the household. But canvas was far too expensive for the poor. By the nineteenth century, however, sheet tin, which was much less expensive and more durable than canvas, was readily available and had become the favorite surface for retablo painters. While retablo painting as a religious art form reached its zenith in the last quarter of the nineteenth century, it remained – and remains – a popular form of private devotion.

A complement to the retablo is the ex-voto, also known as "retablo ex-voto." Ex-votos are often the response to a vow – hence "voto" – made in return for intercession. A supplicant might pray to St. Isidro the Plowman, the patron saint of farmers, for example, for a bountiful crop. In exchange, said supplicant would promise to commission an ex-voto that would include an artistic rendering of the fulfillment of the favor, a depiction of the saint to whom the request was made, and a brief narrative at the bottom explaining the work of the saint. Then the ex-voto painting would be displayed in a church or a pilgrimage site. Unlike retablos, ex-votos were part of a public expression of gratitude. The narrative of one ex-voto, owned by San Diego State University, suffices as an example of the language used in expressing appreciation for the answer to a prayer: "On the Cañada de Negros hacienda in the jurisdiction of P. del Rincón Gto [Guanajuato, Mexico], Navor Pérez was very ill of a tumor which opened up into five pustules on the 5th of July 1924, but her mother M. Josefa Reynoso seeing her in mortal danger, put her in the hands of Christ of the Column who is worshiped in His sanctuary of P. del R. He granted relief and as a reward she dedicated this retablo." (Ex-votos were so ingrained in the Mexican psyche by the twentieth century that even the self-avowed Marxist and atheist Frida Kahlo used the form in some of her most famous work, painting on tin and using her art to tell a story. In her efforts to lay claim to "Mexican-ness," the artist also collected retablos and ex-votos, filling her house with several examples of the religious art.)

An important aspect of ex-votos for scholars is that they give us access to the daily lives of those who often did not leave other records. Likewise, they also reveal the depth of connections between everyday occurrences and faith and culture and faith: relationships that were not severed by all the constitutional acts or legislation passed at the national level. In November 1887, María Dolores presented an ex-voto for the miracle St. Francis de Paul performed by freeing her son from jail. In 1941, Angela Alonso and her family gave thanks through an ex-voto to the Virgin of Guadalupe for curing her husband Benito Gutiérrez of a grave illness. And in 1948, Antonia Lopes thanked El Señor del Monte for saving her two daughters from an illness that proved difficult to cure. For most people, faith went hand in hand with daily life – what theologians such as Ada María Isasi-Díaz call the actual practice of religion in one's everyday activities.

A third means of expressing one's connection with a particular saint was through *milagros*, or miracles. These little charms – most often depictions of some part of the body such as a hand, foot, or heart – were usually fashioned of metal and pinned to the clothing of the saint's statue or placed by the saint's altar as a reminder to the saint of a petition. Once the miracle of healing was granted, the milagro would remain as an expression of gratitude.

THE FORGOTTEN

There were many in Latin America who did not find comfort or help in official religious devotion or in pictoral rendering of religious petitions. They were the ones who felt the church had simply forgotten them or only remembered them when it was beneficial to the church to do so. Such was the case with Carolina Maria de Jesus of São Paulo. Born the illegitimate daughter of a destitute black woman in the very traditional interior of Brazil, Carolina Maria began life with as many strikes against her as anyone could have in the mid 1910s. Her early years were filled with harsh discrimination and ridicule, which some who knew her said resulted in self-hatred and a complicated ambivalence toward other Blacks. (Certainly her diary, which chronicles her forties, could lead to that conclusion.) In addition to the painful realities of the society around her, Carolina Maria experienced rejection from her extended family and constant dislocation as she and her mother moved from one place to another.

Her later years were not significantly better. By the age of thirty-three, pregnant for the first time and having lost her job because she was unwed and expecting a child, Carolina had little choice but to move into Canindé, one of São Paulo's new *favelas*, or shanty towns. There, by scrounging for building supplies, she was able to construct a leaky four-foot-by-twelve-foot shack in which she would eventually raise her three children. She also staked out her foraging area, as was the custom of favela dwellers, and each day would go in search of scrap paper – in trash cans, on the ground, or anywhere she could – which she would then sell for pittances. On lucky days she would find bits of scrap metal to sell.

Some of the paper that Carolina collected she saved for herself, and on those scraps she recorded her life in the favela. Portions of the diary, covering the years 1955 to 1960, were published in Brazil in 1960 – after the efforts of a journalist brought the diary to light – under the title *Quartio de Despejo* (the English translation is titled *Child of the Dark*) and became the best-selling book in Brazilian publishing history up to that time. While a personal diary reveals the experiences of only its author or those about whom the author chooses to write, it does give us a very intimate glimpse into a reality that might otherwise remain shrouded in mystery for many of us.

Carolina Maria wrote of going to get water from the one spigot in the community, fights in the streets, and the commonplaceness of sexual violence and drunkenness, which often went hand in hand. But the one thing that is most striking by its absence is the church – which should not be surprising given the Brazilian Catholic Church's inward focus in the 1950s. When Carolina Maria did mention the church, she did so with cynicism and wonder at its purpose. Yet, paradoxically, she wrote about prayer and the role God played in her life. One might wonder if, for Carolina, God and the Catholic Church were entities unfamiliar with each other. Such an attitude reflects Carolina's early experiences with the Roman church. According to historians Robert Levine and José Carlos Sebe Bom Meihy, Carolina Maria reported to her daughter that when she, Carolina, was young, she was not allowed to enter the local Catholic church because she and her brother were illegitimate. Furthermore, Carolina Maria more than likely never took communion. Yet, interestingly, she described herself as a devout Catholic.

One of her early positive experiences with religion was not with Christianity but with Spiritism. Senhora Maria Leite, a practitioner of Spiritism, was the wife of a landowner near where Carolina lived as a child. Riddled with guilt over her ancestors' slaveowning, Senhora Leite tried to make amends by paying for the education – at a Spiritist school – of several poor black children, Carolina being one of them. From this brief opportunity, lasting only two years before Carolina and her family moved away, the child developed a love of reading and writing, which years later would result in her keeping the diary in Canindé.

Within that diary, if Carolina made reference to anyone affiliated with the church, it was often to Brother Luiz who came to the favela to teach the children their catechism, show them films about the church, or preach homilies about how "God only blesses those who suffer with resignation." With a sense of hopelessness, Carolina wrote that if Brother Luiz had stopped long enough to notice the children eating rotten food out of trash cans he might have spoken about rebellion, not resignation. So distant were he and the church he represented from the realities of life in the favela that when he came to treat the sores of the favelados, Carolina was surprised that he knew they had physical aliments. For Carolina and many like her, the church was an institution whose priests occasionally showed up in cars, handed out some food and platitudes, and then climbed back into their cars and drove away to a place far from the hunger and filth of Canindé.

God, however, was much more present to Carolina. Routinely she wrote of thanking God for a beautiful day, for curing her of some illness, or for protecting her and her children. She wrote of a god for whom all races were equal and who would help her rise above the favela. But Carolina also wrote of a god who had forgotten that the favelas existed and who punished the sins of the parents by afflicting the children with hunger and disease. Clearly the intensely personal faith that sustained, and sometime burdened, Carolina existed outside of – and perhaps in spite of – the bounds established by the institutional church. And when the institutional church did respond specifically to Carolina's writings, it was to hold her up as a symbol of suffering, a role that the fiercely independent Carolina neither wanted nor fulfilled well, often turning on those who would "handle" her.

NEW FAITHS

Operating outside the bounds of orthodox Catholicism was not reserved for those who lived in the Brazilian favelas. The 1920s saw the emergence of a "new" religion largely created by and for middle-sector, urban Whites in Brazil. According to anthropologists Diana De G. Brown and Mario Bick, *Umbanda Pura* came out of the work of disillusioned Spiritists who had been frequenting Afro-Brazilian religious services influenced by Yoruban religious traditions. These Spiritists merged their religious practices with what they liked of the Afro-Brazilian practices to create Umbanda Pura – usually simply called Umbanda.

The early practitioners of Umbanda were from the white middle sector, many of whose members were white immigrants or the children of immigrants. For them, the African elements of the Afro-Brazilian religions were too "primitive," thus, they sought to "whiten" patterns that they found uncomfortable. Paradoxically, the rise of Umbanda was part and parcel of a rise in Brazilian nationalism and an effort to define Brazilianness by glorifying the country's African heritage.

Unlike various "orthodox" Afro-Brazilian religions, such as *Candomblé*, whose practices more nearly reflected traditional African religions, Umbanda tended to be fairly staid in its worship services, placed great emphasis on charity work (particularly spiritual healing), conformed to the rhythms of urban life, and focused on "good" magic that harmed no one. For many practitioners, one of the most attractive elements of Umbanda was the consultation in which those initiated into the faith became possessed of benevolent spirit guides who offered advice to congregants on everything from how to cure an illness to how to deal with problems at work. It is in the pantheon of spirits, however, that we most clearly see the confluence in Umbanda of Catholicism, Afro-Brazilian religions, and Spiritism. God – who had both a European Christian and an African religious identity – reigns supreme. Beneath God is the second tier of spirits who also have dual identities, as minor African deities and as Catholic saints. The saints along with their African deity counterparts rule over and guide the work of seven "lines," or groups of lesser spirits. For example, St. George (Ogun) is responsible for the spirits that protect those in the military while St. Lazarus's (Obalauyê's) line might be consulted about questions of illness. Altars (known as *congas*) in Umbanda religious houses (or *centros*) are routinely decorated with images and statues of Jesus, the Virgin Mary, and various saints, as well as images of the *pretos velhos* ("old Blacks"), who are in the third tier and are the spirits of enslaved Africans who have patience and wisdom borne of suffering. The Brazilian flag also makes an occasional appearance at an Umbanda altar. From Spiritism, Umbanda received the notion of reincarnation as spirits moved up a hierarchy of existence. But why was the "new" religion so readily accepted?

It was precisely the cult of saints that made Umbanda easier for Whites to adopt. Throughout Latin America, saints were viewed as being able to work miracles and answer individual petitions – to which ex-votos are certainly testaments. The leap from an individual asking Our Lady Aparecida (the patron saint of Brazil) for intercession to turning to the *orishas* (deities) of Umbanda for personal guidance was not a large one. In fact, many who routinely attended Umbanda services also considered themselves good Catholics. Additionally, the popularity of Spiritism, with its spirit possessions and the influence of those spirits on everyday life, also paved the way for Umbanda.

In Cuba, another Latin American region with significant African heritage, *Santería*, or Way of the Saints, is a mixing of Catholicism with traditional African religions, primarily Yoruban, brought to the island by slaves. Some scholars of religion argue that the creation of a new faith such as Santería – or Umbanda – is more than using the dominant group's religion (in this case Catholicism) to obscure from the apparently unobservant Whites the continued religious practice of the dominated group. Rather, these scholars argue, what occurs is a type of reciprocity in which elements of one religion – for example, the saints – enrich elements of another – such as the orisha – thereby creating something new. For instance, within Santería the Virgin of Caridad del Cobre has become closely aligned with Ochún, the mother-goddess in the Yoruban pantheon. As historian Olga Portuondo Zúñiga writes, Caridad has neither been assimilated into Ochún nor has she functioned as a disguise for the worship of Ochún. Rather, Caridad and Ochún coexist in parallel and interrelated forms.

Some aspects of the life story of Reyita, an Afro-Cuban woman born in 1902, exemplify the melding of these two distinct religious practices. In 1952, Reyita's husband became very ill, prompting her to pray to St. Lazarus even though the Virgin of Caridad, or the *Virgencita*, as Reyita referred to her, was Reyita's primary religious solace. As part of her bargain with St. Lazarus, she promised his image would share a place of honor with that of the Virgencita. Her husband survived the illness, and Reyita kept her promise. She built a large altar to the saint and bedecked it with flowers, fruit, candy, rum, and tobacco. (Such offerings are an integral part of Santería, with each orisha requiring specific gifts – often animal sacrifices – to remain benevolent.) During a party to honor St. Lazarus, Reyita experienced what she called "radiations," which allowed her to cure those who asked for her help as well as to divine the truth, all with the help of the saint

It is apparent that Reyita was not that different from Carolina Maria de Jesus: They each fashioned a faith that met their needs and reflected the realities in which they lived. Neither found comfort or even relevance in the institutional church, so they turned to and, to some extent, invented a faith that was more immediate and practical.

CONCLUSION

The search for relevance was a hallmark of Christianity in Latin America in the years before the Second Vatican Council – commonly known as Vatican II. Societies became increasingly secular, and the institutional church struggled at first to preserve its old place and finally to have a place at all. Militant Catholics sought to make their faith relevant within society by trying to conform those societies to their religious beliefs. But if the decades between 1930 and 1960 were ones of lost identity for formal Catholicism, they were also a time of change for the church. While such changes varied from country to country and even region to region within each country, in general we can see a slow sea change coming, one that would move the institutional church from master to servant. And for those who had been servants, the decades represented a time of continued religious transformation in which faith could be, and often was, separate from the church.

Chapters 7 and 8, which discuss the beginnings and early development of Protestantism, examine yet another transformative element within Latin American Christianity. With the influx of immigrants and missionaries from Europe and the United States came the "devil" that the Catholics had struggled so hard to keep out: Protestantism. Its arrival would forever alter the face of Christianity in the Americas. Yet, we would be wrong to think that

Protestantism slipped in with the nineteenth-century immigrants and missionaries. It made its first incursions in the area in the sixteenth, seventeenth, and eighteenth centuries, with the interlopers, smugglers, and pirates. These invaders had routine, frequent, and amicable contact with Spanish settlers. And it was through these encounters that Protestantism made its first, though ephemeral, appearance. After independence, newly formed governments began inviting immigrants – of any religious persuasion – to bring their skills and knowledge to Latin America. Those governments of liberal leanings also invited Protestant missionaries to come to their lands largely as a weapon against the conservatives. And come they did.

7

❧

Protestant Immigration

At the same time as Spanish and Portuguese invaders were shaping and reshaping life in the western hemisphere, religion in Europe was also undergoing drastic and even convulsive changes. Hernán Cortés (1485–1547), the conqueror of Mexico, was a contemporary of Martin Luther (1483–1547). In 1521, as Cortés was engaged in the conquest of the Aztecs, supposedly on behalf of King Charles I, Luther was confronting the same ruler, under his other title, Emperor Charles V, at the Diet of Worms. The century of the Conquista is also the century of the Reformation.

The parallelism and contrast between these two events were not lost on Spanish chroniclers of the time. Later in the same century, Friar Gerónimo de Mendieta, a Franciscan missionary in Mexico, decided to write his *Historia eclesiástica indiana* (Church History of the Indies). There he wrote that Hernán Cortés and Martin Luther had been born on exactly the same day – which was not true – and on that basis declared that God

> chose as His instrument this valiant captain, Hernán Cortés, in order to open the door and prepare the way for the preaching of His Gospel in this New World, thus compensating the Catholic Church with the conversion of many souls, and undoing the great loss and evil that would be done by accursed Martin Luther.[1]

Nor was the connection lost on the civil and ecclesiastical authorities in Spain. As a result, a guiding principle of the Iberian enterprise in the New World was to make certain that all Protestant contagion was avoided.

In this they were mostly successful. The one possible exception in the early years of the conquest was a book published by the first bishop of Mexico, Friar Juan de Zumárraga – the same bishop who figures in the stories about the

---

[1] As quoted in Luis N. Rivera Pagán, *Evangelización y violencia: La conquista de América* (San Juan: Editorial Cemí, 1990), 92–93.

Virgin of Guadalupe's first appearances in Mexico. Zumárraga was imbued in the spirit of the Spanish Catholic Reformation, deeply committed to orthodoxy and at the same time profoundly influenced by the call to reformation of Erasmus and other humanists. As a means to reform the church through education and devotional practices, he was instrumental in establishing the first printing press in the New World, which was functioning by 1537. One of the first books published there, under Zumárraga's instructions, was *Doctrina cristiana* (Christian Doctrine), whose purpose was to serve as a handbook for the catechization of the indigenous population. Zumárraga's edition does not name the author, Constantino Ponce de la Fuente, who died a few years later while being held in prison by the Spanish Inquisition under suspicion of "Lutheranism." For several decades, even after Dr. Constantino – as he was generally called – was posthumously condemned as a heretic by the Inquisition, his book continued circulating anonymously in Mexico. To what extent Constantino had Protestant inclinations is questionable. Most likely, he was a follower of Erasmus rather than of the Protestant Reformation.

Despite the very restrictive Spanish and Portuguese policies regarding the presence of Protestantism in their colonies, today there are millions of Protestants in Latin America. How did this come about? As is often the case when a religion enters into new territories, Protestantism in Latin America has a dual origin: immigration and missions. In this chapter, we will deal with immigration and turn to the Protestant missionary enterprise and the further growth of Protestantism in the next.

Even though Protestant immigration into Latin America was mostly a matter of the nineteenth century, there were some earlier settlements, or *antecedents*, which we must consider before we look at the greater wave of immigrants. Then, it is also important to point out that *new political and economic factors* – quite similar to those that affected the life of the Roman Catholic Church at the same time – were involved in the very process of opening up the continent to Protestant immigrants. The immigrants represented several different national origins and streams of Christian tradition. Therefore, after looking at *the first Protestant immigrants*, we must turn our attention to specific groups, such as *the Waldensians in Uruguay and Argentina*, the first *German Lutheran immigrants*, and some very different groups of *North American immigrants* – both African-Americans and Whites – coming to Latin America in the second half of the nineteenth century as a result of the racial tensions in the United States. Finally, in the twentieth century, *the Mennonites*, many of whom were fleeing difficult conditions in both North America and Russia, came to complete the picture as the last of the larger Protestant immigrant communities.

ANTECEDENTS

During the early years of the conquest and colonization, the Spanish and Portuguese ruled the seas, and thus they effectively prevented Protestant and other incursions into their colonies. Their policy, however, was not always successful. Ironically, in spite of stated policies, the first major incursion of Protestantism into South America took place under the umbrella of Spanish authority. Charles V had a sizable debt with the house of Welser. These bankers cancelled the debt in exchange for the privilege of colonizing what is now Venezuela. Among the German leaders of the resulting colony, founded in 1529, was a son of one of the signers of the Confession of Augsburg – the fundamental document of the Lutheran tradition – as well as many other Lutherans. Their purpose, however, was not to bring their faith to a new land but simply to gain wealth through the exploitation of the native population. Abuse and forced labor became the norm, with the natives being expected to produce gold in impossible amounts. When gold was not forthcoming, thousands – perhaps more than a million – were sold into slavery throughout the Caribbean, where the native population was dwindling. As these sources of income diminished, the colony declined and was finally abandoned in 1546.

In 1555, the French established a settlement in Brazil, near today's Rio de Janeiro. The enterprise was under the auspices of Admiral Gaspar de Coligny – known in France for his Protestant convictions and later a victim of the Massacre of Saint Bartholomew. Its leader was Vice Admiral Nicholas Durand de Villegagnon, who at first encouraged French and Swiss Protestants to join the enterprise and start missionary work among the native population. In 1556, a contingent of fourteen pastors and theological students from Geneva was sent by John Calvin. What they found in the new colony was not inspiring. Shortly after arriving, one of the pastors wrote that he had heard some of his countrymen boasting of their debauchery with the native population and even of having joined them in cannibalism. A few months after that, Villegagnon, no longer under Coligny's political patronage and perhaps in reaction to Huguenot criticism of his policies, banned Protestantism from the colony. Most Protestants returned to Europe, a few decided to leave the colony and settle among the native population, and three were condemned to death as heretics. Although many among the aboriginal population of the land supported the French against the Portuguese, by 1567 the latter had destroyed all remnants of the colony. Jean de Léry, one of the Genevan missionaries who chose to remain, left a fascinating account of the impact of European presence among the original population. Commenting on the Tupinambá tribe and their wisdom, and probably thinking of the words of Jesus to the effect that "the people of Nineveh will rise up at the judgment with this generation and condemn it" (Matthew 12:41), Léry declared that this tribe "will rise up in judgment against the plunderers who bear the name of Christians."[2]

Even after the end of the ill-fated Calvinist enterprise, other Protestants found their way to the coasts of South America, but they too did little for the conversion of the natives. Typical of these was Cornishman Peter Carder, who sailed with Francis Drake in his voyage of circumnavigation but was shipwrecked and lived for a time among the Indians in the River Plate region. Although himself a Protestant, Carder did not attempt to bring the natives to his religion. He became a leader among his hosts by teaching them European military methods and leading them into victorious battle with their traditional foes. The same is true of an Englishman by the name of Anthony Knivet, who was captured a few years later by Indians in Brazil. He lived for decades among the Indians, becoming a war leader and a slaver, and was repeatedly made a captive by either Indians or the Portuguese, until he finally returned to England. Both Carder and Knivet left written records of their adventures, the manner in which the Indians lived, and their response to attempts to evangelize them.

In 1562, and then in 1564, two French colonies were established on the coast of Florida, mostly as an attempt to halt Spanish expansion toward the north. Most of the settlers were Protestant. In 1565, the Spanish invaded the area and killed all the settlers – more than six hundred of them – except a few who declared themselves to be Catholic. A sign was left at the place of the massacre, declaring that they were killed "not as French, but as Lutherans." Some years later a friend of some of the victims – although a Catholic – organized an expedition that invaded the place, captured as many Spaniards as they could, and hanged them, leaving a sign that they were killed "not as Spaniards, but as traitors, thieves, and murderers."

The defeat of the Armada in 1588 began to change matters. Now the Spanish and Portuguese control of the seas was challenged by the British, Dutch, French, and others. Pirates and privateers patrolled the sea lanes in search of prey. On occasion, they would land and attack major cities such as Panama, Havana, and Cartagena. Quite often, if captured by the Spanish, these pirates and privateers were accused not of piracy but of heresy and turned over to the Inquisition. Somewhat later, the British began organizing massive attacks against Spanish colonies. In 1638, British buccaneers settled in Belize, which would eventually become an independent, Protestant, English-speaking

---

[2] Quoted in John Hemming, *Red Gold: The Conquest of the Brazilian Indians, 1500–1760* (Cambridge, MA: Harvard University Press, 1978), 16.

nation. Others settled along the coasts of Honduras and Nicaragua, where they established contacts with the Miskito people – many of whom became Protestant through their influence. The greatest British successes were in the Caribbean, where they took several islands – notably, Jamaica in 1655 – and in Florida, which the British received in 1763 in exchange for Havana – held by them since 1762. Likewise, the Dutch also entered the Caribbean, establishing colonies in Curacao, Aruba, Bonaire, and Surinam; and the Danes took possession of some of the Virgin Islands. In all these lands, Protestantism became the dominant religion, but the cultural and political changes also placed them apart from what is commonly considered Latin America. Meanwhile, the buccaneers known as "Brethren of the Coast" settled in Haiti and the nearby islands. Since many of these were French Huguenots who had joined the Brethren fleeing the changing political climate in France, one may say that there was a Protestant presence in Haiti by the 1660s – although religion did not play an important role in the life of most of the Brethren.

Meanwhile, as mentioned in Chapter 3, in 1624 the Dutch had invaded the region of Bahia in Brazil and from there continued expanding to the point that in 1635 they controlled more than a thousand miles along the coast. True to their heritage, the Dutch established a Reformed theocracy in which there was, however, a measure of religious tolerance. They also made significant efforts for the conversion of both the native population and African slaves. All this was possible because at the time Portugal was under Spanish rule and struggling for its own independence. Once this was attained, the Portuguese could turn their eyes once again toward Brazil and seek to evict the Dutch interlopers. This was finally achieved in 1654. The Dutch colony was destroyed, and there does not seem to be any connection between it and the various Reformed churches that now exist in the region.

In 1698, British financier William Paterson dreamed of establishing a colony on the isthmus of Panama, opening a canal between the Atlantic and the Pacific, and thus controlling world trade. He arrived there with more than a thousand settlers – mostly Presbyterian Scots. But the enterprise failed. By 1699, Paterson had returned to England, and the colony was terminated a year later.

In brief, during the entire colonial period Protestant presence in Latin America was sporadic and usually short-lived. It was mostly connected with colonial attempts by Protestant powers and with expeditions and settlements by pirates and corsairs. Those areas in the Caribbean and the Gulf of Mexico where the British, Dutch, and others were able to settle permanently became mostly Protestant, and from that point on their political and religious history was quite different from the rest of Latin America.

NEW POLITICAL AND ECONOMIC FACTORS

Although it is frequently asserted that one of the goals of Latin American independence was to curb the power of the Catholic Church and its clergy, this is not quite true. Of all the major leaders in the struggle for independence, only Simón Bolívar favored the separation of church and state. The rest – Miranda, Hidalgo, Morelos, Moreno, and San Martín, among others – believed that the ancient privileges of the church should be continued, and all agreed that Latin America should continue being Roman Catholic territory. What is true is that when the various nations declared their independence from Spain, most bishops and other prelates opposed it, while many of the local clergy favored independence. This is understandable if one remembers that, as a consequence of the patronato real, bishops were practically appointed by the crown and owed their loyalty to it. For the same reason, the upper echelons of the hierarchy were seldom available to the native born, particularly those lacking contacts in the centers of power in Spain. As a result, most bishops were peninsulares, while criollos tended to serve local parishes. Thus, when the wars of independence erupted, the official position of the Catholic Church was to oppose it.

Once independence was achieved, there was a general exodus of peninsulares – clergy as well as laity – returning to Spain. Power was now in the hands of criollos, for Indians and Blacks were generally excluded from it. As we have seen in Chapter 5, almost immediately after independence, the new criollo elite tended to divide into two parties, which in most countries were known as *conservadores* and *liberales*. The conservadores mostly represented the interests of the landed, whose wealth was based on agriculture and cheap labor. The liberales came mostly from the new and growing merchant class, whose model was the rich industrialized nations of the North Atlantic and for whom an educated and skilled labor force represented greater wealth. They supported free trade and in varying degrees the other freedoms usually associated with it – of speech, assembly, and worship. Conservadores opposed such freedoms, advocating for a more traditional ordering of society and therefore also for the ancient privileges of both the landed aristocracy and the clergy.

For several decades after independence, in most of the new republics the liberales had the upper hand, and governments developed ambitious programs to modernize their nations. They saw promoting immigration from the industrialized nations of the North Atlantic as a means of achieving this goal. One of the leading political thinkers of the liberal party in Argentina, Juan Bautista Alberdi (1810–1884), stated that *gobernar es poblar* – the best way to rule is to promote population growth. In his *Bases y puntos de partida para la organización de la República Argentina* (Bases and Starting Points for the Political Organization of the Argentine Republic), he argued that the nation needed immigrants in order to exploit the underpopulated and fertile lands of the interior, as well as to provide skilled labor for industry and a solid foundation for democracy. He also made it clear that in order to promote the sort of immigration he desired, it was necessary to guarantee religious freedom to prospective immigrants. In this regard, he proposed that "in order to educate our America in freedom and industry, it must be populated with people from that sector in Europe that is most advanced both in freedom and in industry."[3]

THE FIRST PROTESTANT IMMIGRANTS

Thus, the first wave of Protestant growth in Spain's former colonies was the result of immigration fostered by liberal governments whose leaders, while remaining Roman Catholic and having little theological sympathy toward Protestantism, felt that religious freedom was both a value in itself and a necessary concession to prospective immigrants.

As we have seen, the process by which Brazil became independent was somewhat different, but in this case, too, the first permanent Protestant communities were the result of immigration promoted – or at least authorized – by the government. In 1810, while Brazil was still in Portuguese hands, the Portuguese government signed a treaty with the United Kingdom that, among other things, guaranteed freedom of worship to British subjects living in Portuguese lands – including Brazil. The treaty stipulated, however, that the British would not seek the conversion of the Portuguese population, the architecture of their houses of worship would not make them look like churches, and they would refrain from public demonstrations of their faith. This general policy continued after independence, but when Pedro II became emperor of Brazil in 1840, his anticlerical and liberal sentiments led him to favor policies similar to those of the liberal governments of neighboring republics. He, too, fostered the immigration of Protestants and, in order both to promote such immigration and to be true to his own liberal principles, established policies of religious freedom.

So, even though the path followed by the former Spanish colonies was different from that of their Portuguese counterpart, in both cases Protestantism made its first permanent inroads as Protestant immigrants, usually invited

---

[3] As quoted in Pablo Alberto Deiros, *Historia del cristianismo en América Latina* (Buenos Aires: Fraternidad Teológica Latinoamericana, 1992), 619.

by governments, settled in the land. In 1819, following the guidelines of the treaty between the United Kingdom and Portugal, the Church of England dedicated in Rio de Janeiro the first Protestant church built in Latin America – although it did not look like a church. In 1820, nine British immigrants, apparently all Scots, celebrated in Buenos Aires what seems to have been the first Protestant service in Argentina. This was led by Bible Society representative James (Diego) Thomson, whose ministry will be discussed in the next chapter. By 1824, there were Anglican services being held regularly in Buenos Aires. A year later, Argentina signed with Great Britain its first foreign treaty, and this guaranteed freedom of worship to British subjects living on Argentine soil. By 1830, the British community in the city inaugurated its first church. Likewise, Anglicanism and Anglican houses of worship appeared throughout Latin America: Venezuela (1834), Chile (1837), Uruguay (1840), Costa Rica (1848), and Peru (1849).

During the early period after independence, most Protestant immigrants were British. This was the time when Great Britain and France vied with each other in their efforts to fill the vacuum left by Spain and Portugal as they lost their colonies. Indeed, it was at that time that some French authors began referring to the entire area as *l'Amerique Latine*, apparently in an effort to claim a certain kinship with it, because the French, too, speak a Romance language. The French, being mostly Catholic or nonreligious, did not demand that the newly born nations guarantee their freedom of worship, as did the British.

Although mostly English-speaking, not all British immigrants were Anglican. It is true that most of the early churches were Anglican, for they were built with financial support from England. But there were also large contingents of Scots, who were mostly Reformed, and of Welsh, who were mostly Methodist, Baptist, or Congregationalist. Thus, these churches, too, had an early start in the new republics. While most English immigrants settled in the cities, the Scots and Welsh most often moved inland, where they were given land and created small communities in which their language, religion, and traditions survived for generations. (To this day, in the oldest Methodist church in downtown Buenos Aires, there is a men's choir that, although singing in Spanish, is clearly patterned after the musical tradition that the Welsh brought to Patagonia in the 1860s.)

Thus, by the middle of the nineteenth century, there were in various parts of Latin America, but particularly in the Southern Cone – Argentina, Uruguay, Chile, and Southern Brazil – significant Protestants contingents, mostly English-speaking but from various Protestant traditions.

Soon other immigrant groups followed. While they represented much of the vast variety of cultures and religious traditions in Europe, those whose presence was felt most strongly, and whose churches eventually became most numerous, were the Italian Waldensians and German-speaking people from several different religious traditions – Lutheran, Reformed, and Mennonite.

THE WALDENSIANS IN URUGUAY AND ARGENTINA

Late in the twelfth century, in the city of Lyon, Peter Waldo and his "Poor Ones of Lyon" refused to obey the papal order to cease preaching. As a result, they were persecuted and had to hide in the secluded valleys of northern Italy and southern Switzerland, where they were known as Waldensians. There they led a life of isolation until, in the sixteenth century, they learned of the Protestant Reformation and adopted Reformed theology. Still, their life changed little, for they continued working the land in their isolated mountain communities, staying away from much contact with the nearby Italian society, which was mostly Roman Catholic.

This peace was perturbed in the early nineteenth century, not as a result of pressure or violence from their neighbors, but rather of the changing situation in the Alpine valleys themselves. Over the centuries, the Waldensian population had grown to the point that the arable land could hardly sustain it. There was no room for expansion into the encircling and forbidding mountains. Already in the 1840s, a slow process of emigration began, as young people sought agricultural work in southern France. This was staunchly resisted by the leaders of the community, who feared that contamination with the outside world would lead the emigrants to abandon their traditions and faith. Then, in the 1850s, disaster struck. A series of failed crops brought hunger and despair to the land. The leaders of the community were divided as to what course to take. Some saw large-scale, planned emigration as the only solution, while others rejected it as a sign of capitulation after so many centuries of dogged survival.

Eventually, as conditions worsened, the party favoring emigration won the debate. Word arrived from some of the earlier emigrants who had settled in Uruguay. They boasted about the fertility of the land, the healthy climate, and the opportunities that the liberal government then in power was offering immigrants. The first emigrant group, arriving in Uruguay in 1856, had only eleven prospective settlers. But the next year another 72 arrived, and 136 more in 1858. By the end of the century, there were almost four thousand Waldensians living in Uruguay in relatively small rural communities.

The process of settling in the new country was not as easy as the first settlers had promised. Yellow fever ravaged the entire county and with it the nascent Waldensian community. The Catholic priest in a neighboring parish incited his followers to violence against the "heretical" newcomers. The chaplain of the British Legation in Montevideo intervened with the government, which gave its representatives instructions to curb the priest's zeal. Still, the Waldensians moved to a more isolated region where many of their neighbors were British and Swiss immigrants.

Then conflict arose within the community itself. Its first pastor, who had arrived in 1861, insisted on his authority to the point that many felt he was trying to establish a theocracy. The British chaplain who had been their advocate before the government felt compelled to intervene, but the result was only greater dissension. Finally, in 1877, a new pastor arrived. His name was Armand Lugón, and many credit him with being the true founder of the Waldensian community in Uruguay. He worked to reconcile the warring factions – a goal that he eventually achieved. In 1879, as the land allotted to them became insufficient, he petitioned the president of Uruguay for more land, promising that the new colony to be founded there would require no financial support from the government or anyone else and would soon be a center of prosperity. He promoted the founding of primary schools – of which soon there were ten. In 1888, the Waldensians founded a junior college – a *liceo* – which was the first such school in rural areas and the first to admit both men and women.

Shortly thereafter, the Waldensian settlements began expanding beyond Uruguay itself, crossing the River Plate into Argentina. Here land tracts were more extensive, and the terms offered by the government were more favorable than in Uruguay. At first, this process, which began in 1901, was resisted by the Uruguayan Waldensians, who feared that their colonies would become depopulated and those crossing over into Argentina would not keep the faith and traditions as they did in Uruguay. Eventually, however, such suspicions were allayed, and the Waldensians on both sides of the River Plate saw themselves as a single church.

Interestingly, although in their native Italian valleys the Waldensians were a conservative group, staunchly resistant to change, in Uruguay and Argentina they became innovators and inventors. The agricultural methods they had employed for centuries in the Alpine valleys were not appropriate for the vast lands in their new homeland. In response to the challenge, they invented and built farm machinery and experimented with new methods of cultivation. To this day, the descendants of those early settlers run a center for agricultural experimentation and education that makes a significant contribution to the economy of rural Uruguay.

When they embraced the Reformed faith, the Waldensians also embraced that tradition's emphasis on the education of pastors. Paradoxically, in Latin America this resulted in a church that was mostly led by laity, for pastors had to come from Europe and their number was always insufficient. This in turn led to conflicts between the ordained ministry and the laity, for very few ministers were native born, and those sent from Europe had little understanding of the dynamics of their parishioners' lives or the history and circumstances of the Waldensian colonies that dotted the countryside. In 1926, however, the Waldensians began sending their native candidates for ordination to the *Facultad Evangélica de Teología* in Buenos Aires – later known as *Instituto Superior de Estudios Teológicos* (ISEDET). This provided the church with a growing cadre of ordained ministers who had emerged from the Waldensian settlements themselves and were cognizant, not only of life in those communities but also of issues affecting the entire nation – be it Uruguay or Argentina.

The growth of the Waldensian Church in the River Plate area was such that it soon became evident that it was no longer a mission or an extension of the mother church in the Alps. In 1965, the River Plate region was authorized by the mother church to have its own governing *Mesa Valdense* – Waldensian Table – much as the church in the Alps had a *Tavola Valdense*. Less than ten years later, the entire Waldensian community on both sides of the Atlantic took the unusual step of declaring that they were governed by a single synod, whose first session took place in the New Word in February and the second in the old country in August.

By then, Spanish was rapidly surpassing Italian and French as the language of worship in the Waldensian churches in Latin America. Immigration had all but ceased, as free land was no longer available and as both Argentina and Uruguay went through protracted and repeated political and economic crises. While many churches still conducted services in both Spanish and Italian, and while some of the older generations still spoke the old tongue at home, culturally and linguistically the Waldensian community was becoming integrated into its Latin American host nations.

This process of integration into the surrounding society had two major consequences. First, it opened the Waldensian Church to people who were not of Waldensian origin, thus posing for the church itself the challenge of evangelizing its neighbors. This was the result and the cause of growing assimilation of Waldensians into the culture, for the church was no longer identified as an immigrant, isolated community.

Second, the process of integration into the surrounding society meant also that the Waldensian Church was not immune to the struggles that polarized all of Latin American Protestantism, particularly during the decade of the 1960s. As in other churches, one group accused the other of being immoderately conservative and not caring for the plight of the poor, while the other retaliated with the contention that its critics were Communists, intent on establishing Communist regimes in Latin America. However, since such polarization took place in most churches, we will discuss it later, in Chapter 8.

GERMAN LUTHERAN IMMIGRATION

Almost as soon as independence was declared, significant numbers of German-speaking people settled in the new nations. While many of these came from Germany itself, others came from Austria, Switzerland, and even Russia. Most of these early immigrants were Lutheran, although there was also a significant number of people of Reformed (Calvinist) convictions. Later, as conditions in Canada and elsewhere became difficult for the Mennonites, there was also a large influx of German-speaking Mennonites, particularly into Paraguay and some areas of Bolivia and Argentina.

The first large and organized contingent of German immigrants to Latin America arrived in Brazil in 1824, under the auspices of the imperial crown – Brazil was then a recently declared independent empire under the leadership of Pedro I. The new nation needed cheap labor both for its existing plantations and emerging industry and to colonize its vast territories. Thanks to British pressure, and particularly to the intervention of the British navy, the slave trade had practically disappeared. The Indians in Brazil, when pressed into forced labor, simply fled into the hinterlands. Germans were brought in, not as a means to educate the populace, as Alberdi would later propose in Argentina, but simply as cheap labor in substitution for the dwindling slave trade. In this they presented a sharp contrast with the early British immigrants, who were mostly merchants and professionals. Thus, while the Anglican Church in Rio de Janeiro represented privilege, the nascent Lutheran churches in the interior of Brazil were quite the opposite.

The group that arrived in 1824 comprised forty-three persons, mostly Lutherans, and among them was their pastor. They settled in the state of Rio Grande do Sul, where they founded the settlement – still in existence – of São Leopoldo, named in honor of the Brazilian Empress Leopoldina of Habsburg. Since the Indians resisted the settlers, the latter followed a policy of extermination, which they justified with the claim that the Indians were less than human – while they themselves were considered inferior by the ruling Brazilian elite.

These early settlers also faced serious disadvantages. The climate was very different than what they had known all their lives. This required different crops and methods of agriculture, which many were not eager to learn. Disease decimated them. Although they had been invited to immigrate and thus increase the labor force, and although they were granted religious tolerance, the laws of the land still placed them under severe handicaps. Their marriages were not considered legal, and therefore all their children were technically illegitimate. They were not allowed to marry Catholics unless they first renounced their faith. It was not until the Constitution of 1891 that these immigrants – some of them having arrived seven decades earlier – were granted full religious freedom.

Even though firmly settled in Brazil, these immigrants and their descendants continued speaking German and celebrating their services in that language for generations – thus keeping themselves apart from their Brazilian neighbors. Furthermore, as they began organizing themselves, they did so on the basis of regionalisms they had brought from the Old World, thus resulting in a variety of synods competing with each other. (Scandinavian immigrants, although fewer, followed the same pattern, with separate churches and judicatories for Danes, Swedes, and the like.) Circumstances became more difficult for the German immigrant church with the rise of the "German Christians" in Germany and the tendency of many in Brazil to embrace Nazism as part of the Gospel and God's purpose for the German "race." They were opposed by a group led by younger pastors, many of whom found their inspiration in the Confessing Church of Germany and the writings and life of Dietrich Bonhoeffer. Eventually, having had to face bitter struggles on the matter of its own identity, the church that emerged from them was more engaged with the Brazilian reality and more committed to the welfare of the entire nation than before. In 1949, a federation of the various synods was organized, and in 1968 this finally led to a single organization that included most Lutherans in Brazil. This, however, was not achieved without much pain. Some still insisted on the German character of the church, while others countered that the church had a mission in Brazil that could not be accomplished as long as the church remained an ethnic enclave. As in other Latin American churches, dissension arose over social issues and the church's response to them. Particularly during the decades of the 1960s and 1970s, the church was deeply divided over these matters.

At the beginning of the twentieth century, the largest Lutheran body in Brazil – the *Igreja Evangélica da Confissão Luterana do Brasil* (Evangelical Church of the Lutheran Confession of Brazil) – had about a million members, and the *Igreja Evangélica Luterana do Brasil* (Evangelical Lutheran Church of Brazil) – which resulted from a schism in 1890 – had almost a quarter of a million. It is important to remember, however, that not all of these are descendants of German or Scandinavian immigrants, for both of these churches have also grown as the result of missionary work.

In the remote interior of Venezuela, a contingent of almost four hundred Germans – most of them Lutheran – settled in 1834. There they maintained their language and traditions for generations. Eventually, Lutheran missionaries arrived from overseas, which led to greater ties with the surrounding society and to inviting Spanish-speaking Venezuelans to join the community. At the end of the twentieth century, Lutherans were still a small minority in Venezuela. The *Consejo Luterano de Venezuela* (Lutheran Council of Venezuela) had some four thousand members, and the other main body – the *Iglesias Luteranas de Venezuela* (Lutheran Churches of Venezuela) – was about the same size.

In Argentina, the provincial government of Buenos Aires established a policy of promoting German immigration. Here too, as in Brazil, the early German arrivals made common cause with the Anglicans. But as more Germans arrived and social distinctions developed between them and the British, the Germans began founding their own churches (1845) and organizing schools and other instruments for the preservation of their culture and religious traditions. As German settlements and congregations grew, they began establishing systems of government linking them. This led to the Evangelical German Synod of the River Plate, organized in 1899 and comprising churches in Argentina, Uruguay, and Paraguay. As in Brazil, the growth of Nazism presented a serious challenge for the German immigrant community in the River Plate, for many who had linked their faith very closely with their cultural tradition and ethnic origins now saw Nazism as a positive development. And, again as in Brazil, this led to bitter disagreements until Nazism was defeated and its horrors were unmasked. After that time, often having joined forces with churches that had evolved out of Lutheran missions, immigrant churches in Argentina began opening themselves to the society and culture around them – even though many of its members did not favor this development.

At the beginning of the twenty-first century, there were in Argentina eight main Lutheran bodies, most of immigrant origin, but most with a substantial part of their membership resulting from missionary and evangelistic work. German had waned as the language of choice among the descendants of the early immigrants, and as a result most churches conducted their worship in Spanish – or at least bilingually. Among the eight main Lutheran churches, the Scandinavian bodies – Norwegian, Swedish, and Danish – were much smaller, and in general their assimilation into Argentine society and culture had not advanced as much as with the churches of German origin. At any rate, all the Lutheran bodies together had a membership of approximately one hundred thousand. (Other immigrant groups still had their small congregations. The Welsh church, for instance, had slightly more than a thousand members.)

In Chile, the earliest German immigration was composed of merchants, professionals, and, in general, middle-class people who settled mostly in the region of Valparaiso. This small contingent collaborated with the Anglicans, and their most significant achievement was the establishment of a joint Protestant cemetery in that area. This situation changed after the European revolutions of 1848, when large numbers of Germans sought land elsewhere. Thus, while German professionals continued emigrating to Chile, there were now larger numbers of rural people looking for land to till. The Chilean government gave them lands in the southern reaches of the nation, where it was unable to exert control over territories nominally under its rule. Most of these lands were south of the Bío-Bío River – the ancient southern limit of the Inca empire. In these areas, German Lutheran communities continue to this day, although their growth has not been as marked as in Brazil or Argentina.

NORTH AMERICAN IMMIGRANTS

The next large contingent of Protestant immigrants to Latin America were North Americans who decided to leave the United States for reasons connected with the racial issues being debated at the time. Indeed, during the nineteenth century there were many more North Americans emigrating to Latin America than vice versa.

The first to leave were African-Americans who sought refuge in the black republics that had been founded in Hispaniola – Haiti and the Dominican Republic – in order to escape from the racist policies of their native land.

In what is now the Dominican Republic, most of the African-American immigrants were Methodist. The land had been conquered in 1822 by Haiti, and in 1824 the president of Haiti, Jean-Pierre Boyer, decided to follow the lead of other Latin American governments by promoting immigration. He hoped that this would improve agriculture, increase the population, and also counteract the nationalist Dominican spirit, which resented the Haitian invasion. He turned to the United States, inviting African-American settlers to come to the island and settle in its Spanish-speaking area. As Methodists, their connections eventually were mostly with the African Methodist Episcopal (AME) Church.

These immigrants soon began missionary work among their neighbors and were assimilated into the rest of the population to the point that, when the Dominicans finally expelled the Haitians from their territory in 1844, the settlers were allowed to stay, for they were considered citizens of the Dominican Republic. Eventually their descendants became part of the *Iglesia Evangélica Dominicana* (Dominican Evangelical Church) – to which we will return in the next chapter.

Something similar, but much more dramatic, happened in Haiti. Already at the beginning of the nineteenth century there were sufficient African-American expatriates in Haiti that the British Methodists decided to send chaplains to take care of the spiritual needs of the expatriate colony. However, it was after the Civil War in the United States that the first large contingents of expatriates came to Haiti in search of greater freedom and better living conditions. One of these was led by James Theodore Holly, an Episcopal clergyman who had previously visited the island with a view to establishing missionary work there. Now, in 1861, Holly and 109 other African-Americans migrated to Haiti with a dual purpose: better living conditions for themselves and their families and preaching the Gospel on the island. The first few months were tragic. In a year and a half, forty-three of the settlers died – mostly from malaria and typhoid. Holly's own family was reduced from eight to three members. At that point, most of the survivors decided to leave, some for Jamaica and others back to the United States. The settlement was then reduced to twenty persons, led by Holly.

In spite of such tragic beginnings, Holly's work prospered. The mission among the Haitians grew, and other immigrants from the United States joined Holly's group. When the Episcopal bishop of Delaware visited Haiti late in 1863, he found that Holly had prepared three dozen people – immigrants and Haitians – for confirmation, and that he was training a cadre of future pastors. By 1874, the Episcopal Church in the United States was ready to grant independence to the nascent church, the Apostolic Orthodox Haitian Church, and in 1876 Holly was consecrated as its first bishop. When Holly died in 1911, his followers in Haiti asked to become part of the church in the United States, as a missionary district. By then, most of its membership was Haitian, and its services were held in creole or in French.

Significantly, while the churches founded in Latin America by European settlers did not believe that part of their mission was to address their neighbors with their faith, and therefore they long remained ethnic churches, those founded in Hispaniola – the Dominican Republic and Haiti – by African-American settlers followed an entirely different course. From the very outset, they had the dual purpose of seeking a better life for the settlers themselves and preaching the Gospel to their neighbors. As a result, they became assimilated much more rapidly and thoroughly than most other immigrant churches.

Also in the nineteenth century, mostly as a result of the defeat of the Confederate States of America in the Civil War, a number of southern white North Americans emigrated to Brazil. By moving to Brazil, where slavery was still legal, they hoped to reproduce the style of life they had lost in the American south. Some of them, refusing to accept the emancipation of slaves in the United States and free their slaves as the law now required, brought their slaves with them and tried to build in Brazil plantations similar to those they had owned in the lands of the Confederacy. The first such settlers arrived in Brazil in 1866, and other contingents continued arriving during the time of Reconstruction in the former Confederacy. Among these immigrants were Methodists, Baptists, and Presbyterians – the latter being the most numerous. Since each of these denominations had divided as a result of the tensions leading to the Civil War in the United States, their southern branches were very sympathetic with the cause of these staunch southerners who decided to emigrate and provided them material as well as spiritual support.

As we will see in the next chapter, these immigrants – particularly the Presbyterians – were soon joined by missionaries from their own denominations, and this often led to conflicts between the churches founded by missionaries and those resulting from immigration.

THE MENNONITES

The Mennonites were the last major wave of Protestant immigrants into Latin America. As a result, there are Mennonite colonies in Mexico, Bolivia, Argentina, and Belize, but above all in Paraguay, where they have made a significant impact on the country as a whole. This wave of immigration began in 1926, first with immigrants from Canada and then with others from Russia.

The Mennonites had first settled in Russia in 1789, fleeing from persecution in Western Europe and seeking a place where they could practice their religion, keep their traditions, and abstain from violence. As they migrated into that land, they were promised the freedom to continue their religious practices – much to the chagrin of some leaders of the Russian Orthodox Church, who feared the "contagion" of heresy. There they lived for generations, running their own communities and schools with little interference from the outside world. Then, in 1870, conditions changed drastically. The Russian government launched a program of "Russification" that threatened some of the most cherished elements in Mennonite life. The expectation that all Russians would be part of the Orthodox Church was part of this program. In 1873, fearing the course of events in Russia, a Mennonite delegation to Ottawa obtained from the Canadian government the guarantee that Mennonite immigrants would be allowed to continue observing their religious practices and running their own schools. This contrasted with the growing difficulties Mennonites were facing in Russia. In 1881, the Russian government decreed that all the population in Russia was subject to conscription into military service, which made it very difficult for Mennonites to continue their traditional practice of abstaining from all violence and, in particular, from war. Then the government issued new laws on education that threatened the independent schools in which Mennonites had traditionally educated their children and taught them their ways and traditions. By then, more that seventeen thousand had fled the country for North America – ten thousand settling in the United States and seven thousand in Canada. Naturally, as new laws of Russification were enacted, more Mennonites followed that earlier contingent. In the Canadian province of Manitoba, they were given almost half a million acres of rich lands just north of the border with the United States. Others settled in Saskatchewan. There they prospered until World War I.

The war convinced many Canadians that they had been too lax with these immigrants who insisted on their own language and customs and refused to join in the military effort. Their schools were now required to raise the national flag – which for many Mennonites was a military symbol. They also had to teach in English. Their traditional practice of religious education in their schools was no longer tolerated. Once more, many Mennonites felt that they had been betrayed and that the new laws were a breach of promise on the part of the Canadian government.

This led to a renewed exodus. Beginning in 1922, many left for new settlements in Mexico. But the great migration began in 1926, and its goal was the Southern Chaco in Paraguay. The Paraguayan government was interested in populating that region, which was in dispute with Bolivia. In that dispute, which the League of Nations was trying to settle, each party claimed that the other had no real interest in the region and had done little to develop it. The Paraguayan government saw the prospect of Mennonite settlements in the area as a way to strengthen its claim and therefore offered the Canadian Mennonites both land and guarantees that their traditional customs would not be challenged. This included exemption from military service. In 1926, some three thousand people left Canada for the far reaches of Paraguay. Along the way, 168 died and 335 others desisted and returned to Canada. Thus, the early settlers numbered about 2,500. They named their first colony Menno, after the founder of the movement. This initial colony was reinforced by other immigrants from Canada, so that soon it had nine thousand members.

The early Mennonite settlers, who went to Paraguay fleeing the militarization of Canada, soon had reason to question their decision. The tensions between Bolivia and Paraguay, which had moved the latter nation to encourage settlers in the Chaco, rapidly grew worse. In 1928, a series of skirmishes began between Paraguayan and Bolivian outposts in the Chaco. In response, both countries increased their armed forces in the area. Although both the League of Nations and the Pan-American Union tried to mediate, war broke out in 1932. Hostilities continued until 1935, and by then the toll was more than one hundred thousand soldiers dead and many others wounded or maimed. Throughout the conflict the Paraguayan government kept its promise of not drafting the recently arrived Mennonites into the army. But the battlefields were generally near the territory where the Mennonites had settled, and thus they were not protected from the horrors of war. In those circumstances, while refusing to take arms, the Mennonites gained the respect of their fellow Paraguayans by their works of mercy, taking care of the wounded and the displaced. Thus, although finding themselves in the midst of a war that had little to do with them, the new immigrants came out of that conflict with greater assurance that they would not be forced into the military and that their lands, schools, and traditions would be respected.

When they learned of these developments, Mennonites in Russia, whose difficulties had increased with the advent of Communism, also began emigrating to Paraguay. Between 1930 and 1947, four colonies were established in the Chaco area by Russian Mennonite immigrants. Others continued arriving from Canada in the 1940s to the 1960s. Beginning in 1969, many of the more conservative Mennonites who had settled in Mexico in 1922, and who now felt that modern Mexico did not provide the necessary conditions to keep their traditions, also moved to the remoter areas of Paraguay. Finally, between 1967 and 1982, five more colonies were founded by conservative Mennonites – mostly Amish – from the United States.

The native population near the Mennonite settlements was sparse, with many nomads and collectors. When the Mennonites arrived, they found that the life of their neighbors was precarious. It had always been so, and during the nineteenth and early twentieth centuries, the Indians had been decimated by diseases imported from Europe for which they had little or no resistance. Now, with the Chaco War, contacts with soldiers who brought small-pox with them, combined with malnutrition and violence, led to increased mortality and misery.

In response to that situation, some of the Mennonites – particularly those in the firmly established colonies of Menno and Fernheim – felt that their Christian duty was to respond to the needs of their neighbors. Schools, clinics, centers for the treatment of leprosy, and programs to teach agricultural methods were soon established. As this work became known abroad, support began arriving – in the form of both funds and personnel – from Mennonites elsewhere, particularly in the United States. Mostly in order to promote cooperation in service to their neighbors, the various communities joined in 1967 in the *Vereinigung der Mennonitengemeinden von Paraguay* (Union of Mennonite Communities of Paraguay). The facilities for education and health offered by the work of the Mennonites in the area, coupled with the economic development of the region, brought many of the formerly nomadic population to settlements near the Mennonites and also attracted a significant number of Guaraní Indians – the dominant language group in Paraguay – to the Chaco region. By the year 2000, Mennonites in Paraguay reported that there were twenty-four thousand Indians living in twelve settlements, most of them near the older German Mennonite settlements. Of these, about 8,500 had been baptized into the Mennonite community. However, since the descendants of immigrants continued using German as their language both at home and in worship, the two ethnic groups were not fully integrated.

Mention has been made of the economic development of the region. At first, the Mennonite settlers were content with an economy of subsistence and self-sufficiency. Eventually, however, roads were built to connect the settlements among themselves. When the Trans-Chaco highway was built, it gave the Mennonites access to markets – particularly to Asuncion, the capital of Paraguay. At that point, their dairy industry, which they had developed much earlier as a means of subsistence, became their main source of income – and many Mennonites also saw it as a way of improving the diet of the general population of Paraguay. Cooperatives were organized, and large factories were built for the production of cheese, yogurt, powdered milk, and other dairy products. Today, the dairy industry in Paraguay is largely in the hands of Mennonites, who now export their products to other nearby nations.

CONCLUSION

In much of Latin America – particularly in Brazil and the Southern Cone – one of the origins of Protestantism was immigration from Protestant nations. This was fostered by liberal governments that saw in such immigration a way to counterbalance the influence of political and economic conservatism and Tridentine Catholicism. These were generally the same governments that invited and protected Protestant missionaries. This they did for the same reasons that led them to promote Protestant immigration. Thus, although in many ways different, the two original sources of Protestantism in Latin America – immigration and missions – were closely related. Indeed, they were more closely related than either the immigrants or the missionaries realized.

In the view of many among the immigrants and the missionaries themselves, there was a sharp contrast between these two origins of Protestantism, leading to two very different forms of Protestantism and church. Many of the missionaries came from the revival movements sweeping North America – and also Europe, although to a lesser extent. They were convinced that the primary task of every Christian was to witness to others and seek their conversion. Many also believed that Christian living was demonstrated by abstaining from such things as alcohol, tobacco, and dancing. From the perspective of these missionaries and their converts, immigrant churches lacked evangelistic zeal. They seemed content with ministering to their own people and letting the religion of the surrounding society go unchallenged and unquestioned. Furthermore, some of them – particularly Lutherans and Anglicans – seemed too close to Roman Catholicism. Although they conducted their services in their own languages, and in this they differed from the Latin mass, what they actually did and said in those services was very close to what Catholics did and said at mass. And they drank and danced! If from this point of view Roman Catholics were little less than pagans, Lutherans and Anglicans were little less than Catholics!

Similar prejudices existed on the part of many of the immigrants – particularly those, such as the Lutherans, Anglicans, and Scottish Presbyterians, who came from countries where there was a close and official connection between church and state. In those countries, the state churches had long been suspicious of what they called the "free churches" – that is, churches that did not have nor wish to have the support of the state and insisted on their own freedom of worship and organization. From their perspective, Protestant missionaries and evangelists were often seen as fanatics with no understanding of the best of Christian tradition and threatening to upset the delicate balance that the immigrants had achieved with the surrounding Roman Catholic society.

Ironically, circumstances in Latin America changed many of these paradigms and preconceptions. What in other lands were state churches in Latin America had to take on some of the characteristics of free churches, and what elsewhere had been free churches took on some of the characteristics of state churches. Anglican immigrants, for instance, were at first closely related to and supported by the Church of England. But as time went by, their descendants increasingly had to rely on their own resources, thus coming to resemble what in England were free churches. The traditional Anglican position was that in each country there ought to be a single national church. But now Anglicans in Latin America found that their very existence contradicted that position. Furthermore, even though originally conceived as "chaplaincy services" for English expatriates, the passing of time produced new generations that began asking what was the mission of their church in the wider, non-English society. This inevitably led to what an earlier generation of immigrants would have called "proselytizing" and the newer generations called "evangelization."

However, some churches that were born as free churches, and for whom such freedom was part of their identity, took on some of the characteristics of state churches. Since immigration was fostered by the state, it was inevitable that immigrant free churches, such as the Mennonites of Paraguay, be recognized by the state. The Mennonites would not settle in Paraguay without certain guarantees by the state – freedom to worship according to their traditions, exemption from military service, freedom to educate their children in their own schools and according to their customs, exemption from all oaths, and so forth. From the very beginning, this required a relationship with the state that had not been possible nor desirable for Menno Simon and his early followers. Furthermore, once settled in the Southern Chaco, distant from the capital and allowed to organize their own society, the Mennonite settlements became their own government – thus coming to resemble, albeit in a much smaller scale, the state churches of Europe!

These ironies, contradictions, and tensions were complicated by the presence in Latin America of a different sort of Protestantism – one that was not the result of immigration but of missionary endeavors from outside the continent. To these we must now turn.

8

~

An Expanding Protestant Presence

The new conditions that created so many problems for the Roman Catholic Church after independence (Chapter 5) and led to the promotion of immigration from Protestant nations (Chapter 7) also opened the way for the first Protestant missionaries. Liberal governments seeking to counterbalance the influence of the Catholic Church and conservative elements saw in Protestantism a tool for their own political ends. Thus they accepted, and sometimes even promoted and invited, not only Protestant immigrants but also the presence of Protestant missionaries in the hope that their work would undermine conservatism. The political leaders who thus contributed to Protestant penetration into Latin America had no inclination to become Protestants themselves – in fact, most remained active within the Catholic Church, even though in constant tension with its hierarchy.

The very process of independence and its aftermath had also awakened interest in Latin America first in Great Britain, and then in the United States. In Great Britain, the Latin American wars of independence were seen as a valiant struggle against the obscurantism and totalitarian tendencies of Spain, and therefore a number of Britons – including some aristocratic and rich adventurers – crossed the Atlantic in order to join the insurgent armies. In the United States, that nation's own struggle for independence was the window through which many looked at various similar struggles in Latin America. And this sentiment was also reflected among many of the Latin American insurgents, who eventually promulgated constitutions patterned after the Constitution of the United States.

As the United States gained prominence in the world, many of its citizens were convinced that this presented the nation with the burden and the opportunity to promote similar systems of government throughout the hemisphere. This became most apparent in the Monroe Doctrine (1823), which declared the entire hemisphere off-limits to European colonialism but also implied that the new Latin American nations would be under U.S. tutelage and direction. Somewhat later (1846), the notion of the "manifest destiny" of the United States was first proposed. This contributed to the war with Mexico and the expansion of the United States to the Pacific. The same notion was also used later to justify repeated interventions in various Latin American countries – interventions depicted as part of a historic mission to defend and promote democracy throughout the hemisphere.

Even before these events, developments in U.S. religion had prepared that nation for a vast missionary enterprise into Latin America. The American Board of Commissioners for Foreign Missions was founded in 1810, and the American Bible Society in 1816. Although originally both were interested primarily in Asia, the constant news from neighboring Latin America promoted an interest in mission to its new nations. This seemed particularly urgent since Latin American Roman Catholicism was depicted by many Protestants in the United States not only as obscurantist but also as a syncretistic mix that was more pagan than Christian. To this was added the impetus of a religious revival, known as the Second Great Awakening, that swept through the United States from 1795 to 1835 – precisely at a time when the future shape of the newly born Latin American nations seemed to be in the balance. Thus, as the nineteenth century progressed, the number of North American Protestant missionaries to Latin America increased, while the number of British missionaries decreased.

Marked as they were by the impact of the Second Great Awakening, Protestant missions to Latin America reflected the complexity of that movement in the United States. After originating among some of the most educated church leaders in the United States, the revival spread to the masses and by 1801, at the time of the famous Cane Ridge revival, already had a markedly antiintellectual bent. By 1826, it had also led to the founding of the American Society for the Promotion of Temperance. As a result, all of these tendencies and emphases were present in the Protestantism planted in Latin America by U.S. missionaries. Thus, while many of the earlier missionaries presented themselves as promoters of a more advanced form of Christianity and higher and better education than was generally available in Latin America, eventually many of the churches founded by them were swept into the fundamentalist wave that overtook a vast part of North American Christianity in the late nineteenth century.

There was also among some Protestants in the North Atlantic strong resistance to the idea of Protestant missions in Latin America. This was particularly true within the Anglican communion, in which many Anglo-Catholics held that most of Latin America was already a Christian continent and therefore missions to Latin America amounted to proselytism among Christians. The main concessions that Anglicanism in general made regarding its presence in Latin America had to do, first, with providing chaplaincy services to the expatriate British communities in various nations and, second, with missions among the indigenous populations that had not been touched by Roman Catholicism. The latter was done reluctantly, since many Anglicans considered all of Latin America the preserve of Roman Catholicism. In general, Anglican opposition to missionary work in Latin America continued into the early twentieth century, to the point that when the First World Missionary Conference gathered in Edinburgh in 1910, it was necessary to exclude Latin America from the agenda in order to make it possible for Anglicans and some others to participate.

Even so, by the middle of the nineteenth century the Protestant missionary enterprise was present in every country in Latin America. This had resulted in the founding of relatively small Protestant churches as well as schools and other social service institutions in every country. Still, quite often these churches and their members were influential beyond their numbers, for many of them had been formed in excellent schools founded by missionaries. By the beginning of the twentieth century, it was apparent that collaboration among various denominations – although not yet with the Catholic Church – was necessary in order to avoid competition and duplication of efforts. Later in that century, however, Protestants, as well as Catholics, became polarized over issues of church and society – one group accusing the other of Communist leanings, and the other accusing it of supporting injustice and oppression. Eventually, toward the end of the twentieth century and early in the twenty-first, most of these tensions were overcome in favor of a wider ecumenical vision and greater consensus on the role of Christians and their churches in society.

Seeking to summarize these various developments, this chapter will begin with three instances that exemplify *the beginnings* of Protestant missions in Latin America, paying particular attention to *the role of Bible societies*. We will then turn to the first Protestant *missions among the original inhabitants* of the land, then to how *political issues* affected the development of Protestantism, and next to the *institutional development* resulting from those beginnings and that political context. In the next section, we will discuss how Protestantism was affected by the *time of unrest* brought about first by social revolution and then by the Cold War. We will then pay some attention to the *ecumenical beginnings* in a number of continent-wide conferences, national councils, joint programs of education, and other similar enterprises. Finally, taking into account some of the developments within Roman Catholicism as well as the growth of Pentecostalism (with which we will deal in Chapter 10), we will see signs of a quest for new roles for traditional Protestantism.

THE BEGINNINGS

The forerunner of Protestant mission in Latin America – arriving in most countries just as independence was taking hold – was the Scotsman James Thomson, generally known in Latin America as "Diego" Thomson. He first came to Latin America as a representative of the British and Foreign School Society and the educational method it proposed. This was the "Lancasterian method," named after the Quaker Joseph Lancaster, who was not its creator but promoted it widely. In essence, this was a method of education in which students became tutors and mentors for other students, thus learning by teaching and making it possible for an entire school to be run with a single teacher. This was particularly attractive to the newly established Latin American governments, whose liberal ideology led them to consider public education as one of their highest priorities but who lacked the resources – in both money and personnel – to make education widely available. In 1810, Bolívar and fellow Venezuelan patriot Francisco Miranda had visited Lancaster in order to learn of his method – and in 1824, at the invitation of Bolívar, Lancaster himself settled in Venezuela, where he lived for three years.

Planning to reach Venezuela eventually, Diego Thomson first went to Buenos Aires (1818). Since the Lancasterian method used the Bible as its main text, Thomson took steps to see that some selected biblical passages were available to students following this method. Some seven months after his arrival in Buenos Aires, he contacted the British and Foreign Bible Society requesting that copies of the New Testament in Spanish be sent to him. Later he also requested one hundred copies of the Bible and two hundred of the New Testament in Portuguese, because he was beginning to have success getting them into Brazil. (Given his wide interests, and the variety of immigrants present in Argentina, he also requested a smaller number of copies in German, French, and Italian.) He was well received by the liberal elements in Buenos Aires, including many priests and friars who sought greater opening to new ideas. Thus his first school was organized in the facilities of a Franciscan monastery and had the support of the provincial of the order. His work was also encouraged by Bernardino Rivadavia, a social reformer who eventually became president of Argentina. Shortly after his arrival, Thomson reported:

> There was one important difficulty, but it was soon overcome. It was a matter of removing the confusing lessons – and worse than confusing – that were being used in public schools and managing to introduce lessons consisting in selections from Sacred Scripture. I did prepare such lessons as I wished to be introduced, selecting from the Old and New Testaments those sections that I considered most adequate for the instruction of children and for their

understanding. When I presented them before the government, they were accepted without any ecclesiastical oversight, and the order was given that they be printed in the government press and at its expense, in order to be used in public schools. This was quite a liberal decision, considering that the compiler was both a Protestant and a foreigner.[1]

Even so, there were difficulties. The political unrest of the nation, which eventually led to civil war, channeled the interest of government authorities toward more pressing matters, and Thomson complained that it seemed impossible to get them to make decisions on his suggestions and requests. Although the more liberal members of the clergy regarded his work with favor, this was not always the case with others who feared that Thomson was bringing heresy into the nation. Already in 1821 there was a debate in the city council of Buenos Aires as to whether Thomson's work should be allowed, for there was a possibility that in the Lancasterian schools "custom and religion are attacked."[2] The following year, five hundred copies of the New Testament sent by the American Bible Society were held by the authorities, on the grounds that they did not have explanatory notes showing the connection between the biblical text and Catholic doctrine.

While promoting the Lancasterian method, Thomson also gathered a small number of immigrants and in 1820 led them in the first Protestant service ever held in Buenos Aires – not counting services held by invading British troops in 1806 to 1807. At first that group established connections with the Presbyterian Church, but eventually became the nucleus of the Methodist Church in Argentina. Thomson also reported many cases in which his work was having an impact. He cited, for instance, the case of Cualli Piachepolon, a Patagonian chieftain who had found a New Testament on a visit to Buenos Aires and was now communicating its teaching to his people. He also reported of merchants, military officers, and others who had taken upon themselves the task of distributing the Bible.

Early in 1821, Thomson received an official invitation from the government of Chile to establish Lancasterian schools in that nation. His friends in Argentina, as well as government officials, tried to dissuade him. Thomson himself was chagrined to be leaving a country where he had met significant success and where he had not remained for long. But he was convinced that

---

[1] Letter from Buenos Aires, July 26, 1820, published in the British journal *Evangelical Christendom* (1847): 252, as quoted in Arnoldo Canclini, *Diego Thomson: Apóstol de la enseñanza y distribución de la Biblia en América Latina y España* (Buenos Aires: Asociación Sociedad Bíblica Argentina, 1987), 32.

[2] Actas del Extinguido Cabildo de Buenos Aires (March 16, 1821), as quoted in Canclini, *Diego Thomson*, 37.

this was a call from God and prepared to depart. At that point, in recognition for his work in the nascent nation, he was granted honorary Argentine citizenship. He left behind a small group gathering regularly for worship, hundreds of Bibles, and a number of schools –not more than sixteen – that had been reformed according to the Lancasterian method. He also left a Lancasterian Society that continued his work, so that five years later he could report that there were now a hundred such schools with some five thousand students and that five hundred New Testaments had recently been distributed through these schools and their students.

Thomson arrived in Santiago in June of 1821, after a delay in Valparaiso because he had become ill during the voyage around the Horn. He brought with himself sixty copies of the New Testament in Spanish. When customs officials tried to stop them so they could be examined by the rather conservative bishop, Thomson explained that he had been invited by the government in order to promote the Lancasterian method of education. This persuaded the custom officials to allow the importation of the books he brought with him. In Santiago, he was enthusiastically received by Bernando O'Higgins, then head of the Chilean government, and he was soon assigned a large classroom in the university where he could found his first school. There was room for two hundred students, and the school was immediately filled to capacity. In order to promote the Lancasterian method, he organized a *Sociedad escolar* – School Society – whose president was the secretary of state. O'Higgins was one of its members and declared himself to be its "protector."

By now Thomson was clearly shifting his emphasis from education to the distribution of the Bible. Shortly after arriving in Chile, he wrote to the British and Foreign Bible Society:

> Although I present myself before the eyes of South America as a promoter of education and of the instruction of the young, I consider myself in every respect a servant of the British and Foreign Bible Society. I request that you consider me such, and tell me quite freely how I can, either directly or indirectly, promote your blessed work, making the inhabitants of this vast continent more familiar with the words of life eternal.[3]

Thomson did not stay long in Chile. He felt that the School Society was on a firm footing and that the means had been established for the continuing distribution of the Bible when he received an invitation from José de San

---

[3] James Thomson, *Letters on the Moral and Religious State of South America, Written during a Residence of Nearly Seven Years in Buenos Aires, Chile, Peru and Colombia*, ed. James Nisbet (1827): 15–16, as quoted in Canclini, *Diego Thomson*, 62.

Martín, the liberator of Peru, to go to that nation. As Thomson prepared to depart, O'Higgins issued a decree praising his work and announcing that "I have come to the decision of declaring him to be Chilean citizen, to be counted as such, and indeed to be such, having all the rights of the natural citizens of the land, and enjoying all their boons and privileges."[4]

In Peru, San Martín received Thomson even more enthusiastically than O'Higgins had in Chile. Thomson reports that on his arrival San Martín welcomed him with "a most affectionate embrace."[5] The following day, when Thomson was in his room, he was surprised to hear shouts that San Martín was coming. San Martín then entered Thomson's room and sat for an extended conversation. Finally, he invited Thomson to be introduced next day to the entire Cabinet. A few days later, the government ordered that a school for teachers be founded under Thomson's direction in order to teach the system of "mutual instruction" – which was at the heart of the Lancasterian method. This was to be housed at the Dominican Colegio de Santo Tomás, with the instruction that those friars whose presence was not necessary for the actual ministry of the church move to another residence. Finally, the same document declared that in six months all schools that were not conforming to the new method of education would be closed.

These plans were not fully implemented, for there was soon a political crisis that drew attention away from educational policy. The Spanish army retook the city of Lima in a bid to assert its colonial power. The Peruvian army, along with many of its supporters, took refuge in Callao as did Thomson. When the Spanish found it impossible to retain Lima and withdrew, Thomson returned with the revolutionary army, after an absence of five months. During that time, he had been making plans to travel to Cuzco, to Quito, and even into the Amazonian jungle. Thomson abandoned these plans in order to return to Lima and there to greet the victorious troops of Bolívar. But again the city fell to Spanish arms, and this time Thomson decided to remain. He wrote to his supporters in England that he felt as if he were having a nightmare and being transported into Spain, all the while longing to be in to South America. The vicissitudes continued. Although the Spanish government promised its protection, Thomson found that his work became increasingly difficult, in part because of continued military hostilities and in part because the royalist government did not offer the facilities that he had enjoyed until then. Finally, in 1824, he decided to move on, taking his work to *Gran Colombia* – Greater Colombia.

---

[4] Letter from Lima, July 11, 1822, as quoted in Canclini, *Diego Thomson*, 76.
[5] *Gaceta Ministerial*, Santiago, June 15, 1822, as quoted in Canclini, *Diego Thomson*, 71.

His work in Peru was not abandoned. As Bolívar consolidated his power, he proved to be a staunch supporter of the Lancasterian method of education, ordering that in every province a school be devoted to teaching this method and that each province also nominate two young teachers to be sent to England to learn more about it.

Although he did not remain long in Peru, Thomson's impact was significant. Following his vision of Latin America transformed by the power of Scripture, he emphasized the distribution of New Testaments in Spanish, which he sold unless the prospective reader was so poor as not to be able to pay for a copy – in which case Thomson would provide it gratis. He also recruited people to translate the New Testament into Quechua and later into Aymara – the language of much of "Alto Perú," which is now Bolivia. Unfortunately, the translation into Quechua was lost when he sent it to Great Britain to be printed.

By the time Thomson landed in Guayaquil – in what is now Ecuador, but was then part of Gran Colombia – he had officially become an agent of the British and Foreign Bible Society. While he continued promoting the Lancasterian method, this now became a tool for the distribution of Scripture, rather than the purpose of his mission. From Guayaquil he traveled to Quito, distributing more copies of the New Testament than he had thought possible in such a short time and having long conversations on religion with his travel companions. In Quito he found that he had sold all his inventory. When a long-awaited mule train arrived with a new load, he immediately sold most of them – twenty-five to the Franciscan provincial, who ordered that a copy be placed in each cell in his monastery.

He arrived in Bogota early in 1825. There he found the conflict between liberals and conservatives extremely contentious. Although he faced strong opposition from the latter, the former supported him wholeheartedly. He had been in the city less than a month when he began taking steps for the formation of a Bible Society. Although he had done something similar in Buenos Aires, the society there was composed mostly of Protestant expatriates, while the one in Bogota had Colombian Catholics – both lay and ordained – as its members and supporters. This was possible because many liberal Catholics felt that the Bible, even though brought by a Protestant missionary, would enrich their own church. (The Colombia Bible Society did not last long. Enthusiasm waned as other issues came to the foreground. Two years after its founding, it ceased to exist.)

Thomson then returned to England. When in 1826 he was invited by the British and Foreign Bible Society to undertake another tour of South America, he declined. He was recently married and not inclined to repeat his former adventures. Soon, however, the Bible Society offered him the possibility of settling in Mexico City and working from there into the interior of that country. This he accepted. Meanwhile, at Thomson's suggestion, another agent – Lucas Matthews – was sent to continue what he had begun in South America. He, too, traveled throughout the continent, until he disappeared mysteriously while in Colombia.

Thomson himself arrived in Mexico in May of 1827 – just a year after the outbreak of the cristero rebellion, discussed in Chapter 5. He soon reported that all three hundred Bibles he had brought had been sold, as well as 380 out of a thousand copies of the New Testament. He had also undertaken repeated trips into various areas in Mexico, where he distributed Bibles and New Testaments. His many reports often refer to priests, friars, and even bishops who encouraged him in his work and provided letters of introduction and other means of support. Others, such as the Dean of the Cathedral in Mexico City, issued a prohibition on the distribution of Scriptures in the diocese. Thomson felt that this contravened the laws of Mexico, and the government supported his position, declaring the ecclesiastical edict unlawful. Still, similar edicts were issued in several other dioceses. A number of civil officials – including customs inspectors who had to deal with the importation of Bibles – chose to obey the episcopal edicts rather than the law of the land. In contrast, the bishop of Puebla not only supported Thomson's work but also ordered that the Bible be translated into Nahuatl, although this project was aborted by the unexpected death of the bishop. To all of this was added civil unrest that soon exploded into armed conflict. Thomson felt that there was not much more he could do in Mexico and resolved to return to England.

After a brief sojourn in England, Thomson returned to the western hemisphere, although this time to the Caribbean basin. There he worked extensively in Trinidad, Barbados, Antiga, and other islands that were part of the British Empire, distributing Bibles and enlisting support for his endeavors in other lands. He also visited Venezuela, as well as Haiti, Puerto Rico, and Cuba – the latter two still Spanish colonies. In Venezuela, his work and its results were very similar to what had already occurred in other South American nations. In Puerto Rico, his books – both personal and for sale – were retained by customs, and the authorities were reluctant to allow him to disembark. Although he was finally allowed on the island, in the end he was not able to take Bibles into Puerto Rico and decided to leave. He stopped, however, on an island he called "Crab" – possibly Culebra – and found that the political and international muddle there could serve as a way to introduce Bibles into Puerto Rico. The island was claimed by both the English and the Spanish. The former insisted that imports from England were not subject to custom regulations; the latter insisted with equal vehemence that the island was part of Puerto Rico and therefore allowed products to be transported from "Crab" to Puerto Rico without the impediments of customs. Thomson made use of this bizarre situation by leaving in "Crab" a box of Bibles that eventually made their way into Puerto Rico. From Puerto Rico and "Crab," Thomson traveled to Hispaniola, where his experience was similar to earlier ones in South America.

In 1835, Thomson went to Jamaica. While there, but already planning to visit Cuba – the twentieth island he visited in this tour – he learned that the archbishop of Havana was in Jamaica, and Thomson sought to pay him a visit. The archbishop would not receive him and instead issued a circular letter to be distributed throughout his jurisdiction, indicating that Thomson's purpose in distributing Bibles was subversive, trying to promote a slave rebellion. Even so, Thomson traveled to Cuba in 1837, and once there many received him well. A number of booksellers agreed to sell his Bibles and New Testaments – some on commission and others for free. But the opposition was great. His Bibles and New Testaments were not allowed on the island, and when he sought to leave he was told that there was an order for his arrest. After much anxiety, he obtained from the governor an order allowing him to depart for Jamaica.

After this experience, Thomson spent most of the next four years in Canada, where he traveled directly from Jamaica. He then returned to Mexico in 1842. His experience there was very similar to the first time, although now civil unrest made things even more difficult. He was in Mexico when Santa Anna was brought to power by a revolution, and he decided to leave shortly thereafter – just before the Mexican American war. After traveling to Yucatan, and almost being caught up in the complex politics of that area's attempt to secede from Mexico, he returned to Europe, where he would serve the rest of his life – mostly in Spain, Morocco, Andorra, France, and Portugal. During this time, he kept up an ample correspondence with the friends he had made in Latin America and made sure that the British and Foreign Bible Society would continue the work he had begun in those lands. In 1847, he returned to Great Britain, where he lived until his death in 1854. During these last years, he wrote profusely of his travels, and particularly on the religion, geography, and history of Latin America. Among his writings is an autobiographical sketch, which unfortunately has never been published.

The life and work of James "Diego" Thomson amply illustrate many of the features of early Protestant missionary work in Latin America, as well as the difference between the very early beginnings and later Protestant missions. It is clear that he – as many other missionaries of the first generation – enjoyed the support of many who saw in him and his enterprise a way to move their countries into the modern world. The great leaders of Latin

American independence – O'Higgins, San Martín, Bolívar – favored his work, not because they had any personal interest in the Protestant faith, but rather because they saw in it a valuable ally against the archconservatism of many in the ecclesiastical hierarchy, as well as of the schools and other institutions they ran. In contrast to later missionaries, he was encouraged and often supported by members of the clergy who sought to lead the Catholic Church in Latin America into a new day of greater freedom and intellectual creativity. But, like those later missionaries, his work was constantly hindered by bureaucratic inertia and civil and even military unrest. He and they had to navigate through mutually conflicting laws and ecclesiastical edicts. Like many of the early Protestant missionaries, he was convinced that education, democracy, and his faith went hand in hand. They shared his emphasis on education as a means to renew both the church and the body politic. However, he contrasted with those later missionaries in that his purpose does not seem to have been to create a Protestant church in Latin America but rather to refresh and improve the faith and the life of the already existing church in the lands he visited. And yet one can trace lines of continuity between his work and some of the Protestant churches that now exist in Latin America. Like some later missionaries, he endured countless hardships – in Mexico, he had to bury his only two children. But his hardships were greater, for in contrast to most later missionaries, who represented denominations in the United States, his overseas support was scarce and sporadic, and he had to design ways to support himself and his work. In all of this, he both resembled and contrasted with many of his contemporaries who followed in his footsteps.

THE ROLE OF BIBLE SOCIETIES

Diego Thomson's story illustrates the role that Bible societies played in the early presence of Protestantism in Latin America. In the earliest years after independence – Thomson's time – it was the British and Foreign Bible Society that led the way. Although originally not a representative of that agency, from the very beginning Thomson worked hand in hand with the Bible Society, which provided him with the New Testaments – and later whole Bibles – that he distributed and also used in connection with his advocacy for Lancasterian education. This was a time when Great Britain and France vied for hegemony over Latin America, both seeking to fill the vacuum left by Spain and Portugal. Soon, however, the United States entered into the picture. By 1823, President Monroe had announced his famous "doctrine," and as the century wore on, the United States progressively became the dominant power in the region. Similarly, the American Bible Society came to play an increasing role in

Protestant work in Latin America, and the role of the British and Foreign Bible Society waned. This process had already begun in Thomson's time, and we have already noted that Thomson himself, even while representing the British society, did receive materials for distribution from its American counterpart.

A sign of the transition that was taking place is the appointment in 1864 of Andrew M. Milne, himself a Scotsman, to work in Latin America on behalf of the American Bible Society. Milne settled in Montevideo and from there traveled into the rest of Uruguay as well as Argentina, then to Chile, Peru, and eventually even Venezuela. Significantly, just as it was Diego Thomson who organized the first Protestant services – still in English – in Buenos Aires, it was in Milne's home that the first Protestant services in Spanish were held. (Interestingly, the first sermon in Spanish was preached by John F. Thomson, who was not related to Diego Thomson.)

Perhaps Milne's greatest success, however, was in attaining the conversion of Francisco Penzotti, whose name would eventually become synonymous with the presence of the American Bible Society in Latin America and who would be the first great Latin American promoter of Protestantism. Penzotti accompanied Milne and other representatives of the Bible Society on many of their trips and extended his own outreach as far a Central America. It was in Peru, however, that his work was most remarkable. After two earlier visits to that country, in 1888 Penzotti was sent to Peru to promote and oversee the work of the American Bible Society. Although his appointed task was to distribute Scripture and promote its reading, Penzotti was convinced of the need to organize a Protestant Spanish-speaking church. He began holding services in Spanish in an Anglican church, but his nascent congregation had to move when threats came – apparently emanating from among the Catholic clergy – that the church would be bombed. They then moved to a warehouse. Since it was forbidden to hold public Protestant worship in Spanish, Penzotti printed and distributed admission tickets, thus technically making the meeting a private one. In spite of such attempts to circumvent the law, he was arrested but declared innocent when brought to trial. This did not mean that he was free to continue his work. Through a series of legal maneuvers, he was kept in prison – in a dark and stinking dungeon – for more than eight months. While in jail, he found that someone had written on the wall a very pessimistic and despairing poem. Under it he wrote a hymn of hope, joy, and thanksgiving. Finally, the *New York Herald* took up his defense, which became a cause célèbre as an illustration of Peru's backwardness when it came to democratic values. Since at that time Peru was seeking foreign investment and immigrants, Penzotti was set free to continue his work, both distributing Bibles and building a Protestant congregation in Lima. In 1890, this congregation joined the Methodist Church.

At first the version of Scripture that the Bible societies sent to Latin America was a translation from the Vulgate into Spanish by Roman Catholic Father Scio de San Miguel. Eventually, however, the Bible societies turned to the translation from the original languages – Hebrew and Greek – by Protestant Spaniard Casiodoro de Reina, first published in 1569 and then revised in 1602 by Cipriano de Valera. This has generally been acknowledged as one of the jewels of Spain's golden age of literature and soon became the preferred version among Protestants – at least until the middle of the twentieth century, when a number of new translations sought to supplant it, although with limited success.

From the outset, the Bible societies insisted on publishing the Bible "without notes." This was done in reaction to the practice among Roman Catholic presses of including notes explaining how particular texts were to be understood in accordance to Catholic theology. At first, this created difficulties in the distribution of the Bible. Although the version being distributed had actually been translated by a Catholic, ecclesiastical authorities objected that the notes had been omitted, which could open the way for private and erroneous interpretations. Eventually, as laws were liberalized and the hierarchy of the church could no longer determine what books could be sold and distributed, what had originally been a liability became an asset, for the Bible societies could claim that they were simply distributing the Word of God, without taking sides on controverted issues. This allowed them to play an important role in the beginnings of the (Protestant) ecumenical movement in Latin America.

MISSIONS AMONG THE ORIGINAL INHABITANTS

As noted previously, the prevailing attitude among Anglicans, as well as some other Protestants, was that missions to Latin America were not legitimate, for this was a Catholic continent, and to seek to convert its population to Protestantism was an invasive and unwarranted form of proselytism. However, rather than deterring all Anglicans from missionary work in Latin America, this resulted in Anglicans focusing their work on the native populations. Thus, it is significant to note that foremost among the first Protestant missionary efforts in Latin America was the work of an exceptional Anglican family. Allen Gardiner was a British naval captain who had visited Chile during his time of service and had become interested in missionary work among the native population of that land. This he undertook briefly in 1838. In 1846, he visited Bolivia intending to do missionary work there, but the altitude of the Bolivian Altiplano proved seriously detrimental to his health, and he left the country after suggesting that other missionaries be sent from England. (His supporters in England sought to respond to this request in 1847, sending a Spanish Protestant convert, but before he arrived there was a radical political shift in Bolivia and his mission was aborted.)

Seeking to fulfill a calling he felt he had received in 1838 to go to the natives of Tierra del Fuego, Gardiner prepared for this mission by settling in the Falkland Islands (the Malvinas). Finally, he landed in Tierra del Fuego with seven fellow missionaries. The plan was that they would receive supplies every six months. But such supplies did not arrive, and Gardiner and his companions were not able to establish ongoing contacts with the natives. When finally another ship did come to the area, they found that the entire contingent of missionaries had starved to death waiting for supplies. Almost to the very moment of his death (in 1851), Gardiner had kept a diary in which he wrote of the vicissitudes he and his fellow missionaries had suffered and insisted on the need to evangelize the native population of the area. The news of his death touched many in England, and the Patagonian Missionary Society, which he had founded, gained new vigor. A plan emerged for missions in the area based on the Falkland Islands (which had been occupied by the British in 1833, and over which Argentina still claimed sovereignty). Eventually (in 1859), Gardiner's son decided to follow in his father's footsteps. Departing from the Falklands, he undertook a new mission to Tierra del Fuego, where he and his companions were killed and eaten by the people they sought to convert. (Years later, Gardiner's grandson decided to take up his grandfather's original missionary calling to Chile and went to that land to work among the native population as a medical missionary, but he became ill and died shortly after his arrival.)

In 1869, Waite Hocking Stirling, who had previously served as secretary of the Patagonian Missionary Society, was consecrated Anglican bishop of the Falklands. This brought new impetus to the mission in Tierra del Fuego as well as new strength to the small Anglican enclaves in Argentina, which Stirling actively supported. The Patagonian Missionary Society still exists as the South American Missionary Society. Over the years, it has supported missionary work not only in Patagonia but also among the Guaranís in the Chaco region, the Araucanians in southern Chile, and the Miskitos on the Caribbean coast of Central America.

In summary, in its origins Anglican missionary work in Latin America was noted for its interest in "Indian" populations. Anglicans also worked among people of African descent who had been taken to Central America from the English-speaking islands of the Caribbean. Officially, the Anglican Communion refrained from missionary work among Spanish- and Portuguese-speaking Latin Americans, whom they considered to be Roman Catholics. However, as the Anglican residents of the continent became more deeply rooted in the area, their contacts with the rest of the population gave birth to Spanish-speaking Anglican congregations, which eventually were organized into dioceses with their own Latin American bishops.

POLITICAL ISSUES

As was discussed in Chapters 5 and 6, immediately after independence most of the new nations found themselves in a protracted conflict between liberals and conservatives. Obviously, the most conservative elements, in both the Catholic Church and society at large, were royalists, and many returned to Spain or resettled in one of the two colonies that Spain still retained in Latin America: Cuba and Puerto Rico. Yet there remained a core of conservatives who, while not royalists – or at least not avowedly so – wished to keep as much as possible of the former order. This tendency was particularly strong among the clergy and the landed aristocracy, who sought laws protecting their earlier privileges. They were opposed by the liberals, who supported free trade and a laissez-faire economy in which prices and economic policies would be determined by the free market. In general, conservatives also supported the authority of the church over matters such as the civil registry, marriages, cemeteries, and in particular the church's "right" and "duty" to protect the populace from errors by closing the countries to foreign ideas and determining what was read and what books were imported. For all these reasons, liberals tended to make education available to as many as possible – which would also provide personnel for their commercial ventures – while conservatives tended to limit education to a select group and to traditional models.

Given that struggle, and the positions of the two warring parties, it was natural for liberals to consider Protestantism an ally. This did not mean that liberals were not Catholics or that they would consider the possibility of becoming Protestants. It meant rather that they were Catholics, as many would say, *a mi manera* (after my own fashion). But even so, many liberals did promote the entrance of Protestants into their lands, hoping that the new ideas they brought, the schools they founded, and the international connections they represented would undercut the power of conservatives and help move their nations into modernity.

We have already seen that many of the first governments in Latin America – governments led by such persons as Rivadavia in Argentina, O'Higgins in Chile, and San Martín in Peru – encouraged the work of James "Diego" Thomson. They did this because they saw in his Lancasterian method a way to extend education to a large number of students, while still having few teachers. But they did it also because they understood that in other parts of the world the Bible had been used to undercut much of traditional Catholic doctrine and authority, and they hoped the same would happen in Latin America.

While there are many examples of how this favored Protestant missions, a typical case in point is the story of the origins of Presbyterianism in Guatemala. Justo Rufino Barrios became president of that country in 1873, with the double agenda of reunifying Central America and bringing about the changes that liberalism advocated. He failed in the first of these, for he was never able to bring the former "United Provinces" – as Central America had been called – back together. Eventually, he sought to force reunion by military means and was killed in 1885 while leading an invasion of El Salvador. However, he was much more successful in his other agenda, the promotion of liberal practices and values. He was staunchly opposed by the Catholic hierarchy and many among the clergy, and in retaliation he closed monasteries, confiscated church land and other properties, and expelled the Jesuits, who had been reinstated in 1801. As part of his liberal agenda, Barrios promoted public education and encouraged immigration – in part because immigrants would bring with them many of the liberal ideas that Barrios himself wished to disseminate.

As an element in these policies, Barrios wished to introduce Protestantism into Guatemala, in the hope that it too would support and promote liberal ideas and practices. He also knew that Presbyterians were beginning to work in other Latin American countries and that quite often they began this work by founding schools. Therefore, while in New York on other matters, Barrios visited the Presbyterian Board of Missions and invited it to send missionaries to Guatemala. The Board responded positively to this request. Missionary John C. Hill was sent to Guatemala, and the first Presbyterian church in that country was organized in 1884. For the construction of its church building, Barrios made available a lot right in the center of the capital city and adjoining the presidential palace, and the missionaries built a church where the Presbyterian Church still gathers. From the beginning, the Presbyterian mission in Guatemala did extensive educational work. Several schools were opened in both the capital and other cities. It also provided medical services for many who would otherwise have no access to them – although the culmination of this endeavor, the Presbyterian Hospital, was not founded until 1913.

Another country in which the origins of Protestant missions were clearly tied to the liberal agenda was Colombia. There, the liberals held sway from 1849 until 1880. In 1850, the Jesuits were expelled, and a series of measures followed limiting the power of the church – abolishing mandatory tithes, cancelling the right of the clergy to be tried by ecclesiastical courts, seizing church property, and the like. Encouraged by what they saw as a new openness in the country, North American Presbyterians sent their first missionaries in 1859. Most of their work consisted of founding schools where they hoped the younger generations would learn both liberal ideas and the Protestant religion. These *Colegios Americanos* (American Schools) – as they were officially called – played an important role in the development of the Colombian middle class, although the number of converts they produced was relatively small. Other denominations followed a similar course. Although most liberals were not Protestant, practically all Protestants were liberal. Many spoke of Colombia as the showcase nation where the power of the Protestant version of the Gospel would be manifested. But in 1880, the conservatives ousted the liberals. Almost immediately most of the anticlerical laws were rescinded. In 1888, the government signed a concordat with the Holy See restoring most of the rights and privileges of the clergy that had been abolished. Although the constitution guaranteed religious freedom, eventually violence broke out. It was mostly a matter of conservatives attacking and ransacking liberal villages and enclaves, as we have seen in Chapter 6; but since many of these liberals were also Protestant, the initial political violence turned into religious persecution – particularly in the countryside, where legal guarantees could not be enforced. With brief respites when the liberals were in the ascendant, these difficulties lasted well into the second half of the twentieth century.

Finally, still under the general heading of liberalism, one most mention the case of Mexico and the *Reforma* of Benito Juárez. Juárez espoused liberal ideas, but he extended his efforts to include the Indian population of the nation, which he represented. This population had been generally ignored throughout Latin America in the struggle between liberals and conservatives. As was to be expected, Juárez clashed with the Catholic Church and its leadership, and he took many measures similar to those of various other liberal governments, as we have seen in Chapter 5. Although Protestantism had already been introduced into the country, Juárez encouraged its dissemination. More notably, one of his anti-Catholic measures was to encourage the secession from the Catholic Church of a number of Catholics who were disaffected by their church's policies. It appears that he did this hoping that a national Mexican church would emerge. In 1861, under the leadership of two ex-Catholic priests, the *Iglesia Mexicana* was founded (the Mexican Church). This was patterned after the Anglican Church, for it remained Catholic in many ways while seceding from Rome. The membership of this church was not numerous, and eventually its leaders requested that it become part of the Episcopal Church.

Something similar was attempted in 1925, when the growing nationalism surrounding the Mexican Revolution led to the founding of the Catholic Orthodox and Apostolic Mexican Church led by a "Patriarch of Mexico."

This effort, however, did not succeed, and most of its members eventually either returned to the Catholic Church or joined the Episcopal Church.

Similar instances of the connection between liberal and anti-Catholic policies on the one hand and the introduction and development of Protestantism on the other could be cited in several other countries.

The twentieth century, however, brought with it new political issues and social programs. It was marked by a number of political and social revolutions, all seeking to change the order of society, most with strong anti-American inspiration, and a few with relative success. Of these, the two that most profoundly affected their societies as well as the life of the church were the Mexican and the Cuban revolutions. We will return later to the impact of these events on Latin American Protestantism.

INSTITUTIONAL DEVELOPMENT

Up to this point, we have discussed the very early beginnings of Protestant missions in Latin America and have pointed to some of the overarching issues that these missions faced. Later we will return to similar overarching issues in the twentieth century. At this point, however, we must pause to offer a very brief review of the process whereby Protestant missionary work resulted in Protestant churches. In this section, we will follow a geographical outline, moving from one area of Latin America to another.

Since it was in Argentina that both Diego Thomson and James Gardiner began their work, this overview logically begins in the Viceroyalty of La Plata – what is now Argentina, Uruguay, and Paraguay. As mentioned previously, Diego Thomson organized the first Protestant church in Argentina, which eventually became part of the Methodist Church. But services there were held in English, as those attending were almost exclusively immigrants. The first Protestant to preach in Spanish was John Francis Thomson (again, no relation to Diego Thomson), a Scottish immigrant who had studied in Ohio Wesleyan University and returned to Argentina in 1866 with the purpose of evangelizing the Spanish-speaking population. He led the first Protestant public worship in Spanish in 1867 – almost half a century after Diego Thomson's arrival in Buenos Aires. Jointly with the English-speaking group founded under the leadership of that other Thomson (Diego), this would be the beginning of the Methodist Church in Argentina. Somewhat later, the Baptists, who had organized a French-speaking congregation, also began services in Spanish. As previously stated, in Uruguay it was also J. F. Thomson who preached the first sermon in Spanish to a group gathered at the home of Bible Society agent A. M. Milne. Somewhat later, the Christian Church (Disciples of Christ) also entered the country, and in 1878 they joined the Methodists in founding the Crandon Institute, which soon became one of the leading educational institutions of the country. Also in Paraguay, as earlier in Argentina, some of the immigrant groups began recruiting Spanish-speaking members. Most notable among these groups were the Waldensians, who also organized educational and agricultural programs for the surrounding society. In 1871, when political circumstances made it possible, some Paraguayans asked the Methodists to send missionaries to their land. This was not done until 1886 and marked the beginning of organized Protestantism in Paraguay. Here again, as in Argentina and Uruguay, the first missionaries combined evangelization with education, soon founding two schools in Asuncion. Two years after the Methodists, the South American Missionary Society – formerly the Patagonian Missionary Society – began extensive work among the Guaranís, by far the majority of the population of the country.

In the Viceroyalty of Peru and the Andean region in general, Protestant progress was slower than in the River Plate region. The country with most significant Protestant presence in the nineteenth century was Chile. It was North American missionary David Trumbull, sent by the Foreign Evangelical Union in the United States, who began holding Protestant services in Spanish. Opposition on the part of the Roman Catholic leadership was severe. When the first church – still for a congregation that was completely English-speaking – was built in 1855, the authorities required that a high wall surround it and hymns not be sung loudly enough that passers-by might be enticed to investigate. With the support of a number of liberals, Trumbull worked assiduously to have such laws changed. Finally, he was able to organize the first Protestant church in Chile where worship was public and in Spanish. This was in 1868, twenty-two years after his arrival, and at that point the church had four Chilean members.

A different sort of missionary enterprise in Chile – and in parts of Bolivia that now belong to Chile – was led by Methodist William Taylor. He traveled along the coast, seeking English-speaking immigrants who wished to have schools and religious services in their own native tongue. He would then recruit people from the United States who were willing to go to Chile as missionaries knowing that they had to find their own means of subsistence. They usually achieved this by charging tuition in the schools they founded and from the offerings collected in the churches they also founded. The result was that the Pacific coast of Chile was dotted with English-speaking Methodist churches.

Although Taylor's work dealt mostly with English-speaking people, the consequences of his work may still be seen in Chilean vocabulary. A Spanish ex-Jesuit – who was also an ex-Presbyterian – by the name of Juan Canut de Bon found renewed faith in one of Taylor's churches. He then returned to Santiago, where he eventually became an active preacher. In 1890, he became pastor of a small Methodist congregation that continued the work begun by Trumbull. He lived only six more years. But during that time, his zeal and impact on the community were such that from that time Protestants in Chile were popularly, and often pejoratively, known as *canutos* – followers of Canut.

Several other denominations soon began work in Chile: the Christian and Missionary Alliance in 1897, the Baptists and Presbyterians at about the same time, and the Salvation Army in 1909.

In Peru, Spanish-speaking Protestantism is the direct result of the work of the Bible societies. Both Diego Thomson and Lucas Matthews had visited the country. But it was Francisco Penzotti – whose work and trials we have already mentioned – who founded the first Spanish-speaking Protestant congregation in Peru. Later, other denominations joined the initial Methodist presence – the interdenominational Peruvian Mission among them.

In Bolivia – originally known as "Alto Perú" – there were repeated and not very successful visits by agents of the British and the American Bible societies throughout most of the nineteenth century. It was in 1883, through the efforts of both the British and Foreign Bible Society and the American Bible Society, that the importation of Bibles was legalized. Only in 1896 were the Canadian Baptists finally able to gain a toehold in the nation. (Taylor's work did include a number of Bolivian towns, but these became part of Chile when Bolivia's outlet into the Pacific was cut.) Thus, most Bolivian Protestantism dates from the twentieth century. The main exception is the work undertaken among the Bolivian Quechuas and Aymaras, mostly under the inspiration of Captain Gardiner and the Patagonian Missionary Society.

The first of the nations of Gran Colombia where there was Protestant missionary work among the Spanish-speaking was Colombia. This was not the result of a preconceived plan. In 1855, a Spanish ex-friar convert to Protestantism, Ramón Montsalvage, was shipwrecked near Cartagena while en route to Venezuela. He remained in Cartagena for over a decade, preaching and teaching, and was able to gather a congregation. Unfortunately, little more is known about the rest of his life or the later history of that congregation. The first permanent Protestant presence in Colombia began with the work of Presbyterian missionary H. B. Pratt, who arrived in 1856. Five years later, a Presbyterian church was organized in Bogota, but its first Colombian members joined in 1865. As was the case elsewhere, the Protestant presence in the nation was most noticeable in the field of education, where Presbyterian schools were admired for their excellence. As was already stated, this nascent church suffered persecution as the conservatives came into power and unleashed violence against liberals. Also in Venezuela, Protestant missionary work – apart from visits from Bible society representatives, and of churches for immigrants and expatriates – began relatively late. Apparently, the first missionaries were Southern Methodists who arrived in 1890 and in 1900 transferred their work to the Presbyterian Church. In Ecuador, the first missionaries arrived in 1896, responding to an invitation by the liberal government of Eloy Alfaro.

The first Protestant endeavors in Brazil date from 1557, in the already mentioned Genevan settlement under the leadership of Villegaignon. Much later, in 1835, Protestant denominations began exploring the possibility of sending missionaries to Brazil. Some did send missionaries, and a few schools were founded. But this work did not continue. It was in 1858 that the first Brazilian convert to Protestantism was baptized by Scottish doctor Robert Reid Kalley. His story once again illustrates the early connection between Protestantism and political liberalism. Kalley had worked as a medical missionary in the Portuguese island of Madeira, but his very success in gaining converts led to persecution by the Portuguese government. Kalley went to the United States, and it was there that he heard of the liberal anticlerical leanings of Brazilian Emperor Pedro II. This led him to settle in Brazil, where much of his work had to do with encouraging the political inclinations of the emperor, thus assuring freedom to teach and preach. This made it possible for his own Brazilian colleagues, whom he had trained, to preach, teach, and found churches. It also opened the way for other missionaries. Among these, the Presbyterians arrived in 1859, founding a number of churches and finally organizing the Presbytery of Rio de Janeiro in 1865.

One of the most interesting Protestant personalities in Brazil in the nineteenth century was José Manuel da Conceição, an ex-priest from São Paulo. He was about forty years old when he was profoundly shaken in his faith. His crisis – like Luther's – had to do with justification by faith, the work of grace in salvation, and the traditional Catholic teachings on salvation by merit and on indulgences. He then withdrew from the priesthood and sought refuge in a rural area where people came to know his as "the Protestant father." There a Presbyterian missionary contacted him, and in 1864 he joined the Presbyterian Church of Rio de Janeiro. He then began traveling, mostly to his former parishes, trying to correct what he now saw as the errors of his former preaching. He was not concerned with founding Protestant churches but simply with letting his former Catholic parishioners know and experience the deeper riches of the Gospel. This prompted the leadership of the Presbyterian Church to distance itself from the "Protestant father" – or "the crazy father," as his Catholic critics called him. He continued preaching and traveling incessantly in spite of ill health. He finally collapsed on the road and was attended until his death by a passerby who had never met him. Conceição's witness in the very process of dying was such that this passerby resolved to inquire more about Conceição's faith and life, become a Protestant, and eventually write a biography of Conceição.

In spite of much success, the Presbyterian Church in Brazil was racked by inner conflicts and eventual schism. Originally, the dispute was among three parties: the Southern Presbyterian missionaries, the Northern Presbyterian missionaries, and the emerging native leadership. This latter group was headed by Eduardo Carlos Pereira, who insisted that the funds employed in missionary schools be invested rather in direct evangelization and the training of Brazilian ministers. Being an able politician, Pereira recognized that the missionaries were still the majority of ministers, and therefore he sought to exploit the differences between those from the South and those from the North. His proposal, however, was not supported by the Boards of Missions of the two churches in the United States – particularly the Northern church – and the matter seemed to have been resolved, with most of the money going to schools. But then another issue came to the foreground: Could a Christian be a Freemason? Many of the missionaries were Masons, and so were some national pastors. Many saw in Masonry a natural ally against conservatives, particularly conservative Catholics. But Brazil was a nation that had been profoundly affected by philosophical positivism, with its emphasis on human achievement and the power of reason – hence the national motto of "order and progress." Pereira felt that Christian Masons played into the hands of philosophical positivism. He saw their positive view of human capabilities as contrary to the basic tenets of Christianity – and particularly to the Reformed tradition that Presbyterians were supposed to uphold. He therefore insisted that true Christians could not be Masons. When the Presbyterian synod refused to adopt Pereira's position, he and his followers abandoned the meeting, clearly dominated by missionaries, shouting, "down with Americanism." They then formed the *Igreja Presbiteriana Independiente* (Independent Presbyterian Church), still in existence.

Other denominations from the United States also established permanent work in Brazil during the nineteenth century: the Methodist Episcopal Church in 1870, the Baptists in 1881, and the Episcopalians in 1888. In 1893, the Congregationalists in the United States founded a missionary agency called "Help for Brazil."

The story of Protestantism in Central America during the nineteenth century is similar to what we have seen in the rest of the area. After a number of preliminary visits, Protestantism established its first permanent role in Guatemala when – as stated previously – liberal President Justo Rufino Barrios invited missionaries into his country. Although at first a church of the Guatemalan liberal middle class, the Presbyterian Church made significant inroads among the original inhabitants of the land, particularly the Mams and the Quichés. In 1899, the Central American Mission – not to be confused with the Latin American Mission, founded much later, in 1921 – entered Guatemala. This was a radical dispensationalist movement, organized in Texas in 1890 by Congregationalist pastor Cyrus Scofield, who was made famous by the "Scofield Bible." Its proclamation of the impending end and its claim to be able to unlock the mysteries of the Apocalypse gained it many converts. Although other denominations settled in Central America late in the nineteenth century, the Central American Mission remained the dominant Protestant force until well into the twentieth century – thus giving Protestantism in Central America a radically dispensationalist image.

In Mexico, as elsewhere in Latin America, James "Diego" Thomson was the forerunner of Protestantism. Later, other representatives from the American Bible Society visited the country and distributed Bibles. It was, however, the Mexican-American War (1846–1848) that opened the way for Protestantism. The oldest Protestant denomination in Mexico, the Episcopal Church, dates its origins from 1853, when American missionary E. C. Nicholson founded the Apostolic Mexican Society. Then in 1861, two Roman Catholic ex-priests founded the *Iglesia Mexicana*, which – as stated before – was patterned after the Church of England. This eventually came to be called the "Church of Jesus" and in 1909 joined the Protestant Episcopal Church of the United States. Shortly after the founding of what would eventually become the Episcopal Church, several other denominations, attracted by both the constant news about Mexico following the war and the liberal policies of Benito Juárez, began work in Mexico. The Congregationalists arrived in 1866, the Presbyterians and Quakers in 1871, the Methodists in 1872, the Baptists in 1891, and the Disciples in 1894. All of these churches experienced moderate growth, and most of them combined evangelism with educational work, founding schools as well as churches.

The islands of the Caribbean had a varied history during the nineteenth century. Haiti, under the leadership of Toussaint Louverture, who profited from the chaos of the French Revolution and the Napoleonic wars to declare independence and issue a national constitution in 1810, broke away from France. We have already told the story of this new nation's allure for North Americans of African descent, and how this led to the founding of the Episcopal Church in Haiti. Other African-American churches – notably the African Methodist Episcopal Church – followed, mostly toward the end of the nineteenth century.

Until the Dominican Republic gained its independence from Haiti in 1844, African-American immigrants to what was then Haitian territory were practically the only Protestant presence. However, the main Protestant mission to the Dominican Republic was organized early in the twentieth century, when the Evangelical Union of Puerto Rico requested support from various North American boards of missions to begin joint missionary work in the neighboring republic. This resulted in a missionary enterprise staffed mostly out of Puerto Rico and with the support of Congregationalists, Disciples, Methodists, Presbyterians, and United Brethren.

After the independence of most of Latin America early in the twentieth century, Cuba and Puerto Rico remained the only two Spanish colonies in the western hemisphere – a situation that came to an end in 1898, as a result of the Spanish-American War. In Cuba, the struggle for independence had begun in 1868, thirty years before American intervention. As a result of this struggle, many Cubans had gone into exile in Tampa and Key West. There some became Protestants and organized their own congregations. These congregations began sending Bibles to Cuba, and eventually some of their members followed as missionaries. In 1884, the first Protestant congregation was organized in the city of Matanzas. This would eventually become the seed for the Episcopal Church of Cuba. Six years later, the Board of Missions of the Presbyterian Church, U.S. – the Southern Presbyterians – received an unexpected letter informing them that its writer, Evaristo Collazo, had founded three Protestant churches and a girls' school in Cuba and was requesting the Board's help. This assistance came in the form of a missionary who had been working in Mexico and who organized Collazo's congregations as Presbyterian churches. Finally, at the point when the end of Spanish rule made it possible, several Cuban pastors who had been serving in Florida returned to the island – some of them with part of their congregation.

Puerto Rico did not attain independence as a result of the Spanish-American War but became a territory of the United States. It was at that time – 1898 and shortly thereafter – that Protestant missionary work began on the island. However, much earlier, in 1868, a man by the name of Antonio Badillo Hernández had been visiting the island of St. Thomas when he came across a Bible. He brought it back to his native city of Aguadilla in Puerto Rico, and he and his family began studying it. The result was that when the first Protestant missionary arrived in Aguadilla in 1900, he found there a group calling itself "Believers in the Word." This became the first nucleus for the Presbyterian Church in Puerto Rico.

Having sorted through all the details, dates, and names comprising this summary, several general conclusions may be drawn. The first is that, although

Protestant missionary work dates from 1818, most denominations entered the area during the second half of the century. Second, what was said earlier regarding the connection between political liberalism and Protestant presence is confirmed by the history of Protestantism in almost every country. Third, this connection with liberalism was frequently manifested in the notion that education would solve many of the nations' problems and therefore in the founding of Protestant schools. Fourth, although at first most Protestant work in Latin America – particularly in its southern areas – was connected primarily with Great Britain, this changed over the course of the nineteenth century as the United States grew in power and North American Christians became increasingly interested in their southern neighbors. Fifth, in many instances Protestantism did not enter a country through the work of official missionaries; rather, when the missionaries arrived they found small congregations and groups of believers already there.

Finally, a word must be said about the social composition of this early Latin American Protestantism. As one looks at the records of churches, where they gathered, who their members were, and so forth, it becomes apparent that early Latin American Protestantism was mostly an urban movement. In general, while many of the leading liberals, entrepreneurs, and merchants favored Protestantism, this new aristocracy of money remained at least nominally Catholic. Due in part to Protestantism's connection with political liberalism and education, most of its members belonged to the lower middle classes – teachers, clerks, people involved in retail sales and in small scale trade, and lower-echelon government officials. The main exception were those from among the original inhabitants of the hemisphere who had become Protestants – Aymaras, Quechuas, Araucanians, Guaranís, Mams, Quichés, and so forth. By and large, by the end of the nineteenth century Protestantism had made few inroads among the higher reaches of society, the urban poor, or the rural poor creole farmers and peasants.

A TIME OF UNREST

The twentieth century was marked in Latin America by a series of revolutions seeking or promising to heal social ills and eliminate economic injustice and inequality. The first of these was the Mexican Revolution, already discussed in Chapter 5, particularly in connection with its impact on Roman Catholicism. We must now say a word about Protestant participation and reactions to it. Protestants had played an important role – including a military role – in Juárez's campaign to oust Emperor Maximilian, who had been imposed on the nation by French invaders. Historian Jean-Pierre Bastian has compiled a partial list of military leaders of that effort who were Protestants or had strong ties with Protestantism. This includes two generals, eighteen colonels, and a vast number of lesser officers. Many of these became Protestants after their military action, thus indicating that the relationship between Protestantism and liberalism was a two-way street, each providing recruits for the other. As the nineteenth century was closing and the twentieth was dawning, there were many liberals in Mexico who felt that the achievements of the Reforma led by Benito Juárez were being seriously eroded. This was particularly true regarding the power of the Catholic clergy, which Juárez had curtailed. Although most of his laws were still on the books, increasing pressure from conservative clerics and lay people led many in the government to ignore them. This caused many Protestants to fear that the freedoms they had attained would be lost. They thus joined forces with the more radical liberals who were beginning to emerge and whose actions would lead to the Revolution. When in 1900 a group of liberals in Potosi issued a call to action, Protestants were at the forefront of the ensuing movement. At first, the main note of the movement was anti-Catholic, with limited emphasis on the restoration of the policies of Juárez for the greater participation of the indigenous population and others in the life and wealth of the nation. But soon the emphasis began to shift toward land reform and social justice. In this process, a number of Protestant leaders – many of them pastors – played an important role.

This connection between Protestantism and the Mexican Revolution may be seen, among many, in the career of Methodist pastor José Rumbia, who had studied at the Mexican Methodist Institute in Puebla under liberal teachers. As a pastor, he sought and eventually obtained permission to offer evening classes to prisoners, organized a sort of union of laborers in the textile industry, and opened a day school for the children of laborers. In this he illustrated a process that had begun to develop in Mexico some years earlier – a process in which the Methodist Church, and to a lesser degree other denominations, began penetrating the ranks of the dispossessed, in both towns and some rural areas. Significantly, at the time when Rumbia was organizing textile laborers, their employers – with the support of the authorities – had outlawed meetings of more than three such laborers. In 1902, at a vast gathering of laborers and peasants, Rumbia was the main speaker – and one of the other two was a Methodist layman. As the conservative authorities exerted increasing pressure on Rumbia and his fellow liberals, they became increasingly radicalized. By 1906, Rumbia was writing against those who seemed to believe that "light and freedom were created only for those of high birth and those who have a monopoly over knowledge as if it were a commodity."[6] From that point on, he became generally known as one of the best orators promoting radical change. Eventually, as the Revolution broke out, he was ready to become the personal secretary of the revolutionary governor of his state. In 1913, when opponents of the Revolution gained the upper hand, Rumbia was executed by a firing squad.

Rumbia's case was not exceptional. On the contrary, Protestant participation in the revolutionary process was extensive both at the level of the rank and file and among the leadership. Again, Jean-Pierre Bastian has collected impressive lists of Protestant leaders in the Revolution, indicating that many of the groups organized in various sections of the country were led by Protestants. This clearly shows that early in the twentieth century Mexican Protestants were actively involved in the political life of the nation and generally supported social and agrarian reforms proposed by the revolutionaries, and not only their anti-Catholic stances.

Although the Mexican Revolution was not adverse to Protestants, it still brought about upheavals that affected the life of the churches. Pastors and lay leaders left in order to join the ranks of the military or those working for the revolutionary governments. Thousands of Mexicans were uprooted – many emigrating to the United States – and this included many of the Protestant rank and file. The internecine warfare among revolutionary factions spilled over into the churches – particularly those most actively participating in the Revolution. Additionally, as missionaries left the country because of the generalized violence, there was a serious lack of both personnel and funds. By the time the revolutionary process slowed down, there were many Protestants who feared the repetition of those events and unending conflict and therefore became more conservative than they had been at the beginning of the Revolution. Many Protestants came to feel that the church ought to limit its work to the strictly religious and not become involved in political or social action or debate. Still, there remained within Protestantism a strong cadre of those who believed that their faith should result in social action and advocacy. Many of these were also strong nationalists seeking ways to be both Protestant and thoroughly Mexican.

A clear example of these interests is Alberto Rembao, who fought in the Revolution and was rescued from a wagon-load of corpses by a missionary who heard him moaning. She nursed him to health and spoke to him of her

[6] José Rumbia, "Y dijo Dios, la Luz sea y la Luz fue," *ACI* (September 13, 1906), 302–303, as quoted in Jean-Pierre Bastian, *Los disidentes: sociedades protestaxtes y revolucion in Mexico, 1872–1911* (Mexico City: Fondo de Cultura Económica, 1989), 241.

faith. In later years, Rembao would say that he had lost a leg as a result of his wounds but had gained a faith. After his studies, Rembao attended several of the missionary conferences to be discussed in the next section of this chapter – Panama in 1916, Montevideo in 1925, and Havana in 1929. His book *Discurso a la nación evangélica* (An Address to the Evangelical Nation) broke new ground in Latin America on the matter of the relationship between faith and culture and argued that it was indeed possible to be both Protestant and Latin American – although he also argued that true Protestants would be different from other Latin Americans. As editor of the journal *La nueva democracia*, published in New York, he set the pace for theological reflection and literary expression in a new, Latin American mode – although his own literary style, sometimes convoluted, limited the impact of the journal. At the same time, throughout his life he maintained the strong national pride that had originally led him to join the forces of the Revolution. He died in New York in 1962, leaving behind a younger generation of leaders and theologians to whose formation he had contributed significantly.

The Mexican Revolution was more than a national phenomenon. It also presaged a change that was taking place in Latin America. This was a movement beyond the traditional tenets of liberalism and toward more radical ideas. When Rumbia and others began protesting against the encroachments of the clergy and other conservatives on the achievements of Juárez and his followers, they were concerned mainly with traditionally liberal issues – freedom of the press and of religion, the right and responsibility of the state, rather than the church, to keep civil records, and free trade. By the heyday of the Mexican Revolution, the issues had become agrarian reform, the dismantling of the neocolonial economic and political order that had placed many of Mexico's assets in foreign hands, and the rights of those who had been marginalized by reason of birth, race, or culture.

The two World Wars both delayed and exacerbated the revolutionary process (which is discussed in more detail in Chapters 6 and 9). They delayed it by bringing economic prosperity to Latin America. This was in part the result of the war effort itself, but mostly due to the need of the United States to turn to Latin America for raw materials and other resources. The wars exacerbated the revolutionary process by making Latin American economies increasingly dependent on the United States. When, after World War II, trade resumed across both the Atlantic and the Pacific and as the Latin American economies generally declined and their foreign dependence was made manifest, revolutionary sentiments grew. To this was added the Cold War, which turned the attention of the United States further away from the hemisphere and across the oceans. Then, in 1959, the Cuban Revolution resulted in the Cold

War heating up in Latin America. For many throughout the continent, Cuba became a symbol of justice and liberation. For others, it became a symbol of tyranny and the chaos of revolution. The result was a polarization of the continent, as military governments insisting on "national security" (see Chapter 9) persecuted those whom it considered subversive, and the latter gained strength among the masses and the intellectual elite. Eventually, a series of wars broke out – mainly in Central America – in which the two sides of the Cold War fought by proxy. The demise of the Soviet Union in 1990 and the clear decline of Cuba's revolutionary economy meant an end to the Cold War. But revolutionary and anti-American sentiments did not disappear. Ernesto "Che" Guevara, one of the original leaders of the Cuban Revolution, became an icon throughout the continent. Early in the twenty-first century, a series of governments arose – for instance, in Venezuela, Brazil, and Bolivia – that challenged the long-standing U.S. hegemony over the region. That some of these governments may have been led by demagogues who used anti-American and revolutionary sentiments for their own ends does not change the fact that such sentiments were widespread.

By the end of the twentieth century, "liberal" – by which was meant above all being a proponent of free trade and economic globalization – was often used as an insult. A "liberal" in this context was roughly similar to what in the United States was a "conservative" – someone in favor of free enterprise and believing that the market by itself would eventually correct the economic inequities of society.

For Protestants, this meant that their earlier connection with liberalism had played itself out. Churches that had entered Latin America in the nineteenth century as champions of democracy, and therefore seemed to represent the wave of the future, now were left behind by events. Many of the liberal ideals they had espoused – freedom of religion and of the press, for instance – were now generally accepted, so that in this respect these churches had little new to say. At the same time, many of them had developed a relationship of dependency with their North American counterparts. Indeed, during the first half of the twentieth century, most of them were an integral part of their mother denominations, and it was not until the second half of the century that they became autonomous churches. But even then, economic, theological, and ideological dependency continued.

This led to the polarization of much of traditional Protestantism. On the one hand, there were those who felt that the ministry and preaching of the church should still be what it had been for generations. On the other hand, others insisted that the new revolutionary times required that the church be present in the revolutionary processes. In the 1960s, this cause was taken up by several organizations, at both the national and international levels. In the international scene, the leading voice in this direction was the organization *Junta Latinoamericana de Iglesia y Sociedad* (Latin American Board of Church and Society, ISAL), whose stance was supported by other organizations such as the *Unión Latinoamericana de Juventudes Evangélicas* (the Latin American Union of Evangelical Youth,ULAJE) and the *Comisión Evangélica Latinoamericana de Educación Cristiana* (the Latin American Evangelical Commission on Christian Education, CELADEC). Support from outside came from the Word Council of Churches, the missionary agencies of some denominations in the United States, and the World Student Christian Federation – the latter at that time radically opposed by the more conservative Inter-Varsity Fellowship. In the 1970s, as liberation theology spread, many of the publications of these agencies used tools taken from Karl Marx to analyze the structure of Latin American society (discussed in Chapter 9). This in turn polarized the situation even more, for the more traditionalist elements felt that many in the church were embracing Communism. The political and theological polarization of the church led many to demonize the leading Protestant theologians who advocated for new social structures – among them José Míguez Bonino (1924–), Rubem Alves (1933–), and Elsa Tamez (1950–).

Toward the end of the twentieth century, as the Cold War waned after the fall of the Soviet Union, this polarization began to disappear. The more radical elements came to realize that the solution to the social ills of Latin America was not just around the corner of the next revolution. Moderate conservatives also realized that traditional liberalism had its flaws – particularly in economic and social matters – and that dependency on the United States was not an asset. Slowly, the two poles began to move toward a common center.

Even in the midst of these conflicts, traditional Protestantism continued to grow throughout the continent. In most countries, it far outpaced population growth. But as one looks at the membership figures at the beginning of the twenty-first century, it is clear that these churches were far outpaced by another form of Protestantism – Pentecostalism, to which we will turn in Chapter 10. Again, this reflected the new conditions in which traditional liberalism had lost much of its attraction.

ECUMENICAL BEGINNINGS

Some of the earliest Protestant missionaries to Latin America – James "Diego" Thomson among them – did not seek to found Protestant churches. They were content with spreading the Bible, raising questions about traditional religion, and then letting the Word take its course, which they hoped would lead to the birth of Protestant churches as well as a renewal and purification of Catholic faith. This made it possible for people such as Thomson to work with liberal priests, among whom he found many of his strongest supporters.

Soon, however, the spirit of antagonism of the Catholic Church toward Protestantism led to a Protestant church that tended to define itself in terms of opposition to Catholicism. Thus, when one speaks of ecumenism in Latin America – at least before the time of the Second Vatican Council – one is actually referring almost exclusively to relationships among Protestant denominations.

Most historians point to the World Missionary Conference held in Edinburgh in 1910 as the beginning of the modern ecumenical movement – and it is clear that it set the stage for the birth of the World Council of Churches in 1948. However, that World Missionary Conference explicitly excluded Latin America from its agenda. This was due, as we have mentioned, to the opposition of Anglicans and Lutherans, who insisted that Latin America was already a Christian continent. However, this very exclusion led a number of missionary leaders to plan a meeting in which the specific issues facing Protestantism in Latin America were to be discussed. This took place in Panama just six years later, in 1916. This *Primer Congreso de Acción Cristiana en América Latina* (First Congress of Christian Action in Latin America) was clearly dominated by foreign missionary personnel and interests – out of 304 delegates, 28 were born in Latin America, although the meeting was presided by Professor Eduardo Monteverde, from Uruguay. The rest were mostly from Europe and the United States. As a result, many have said that the Panama Congress was for the most part a North American project and even that it was an unwitting expression of growing North American imperialism. (The Panama Canal had been opened two years earlier, and in order to make its construction easier, the United States had incited and supported Panama in its secession from Colombia.) Even so, in his report on the meeting, Brazilian Erasmo Braga stated that "throughout Latin America, particularly in Mexico, Peru, the River Plate and Brazil, the ideal of the nationalization of evangelism, of creating a ministry and a church identified with national life, stirs Protestants."[7]

As a result of the meeting in Panama, the Committee on Cooperation in Latin America was formed. Like the Panama Congress itself, this was dominated by North American missionary agencies. It did produce a series of cooperative enterprises in fields such as publications, theological education, and comity agreements whereby various missionary agencies agreed on the areas in which each of them would work. (Many Latin Americans felt that

---

[7] Erasmo Braga, *Pan-Americanismo: Aspectos religiosos* (New York: Sociedad para la Educación Misionera en los Estados Unidos y el Canadá, 1917), 38–39.

these agreements were an expression of the imperialistic attitude of boards of missions, meting out territories as if they owned them.) It also planned the two next conferences held in continuation of the one in Panama: Montevideo (1925) and Havana (1929). In these conferences, Latin American presence and participation increased, and it became evident that interdenominational cooperation in the continent was a concern not only of missionary agencies but also of the emerging national churches and their leadership.

Although not quite as rapidly as among other Protestants, cooperation had also been developing among Latin American Evangelicals. The *Primer Congreso Latinoamericano de Evangelización* (First Latin American Congress for Evangelization, CLADE I) was held in Bogota in 1969. Significantly, although this meeting was seen by many as an alternative to the social activism of the agencies just mentioned, and even though this was the time of greatest polarization in Latin American Protestantism, CLADE I too recognized the urgency of addressing the social ills of the continent: "The time has come when we Evangelicals acknowledge our social responsibilities."[8] CLADE I also led to the founding in 1970 of the *Fraternidad Teológica Latinoamericana* (Latin American Theological Fraternity, FTL). Its members were mostly pastors and theologians of Evangelical convictions who were also deeply concerned with both the social ills of the continent and the apparent extremes of the more radical elements in the churches. While insisting on the need for evangelism, the FTL also emphasized the social dimensions of the Gospel. Ten years later, CLADE II met in Lima. It, too, was closely connected with the worldwide evangelical movement. CLADE II followed the lines of the Lausanne congress of 1974 in which Evangelicals had taken a stance in favor of social justice. In its final report, CLADE II declared: "We affirm our adherence to the Declaration of the First Latin American Congress on Evangelization and to the Covenant of the International Congress on Evangelization held at Lausanne, Switzerland, in July, 1974."[9] The movement continued with CLADE III, held in Quito in 1992, and CLADE IV, again in Quito, in 2000. It is possible to trace in the history of this movement a growing awareness, first, of the social dimensions of the Gospel, and then, of the structural dimensions of the social and economic problems of Latin America. This was another sign that the polarizations of the 1960s and 1970s was being questioned – even though it would continue well into the 1980s – and that Protestants in Latin America from very different

---

[8] CLADE I, "Declaración Evangélica de Bogotá," *Boletín Teológico* 1 and 2 (1979): 41, as quoted in Carlos F. Cardoza Orlandi, "Ecclesiology in the Latin American Theology Fraternity" (unpublished paper, Princeton Theological Seminary, 1992), 10.

[9] René Padilla and Chris Sugden, *Texts on Evangelical Social Ethics* (Nottingham [England]: Grove Books Limited, 1985), 5, as quoted in Cardoza Orlandi, "Ecclesiology," 31.

theological backgrounds were reaching a general consensus as to the nature and scope of their mission.

All of this was supported by an entire generation of Protestant leaders who had been formed in seminaries that themselves were the result of interdenominational cooperation – among them the *Facultad Evangélica de Teología* in Buenos Aires, the *Seminario Evangélico de Puerto Rico*, and the *Seminario Evangélico de Teología* in Matanzas, Cuba. The *Seminario Bíblico Latinoamericano* in San Jose, Costa Rica, although different in origin, by the 1970s had adopted an openly ecumenical stance.

An outcome of these ecumenical beginnings, as well as of the support of the World Council of Churches and the Student Christian Federation, was that a number of interdenominational agencies and movements developed. Some of these have already been mentioned – ISAL, ULAJE, and CELADEC. But the most notable development out of the history begun in Panama was the birth in 1982 of the *Consejo Latinoamericano de Iglesias* (Latin American Council of Churches, CLAI) in close connection with the World Council of Churches and including not only the traditional Protestant churches founded mostly in the nineteenth century but also many Pentecostal and Evangelical churches for which a few decades earlier the very word 'ecumenism' was anathema. Still, in the polarized atmosphere of the time there were some who felt that the World Council of Churches, which strongly supported the birth of CLAI, was too radical in its political positions, as well as too open-minded with reference to theological differences. The result was the founding, also in 1982, of the *Confraternidad Evangélica Latinoamericana* (Latin American Evangelical Confraternity, CONELA), in direct opposition to CLAI, the World Council of Churches, liberation theology (discussed in Chapter 9), and even those Evangelicals who had sought to combine evangelism and strict orthodoxy with social action – including those Latin American leaders who twelve years earlier had founded FTL.

As we will see in Chapter 11, by the end of the twentieth century not only had ecumenism progressed among Protestants in Latin America, but these Protestants were also making significant contributions to a number of ecumenical and interdenominational endeavors beyond the limits of their continent and hemisphere.

CONCLUSION

As one now looks at the total picture of Christianity in Latin America, it is clear that, numerically speaking, traditional Protestantism – what in the United States is called "mainline denominations" – has fallen far behind both Roman

Catholicism and Pentecostalism. As stated previously, the process throughout the twentieth century whereby political and economic liberalism – in
the traditional sense, and not in the sense in which it is employed in the United
States – lost it allure meant also that Protestant churches that had entered
the continent and grown under the auspices of such liberalism lost much
of their appeal and uniqueness. Then the Second Vatican Council brought
about changes in the Roman Catholic Church that made it more difficult for
Protestants to continue promoting their faith and their churches, as they had
done before, by criticizing Catholic practices. Now the mass was said in the
language of the people. Now the Bible was being read and studied in Catholic
circles. Now more and more churches placed the images of the saints to a
side and focused on Jesus Christ. Now many Catholic leaders questioned the
traditional ties of their church with the ruling oligarchies and its neglect of
the poor.

In the twentieth century, as Pentecostalism grew, these churches and
their institutions had provided books, theological education, and other such
resources for the training of Pentecostal leaders. After the Second Vatican
Council, they provided the Catholic Church with their expertise in the translation and distribution of Scripture, and in some cases with their expertise
in preaching and interpreting Scripture for their congregations. During the
same period – the first years after Vatican II – those traditional Protestant
denominations sometimes served as a bridge facilitating the dialogue between
Catholicism and Pentecostalism. During the last decades of the twentieth century, these churches had expanded their educational outreach by founding a
number of universities – many of them quite respected.

By the end of the century, however, it was clear that these functions were
becoming less necessary. Pentecostalism was developing first-class educational
institutions and scholars. The Roman Catholic Church had organized thousands of 'base ecclesial communities' in which the Bible was studied and
discussed. In an increasing number of settings, Pentecostalism and Roman
Catholicism were communicating directly, without the need for a bridge.
Thus, the fundamental question that many thoughtful leaders in the more
traditional denominations were asking was what should be the role of their
denominations in the emerging Latin American picture. This was a question
that only the ensuing decades of the twenty-first century could answer.

9

❧

Catholicism after Vatican II

We must now continue the history of Roman Catholicism beyond the point at which we left it in Chapter 6 – just after the middle of the twentieth century. In the latter half of the twentieth century, there were in the Roman Catholic Church momentous changes that would be felt in Latin America and throughout the world. These changes were connected mostly with Pope John XXIII and the ecumenical council he convened, *Vatican II*. Roughly at the same time this council was convening, there were in Latin America serious and far-reaching *discussions on poverty and its causes*. Partly as a result of Vatican II, but also in continuation with earlier initiatives, the *Consejo Episcopal Latinoamericano* (Latin American Bishops' Council), commonly known as CELAM, was organized in 1966. Although issues of poverty and social justice were not originally a very high priority in its agenda, they became such in CELAM's second general session, held in Medellin, Colombia, in 1968, and simply known as *Medellin*. While most of its statements were fairly moderate, Medellin opened the way for *base ecclesial communities* (*comunidades eclesiales de base*, or CEBs) and for their concomitant *liberation theology* – both of which made a significant impact not only in Latin America but also throughout the world. All the foregoing had as its context the *political polarization and violence* that took place in Latin America as a reflection of the Cold War, and this polarization and other factors were tied to *resistance and opposition* to both CEBs and liberation theology. At the same time, *the piety of the people*, often at odds with official church teaching, remained strong and varied. Latin American Catholicism had to take into account all of these factors as it moved *into the twenty-first century*.

VATICAN II

The Catholic faithful were mildly surprised in 1959 when, just a few months after his election, Pope John XXIII announced his intention to convene a council of the church. Many had believed that, since Vatican I had confirmed the enormous and centralized power of the Papacy, the time of the ecumenical councils was past, for now the pope had authority to make all decisions without their input. Others pointed out that in the past most councils had been called in order to deal with a major heresy or some other threat to the church, and this did not seem to be the case with the one being proposed. It was reported that, when asked about his purpose in convening a council, Pope John opened the windows and responded, "to let fresh air in." Pope John himself declared that the purpose was an *aggiornamento* – updating – of the church. This was significant, since for the last century and a half the Roman Catholic Church, led by the papacy, had resisted and condemned the changes brought about by modernity. Now, Pope John felt, the time had come to engage the modern world in ways that his predecessors had not.

When the council gathered in 1962, it brought together an unprecedented number of bishops and other prelates, as well as of theologians with expertise in various fields – the *periti* – and non-Catholic observers, Protestant as well as Eastern Orthodox. At that point no one knew what to expect. There was a vast array of subjects to be discussed, from the liturgy of the church to its relationship to other Christians and other religions. It was the first such gathering in which the majority of voting participants came from the Third World. However, church historian Enrique Dussel points out that Latin America was still underrepresented. While 38 percent of all Catholics lived in Latin America, only 22 percent of the "conciliar fathers" were from the area. In the team of periti, Latin America had 50 members, while the Vatican curia had 318 and Europe another 219. Furthermore, Latin American prelates were fairly passive participants, waiting to see what the pope wanted and only one – the bishop of Talca, in Chile – took a decisive part in the deliberations.

The mild surprise at the convening of the council turned into shock as reports came from each of its ten sessions. The Vatican curia had prepared a series of documents with the implicit expectation that the council would discuss, amend, and finally vote their approval with only minor changes. But this was not to be. There were too many prelates present who in their own jurisdictions were experiencing first-hand the profound crisis of the church in its alienation from the modern world and who insisted on rewriting every document so as to deal with that crisis. While this is not the place to discuss all the documents that the council approved in terms of liturgy, religious freedom, other religions, the training of clergy, and so on, the first few words of the *Pastoral Constitution on the Church in the Modern World* – generally known as *Gaudium et spes* – suffice to show the changed mood of a church that for generations had remained aloof from much of the suffering, pain, and injustice in the world:

> The joy and hope, the grief and anguish, of people today, particularly of those who are poor or in some way afflicted, are also the joy and hope, as well as the grief and anguish of those who follow Christ. Nothing truly human is foreign to their hearts, for their community is composed of people – people who, joined in Christ and guided by the Holy Spirit, march towards the Kingdom of God the Father and carry a message of salvation for all.[1]

As expressions of this attitude, vast changes were decreed that would surprise many Catholics throughout the world. Probably the most immediately evident was the celebration of the mass in the vernacular language of each nation and the call to relate worship to the various cultures in which it took place. Also as a result of the council, there was an emphasis on preaching and on the centrality of Christ, and this seemed to imply a "demotion" of many of the saints that had long been the object of popular devotion in Latin America and elsewhere. After a period when the Roman Catholic Church had seen all other Christian bodies as heretical competition, the council opened the way for conversations with other Christians – Protestant as well as Eastern Orthodox. Furthermore, the council also encouraged conversations with other religions.

The council's decisions left many of the more traditional members of the church quite perplexed. The priests and bishops who were instructed to implement the various reforms ordered by the council had little idea how to do so. The more conservative believers were appalled at the mass in the vernacular, at having the altar moved so that the priest celebrating mass was facing the congregation instead of with his back to it, and at a number of other changes. Most notable among the elements of resistance to these changes was the Opus Dei. This was an organization, founded in Spain in 1928, devoted to preserving both orthodox Catholicism and the traditional and hierarchical structure of the church. It often promoted dictatorial or even Fascist governments, as long as they supported the church.

Returning from the council, most of the prelates in Latin America did not know what to do with the new directives. They found in Latin America

---

[1]   *Pastoral Constitution on the Church in the Modern World*, in *Documents of Vatican II*, ed. Austin P. Flannery (Grand Rapids, MI: William B. Eerdmans Publishing Co., 1975), 903.

strong pockets of resistance to the decisions of the council. These pockets were often connected with the program known as *cursillos de cristiandad* – short courses on Christianity – discussed in Chapter 6, and often accused of having connections with Opus Dei. Although eventually the nature of the *cursillos* mellowed in response to Vatican II, at first many of their members and followers resisted the changes proposed by the council.

The bishops charged with implementing the council's decrees had been formed in a previous age – most of them under Pius XI and Pius XII, two popes not known for their openness to the modern world or its democratic ideals. In all their training, these bishops had been led to conceive of their task as maintaining ecclesiastical structures and promoting the growth of the church, not as responding to its members and to society's needs. Once having joined the church, people were expected to follow and support the bishops and other church leaders. Now these bishops had to organize and celebrate liturgies in Spanish and Portuguese as well as a host of indigenous languages, promote preaching, and show openness toward Protestants and even members of other religions. The task was certainly daunting.

DISCUSSIONS ON POVERTY AND ITS CAUSES

Even before Vatican II, there were in Latin America certain beginnings and stirrings, in both the church and society, that would give the implementation of Vatican II in the continent a particular flavor. The need to respond to poverty, and to do so taking into account that it was not only a matter of changing attitudes but also a structural issue, was brought forth in the 1960s by a series of secular publications of which the diary of Carolina Maria de Jesus – discussed in Chapter 6 – is a prime example. In 1961, Oscar Lewis published the results of his research on the culture of poverty in Mexico, *The Children of Sanchez: Autobiography of a Mexican Family*, and shortly thereafter he published similar research on a Puerto Rican family: *La Vida*. All of these, and many more like them, laid bare the often forgotten realities of life in extreme poverty.

At the very time when Vatican II was meeting in Rome, large numbers of priests in Latin America were questioning the traditional explanations of the origins and reasons for poverty and inequity in the region. Those traditional explanations had been given by both secular and Catholic scholars and institutions that for years had been studying the situation in Latin America "scientifically." One of these was the Catholic *Centro de Investigación y Acción Social* (Center for Social Research and Action) in Chile, whose documents suggested that the problem was one of mindset, with the poor envying the rich and the rich not helping the poor, and that what the church should do was to work for a change in the mentality of all. These theoreticians also worked on the premise that Latin America's economic and social woes were due to underdevelopment and that their solution rested simply on finding ways to encourage development – mostly through foreign capital investment.

Many of those working among the poor came to see this explanation of poverty as a fallacy, and even as a way of supporting the status quo while claiming to work for the benefit of the poor. For them, the problem in Latin America was not caused by underdevelopment but by neocolonial dependency. They saw this dependency as leading to the sort of "development" desired and determined by investors – both national and foreign – and by foreign markets. From this perspective, shared by an increasing number of Latin Americans, *desarrollismo* – developmentalism – came to be seen as at best a misconception of both the problem and its possible solutions, and at worst an attempt to keep the poor subservient. Those who supported desarrollismo, and particularly its expression in the Alliance for Progress sponsored by the United States under President Kennedy's leadership, were accused of being neocolonialists. Within the context of religious discourse, Christians supporting desarrollismo were often called "Herodians" – and epithet meaning that these religious leaders were akin to Herod and his followers, willing to betray the interests of their people and even the very heart of their religion in order to serve a foreign empire.

While the council met in Rome, in Latin America the more radical priests began to organize. In 1965, in Argentina, sixty of them gave birth to *Sacerdotes para el Tercer Mundo* (Priests in Favor of the Third World). They openly confronted bishops and other prelates who embraced desarrollismo, as well as those who refused to take action on behalf of the people and seemed to be more concerned with running the church than with making it an agency for service and change. In the same year, an article in a Brazilian religious journal declared that the salvation of the world was intrinsically connected to finding a solution to the tragedy of hunger and to "the liberation of peoples that have been colonized economically and politically."[2] Soon the movement begun in Argentina spread throughout the continent, with parallel organizations in various countries. In 1968, fifty priests gathered in Colombia at a farm called Golconda. They adopted an even more radical stance: the church must support revolution. (Shortly thereafter, the leader of the "Golconda priests,"

---

[2] L.A.G. de Souza, "El postconcilio o el riesgo del ghetto narcisista," *Víspera* 11 (1967): 40, as quoted in Prien, *La historia del cristianismo*, 864.

Camilo Torres, joined a revolutionary guerrilla movement and was killed.) Throughout the continent, voices were echoing similar feelings. Many of these Roman Catholic leaders were in close conversation with those Latin American Protestants who were embracing the "theology of revolution" proposed in 1966 in the Conference on Church and Society that gathered in Geneva under the auspices of the World Council of Churches.

Although most of the bishops and other prelates bemoaned and even condemned all of this, radical Latin American priests also drew strength from the *Declaration of Bishops of the Third World*, issued in 1967 under the leadership of the bishop of Recife, Brazil, Dom Hélder Câmara. This document, signed by seventeen bishops, declared that it was time to "end the concubinage of the church with money" and "free our church from all servitude before the great international financial systems, for one cannot serve God and mamon."[3]

MEDELLIN

While these discussions and priests' organizations would provide the intellectual energy for a new day, a region-wide organization was needed to carry forth the renewal for which they called. This was provided by CELAM. The beginnings of CELAM were fairly conservative. Concerned primarily with the lack of priests and the "Protestant danger," authorities in Rome encouraged the bishops in Latin America to come together to develop a strategy to deal with these matters. Although from its first session in 1966 CELAM included social issues among the items to be discussed, it focused primarily on matters concerning the internal life of the church and challenges to its dominance. This included the recruitment and formation of priests as well as ways to counter Protestantism, secularism, and Communism. The main initiative for change was perhaps the restoration of the permanent diaconate. Following the instructions of Vatican II, married men were ordained deacons, not as a step toward the priesthood but as a recognition of their particular forms of ministry. Many hoped that this permanent diaconate would enroll large numbers of men devoted to social services. But soon studies – particularly in Chile – showed that the vast majority of those seeking the permanent diaconate were men wishing to imitate or have a part in the ministry of priests. They were therefore more interested in their liturgical functions than in a ministry of service outside the confines of the church. Some bishops rejoiced, hoping these men would provide a partial answer to the constant problem of the lack

[3] Alain Gheerbrant, *La iglesia rebelde de América Latina* (Mexico City: Siglo Veintiuno Editores, 1970), 119, as quoted in Prien, *La historia del cristianismo*, 861.

of priests. Yet in most cases the permanent deacons served merely as assistants to priests, and thus their ministry was fairly limited.

All of this set the stage for the Second General Conference of CELAM, which began in Bogota in 1968 but held most of its sessions in Medellin. At the outset, the meeting was not very promising. As the news spread that Pope Paul VI would come to Bogota to open the sessions – the first time a pope had visited Latin America – the increasing political polarization among the faithful became evident. While many simply rejoiced in the blessing of having His Holiness visit their land, many others demanded that the pope show his solidarity with the suffering people rather than with the government and the elites. They urged him to break the tradition of having the church legitimize abuses by governments; to acknowledge the complicity of the church in the oppression of the poor; not to "betray the poor" by blessing a planned International Eucharistic Congress that would avoid addressing the more pressing issues of justice; and to condemn those who had killed Father Camilo Torres. Apparently paying no heed to these requests and strong suggestions, the pope arrived in a military helicopter – a conveyance that for many had become a symbol of military raids on peasants and rural villages. His main concession to the more radical demands before him was to call for a church of poverty:

> [T]he Church today finds herself faced by the vocation of Christ's poverty. Some there are in the Church who already feel poverty's inherent discomforts due to the insufficiency sometimes of bread and often of means. May they be encouraged and aided by their brothers and by the good faithful, and may they be blessed. The poverty of the Church, in its decorous simplicity of form, is a testimony of fidelity to the Gospel.[4]

Such a statement, however, was not very satisfactory to those who demanded that the church take action against the prevailing social and economic structures causing poverty. The reference to the "discomforts" of poverty seemed to indicate a lack of understanding of its tragic dimensions. Furthermore, the pope's speech still focused on the problems of the church as an institution, on the need for more and better clergy, and on keeping all in line with the directives of the hierarchy:

> If a bishop were to concentrate his most constant understanding, patient and cordial attention on the formation, the assistance, the listening to, the

---

[4] Second General Conference of Latin American Bishops, *The Church in the Present-Day Transformation of Latin America in the Light of the Council*, vol 2: *Conclusions* (Washington, D.C.: USCC, Division for Latin America, 1973), 19.

guidance, the instruction, the exhortation and the encouragement of his clergy, he would have well employed his time, his heart and his activity.

Provision should be made to give to councils and priests and pastoral councils the solidity and functionality which the council wishes. Prudently and with paternal understanding and charity, every irregular and undisciplined pronouncement of the clergy should be forestalled, as far as possible.[5]

In other words, the pope saw the work of the leadership of the church essentially as making sure that priests were able to perform their duties and did not step out of line.

After the pope left, the sessions of CELAM moved from Bogota to the relative seclusion of a seminary in Medellin. The gathering included as voting members the presidents of each of the national conferences of bishops and one more bishop for every twenty-five. Besides – as earlier in Vatican II – there were a number of periti, as well as observers, including some Protestants. Most of the participants still had as their first priority the inner life of the church, particularly its growing lack of impact on society at large and its long-lasting need for more clergy. Still, there were others who insisted that the church must respond to the ills of society, not simply for the sake of the church and its prestige, but also for the sake of society itself, and because the Gospel demands it. Foremost among those were Hélder Câmara of Recife, Brazil, and Sergio Méndez Arceo of Cuernavaca, Mexico. Among the periti were a number of theologians who had long been arguing for the need to analyze the ills of society – and particularly the matter of poverty – in structural rather than individualistic term, and thus to seek and promote structural remedies. Others at the gathering feared that these ideas sounded too much like revolution, perhaps even like Communism, and must therefore be rejected.

Eventually, the gathering resulted in sixteen documents that may be organized around two main themes: the first five deal with human life and societal issues, and the other eleven focus mostly on the inner life of the church and what the church must do in order to reach various groups with its message. Thus, document six deals with the "Pastoral Care of the Masses"; document seven, with the "Pastoral Care for the Elites"; documents eleven to thirteen, with priests, religious, and the formation of clergy; and so on. However, even in these documents issues of justice, poverty, and the social order repeatedly appear. This is particularly true of document fourteen, "Poverty of the Church," which in a way connects the inner life of the church with the pressing issues of poverty among the population at large.

[5] Ibid., 17.

This fourteenth document distinguishes among three kinds of poverty. The first is material poverty, the "lack of goods of this world necessary to live worthily."[6] The second, spiritual poverty, is "the attitude of opening up to God, the ready disposition of one who hopes for everything from the Lord."[7] The third is poverty "as a commitment, through which one assumes voluntarily and lovingly the conditions of the needy of the world in order to bear witness to the evil which it represents and to spiritual liberty in the face of material goods."[8] The document then quotes the pope's opening address, in which he called on believers to "break the bonds of the egotistical possession of temporal goods," and invites all Catholics – bishops, priests, religious, and lay people – to embrace "the spirit of poverty."[9] It then insists on the poverty of the church as indissolubly tied to its mission; but it is not altogether clear how this poverty is to be achieved or manifested.

Commenting on the documents having to do with the inner life of the church, historian Hans-Jürgen Prien reaffirms the judgment of many who said that the bishops gathered at Medellin, while ready to pronounce judgment on the evils of society, were less willing to do likewise regarding the ills of the church.

The first five documents deal more directly with the social and economic issues that were rapidly coming to the forefront in much theological and pastoral reflection. From the outset, the first document acknowledges the evils of both Communism and capitalism:

> The system of liberal capitalism and the temptation of the Marxist system would appear to exhaust the possibilities of transforming the economic structures of our continent. Both systems militate against the dignity of the human person. One takes for granted the primacy of capital, its power and its discriminatory utilization of the function of profit-making. The other, although it ideologically supports a kind of humanism, is more concerned with collective man, and in practice becomes a totalitarian concentration of state power. We must denounce the fact that Latin America sees itself caught between these two options and remains dependent on one or the other of the centers of power which control its economy.[10]

As a way to promote greater justice, and to bring about a sort of development that does not augment injustice, the document calls on business and government leaders to "radically modify" the way in which they do business

---

[6] Ibid., 189.
[7] Ibid.
[8] Ibid., 189–190.
[9] Ibid., 191.
[10] Ibid., 45.

and evaluate the results. It also calls for a new political order in which power would not be concentrated in the hands of a few and policies would no longer favor privileged groups. Workers are encouraged to organize so that they might participate actively in shaping economic and social policies and benefit from them. The document asserts that it is also necessary to establish "small basic communities" to counterbalance the elite that holds power. All of this was to be done in collaboration with "non-Catholic Christian Churches and institutions dedicated to the task of restoring justice in human relations."[11] Most of these statements could be interpreted – and many did interpret them – as calls for a change of mind and for moderate policy changes, mostly of a voluntary nature.

These fairly mild statements, however, are accompanied by others calling for more drastic changes, such as "an authentic and urgent reform of agrarian structures and policies." And, in a declaration that would encourage the more revolutionary elements within the church, the bishops affirmed that "faced with the need for a total change of Latin American structures, we believe that change has political reform as its pre-requisite."[12]

While the first document dealt with "Justice," the second took up the subject of "Peace." As could be expected, this document warns against revolution and "the temptation of violence." But surprisingly it also declares that injustice is "institutionalized violence," and that this too destroys peace. This was a crucial statement, implying that violence is not limited to overt acts but also includes structures and conditions of oppression.

The other three documents, three to five, deal respectively with "Family and Demography," "Education," and "Youth." While not as radical as the first two, they are remarkable in their use of sociological and economic analysis and in a pastoral concern that focuses on the people themselves, rather than on the church.

In brief, while not committing the church to revolutionary processes – and even while discouraging them for fear of chaos and violence – Medellin also opened the door for a more radical understanding of the mission of the church in society and of its role in promoting structural political, economic, and social change.

BASE ECCLESIAL COMMUNITIES

The Medellin conference had spoken of the need "that small basic communities be developed in order to establish a balance with minority [meaning

---

[11] Ibid., 50.
[12] Ibid., 47.

elite] groups, which are the groups in power."[13] These communities came to be known as the *comunidades eclesiales de base* (CEBs). Their name and its meaning may require explanation. In this context, *de base* refers to the base, the grassroots of the church. Thus, CEBs are small grassroot communities. The term *eclesial* (ecclesial) was used in order to make it clear that these communities, while ecclesial in nature, were not churches – they were not "ecclesiastical" communities.

The CEBs had their roots in practices that had developed long before Vatican II and Medellin. Although parallel events were taking place in other countries, it was in Brazil that such roots grew most rapidly both before and after Medellin. Some Brazilian bishops, faced by the endemic lack of priests, began developing new means of evangelization and pastoral care. Instead of expecting people to come to church for all their religious education and support, small grassroot groups were created, often meeting in homes, schools, or other facilities, and under lay leadership. These groups engaged in prayer and other religious exercises as well as in projects for improving their communities – adult literacy programs, community clean-up, lessons in hygiene and child care, crafts programs, and the like. What had begun as a policy for providing church services where priests were lacking, soon took wider dimensions. President Jânio Quadros of Brazil, apparently with a view to gaining popularity among the masses, lent his support to this program, particularly as it was organizing small groups in order to promote literacy and other education. This was supported by radio programming through which the small groups – numbering more than seven thousand by 1963 – could be led in their educational and organizational efforts. Those elements from Catholic Action that had specialized in youth and students joined this and other similar efforts, at the same time calling for more decisive action on behalf of the poor.

This entire movement to promote adult education was deeply influenced by Brazilian educator Paulo Freire (1921–1997), who rejected what he called the traditional "banking" view of education. In that view, Freire argued, education is like a "deposit" that teachers are to transmit to students. The result is a structure of power and authority that makes students dependent on the teachers – and that ultimately justifies a social order in which those who have either money or education have the right to determine the lives of those who do not. In contrast to this, Freire proposed a "liberation" view of education, whose main purpose is to affirm students – particularly adults – in their role as producers of culture and not merely as consumers. This in turn empowers

---

[13]   Ibid., 49.

them to question the existing order and become active elements in the shaping of their own culture, identity, and future.

As these developments were taking place within the church, there were significant political shifts throughout Latin America. In 1964, a coup d'état overthrew the elected president of Brazil and put the military in power. One of the excuses given for the coup was the growth of "subversive" elements and the need to preserve "national security." This justification for political oppression was often used by governments in other nations, and for that reason these regimes came to be known as "governments of national security." While such governments of national security suppressed many of the groups that had developed in earlier years, they also radicalized individuals who felt that the suppressed groups represented the best hope for both their church and their nations. While not supportive of the more radical elements within the movement, most Brazilian bishops were still convinced that small gatherings of believers – now taking shape as CEBs – were the only workable approach if the church was to provide ministry to the people at large. As Vatican II was coming to a close, the Brazilian bishops issued a pastoral plan in which all believers were invited to become involved – the *Plano de Pastoral de Conjunto*, or Plan for a Joint Pastoral Practice. As justification for this plan and its reliance on CEBs, the bishops declared that these small community-based groups provided the best way "to renew our parishes, whose structures are increasingly revealed as inadequate."[14] Throughout Latin America, church leaders were making similar experiments and proposals.

Although many in the church hierarchy conceived of CEBs as a way to provide ministry to the masses, and perhaps even to regain the control that was being lost for lack of priests, many among the grassroots viewed them in a different light. Traditionally in Latin America, when people referred to "the church," they meant its hierarchy, its priests, and monastics. However, even before Medellín there had been a growing sense among Latin American Catholics that the church actually belongs to the people – that the church is the people and not the hierarchy. Justification for this emphasis was found in the renewed understanding of Vatican II, of the church as the "people of God." All over the continent, often quite apart from any official policy to create CEBs, groups of lay people gathered – not necessarily as formal CEBs – to discuss their faith and often to oppose the policies and decisions of the leadership of the church. Many such groups became increasingly radicalized. In Buenos

---

[14] Raimundo Caramuru de Barros, *Brasil: Uma igreja em renovação: A experiencea brasileira de planejamento partoral* (Petropolis [Brazil]: Vozes, 1968), 105, as quoted in Prien, *La historia del cristianismo*, 1075.

Aires, for instance, the congregation of the church *Corpus Domini*, upon learn-ing that a parish priest had been appointed without consulting them, simply occupied the church building and forced the hierarchy to negotiate with them. In 1968, a group of approximately two hundred Catholics – including eight priests – locked themselves in the cathedral of Santiago, Chile, demanding that the church take a more active stance in favor of social reform. Actions such as these, and the sentiments behind them, were to be found also in other countries, and some historians see a connection between these groups and the shape that the CEBs eventually took.

The most common agenda for CEB meetings included a time of sharing and solidarity, discussion and analysis of the social conditions in their own communities and their causes and possible solutions, prayer, and Bible study. As time went by, the method emerged of looking at issues in three steps: *ver, juzgar y actuar* – to see, to judge, and to act. "To see" means that Christians should look around in order to identify the most pressing issues – particularly issues of injustice and grief – affecting them and their neighbors. "To judge" means that one must not simply accept the most common explanations for these problems but rather seek their underlying causes. For instance, it is not enough to say that children are dying because the community is unsanitary. One most move beyond this, asking why the community is unsanitary, who makes it so, who profits from not providing the necessary services, and what could be done in order to change conditions. Finally, "to act" means that it is not enough to understand a problem and its causes; Christians must go beyond judging, taking whatever actions seem advisable and possible in order to remedy the situations that they are seeing. The process, however, does not end there, for in judging and acting the community comes to see things in a different way. This new seeing leads to further judging and acting, and so on.

Bible study and discussion were an integral part of this process. Vatican II had called for renewed study of the Bible among the faithful. Following these guidelines, several new and readable versions of the Bible were produced, and most of the hierarchy of the church promoted the distribution and the study of the Bible. While in some dioceses and parishes Bible study was conducted by priests, there clearly were not enough of such leaders. It was necessary to train vast numbers of laity to lead Bible study and discussion among the people. These trained teachers of the Bible became known in many dioceses as "delegates of the Word." They often traveled deep into the countryside, where priests were seldom seen, and there conducted Bible study, quite often within CEBs that they also organized.

While those who promoted this program seem to have thought at first that the delegates of the Word would simply carry the message they had been taught, the results were quite different. It soon became evident that people who had never had the opportunity to read the Bible, but who had long believed that this was the Word of God, were reading Scripture with an unexpected freshness and enthusiasm. They were doing so with the encouragement of delegates of the Word as well as of some priests. The CEBs – thousands in each country – were not reading the Bible merely as a tool for religious instruction or – as was generally done by both Protestants and Catholics – to learn correct doctrine. They were reading it as a guide to life and as a clue to understand the world around them. They were thus discovering things in otherwise commonly known passages that the hierarchy of the church did not expect. This seemed to prove Paulo Freire right, pointing to a sort of education in which, rather than having people simply receive what their teachers transmitted to them, the learners themselves would take charge not only of their education but also of their understanding of both themselves and the social order.

Clearly, however, there was still a role for the teacher or study leader. Semi-literate people reading the Gospel of Matthew, for instance, needed someone to explain to them what is a Pharisee or a publican. Ideally, if Freire's method was to be strictly followed, this was the function of the delegates of the Word and the priests and others who organized and led CEBs. But this was also a time when radical views of social change, including calls for revolution, were common. Thus, radicalized priests and delegates of the Word led many CEBs to read the Bible from the perspective of a situation of oppression and the hope for liberation through revolution.

It is impossible to know all that was being discussed in the thousands of CEBs throughout Latin America. There are, however, sufficient reports to be able to gather a general view of such discussions. Particularly enlightening are the conversations recounted in Ernesto Cardenal's *The Gospel in Solentiname.* Cardenal (1925–) is a priest, a poet, and a monk. He founded a CEB on the island of Solentiname, in Lake Managua. There he promoted discussions of the Gospel readings for each Sunday. Impressed by what people were discovering in the Bible, he began recording these conversations, which were eventually published as *The Gospel in Solentiname.* Reading these reports, one is struck by both the newness with which people read well-known stories and the degree to which they expressed a revolutionary ethos that clearly reflected Cardenal's own views. The revolutionary bias may be seen, for instance, in the declaration of some in the group that when Mary urged Jesus to perform a miracle at the wedding in Cana, even though his "time has not come," she was like a revolutionary mother urging a son to join the revolution. The ability to see in Scripture what most others missed is evident in the same discussion about the wedding at Cana. One of the participants expressed concern that

Jesus turned the water for the rites of purification into wine, thus making it impossible for religious folk to purify themselves. What would happen then, if someone came seeking water for the religious rite? With a freshness that borders on the disrespectful, another participant responded that Jesus would simply say, "It is time for a party. Here, have a drink." On another occasion, while the group was discussing the story of the "wise men" in Matthew, one of the participants commented that they were not so wise after all, for they went to Jerusalem, Herod's capital, asking where was this new king who had been born. This would be like someone going to Dictator Somoza's palace in Managua and asking where was the new revolutionary leader who was emerging!

LIBERATION THEOLOGY

Much of the ethos of the CEBs found its expression in what became known as *liberation theology*, many of whose main exponents had been and continued being part of CEBs and therefore claimed that in a way they were expressing the actual theology of the people. Among the many theologians of liberation in Latin America three of the most vocal and creative figures were Dominican Gustavo Gutiérrez (1928–), Jesuit Juan Luis Segundo (1925–1996), and Franciscan Leonardo Boff (1938–).

Gutiérrez is commonly credited with the founding of Latin American liberation theology, for in 1971 he published the first major work on the subject, *Teología de la liberación: Perspectivas*. He is a mestizo, born and raised in a poor family, who was involved in various movements of support for the poor since his student days. After studying several other disciplines in Lima, he decided to join the Order of Preachers – the Dominicans – and received an outstanding education, not only in his native Peru, but also in Chile, Italy, Belgium, and France, where he received his doctorate from the University of Lyon. When CELAM met in Medellin, he was one of the periti, and his hand may be seen in several of the documents issued by that historic gathering. After 1971, he continued writing prolifically, further developing the principles of liberation theology, and joining it with the earlier history of Latin America – particularly in his book on Bartolomé de las Casas, published in 1992 under the title of *En busca de los pobres de Jesucristo* (Las Casas: In Search of the Poor of Jesus Christ).

One of Gutiérrez's most commonly misunderstood tenets is the centrality of *praxis* for theology. He insists that theology is always a process of reflection on praxis, and therefore one cannot properly do theology first and then engage in praxis, as if the latter were the mere application of theology. Many – particularly in the North Atlantic – understood this as simply meaning that there is a connection between theology and practice. But Gutiérrez made a very clear distinction between practice and praxis. The first is mere action; the latter is a critically committed engagement. In praxis, one not only does things but also does them out of a commitment to God's justice and with a critical perspective that moves naturally into reflection. This reflection in turn leads to renewed praxis, further reflection, and so on. Thus, Gutiérrez's view of the relationship between praxis and reflection is parallel to the method of seeing, judging, and acting.

Segundo was a Uruguayan Jesuit who had also studied in both Latin America and Europe – Buenos Aires, Louvain, and Paris. Among his many works, two stand out: the five volume *Teología abierta para el laico adulto* (An Open Theology for the Adult Lay Person, published in English as *A Theology for Artisans of the New Humanity*) and *The Liberation of Theology*. In Montevideo, he founded a center for the sociological study of religion whose purpose was not only to study religion as a sociological subject but also to develop theological perspectives that would result in sociological change. He was profoundly influenced by French theologian and paleontologist Pierre Teilhard de Chardin and his non-Darwinian understanding of evolution and its place in God's purposes.

Boff is a Brazilian and former Franciscan who studied systematic theology in Germany under Karl Rahner – arguably the most outstanding Catholic theologian of the twentieth century. Boff focused on the doctrine of the church – ecclesiology – proposing new paradigms for understanding the church and its mission. When he published his major book on the subject, *Church, Charisma and Power*, he was temporarily silenced by the Vatican (1985). Eight years later, when threatened once again with an order of silence, he left the priesthood, although remaining a Catholic. He then became a professor at the University of the State of Rio de Janeiro, where he continues publishing, now joining his ecological concerns with his long-standing advocacy for the oppressed – arguing that the earth, too, is oppressed by anthropocentrism as well as by capitalism and industrial "development."

As one looks at the theology of these three, as well as of the many other liberation theologians, it is important to point out that the phrase "theology of liberation" does not mean a theology *about* liberation. In this, Latin American liberation theology differs radically from earlier movements such as the theology of development or the theology of revolution. It insists that, like any theology, it is about God, God's workings in creation and history, and human salvation and responsibility. Those other theologies took traditional theological and doctrinal statements and then sought to apply them to concerns such as development or revolution. Liberation theology, in contrast, seeks to reread all of theology and Scripture from the perspective of a people oppressed and hoping for liberation. Thus, for instance, the five volumes of Segundo's *A Theology for Artisans of the New Humanity* deal respectively with the church, grace and the human condition, God, the sacraments, and "evolution and guilt" – in this last volume showing the profound influence of Teilhard. Other liberation theologians published books on specific aspects of Christian theology, all of them dealing with traditional doctrine and looking at it from a new perspective. One such case is the work of Spanish Jesuit Jon Sobrino (1938–), *Christology from Latin America*, which takes traditional Christological dogma and reinterprets it from a perspective of liberation as he had experienced it over many years of living in El Salvador.

This new theology also required its own methodology. At its very foundation was the notion that it is not only how one thinks that determines how one lives but also how one lives that determines how one thinks. This principle had been proposed by Karl Marx a century earlier, and now liberation theologians took it to heart. They insisted, for instance, that the traditional doctrine of God reflects the social perspective and experience of those who formulated it, and that therefore when interpreted from a different perspective – that of the poor and the oppressed – it is shown to be something else. This meant that one should no longer take for granted that the study of philosophy was the best preparation for theology, because the social sciences – particularly economics and sociology – promised to lead theology, and therefore the church, in different and better directions. Furthermore, claiming to be an expression of reflection on praxis among the poor and the oppressed, liberation theology often followed a method of dialoguing with those it claimed to represent.

The writings of Karl Marx had a profound impact on most liberation theologians – as they did on many others in Latin America. In the press, these theologians were often described as Marxists, and therefore, by implication, as supporters of Communism and even of the Soviet Union. There is no doubt that, the Soviet Union being more distant and less influential in Latin America than the United States, liberation theologians and their followers tended to be more critical of North American than of Soviet policies. But most Latin American liberation theologians insisted that they used Marx's work as a tool of analysis and not as a source for a programmatic solution for the ills they were analyzing. For this reason, some preferred to use the adjective "Marxian" rather than "Marxist" to express their connection with Marx's theories. In this regard, it must also be pointed out that, while the international press often depicted them as advocates of violence, most liberation theologians pronounced themselves in opposition to all violence – although insisting, as Medellin had done before them, that violence is not only what a revolutionary may do, but also what a capitalist oppressor does. Thus, liberation theology was highly critical of capitalism and the social structures it had created.

One of the most cogent discussions of the method of this theology is found in Segundo's *The Liberation of Theology*, published in Spanish in 1974 and in English in 1975. There he proposes what he calls the "hermeneutical circle" – or the circle of interpretation. He insists that the subject of theology is not primarily society or history but the interpretation of Scripture and Christian doctrine, and therefore the task of theology is always one of interpretation – a hermeneutical task. Hermeneutics, however, is not a simple one-way relationship with the text, nor is it even a two-way relationship; it is a circular relationship. The hermeneutical circle thus consists of four basic steps:

> *Firstly* there is our way of experiencing reality, which leads us to ideological suspicion. *Secondly* there is the application of our ideological suspicion to the whole ideological superstructure and to theology in particular. *Thirdly* there comes a new way of experiencing theological reality that leads us to exegetical suspicion, that is, to the suspicions that the prevailing interpretation of the Bible has not taken important pieces of data into account. *Fourthly* we have our new hermeneutic, that is, our new way of interpreting the fountainhead of our faith (i.e., Scripture) with the new elements at our disposal.[15]

Since this is a circle, the fourth step it also the beginning of a new round of suspicion, reinterpretation, and rediscovery. Thus, what Segundo proposed was very similar to the cycle used by the CEBs of seeing, judging, and acting and Gutiérrez's understanding of praxis leading to reflection and reflection to praxis.

The "ideological suspicion" that Segundo mentions here lies at the core of all liberation theology. In this context, "ideology" is not to be understood in the common sense, as simply a system of ideas and ideals. Ideology is the conscious or unconscious use of ideas and ideals to promote particular social and economic perspectives and agendas. Here again, the presence of Marxian influences is clear: an ideology is a superstructure by which those who control society justify their position of power and privilege – and which those not in control often accept, thus acquiescing to their own marginalization and oppression.

Another principle at the heart of liberation theology is the "preferential option for the poor." This is not grounded merely on a sense of compassion or even of justice, but rather on God's own actions in Scripture, showing particular concern for the poor, the widow, the orphan, and the alien – in other words, for all who are weak and marginalized – and calling the people

---

[15] Juan Luis Segundo, *The Liberation of Theology* (Maryknoll, NY: Orbis Books, 1976), 9.

of God to act in response to this divine concern. This does not mean that God does not love the rich. But it does mean that God rejects the notion that some are justly rich and others are justly poor. It also means that for the rich obedience to God – and true religion – has different and perhaps more demanding dimensions than for the poor.

After the first generation of liberation theologians, a second generation arose that was more concerned with spelling out the implications of a liberationist perspective for various aspects of theology, as well as for the life of the church and of society. Many wrote commentaries on various books of the Bible from a perspective of liberation. Others wrote on specific doctrines – the Trinity, Christology, ecclesiology, the human creature, ecology, the nature of the Christian hope, and so on. Still others sought to refocus theological reflection on concrete sets of circumstances – for example, urban laborers, native populations, peasants, particular political conditions in a given country. This second generation also included a number of women whose perspective critiqued and enriched much that earlier theologians of liberation had said. Brazilian Ana Maria Tepedino (1941–) published in 1990 a widely read book, *The Women Disciples of Jesus*. Mexican María Pilar Aquino (1956–) and others wrote on the significance of *lo cotidiano* – the everyday – for Christian praxis and theology, and of the particular experience of women regarding it. In 1998, she and Tepedino published *Between Indignation and Hope: Latin American Feminist Theology*.

These further developments of Latin American liberation theology prompted many to point out that it would be more exact to speak of "liberation theologies" (in the plural). Besides the developments just mentioned, other differences and nuances began to emerge. Dom Hélder Câmara, who had been among the forerunners of liberation theology, rejected Marxism altogether and also insisted on the centrality of the church and its doctrine for the future hope of Latin America. In contrast, Brazilian Hugo Assman (1933–), who had been one of the first to propose Marxism as an instrument of social analysis, was more inclined to take his point of departure from the social conditions of the people, and some interpreted him – although with some exaggeration – as altogether rejecting revelation in favor of social experience and liberating praxis as the starting point of theology.

POLITICAL POLARIZATION AND VIOLENCE

The second half of the twentieth century was marked in Latin America – as elsewhere – by the polarization brought about by the Cold War. Until the very early 1960s, this tension was relatively mild. But during that decade, as the Cuban Revolution increased its economic, political, and ideological links with the Soviet Union, the struggle between the two great superpowers and the systems they represented was directly projected into Latin America. Out of Cuba, Fidel Castro tried to export revolution, and to that end Ernesto "Che" Guevara was sent to organize guerrillas in the Andean region, where he was killed in 1967. In spite of that setback – and perhaps in a measure because of it, for Guevara became an icon among revolutionary youth throughout Latin America – the spirit of revolution, and the quest for a socialist solution to the ills of Latin America, spread far and wide. In several countries, openly pro-Soviet parties – often called "Partido Socialista Popular" – increased in membership and influence. Other revolutionary groups – though less openly pro-Soviet – emerged in various countries. In 1970, Chile elected socialist Salvador Allende as its president. Allende announced a program of social and economic reform, including the nationalization of private banks and the copper industry. All over the region, candidates with socialist leanings gained ground. In several countries, most notably in Nicaragua, Peru, and Colombia, leftist guerrillas, both rural and urban, gained popularity as enemies of dicta-torial governments. In 1978, Sandinista guerrillas stormed the national palace in Managua, took more than a thousand hostages, and gained the freedom of fifty-nine political prisoners. They also received a large quantity of cash, and safe conduct to Cuba. By the next year, the long-standing dynasty of the Somozas, who had ruled Nicaragua with an iron hand, came to an end, and the Sandinistas attained power.

The response to these leftist upheavals was neither slow nor mild. We have already indicated that in 1964 the armed forces overthrew the elected govern-ment of Brazil. In 1973, clearly with the support of the Central Intelligence Agency (CIA) of the United States, Allende was overthrown, apparently com-mitted suicide, and was succeeded by a strong-hand military government under the leadership of Augusto Pinochet. Although not as openly as in Chile, the CIA and Latin American conservative elements sought similar results throughout the region. In 1976, the Argentine military took over the govern-ment in Buenos Aires. By the end of that decade, most of Latin America was under military rule. Furthermore, these military governments shared a com-mon ideology whose basic value was *la seguridad del estado* (national security), particularly against leftist subversives. This security allegedly required the sup-pression of most dissenting groups – although some governments allowed a measure of moderate dissent, apparently in order to claim that they respected civil rights. The various governments of national security – and according to some the intelligence services of the United States – shared information regarding "subversives." The collaboration among these governments meant that it was no longer possible for dissenters to seek refuge in a neighboring country, for it was quite possible that they would simply be returned to their country of origin. Latin American dissenters testified before the American Congress that the United States was providing equipment and intelligence to the forces of repression of the governments of national security; these witnesses were generally ignored by Congress. The victory of the leftist Sandinistas in Nicaragua, and the fear that other countries in Latin America would follow a similar route, led to armed conflicts in which citizens of countries such as Guatemala and El Salvador fought proxy wars on behalf of the United States on the one hand and the Soviet Union and Cuba on the other.

What is here told in a few paragraphs actually spelled death, torture, and tragedy for thousands of Latin Americans. Entire villages were wiped out overnight. Claiming that their countries were threatened by subversive and terrorist guerrillas, right-wing extremists formed "death squads." These paramilitary groups – quite often the military themselves, but wearing civilian clothing – would invade a home in the middle of the night, carry away several members of a family, and make them "disappear." Thousands "disappeared" under similar circumstances, never to be heard from again. Bodies of "unknown persons" were frequently found by the roadside – often with clear signs of brutal torture. Women were raped as a "lesson" to their husbands and children. Many used the excuse of "national security" and the defense against terrorism and subversion for their own purposes. Indian communities were strafed by military aircraft so that someone with ties to the government could take their lands. In Argentina, childless women with political connections secretly adopted the children of those whom their husbands or others in the military had killed.

While all of this was going on, the Catholic Church was once again divided between the "two faces" that we have seen in earlier chapters. On the one hand, some staunchly defended the governments of national security as bulwarks against "atheistic Communism." After the fall of the military regime in Argentina, officers of the Air Force told of priests blessing their endeavors as they took off in helicopters carrying suspected "subversives" to be dumped alive into the ocean miles away from land. Some church leaders in Chile celebrated the death of President Allende and the rise of dictator Augusto Pinochet with thanksgiving masses. There were attempts to suppress CEBs that were accused of having embraced radical views. Liberation theologians were dubbed "Communists," and their orthodoxy was repeatedly questioned in religious periodicals. Thus, there clearly was a segment of the church that generally shared the view of the governments of national security and approved of their actions.

However, many of those who were killed were church leaders and workers. In Guatemala, dozens – perhaps hundreds – of delegates of the Word were killed as well as several priests and other church workers. In December 1980, members of the National Guard of El Salvador intercepted a van carrying four American churchwomen. The four women were never again seen alive. They had been raped and killed, and their bodies dumped for passers-by to find. Although there were many signs indicating who the perpetrators were, they were not brought to justice. Nine years later, six Jesuit priests, their housekeeper, and her fifteen-year old daughter were killed with impunity by members of the "Atlacatl" Battalion who had been trained in the School of the Americas in the United States. The number of delegates of the Word and other such workers killed – and considered martyrs by many – rose into the thousands.

Probably nothing illustrates the struggles of the church and its leaders as well as does the life of Archbishop Oscar A. Romero of San Salvador. He had been ordained as a priest in 1942 and was quite content with the existing order of things in El Salvador. After being made a bishop, he became Secretary General of the National Bishops' Conference of El Salvador in 1967. Even though Vatican II had concluded two years earlier, Romero saw no great need for changes in the life of the Salvadoran church. After the conference in Medellin in 1968, he was still warning against the "demagoguery" of people whose opposition to the military regime in El Salvador reflected their desire to implant Marxism. As the editor of the Catholic magazine *Orientación*, he supported the status quo, arguing that peace was to be sought above any other value and that therefore "subversives" must be repressed.

Romero's attitude changed drastically in 1975 when the National Guard raided the village of Tres Calles in his diocese of Santiago de María. The Guard went from house to house, supposedly looking for concealed weapons, pulling people out and cutting them into pieces with machetes. Romero was shocked and incensed. At the victims' funeral mass, he preached his first sermon defending human rights and condemning those who violated them under the pretense of preserving peace. He also wrote to the president of El Salvador protesting what had happened. When the president ignored his appeal, Romero became convinced that what had happened at Tres Calles was not an isolated incident but actually a matter of policy.

His protests and calls for justice turned the ruling elite against Romero. When the Vatican named him archbishop of San Salvador, there were loud protests from many in the aristocracy. Romero replied by insisting on the need for justice for the poor. Rather than living in the bishop's palace, he took up residence in a hospital for indigents. He was preparing to assume his duties as head of the Salvadoran church when dozens of civilians protesting what were clearly rigged elections were machine-gunned by the military. Romero then ordered all priests in his diocese to offer sanctuary to anyone who was fleeing the military and its death squads.

The death squads took up the challenge. Romero's friend Rutilio Grande, a Jesuit, was shot and killed together with two companions. Romero wept openly while holding Father Rutilio's remains. After the funeral, he excommunicated those who had murdered his friend and ordered all services in the city cancelled, while a single mass was celebrated outdoors in the plaza facing the cathedral. Leading voices in government and among the national elite protested the bishop's attitudes and actions, and Romero was summoned by the Vatican. But when he returned he declared that the pope's response to his explanations was simply, "Courage!" His opponents circulated leaflets with a simple message: "Be a patriot. Kill a priest." More villages were attacked, and people massacred. Four Jesuit priests disappeared, and their tortured bodies were later found across the border in Guatemala.

Romero knew that he was marked for death. There were threats and attempts on his life – including a plot to blow up the cathedral. He declared that if he was killed he would still live on in the soul of the Salvadoran people. On March 24, 1980, the end came. Romero was preaching at a funeral mass in a chapel. His theme was Jesus's saying, "Whoever would save his life will lose it, and whoever loses his life for my sake will find it." He also referred to Paul's words in I Corinthians 15, to the effect that a grain of wheat cannot produce life unless it dies first. On a recording of that occasion one hears him declaring:

> Those who give themselves up in service to others for love of Christ, they will live. Just as the grain of wheat seems to die, but does not. If it does not die, it will remain alone. There is a harvest because it dies, because it allows itself to be sacrificed in the soil, to be undone, and by being undone it produces the harvest.

And then, referring to the host and the chalice, he continued:

> May this broken body and this blood shed for humankind nourish us, so that we too may give up our bodies and our blood to suffering and to pain, like Christ – not for ourselves, but to bring forth visions of justice and of peace for our people.
>
> Let us therefore come closely together in faith and in hope as we pray both for doña Sarita [the deceased] and for ourselves.

He never finished his words, for at that precise moment a shot was fired – his death a dramatic fulfilment of his own sermon.

At his funeral, in the cathedral of San Salvador, a quarter of a million people were present. Only one of all the bishops in the entire country was there. A bomb exploded, and in the resulting panic forty people were killed. Repression became even fiercer. More than thirty-five thousand people were killed or simply "disappeared." More than one out of every eight Salvadorans fled the country. Still, his memory sustained those who continued the struggle. His tomb became a place of pilgrimage. Pope John Paul II visited it and then appointed as Romero's successor the only bishop who had dared attend his funeral. Christians worldwide acknowledge Romero's courage and sacrificial stance. The Church of England included his name among the twentieth-century martyrs to be venerated, and a statue of Romero was placed above a door in Westminster Abbey. In 1997, a formal process was inaugurated for the beatification of Romero – the first step toward canonization into sainthood.

The very life of Oscar Arnulfo Romero is one more instance of what we have seen throughout this history, that Christianity in Latin America has often had two faces: one that supports the status quo, blesses or at least condones injustice, and whose main concern is the survival and prosperity of the church; and another that questions and challenges the status quo, denounces injustice, and is primarily concerned with the well being of the people. In a singular way, Romero's spiritual pilgrimage parallels that of Las Casas. Like Las Casas, he set out as simply one more among the many who saw no contradiction between the prevailing injustice of his time and the Gospel in which he believed. And, like Las Casas, when he did come to see that contradiction he devoted the rest of his life to the struggle for justice.

RESISTANCE AND OPPOSITION TO LIBERATION THEOLOGY AND THE CEBS

Many of the groups that the governments of national security considered subversive were precisely the CEBs that were meeting to study Scripture, analyze social conditions in their communities and countries, and seek answers to them. These governments – and many in the church who supported them, often out of a fear of Communism – regarded liberation theology as a subversive movement intent on overthrowing them as well as the existing social and economic order. Thus, many of those who were killed by death squads were liberation theologians, or at least supporters of liberation theology. The decades of the 1970s and 1980s were not easy times for theologians of liberation nor for their followers.

Parallel to the physical persecution already described, liberation theology was challenged or threatened in three other ways: first, by a simplistic distortion of its tenets; second, by official actions by church authorities; and third, by having its language coopted into traditional contents and thus rendered innocuous.

The oversimplification and even demonization of Latin American liberation theology began almost as soon as it appeared – and in the minds of many justified attempts to suppress it in the name of national security. Since it made use of Marxian social analysis, and since it was radically critical of the policies of the United States and of free-enterprise capitalism in general, it was vulnerable to the charge of being either pro-Communist or simply Communist. The obvious sympathy of some liberation theologians for the Cuban Revolution made this accusation more believable. The secular press, both in Latin America and elsewhere, affirmed that liberation theology was encouraged and even supported by the Soviet Union – or if not, by Communist China or Fidel Castro. Even the religious press – particularly the Catholic press sympathetic to the Opus Dei – followed suit, making it appear that liberation theologians were anti-church, that they did not believe the essential doctrines of Scripture and the church, and that their central goal was revolution rather than obedience to the Gospel. Some went so far as to call for a "crusade" against the new infidels. Fortunately, the leading liberation theologians – people such as Gutiérrez, Segundo, and Boff – had received the best traditional theological education possible and thus generally avoided making themselves vulnerable to easy accusations of heresy.

More difficult was the growing official opposition – or at least resistance – on the part of church bodies and authorities. Pressure was exerted from Rome. At the 1972 assembly of CELAM that took place in Sucre, Bolivia, Monsignor Alfonso López Trujillo, a conservative who feared the content and the consequences of liberation theology, was elected general secretary. The assembly itself produced fairly conservative documents that in many ways contradicted or at least weakened what had been declared at Medellin.

As the debate grew, all eyes turned toward the meeting of CELAM scheduled to take place in Puebla, Mexico, in 1979. Many expected liberation theology to be condemned outright. Interest in this assembly was such that more than three thousand journalists and observers from all around the world were present. In contrast to Medellin, liberation theologians and their sympathizers were given no role in the preparatory documents or in the actual discussions. The fear that liberation theology and its leaders might be condemned, however, produced an outcry among Catholics and other Christians, both in Latin America and elsewhere. Additionally, since many countries were under "national security" military governments, church leaders at CELAM feared that an outright rejection of liberation theology might appear to be an official endorsement of those clearly unpopular, and in many cases murderous, regimes. The result was that Puebla produced a series of documents that, while not reaffirming the more radical views of Medellin, refrained from an outright condemnation of liberation theology.

Official opposition was also coming from the Vatican. In 1984, the Sacred Congregation for the Doctrine of the Faith, under the leadership of Cardinal Joseph Ratzinger – later to become Pope Benedict XVI – issued an *Instruction on Some Aspects of Liberation Theology*. This was a negative judgment on liberation theology in general, calling it "a severe deviation from Christian faith" and caricaturing it as a purely humanistic theology with little or no place for revealed truth and as an espousal of Marxism that would lead to atheism. The document declared that it was not intended to discourage a genuine concern for the poor and a quest for justice but rather to "call the attention of pastors, theologians and all the faithful to the deviations and perils of deviation, ruinous for faith and for Christian living, implied by certain forms of liberation theology."[16]

The *Instruction* did not have the intended results. While deploring what it said, liberation theologians in general declared that, since the document did not describe their own positions but a caricature thereof, it did not actually refer to them.

Although the *Instruction* stressed the connection between Marxism and the theology of liberation, many in Latin America and elsewhere thought that at a deeper level it showed the concern of Ratzinger and other authorities in the Vatican: that the Latin American church was moving in directions that were undermining the power of both its own local hierarchy and the Vatican. This was particularly true in that the CEBs had become a movement beyond the control of bishops or even of priests. In many parishes where priests disagreed with what was taking place in the CEBs, these simply continued existing on their own, often in open conflict with the parish priest and even with his bishop.

Given the widespread negative response to, and the general ineffectiveness of, the first *Instruction*, Ratzinger issued a new one in 1986, the *Instruction on Christian Freedom and Liberation* – often simply called the *Second Instruction*. This was more subtle than the first. It strongly condemned the inequities existing in Latin America, as well as several other social ills; it called on Christians to take action against injustice; and it even recognized some of the contributions of liberation theology. Yet, in a carefully nuanced response, Gutiérrez was able to claim that this *Second Instruction* did not preclude his teachings and even that it showed a measure of support for liberation theology.

[16] Sacred Congregation for the Doctrine of the Faith, introduction to *Libertatis nuntius: Instrucción sobre algunos aspectos de la "teologia de la liberación,"* issued in Rome, August 6, 1984.

These documents were parallel to more concrete, although largely unsuccessful, actions against individual theologians of liberation. As already mentioned, in 1985, a few months after the first *Instruction*, and as a response to his
book *Church, Charisma and Power*, Leonardo Boff was officially "silenced" by
the Sacred Congregation for the Doctrine of the Faith – that is, he was prohibited from publishing or giving public addresses. After this ban was lifted,
he was threatened by another, and at that point he decided to leave the priesthood. Gustavo Gutiérrez was never officially condemned by Rome. Instead,
Cardinal Ratzinger called the Peruvian Conference of Bishops to Rome and
there pressured them to condemn Gutiérrez. The bishops, however, refused –
apparently in part because they felt such a condemnation was inappropriate
and in part because they were appalled by Ratzinger's action, which undermined their own authority.

The resistance to liberation theology was not manifested only in simplistic
distortions by the press and conservative Catholics and governments and in
official documents and actions of the church; it was manifested also, in a subtler
way, in attempts to coopt its language and thus render it ineffective. This was
done most notably by Cardinal López Trujillo – mentioned previously as a
secretary general of CELAM. In his many writings, he used the same language
of liberation theologians but gave it an entirely different content. According to
him, liberation from oppression was indeed at the very core of the Gospel, but
this was to be understood in terms of liberation from the oppression of sin.
The poor did merit special attention, but this was "the poor in spirit." López
Trujillo's actions had two immediate results. On the one hand, much of the
language that liberation theologians had been using now became common
in many of the official documents of CELAM and other church authorities.
On the other hand, it forced liberation theologians to clarify further what
they meant by "liberation," "the preferential option for the poor," "praxis,"
and many other terms and phrases. The net result was that the language of
liberation theologians became more precise, thus helping clarify its meaning
and its connection with both traditional Christian doctrine and the social
issues of the time.

With the demise of the Soviet Union in 1990, many predicted that liberation
theology would also disappear. This prediction was mostly based on the perceived connection between that theology and Communism. Certainly, there
was a change in mood among liberation theologians. The earlier expectation
of many among them, that a liberating process already in existence would
soon bring about a more just social order, was postponed. It now seemed
that there was little opposition to liberal capitalism and that the increasing
inclusion of Latin America into a global economy would lead to even more

inequity and poverty. Indeed, whereas in earlier times liberation theologians focused on the exodus from Egypt as the paradigm through which they read Scripture, there was now more interest in the exile in Babylon as a paradigm showing how to keep the faith while in an alien land and under oppressive regimes. Yet, the new world order in which the Soviet Union was no longer a superpower also made it easier for theologians of liberation to express their analysis of the ills of society without being accused of being Communists – an accusation that had lost much weight.

THE PIETY OF THE PEOPLE

Vatican II had insisted on the centrality of Christ for Christian religion. For many, this meant that devotion to the saints had to be pushed aside. In many church buildings throughout Latin America, the saints and their images were placed in less conspicuous places, making it clear that Christian devotion should focus first of all on Christ himself. The word from Rome was that a number of saints who had never existed – St. Christopher, for instance – were to be expunged from the list of saints. Some reformist priests felt that the time had come to purify the church of the many "pagan" accretions and baseless religious traditions that had accrued over the centuries. There was, for instance, an attempt to make the laity understand that St. Lazarus was not the poor man, covered with sores, of the parable of Jesus but the brother of Mary and Martha. But St. Lazarus, covered with sores and surrounded by dogs licking them, had become a powerful center of devotion for many in Latin America, particularly among the poor. He had also been identified with a particular god of the African pantheon and was thus an important element of Afro-Christian religion. In spite of all the "enlightened" efforts to explain the historical truth about St. Lazarus, the allegiance of the people remained with the Lazarus in rags and surrounded by dogs.

In general, the efforts of reformist priests to "purify" Catholicism met with little success. Many believers felt that it was easier to approach the saints than it was to approach Jesus – particularly since they had been taught that the highest form of the presence of Jesus was in the Eucharist, and this had to be performed by a priest. When images of saints were removed from their traditional places of prominence, many of the faithful still sought them out in order to pray before them. It soon proved impossible for the church simply to ban such devotional practices – as well as the ex-votos and retablos discussed in Chapter 6.

Eventually, there was a growing consensus among Latin American Catholic theologians that such "popular religiosity" was not to be condemned but rather affirmed as an expression of the faith of the people. A number of liberation theologians pointed out that what made such religiosity popular was precisely that it was beyond the control of the established authorities of the church and was therefore a truer expression of the faith of the people. Eventually, some argued that to speak of a popular *religiosity* was to make this faith and its practice inferior to the official religion of the church, and that therefore it was best to speak of popular *religion*. Thus, as the twentieth century came to a close the effort to purify the faith of the people, which had been quite strong in the 1970s, had been practically abandoned, and much theological work was devoted, for instance, to show the relevance of the Virgin of Guadalupe and what her story reveals about the nature of God and God's relationship with the marginalized.

CONCLUSION

The CELAM conference of Santo Domingo opened on October 12, 1992 – exactly five hundred years after the "discovery" of the western hemisphere. Many feared that this event would polarize the church, for while some planned great celebrations to commemorate the arrival of Christianity in the Americas, other saw that date as the beginning of the oppression and decimation of the native populations and the destruction of their ancient cultures as well as a herald of other tragic events in Latin America's later history. The conference of Santo Domingo, however, showed that the time of radical polarization had passed. Its final document, included in a collection edited by Alfred Hennelly, spoke of a "new evangelization." The conference explained the meaning of this phrase as indicating, on the one hand, that the original evangelization in times of the conquest was true evangelization, for people were brought to believe in Christ; and, on the other hand, that this original evangelization was insufficient and often mixed with injustice and abuse. Reviewing much of the history of Christianity in Latin America, the conference claimed the value of the work done by missionaries and other Catholics throughout those five hundred years. But it also acknowledged that much of the work of the church had been done in complicity with violence, oppression, and injustice. Thus, what CELAM now proposed was a "new evangelization" that was to be carried out by all true believers – lay as well as ordained – and which must include issues of justice and liberation.

The tenor of the conference in Santo Domingo showed that the polarization of earlier decades was slowly being resolved. Many of the original tenets of liberation theology had now become part of the official position of CELAM. At the same time, the authority of the church and its hierarchy and the value of traditional Latin American Catholicism were reaffirmed.

All of this was a sign that a new age was arriving in which the challenges before the Roman Catholic Church would be different and which would require different policies and initiatives. Foremost among these was the growth of Protestantism. The numeric growth of traditional Protestantism had been relatively slow in most countries. But as the twentieth century came to a close, Pentecostalism was growing at a rate that Catholic leaders found alarming. Many of them felt they were struggling with Pentecostalism for the very soul of Latin America. They feared that this vast region, which had long been almost exclusively Catholic and where fifty years earlier more than a third of all Catholics in the world had lived, would become a Pentecostal region.

To these developments we will turn in Chapter 10.

Pentecostalism and Autochthonous Movements

Early in the twentieth century, a movement began that would eventually sweep through much of Christianity. This is usually called the Pentecostal or Charismatic movement. These two words, "Pentecostal" and "Charismatic," are often used interchangeably.

Etymologically, the first refers to the outpouring of the Spirit over the early disciples, as told in the second chapter of the book of Acts, which took place on the day of the Jewish feast of Pentecost. The second comes from the Greek word for "gift," *charisma*, and refers to the gifts of the Spirit – particularly to extraordinary gifts such as speaking in tongues, healing, and prophecy. However, in this chapter we will not use those two words interchangeably. Since the word "Pentecostal" appears in the name of many a denomination, we will use it for those parts of the movement that did become denominations or independent churches and reserve the term "Charismatic" for those, Protestant as well as Catholic, who remained in their traditional denominations but emphasized the extraordinary gifts of the Spirit. It should also be noted that there are in Latin America thousands of independent congregations that, although not having the word "Pentecostal" in their name, are in fact Pentecostal.

Although there may have been similar events at roughly the same time in various parts of the world, historians usually place the beginning of Pentecostalism at the Azusa Street Mission in Los Angeles in 1906. There had long been a history of revivalism in North American Christianity, marked by the Great Awakening toward the end of colonial times and the Second Great Awakening in the nineteenth century. Early in the twentieth century, what could well be called the Third Great Awakening began. This movement was characterized by speaking in tongues, visions of divine guidance, and an extraordinary zeal in spreading the faith. It rapidly expanded from Azusa Street to believers throughout the United States, particularly at first among people of the Wesleyan

Holiness tradition, then among Baptists, and finally among members of every other denomination. In Latin America, over the course of the next hundred years, it would radically change the total picture of Christianity.

The history of Pentecostalism in Latin America still needs more thorough research. Most of the early leaders and members of the movement left few detailed records, and not many of these have been properly compiled, classified, and studied. Furthermore, the movement resulted in hundreds of new denominations and thousands of independent churches. As a by-product that Pentecostals themselves rejected, messianic movements appeared, many of them claiming to be led by a new incarnation of Christ or the Holy Spirit. It is therefore impossible at this time to present an orderly and critical review of the origins and growth of the movement in the entire region and much less of the history of the various denominations and new religions that have resulted from it. Therefore, our goal in the present chapter will not be to give a detailed account of the history of the movement but rather to provide the reader with a wide panorama of its nature, growth, variety, and impact on religion in Latin America. We will deal first with the history of the movement in some of the areas where it is best documented, beginning with *Chile*, the first country in which Pentecostalism made a significant impact. After surveying parallel histories of the early stages of the movement in *Brazil* and *Mexico*, we will turn our attention briefly to *the Charismatic movement in other denominations* – including Roman Catholicism. Then we will deal with some of the groups that most leaders of the movement itself – as well as Catholics and traditional Protestants – considered *heterodox or questionable movements*. Finally, we will present a panoramic view of the movement as a whole in Latin America.

CHILE

Protestantism had been in Chile since the early days of independence, when the first immigrants and the first missionary (James "Diego" Thomson) arrived. By the beginning of the twentieth century, although it had attained moderate growth, it was still mostly a foreign import. The census of 1920 reported that there were fifty-four thousand Protestants in Chile, of whom seventeen thousand were foreigners and another ten thousand naturalized German immigrants. Thus, only one half of all Protestants were native Chileans. Most of these belonged to churches that were highly dependent on foreign leadership and financial support. Protestantism had entered the nation in association with liberalism, which in turn was strong mainly among the rising middle class of industrialists, merchants, and professionals. The emphasis of Protestantism on education and its work founding schools further identified it with the rational, modern mindset of the middle class and tended to alienate it from the masses. Furthermore, in its efforts to organize churches after the pattern of their mother denominations in the United States, it had often become top-heavy with bureaucracies that absorbed most of its resources.

The one denomination that was experiencing remarkable growth at the end of the nineteenth century and the beginning of the twentieth was the Methodist Church. In the ten years between 1897 and 1908, it had grown eightfold – from five hundred to four thousand members. One of the main reasons for this growth can be traced to the policies established by William Taylor in 1877, which we discussed in Chapter 9. His policy, it will be remembered, was to develop a self-supporting church by recruiting missionaries in the United States who would come to Chile and there earn their own keep – mostly by working in schools for English-speaking expatriates. It was only after 1897, twenty years after Taylor began his work, that the Board of Missions of the Methodist Episcopal Church in the United States began supporting the church in Chile with funds and missionaries. In the United States, Taylor's recruitment of missionaries had been most successful among Methodists of revivalistic tendencies, many of them members of the lower classes and with relatively little education. These missionaries, like Taylor himself, were often more comfortable among the poor and uneducated than among the educated middle class. Thus, while denominations such as the Presbyterians were represented in Chile by highly educated missionaries, this was not generally the case with those recruited by Taylor or with most other Methodists. Indeed, in 1906 Presbyterian missionary Florence Smith boasted that the Presbyterian Church was far ahead of the Methodist, "among other things, in culture and education."[1] She referred specifically to Methodist pastor Willis Hoover as being close-minded and fanatical but having significant success in preaching to the poor. Leaders in other denominations expressed similar sentiments, boasting of their work as bringing Latin America into modernity and rationality – although this actually touched only a minute section of the population.

Willis Hoover had arrived at Iquique, Chile, in 1889, and in 1902 – after thirteen years serving as a pastor in various churches – was appointed to Valparaiso. All seemed to be going well – the congregation was growing and there were plans to build a new church – and in 1904 Hoover visited the United States, where he made contact with the strong revivalist movement. Then difficulties began in Valparaiso. In 1905, there was an epidemic of smallpox. In 1906, an earthquake destroyed much of the city, including the building

---

[1] Luis Orellana Urtubia, *El fuego y la nieve: historia del movimiento pentecostal en Chile: 1909–1932*, vol. 1 (Concepcion [Chile]: CEEP, 2006), 28.

where Hoover's church gathered for worship. There seemed to be no option but to meet in small groups in the homes of believers. This in turn led to the development of strong leadership among lay people who were not highly educated and whose knowledge of theology was minimal but who preached with conviction and effectiveness. A year later, the church began meeting once again as a whole, although now under a tent. In these renewed services, it became clear that the new leadership had much to contribute. The church continued growing. The congregation decided to build a place of worship with its own resources, and by 1908 it had completed what was then the largest Methodist church in Chile – with a seating capacity of a thousand people.

It was in that building, on the very eve of New Year, 1909, that the Pentecostal revival began. Hoover tells the story as follows:

> After opening the meeting there was a call to prayer, with the usual words, and it was expected that one person would lead, then another, and so on, as was our custom. But that is not what happened this time; on the contrary, all with a single voice began praying in a loud voice, as if it had been planned beforehand. It was as if a whole year's prayer had been held bottled up, and at this moment all one could do was to break the vase and spill out the contents. This noise, "as of many waters," lasted about ten or fifteen minutes, and little by little calmed down, and we arose from our knees. I think all were as surprised as the pastor [Hoover himself]; but they too, like him, knew that this was a manifestation of the Holy Spirit.[2]

The possible connections between Hoover and the Azusa Street revival are not altogether clear. There is no doubt that he knew about the emerging movement not only in the United States but also in other parts of the world, for he and his wife had contacts with similar movements in India and Norway. At any rate, the events that had begun in Valparaiso on New Year's Eve continued for months. Some people wanted to remain in prayer, and thus *vigilias* (all-night prayer sessions) were formed. Some who had committed grave sins confessed them before the congregation. Others who had been carrying grudges and feuding among themselves were publicly reconciled. Some young people would fall prone on the floor, where sometimes they would remain silent and other times would sing; but as they arose, Hoover tells us, they were different persons. And, Hoover adds, "some were taken by the Spirit to heaven, where they enjoyed marvelous visions, they flew, they ate delicious fruit, and they spoke with the Lord."[3]

---

[2] W. C. Hoover, *Historia del avivamiento pentecostal en Chile* (Valparaiso [Chile]: Excélsior, 1948), 17.
[3] Ibid., 32.

Although it does not appear to have been part of the very first experience on New Year's Eve, soon speaking in tongues (glossolalia) became common. This would happen most often during congregational singing or in prayer vigils. From the very beginning, Hoover and his associates took very seriously St. Paul's injunction that when someone speaks in unknown tongues, others should interpret. Being able to interpret tongues was as much a gift of the Spirit as was the actual speaking in tongues. In 1910, Hoover wrote a letter in which he marveled at this particular gift of interpretation. He spoke of its rhythm, so that a person would speak a phrase in an unknown tongue and then give time for another to interpret what was being said, and he compared it to the experience and the rhythm of his earlier practice of translating for visitors who did not speak Spanish. He also declared that, just as the Spirit chose those who would speak in tongues, the Spirit also chose those who would receive the gift of interpretation.

Another practice that had already existed to a limited degree in Methodism but came to full bloom in the *Iglesia Metodista Pentecostal* (Methodist Pentecostal Church) was the *testimonios* (acts of witnessing), which had an important place in Pentecostal worship. In these testimonios, people would come to the pulpit and there tell what God had done for them and in them. They would speak of experiences of forgiveness of sin, acts of reconciliation, miraculous healing, God providing for their needs, and so forth. Often connected to these testimonios were prayers for the sick and the bereaved, the imposition of hands – a practice not limited to those in official authority – and prophecies uttered by those who claimed that particular gift.

Perhaps the most surprising of all was the new zeal with which believers witnessed to their faith. They would go out and preach in the streets, inviting people to believe in Christ and often also to follow them to church. Hoover himself expressed surprise that "boys and girls and shy women would speak with a power that would overcome their hearers, sometimes even making them cry or tremble."[4]

Meanwhile, similar events were taking place miles away, in Santiago. On a Sunday morning service at the Second Methodist Church of Santiago, a woman known as Sister Elena, who claimed to have the gift of prophecy, asked the pastor for an opportunity to speak to the congregation. The pastor refused, and there were protests by some in the congregation that she should be allowed to speak. That afternoon, in one of the missions of Second Methodist, Sister Elena once again asked to speak. When the pastor again refused, she went out

[4] Ibid., 52.

to the backyard, and many followed to hear what she had to say. The pastor was furious, and a scuffle ensued in which he was cut on the scalp. Elsewhere in Santiago, as First Methodist Church prepared to celebrate its evening service, its pastor, having heard what had happened at Second Methodist, invited the police to be present to keep order. When Sister Elena sought to speak, the pastor ordered her to be silent. She would not obey him and was arrested for disorderly conduct. The result was great tension within the Methodist Church, as some people welcomed these unusual religious expressions such as Sister Elena's gift of prophecy, and others bemoaned them.

Back in Valpariso, news of what was happening there spread throughout the country, as first the local newspapers and then others with wider circulation began reporting on them. Some of the missionaries who had positions of leadership in the church became worried, in part because Methodism was being rent asunder over differences in response to this new religious fevor and in part because what was happening first in Valparaiso and then in Santiago might mar the image of the church. Word was sent to the missionary headquarters in New York. A delegation that included missionaries as well as the American consul in Valparaiso was sent to inquire on the matter. A judge who had received complaints from the church's neighbors reaffirmed the right of believers to continue their services and practices but ordered that such services should not continue past midnight. Concern abounded from all quarters.

Shortly thereafter, the Annual Conference – the governing body of the entire Methodist Church in Chile – gathered in Valparaiso. Charges of insubordination bordering on heresy were brought against Hoover. Given the venue of the Conference, precisely in the city that was his stronghold and the obvious numerical growth of the congregation under his leadership, Hoover was acquitted. However, the Conference did issue a condemnatory statement against the sort of extraordinary events that were taking place in the church of Valparaiso. Hoover resigned, but the bishop did not accept his resignation. All of this did not put an end to the matter but rather made the conflict worse. Two months later, while being visited by the Methodist district superintendent, Hoover's congregation decided that it was being treated unfairly by denominational authorities, and most of them left the Methodist Church. About five hundred Methodists left the church in Valparaiso – out of a denomination that in the entire nation did not count more that five thousand members. They invited Hoover to become their pastor, and he accepted, creating the Iglesia Metodista Pentecostal.

Events in Santiago followed a parallel route. Having heard of the rejection of Pentecostal practices by the Annual Conference, the two groups of similar leanings in the capital city decided to leave the Methodist Church.

Those who left the *Primera Iglesia Metodista* (First Methodist Church) became the *Primera Iglesia Metodista Nacional* (First National Methodist Church), and those leaving the *Segunda Iglesia Metodista* (Second Methodist Church) became the *Segunda Iglesia Metodista Nacional* (Second National Methodist Church). They then invited Hoover to be the superintendent of the nascent denomination. Hoover agreed, and the Iglesia Metodista Pentecostal became a new denomination, now with three congregations.

The name that the two dissenting churches in Santiago gave themselves, *Nacional,* is an indication that the conflict had dimensions other than the obvious matter of forms of worship or even doctrinal differences. It was also a conflict between the more recently arrived missionaries, who valued education and order and who envisioned a church following the mores of the middle class that they represented, and the emerging national leadership, joined by some of the earlier missionaries and by Hoover himself, who felt more at ease working among the impoverished masses of urban centers such as Santiago and Valparaiso. This is confirmed by events in 1910 in the Presbyterian Church in Concepcion, where a number of members collided with the missionaries and left the church, creating an independent congregation that in the following year (1911) joined the Iglesia Metodista Pentecostal.

To these nationalistic tendencies other conflicts were added. Traditional Methodism had come to emphasize doctrine, rationality, and order, while the new movement emphasized emotion, freedom, and spontaneity. The one had come to insist on the need for an educated clergy, deriving its authority in part from education; the other offered all believers the opportunity to express themselves in their own way and the possibility to attain positions of leadership. The one was designed to serve a culture of the written word; the other was best adapted to an oral society. The one had created a superstructure that weighed heavily on its mission; the other insisted that mission and witness were more important than structure, and freed itself – at least for a time – of the added burdens of a denominational bureaucracy.

There are many examples of the manner in which the new movement enabled people to attain positions of leadership. One notable, but not atypical, case is that of Manuel Umaña. He had been a lay preacher in the Methodist Church, and in 1911, after he became a Pentecostal, Hoover named him as interim pastor of the First Methodist Pentecostal Church in Santiago. By all accounts poor, ignorant, and uneducated, at first Umaña floundered in his new position. He heard a voice telling him to abandon his secular work, and for a while he and his family struggled to have enough to eat. He later told of a day when they had reached their economic limit and were despairing. While he and his wife were praying behind closed doors, they had a vision of a young man who told them that they should not worry, for God would take care of them. The young man then showed his true being as an angel. Umaña and his wife decided to trust this vision, and he continued devoting himself entirely to the church. After that time, conditions improved so rapidly that a year later the journal *Chile Pentecostal* commented: "It is admirable that a congregation of poor people is able to give such a large amount of money, particularly in these difficult times. Only God's providence can work such marvels."[5] By 1928, this church was known as the *Iglesia de Jotabeche* – (Church of Jotabeche) the name of the street where it had built its sanctuary. It had thousands of members. Lay people would preach at a street corner, gather a group, and invite them to follow them to church. There are many reports of visitors in Santiago astounded to see masses of people, many of them carrying Bibles, flowing like rivers toward Jotabeche. Umaña, named as "interim" pastor in 1911, remained as the pastor of this church until he died in 1964.

The openness of the new movement to new forms of leadership was also manifested in the role of women. From the very beginning, women would give their testimonios from the pulpit to the entire congregation. They too became preachers. Many of these women were particularly active preaching in tenement houses, where they were accepted because they belonged to the same social echelons as the residents and received a respect and attention not granted to outsiders.

The Iglesia Metodista Pentecostal claims the honor of being the first independent and self-supporting Pentecostal church in the Third World. Declaring itself more truly Wesleyan than the Methodist Church, for the latter had abandoned the zeal of early Methodism in both worship and evangelism, the Iglesia Metodista Pentecostal organized itself along traditional Methodist lines. It retained infant baptism – which many of the later Pentecostal churches rejected – but, as Methodists and other Protestants in Latin America were beginning to do, rebaptized Roman Catholic converts. Following earlier Methodist tradition, Hoover took the title of "superintendent" rather than "bishop" – but he actually had more authority in the Iglesia Metodista Pentecostal than most Methodist bishops. Tithing was also strongly encouraged and became the standard practice of most members. It required not merely setting aside 10 percent of one's income for the church and works of charity but rather setting that amount aside for the church and still performing works of charity out of the remaining 90 percent.

---

[5] José Quiroga, "Santiago, Junio 9 de 1912," *Chile Pentecostal* 24 (September 1, 1912), 2, as quoted in Luis Orellana Urtubia, *El fuego y la nieve*, 53.

The movement soon resulted in the birth of a vast number of independent churches and smaller denominations – often motivated by personality conflicts. For instance, in 1911 a lay pastor of the Christian and Missionary Alliance who had earlier been a member of Second Methodist Church in Santiago left the Alliance with many of his flock and founded the *Iglesia del Señor* (Church of the Lord). After he died in 1933, this denomination split into many others – among them the *Iglesia Apostólica del Señor* (Apostolic Church of the Lord), the *Iglesia del Señor Misionera* (Missionary Church of the Lord), and the *Iglesia del Señor la Cual Ganó con Su Sangre* (Church of the Lord Which He Purchased with His Blood).

At first the Pentecostal movement grew primarily among Protestants who left their more traditional churches – sometimes in large groups – in favor of the Iglesia Metodista Pentecostal or another similar body. But soon it began drawing converts from among the nominally Catholic population in the main urban centers – a population marginalized by its poverty and seldom receiving pastoral services from the Catholic Church, which suffered from an endemic lack of priests. People heard preaching and witnessing in the streets; they noticed the joy and sense of community that seemed to pervade Pentecostal congregations; they were told of experiences with the Holy Spirit and of miracles of healing; they inquired about this unusual movement; and they joined it. Also, from the outset, the Iglesia Metodista Pentecostal would send "workers" – usually volunteers – to open places of worship in new areas. These workers would begin celebrating worship in their own homes – normally rented. When the group gathering regularly reached two or three dozen, they were formally organized into a congregation, and the worker who had founded it became its pastor – usually beginning work with little or no salary. When it outgrew the pastor's home, the new congregation would rent a space to meet. Eventually, when the need was obvious and the group could afford it, they would build a church.

In other places, the movement spread without such workers. A family would move to a new area and would begin gathering a group in their living room, or people would go to the city, become Pentecostals there, and share their faith upon returning home – sometimes requesting that a church worker be sent to them. Out of such beginnings a new congregation would emerge.

Two problems that have frequently plagued Pentecostalism – in Chile as well as elsewhere – are the constant threat and frequent reality of schism and the authoritarian attitude of some of its pastors and leaders. The Iglesia Metodista Pentecostal was not immune to this and suffered a number of schisms originating from questions of authority and leadership. Interestingly, a decade and a half after the Iglesia Metodista Pentecostal was born out of schisms in the

Methodist churches of Valparaiso and Santiago, another denomination was born out schisms in the same two cities – and in both cases such schisms were led by people questioning the authority of very strong pastors. In Valparaiso, Hoover had ordained Vicente Mendoza, whom he named his assistant, and who was left in charge of the church when Hoover was absent. After almost ten years of working with Hoover, Mendoza felt ready to suggest a reorganization of the congregation that would give other leaders greater participation. Apparently, Hoover took this as a personal assault on his authority, and he expelled Mendoza from the Iglesia Metodista Pentecostal. Mendoza was followed by a small group from the church in which he had been serving, and this group became the nucleus for a new church in the city.

Shortly thereafter, the church on Jotabeche street in Santiago also suffered a schism. Here again it was a matter of authority. A group of officers of the local church tried to organize a fund for the support of the needy within the congregation and to create a commission to manage it. Pastor Umaña took this as an attack on his authority and a lack of trust in his management of money. He expelled the six officers guilty of such disrespect, and when they left they were followed by some eighty people, who defiantly marched out of the church singing a hymn. Soon the two dissident groups, one in Valparaiso and the other in Santiago, joined to form a new denomination, the *Iglesia Evangélica de los Hermanos* (Evangelical Church of the Brethren).

Similarly, other groups were leaving the Methodist as well as other traditional churches and founding new Pentecostal denominations. For instance, in 1928 a group of former Methodists founded the *Iglesia Wesleyana Nacional* (National Wesleyan Church). Note, once again, in the very name of the church an indication of the conflict in the traditional churches between foreign missionaries and native leadership who resented their excessive power. Commenting on this and parallel cases in Brazil, historical sociologist Emilio Willems explains:

> Most schisms in the Protestant churches of Brazil and Chile seem to be directly or indirectly related to "nationalism." This term covers a variety of things, especially in connection with the activities of foreign missionaries.... It was assumed that at some point in the development of a new church the "natives" would have "matured" enough to "take over." One may expect natives and foreigners to disagree sometimes about *when* exactly church development had reached the point of maturation.[6]

---

[6] Emilio Willems, *Followers of the New Faith: Culture Change and the Rise of Protestantism in Brazil and Chile* (Nashville, TN: Vanderbilt University Press, 1967), 104.

The existence of an increasingly confusing number of new denominations and independent congregations was a matter of concern for many Pentecostals, but there seemed to be little that could be done to remedy the situation. In 1932, a number of those most concerned with the existing divisions sought to remedy them by creating the *Misión Evangélica Nacional* (National Evangelical Mission), bringing together people from the *Iglesia Evangélica Pentecostal* (Evangelical Pentecostal Church), the Iglesia del Señor, the Iglesia Evangélica de los Hermanos, and the Iglesia Wesleyana Nacional, as well as from several other Pentecostal groups. They were also joined by Methodists and some Presbyterians who were ready to become Pentecostals. The hope of the Misión Evangélica Nacional was to unite all these denominations, thus presenting a common witness, avoiding duplication and competition, and becoming more effective in their ministry. However, the eventual result was that the Misión Evangélica Nacional simply became one more denomination among many.

By the beginning of the twenty-first century, 36 percent of all Chileans were affiliated with Pentecostal churches, either as members or as adherents.[7]

BRAZIL

The early history of Pentecostalism in Brazil parallels what we have seen in Chile. Its founder was Luigi Francescon, an Italian immigrant to the United States. He and his wife, Rosina Balzano, were living in Chicago, where they began attending a church profoundly influenced by the Azusa Street revival. There Rosina suddenly had the experience of being "baptized in the Holy Spirit," and Luigi's similar experience followed a month later. Shortly thereafter, Francescon was convinced that the Lord had commanded him to abandon his employment and travel to South America as a witness to Jesus, particularly among the Italian immigrant community in that continent. He arrived at Buenos Aires in 1909 and a few months later moved on to São Paulo, which would become the center for his missionary work. There he contacted the Presbyterian Church and for a while worked within it. When he began speaking in tongues and inviting others to seek the baptism of the Holy Spirit, he was expelled from the Presbyterian Church. He took with him a dissident group that decided to abandon the Presbyterian Church and with them and others recruited from other churches – Methodist, Baptists, and

---

[7] David B. Barrett et al., *World Christian Encyplopedia: A Comparative Survey of Churches and Religions in the Modern World* (Oxford: Oxford University Press, 2001), 1 :186. Other statistical data in the present chapter are taken from this source.

Catholics – founded the *Congregacāo Cristā no Brasil* (Christian Congregation in Brazil). After its first generation, the new denomination grew explosively. Between 1952 and 1996 it baptized more than 2.34 million people – although not all remained members of the church. In its own annual publication for 1998, the Congregacāo Cristā no Brasil reported that it was present in 3,996 towns and that it had a total of 12,132 "houses of prayer" – as the denomination called its church buildings. As is the case with most other Pentecostal churches in Latin America, this growth was mostly urban.

The Congregacāo Cristā no Brasil had no ordained or salaried ministers. Francescon himself did not move to Brazil but continued living with his wife in Chicago and traveling regularly to Brazil. The denomination was governed by a team of elders and deacons – all volunteers. The tithe was expected of all its members, but at the same time the church insisted that this was a matter for the conscience of believers. Therefore, it instructed its members not to present their contributions by check but only in cash, so no one would know how much other members contributed. It frequently claimed that it was the only true church of Christ and therefore rejected all others – including other Pentecostal denominations.

A church whose origins illustrate the connection between early Pentecostalism in Latin America and North American denominations is the Brazilian Assemblies of God. This denomination was not founded by missionaries sent by the Assemblies in the United States but rather by independent North American missionaries whose work resulted in a national Brazilian church. This group then established contact with the Assemblies of God in the United States and took their name. As was the case with the Congregacāo Cristā no Brasil, the *Assembléias de Deus* (Assemblies of God) in Brazil have their roots in the Pentecostal movement in the North American Midwest. They too were founded by Europeans who had emigrated to the United States, joined the Pentecostal movement in the Midwest, and then received a call to go to Brazil. However, while the Congregacāo was founded by an Italian, the founders of the Assembléias were Swedes.

Fleeing poverty in Sweden, Daniel Berg arrived in the United States in 1902, when he was eighteen years old. Gunnar Vingren arrived the following year and was six years older. For a while, their careers followed different courses. Vingren studied theology and became the pastor of a Baptist church in Menominee, Michigan. Berg was much less educated and made a living by working in a store in Chicago. While visiting the First Swedish Baptist Church in Chicago, where the influence of the Azusa Street revival was marked, Vingren received the baptism of the Holy Spirit and began speaking in tongues. When he attempted to lead his church in Menominee to similar experiences, he was expelled from his post. He then took up the pastorate of another Baptist church, this time in South Bend, where he met Daniel Berg.

As Vingren and Berg later related the story of their calling to Brazil, this was entirely and mysteriously revealed to them by God. In the summer of 1910, in his kitchen in South Bend, one of the members of Vingren's church who had the gift of prophecy declared that God was calling Vingren to a great mission elsewhere. A few days later, the prophet told Berg essentially the same. The prophet did not know where their mission was, but he knew that the place was called Para, and that the two were to sail from New York on November 5. Since no one knew where Para was, Vingren and Berg went to the library and there discovered that there was a state by that name in northern Brazil. They then traveled to New York, where they learned that there was a ship, the *Clement*, leaving New York for Para on November 5! Without further arrangements, they bought two passages in steerage and arrived in Belem do Para two weeks later, with 90 dollars between the two of them and without knowing one word of Portuguese.

Rapidly learning some Portuguese, and with the help of those they found in Para who spoke English, they began their ministry. They lodged at first with the Baptist pastor of Belem, who also gave them the opportunity to speak in worship services and encouraged their efforts to learn Portuguese. But soon the pastor realized that what the two Swedes were preaching was different from what he had been taught, and he began questioning their teachings. The result was that the church divided. The two Swedes and their followers then founded the *Missão da Fé Apostólica* (Mission of the Apostolic Faith). This was in June, 1911, scarcely half a year after they had arrived at Belem with practically no resources other than their conviction that God was calling them to this mission.

At about the same time, in the United States, a number of those affected by the Azusa Street revival decided that they should come together to form a common organization. The result was the Assemblies of God, founded in 1914. In 1918, in Brazil, the Missão da Fé Apostólica decided to take the name of Assembléias de Deus and established links with the young denomination in the United States.

During the first few years, the growth of the Assembléias was relatively slow – slightly less that four hundred were baptized between 1911 and 1914. But by 1920, the Assembléias were present in every state in the north and northeast of Brazil. By 1944, they had work in every state of the nation. By 1950, they had almost a hundred thousand believers. In 1997, they hosted the Eighth World Pentecostal Conference, which seven hundred thousand attended and made an enormous impact on the nation. By the beginning of the twenty-first century, they had 14.4 million members. In total, some 47 percent of all Brazilians were affiliated with Pentecostal churches, either as members or as adherents.

MEXICO

The origins of Pentecostalism in Mexico – as in several other countries in Latin America – are obscure. In 1900, while visiting the capital of his state of Sonora, Gabriel García crossed the border into Arizona and there obtained a Bible. This he took back to his small village, Valle de Tecupeto. His wife Lucía García also read the book, and soon the entire village was gathering to read the Bible, with García functioning as their pastor. In 1907 – apparently with no connection with the Azusa Street revival – there was a great wave of glossolalia, and it is reported that almost three out of every four persons in the village spoke in tongues. This led to a revival throughout the state of Sonora, where people gathered to study Scripture and often received the gift of tongues – although they did not organize as a church. In 1918, Congregationalists from the United States began working among them but with little success, for the people in Sonora who had received the Spirit felt that the Congregationalists did not understand or share their experience. Eventually, a number of Pentecostal denominations – notably the Assemblies of God in 1933 – established contact with these scattered groups, many of whose members joined them.

Meanwhile, another Pentecostal movement was emerging that would have much greater impact in Mexico and beyond. In 1910, fleeing from the insecurity of the Mexican Revolution, Romana Carbajal de Valenzuela and her husband left her native village of Villa Aldama in the state of Chihuahua – where they had been Congregationalists – and settled in Los Angeles. Two years after their arrival in California, they joined a Mexican congregation that had grown out of the revival in the Azusa Street mission. In those years when Carbajal was living in Los Angeles, there was a strong debate among Pentecostals as to whether baptism was to be "in the name of the Father, and of the Son, and of the Holy Spirit" or simply "in the name of Jesus," as seemed to be the common practice in the book of Acts. Although later some began speaking of those who insisted on the latter formula as "unitarians," this is not quite exact, for they did not reject the divinity of the Father, the Son, and the Holy Spirit, or the distinctions among them. They simply insisted that, since in their view the early church baptized "in the name of Jesus," they should do likewise. For this reason, some preferred to refer to them as "uni-Pentecostals" rather than as "unitarian Pentecostals." At any rate, Carbajal's church in Los Angeles took the stance that baptism should be only in the name of Jesus.

In 1914, she decided she must return to Chihuahua to see if her relatives had survived the turbulent years since she had left and to bring to them the good news of what she had experienced. It was a difficult time, and many of the upheavals of the revolution were still to come. Her husband remained in Los Angeles, and from that time it was mostly she who traveled repeatedly to Mexico and is therefore credited with being the founder of the church that resulted from her work.

In Chihuahua, she learned that her extended family had indeed survived the intervening years, and she was received enthusiastically by all until she began telling them about her experience of the Holy Spirit. The family was already divided between those who had remained Catholic and those who had joined the Congregationalist Church. Now her teachings brought further division, for Catholics as well as Congregationalists rejected what she had to say. She persisted, with the result that her nephew Miguel García, together with eleven others, had the Pentecostal experience of speaking in tongues. Carbajal was convinced that this nucleus of believers should be organized as a church and returned to the United States seeking a pastor to lead them. When such a person could not be found, she decided to look in Mexico itself. She set her sights on Methodist pastor Rubén C. Ortega. She told him about the events that were taking place in Villa Aldama and invited him to baptize these new believers, but with two conditions: they were to be baptized only in the name of Jesus, and they were not to become Methodists. Ortega paid no heed to her until, in one of her insistent visits to his house, a member of the Methodist Church asked her to pray that he would receive the gift of tongues. She prayed for him in Ortega's living room, and the man immediately began speaking in tongues. This so impressed Ortega that he decided to accept Carbajal's invitation. She traveled with him to El Paso, Texas, to an African-American uni-Pentecostal church where he was baptized anew – this time only in the name of Jesus. He then returned to Chihuahua, where he served as pastor of both the church in Villa Aldama and another group that was emerging in the capital city. The denomination that was thus born is the *Iglesia Apostólica de la Fe en Cristo Jesús* (Apostolic Church of Faith in Jesus Christ) – commonly known as the *Apostólicos* (the Apostolics) and not to be confused with the "apostolic networks" discussed later in this chapter.

Ortega's ministry among the Apostólicos did not last long. His increasingly extremist religious notions led many in the church to question his authority, and he died two years after joining the church, by then clearly insane. At that point, Miguel García – Carbajal's nephew – was made pastor in Villa Aldama. Meanwhile, Carbajal had continued her mission, in both the state of

Chihuahua and the adjoining state of Sonora. There she recruited a number of former Presbyterians and Methodists, and new churches were organized.

At first, the Apostólicos continued baptizing children, as they had learned from their early Methodist, Congregationalist, and Presbyterian contacts. Eventually, through the influence of other Pentecostal churches, they came to limit baptism – always and only in the name of Jesus – to adult believers.

The early years of the new denomination were turbulent. Few of its leaders proved to be reliable. Miguel García himself, having experienced family problems, left for the United States. How the new leaders were to be chosen and validated became a matter of great confusion. Preachers of extreme doctrines and practices repeatedly divided congregations. Such was the case, for instance, of the church in Torreon, where "Saul" and "Silas" – of whom more will be said later – had an enormous impact. There was also the question of order in worship. While some insisted on speaking in tongues endlessly, others felt that some order was necessary. Eventually, an unwritten rule of practice developed. There were times when all prayed out loud, some in Spanish and some in various tongues. But after a while the loud prayers would begin to subside. If at that point someone continued speaking in tongues, the rest of the congregation would remain in reverent silence or murmuring their prayers for a few minutes. But after that the pastor would let the person speaking in tongues know that it was time to be quiet. In some churches, there was a little bell that the pastor rang to convey this message. In others, the pastor would simply begin speaking or direct the congregation to sing. In contrast to other Pentecostal churches, there was little or no effort to "interpret" what someone said in an unknown tongue.

In 1946, the Apostólicos adopted a constitution regulating the government of the church. This resulted in an organization that was highly hierarchical in both its governance – with bishops who, although elected by the church at large, had great power – and its economic order – with each level of that hierarchy (individuals, congregations, districts, and conferences) tithing to the one above it.

By the beginning of the twenty-first century – less that a hundred years after Romana Carbajal had her Pentecostal experience – the Iglesia Apostólica de la Fe en Cristo Jesús boasted more than a million members not only in Mexico but also throughout Latin America and in the United States.

While the Apostólicos were in turmoil after the loss of the first generation of leaders, other Pentecostal churches were organized, not as a result of official missions from Pentecostal churches elsewhere but simply as a result of the expanding power of the movement. A case in point is the *Iglesia Evangélica Cristiana Espiritual* (Christian Evangelical Spiritual Church), which was mostly

the result of the efforts of Scotsman Joseph Stewart. Stewart was a highly educated man who had grown up in a traditional Scottish Presbyterian family,
but in 1893 he met a group of Egyptian missionaries who were proclaiming
the baptism of the Holy Spirit and insisting on baptism only in the name
of Jesus. (The date is significant, for this was more that a decade before the
Azusa Street revival, thus showing that Pentecostalism did not have a single
origin, and that the events in Azusa Street were part of many taking place at
roughly the same time in other parts of the world.) At first these Egyptian
missionaries were allowed to preach in the Presbyterian Church, but they
were expelled when Stewart received the baptism of the Holy Spirit and began
speaking in tongues. The missionaries returned to Egypt, and Stewart went
with them, to be baptized in the Nile in the name of Jesus. He then traveled as
a missionary in Africa as well as various nations of the western hemisphere –
such as Argentina, Canada, and the United States – until he finally arrived in
Mexico in 1924. There he preached in several traditional Protestant churches –
Methodist, Baptist, and Presbyterian – but was eventually expelled from all of
them. From these churches he drew a number of followers. Apparently, the
church he founded, the Iglesia Evangélica Cristiana Espiritual, experienced
most of its earliest growth by attracting Apostólicos who were unhappy with
the chaos that reigned in their own denomination.

Early in the twenty-first century, there were in Mexico dozens of other
Pentecostal denominations as well as thousands of independent churches.
Most of the larger Pentecostal churches had not originated through the efforts
of denominations or missionary societies and boards in the United States,
but they – like the Apostólicos – were the result of the work of Mexicans who
had become involved in the Pentecostal revival and then founded their own
churches. Such were, among many others, the *Iglesia Cristiana Betel* (Bethel
Christian Church), the *Iglesia de Dios en la República Mexicana* (Church of
God in the Mexican Republic), and the *Iglesia Cristiana Interdenominacional*
(Interdenominational Christian Church). At that time, roughly 13 percent of
all Mexicans were affiliated with Pentecostal churches, either as members or
as adherents.

THE CHARISMATIC MOVEMENT IN OTHER DENOMINATIONS

It should be clear from the foregoing that much of the early growth of Pentecostalism came from divisions within the more traditional Protestant denominations. It should also be clear that as the movement grew it began drawing
increasing numbers from the nominally Catholic – although some Protestant individuals and even entire congregations continued leaving their own

denominations in order to become Pentecostals. But the impact of Pentecostalism on other denominations was not limited to drawing members from them. On the contrary, during the course of the twentieth century every major Protestant denomination, as well as the Catholic Church, was influenced by the Pentecostal movement and its practices – particularly in worship. Pentecostal worship styles were adopted by many congregations, which often led to schism within the congregation itself. Testimonios, the repetitive singing of simple choruses, speaking in tongues, several people praying aloud at the same time, the waving of hands as a sign of praise, and many other such Charismatic practices were soon found in every other major denomination in Latin America. Thus there were Methodist Charismatics, Anglican Charismatics, Presbyterian Charismatics, and the like.

Special mention should be made of Roman Catholic Charismatism. This movement originated in the United States in 1967 but soon extended into Latin America. In the United States, it worked mostly through prayer groups in which people gathered to pray, study Scripture, seek the extraordinary gifts of the Spirit, and share experiences. In Latin America, the same procedure was adopted, except that in a number of cases the Charismatic prayer groups coalesced with base ecclesial communities (CEBs, discussed in Chapter 9), thus leading to groups that were both Charismatic and very active in seeking to change the structures of society.

The Catholic Charismatic movement was viewed askance by many church authorities who feared that it would undercut the authority of the hierarchy, divide the church, and open the way for Pentecostal Protestantism. Others saw in the movement a way to revitalize the church and counter what they viewed as the Pentecostal threat in Latin America. The actual development and outcome of the movement vindicated both positions. On the one hand, Charismatic Catholics contributed significantly to the vitality of Roman Catholicism in Latin America toward the end of the twentieth century. By introducing more lively worship, with greater freedom of expression, it appealed to many young people who had abandoned the church. Charismatic parishioners made it a habit to pray for their priests, study Scripture, visit the sick, and speak of their faith to others.

On the other hand, the movement did not always remain within the bounds of acceptability for church authorities and thus gave rise to new Charismatic denominations whose members had not come from other Protestant denominations but directly from Catholic Charismatism.

The happened, for instance, in Peru, where Father Rómulo Falcón, a member of the order of Missionaries of the Sacred Heart, who had served as a priest for more than twenty-five years, joined the Charismatic movement.

Before that, he had been a very respected director of spiritual formation for seminarians in the city of Trujillo. It is reported that he had been having misgivings about his faith and had written to Rome requesting that he be relieved of his ministry. He was invited to speak in a remote village where he was surprised and even offended when a young man addressed him by his first name. But when the man said, "Rómulo, you are not a Christian," he was shaken. He then began speaking in tongues and would later declare that this was the moment of his true conversion to Christ. Although he was then invited to join the Pentecostal church, he refused, saying that he had been born a Catholic and that it would be his task to bring the experience of baptism in the Holy Spirit to the Catholic Church. This he did, organizing what he called *escuelas de servidores* – servants' schools – devoted to Bible study and service to others. For a while, he had the support of his bishop – some say, even to the point of being authorized to establish contact with Pentecostals in the United States – and in 1984 he was named National Coordinator of Catholic Charismatic Renewal. Father Falcón had been closely connected with CEBs in the mountains of Peru, and now he organized the movement he headed along similar lines.

The movement soon began to split. Some said that the experience of the Holy Spirit and the study of Scripture required that they abandon the veneration of the saints and the Virgin. They began calling themselves "Renewed Charismatics" and dubbing the others "Traditional Charismatics." For some time, Father Falcón was able to keep the movement together. But in 1984 he was called to Europe – some say to respond to accusations against him in Rome – and died while in Germany. At that point the movement divided, and some of its members became staunchly anti-Catholic – some even suggesting or implying that Father Falcón's death had not been purely natural. While the Traditional Charismatics remained in the Catholic Church, the Renewed Charismatics left it. Some joined existing Pentecostal churches, and some became an independent movement, consisting of a large number of independent Charismatic churches.

This new movement insisted that it was Charismatic, but not Pentecostal. While continuing to value the gift of speaking in tongues, they pointed out that at Pentecost this gift was for the communication of the Gospel and that therefore God gives it, not just so that believers may rejoice in it but also to call them to witness to others. They emphasized service and often referred to their leaders as "servants" – a title reminiscent of Falcón's escuelas de servidores. They also claimed that in order to receive the Spirit it was necessary to receive it from another who already had it – in which some have seen echoes of the traditional Catholic doctrine of apostolic succession. For almost two decades, this movement refused to join other churches in interdenominational activities and evolved into several groups and independent congregations, of which the best known is *Agua Viva* (Living Water), claiming to be the largest Peruvian church. In some areas, the movement also experienced significant tensions between those who sought to make it as similar as possible to other Charismatic movements, particularly in the United States, and others who emphasized its autochthonous character.

HETERODOX OR QUESTIONABLE MOVEMENTS

The freedom provided by Pentecostalism for all to become leaders, combined with the ease with which churches divided, made it possible for a number of movements to develop that many considered at least questionable and even heretical. Some of these diverged from more traditional Protestantism not so much in their doctrines as in their practices. Others turned religion into a system of obtaining from God whatever one wanted and the Gospel into a promise of prosperity for the faithful. Still others took on messianic characteristics, seeing messiahs in their leaders and even turning them into deities.

There were many such cases. In Mexico, the Apostólicos had several such occurrences. Pastor Rubén Ortega, apparently on the way to the mental disease that finally took over, declared that he was the Messiah. Shortly thereafter, while still under Manual García's leadership, the Apostólicos had to confront one of their members, Juan Rodríguez, who also claimed to be the Messiah and insisted that all true believers should accept him as such. He did develop a following, and the conflict between him and García turned into a public scandal that landed García in jail. Eventually Rodríguez's group dissolved, and Rodríguez himself emigrated to the United States.

We have already mentioned "Saul" and "Silas." In a visit to another church, the pastor of the Apostolic church in the city of Torreon met these two people who refused to divulge their names – we now know that they were Antonio Muñoz and Felipe Flores – and who declared that the Holy Spirit had ordered them to adopt their biblical names. Hearing them declare that all things were to be done in the church in strict accordance with the guidance of the Holy Spirit, this pastor invited them to come to Torreon and work with him. Soon the preaching of Saul and Silas gained widespread following among the Apostólicos. At the same time, their teachings and demands became increasingly bizarre. They would wear long robes and beards, as they were convinced the apostles did. They would not bathe, for bathing was a sign of sinful preoccupation with the body. God would reveal to them the new name – always a biblical name – by which each convert was to be known. Those who did not use such names were deemed unfaithful. They ordered that believers should live apart from the rest of society, either in villages of their own or in common houses, and that all things were to be held in common and administered by Saul and Silas themselves. They would receive revelations telling them who should marry whom and what marriages should be dissolved – often, but not always, on the grounds that they had been performed by "pagan" Catholic priests. They forbade the wearing of perfume, jewelry, makeup, and so forth. They decided that the ill should trust only in the Lord for their health and that those who went to physicians, clinics or hospitals – or even took an aspirin – were simply showing a lack of faith. Others – "Abraham," "Moses," "Barnabas," and so on – spread their teachings, always declaring that Saul and Silas were God's delegates and should be obeyed in all things.

Eventually the movement died. But some suggest that there is a connection between its remnants and the much larger *Iglesia La Luz del Mundo* (The Light of the World Church). The full name of this organization is *La Iglesia del Dios Vivo, Columna y Apoyo de la Verdad, La Luz del Mundo* (The Church of the Living God, Column and Foundation of Truth, The Light of the World). Its origins are traced to Eusebio Joaquín González, who in 1926 had a vision telling him that henceforth he would be called "Aaron" – an event with overtones of the movement of Saul and Silas. His calling was to restore primitive Christianity. When he died in 1964, he was succeeded by his son, "the Anointed," known as "Brother Samuel," or as "Samuel Joaquín," for his birth name was Joaquín. Aaron and Samuel were considered the two apostles called by God to restore Christianity, which had fallen into apostasy when the original apostles died. The high regard in which these two apostles were held may be seen in one of their hymns, which says: "Samuel Joaquín, apostle powerful in word, brings forgiveness to earth, like Christ in Galilee." One of the great feast days of the movement was August 14, the birth of Aaron. A hymn for this occasion says: "Peace to the word, Aaron is born, our King is now born, now the heart has light and his holy flock has peace." And, in another parallelism with Jesus, we are also told that when Samuel returned from a trip abroad, he entered the town driving a big white convertible, "and all the people went out to greet him with palm fronds in their hands, waving them and shouting: 'Blessed is he who comes in the name of the Lord!'."[8]

La Luz del Mundo also rejected the doctrine of the Trinity and insisted on baptism only in the name of Jesus. But, in contrast with the Iglesia Apostólica

---

[8] Ricardo Becerra and Luis C. Reyes, "La Luz del Mundo," http://www.sectas.org/articulos/luzdelmundo.html.

discussed previously, they rejected the very notion of the eternal divinity of Jesus. It was at his baptism that he became Christ and therefore divine. In order to be saved, one had to be baptized in the name of Jesus only, and this had to be done in the church La Luz del Mundo, for all others were false, and there was no salvation in them.

Members of La Luz del Mundo were told to lead austere lives. Women were not to wear pants or makeup. In church, they had to sit to one side, and men to the other – a common practice in several Pentecostal churches. Men could not wear long hair, and women could not trim theirs. Worship included no musical instruments, for they were seen as an abomination unto God.

Part of the attraction of La Luz del Mundo was in its social services, for it lent significant support to its members by both direct assistance and the development of cooperatives. By 1992, this movement, with headquarters in the city of Guadalajara, claimed to have two hundred thousand followers in Mexico and a total of more than one million throughout the world.

Another movement that has enjoyed explosive growth is the *Igreja Universal do Reino de Deus* (Universal Church of the Kingdom of God), often known as "Stop Suffering," for this is the sign and invitation that marks its places of worship, literature, and media programs. It was founded in 1977 by Edir Macedo, who rented a warehouse in Rio for its first gatherings. The main characteristic of this movement is its insistence that – as its official website declares – "Prosperity is a promise of God and must be part of the life of all who are faithful and act in agreement with Holy Scripture."[9] Since one of the things that Scripture commands is tithes and offerings to God, one of the reasons why people do not prosper is that they do not give to God what is God's due. Thus, a common theme in the preaching of Stop Suffering is "When you give freely, you will prosper," or "If you do not give, this shows that you do not love God, and therefore God does not have to solve your problems." This prosperity is not only financial success. It also involves health – God heals those who are faithful and obedient – as well as family relations, and therefore there are special days every week devoted to each of these and similar issues. One feature of the Igreja do Reino de Deus is that its worship buildings never close. People are invited to come in and pray at any time – which in Latin America has long been the tradition in Catholic but not Protestant churches.

The impact of the movement in Brazil, throughout Latin America and elsewhere, was enormous. (Some claimed that this was due in part to its use of the latest marketing and publicity techniques.) Early in the twenty-first

[9] Edir Macedo, *Igreja Universal do Reino de Deus*, http://www.igrejauniversal.org.br.

century, the Igreja Universal do Reino de Deus was present in ninety different countries, and some claimed that it was the largest international franchise based in Brazil. Macedo's fortune was estimated at one hundred million dollars, and there was talk of his thinking about running for president of Brazil – while his critics claimed that his goal was to turn the nation into a theocracy.

Another movement that was much discussed in Latin American circles was the "apostolic networks." The origins of this movement are not completely clear. Some trace it to Chicago in 1995, when Apostle John Eckhardt founded International Ministries of Prophetic and Apostolic Churches Together (IMPACT). Others place its roots in Latin America – where more than one "apostle" claimed to have founded the network or to have been among its founders. At any rate, late in the twentieth century the movement spread throughout Latin America, causing grave concern among some of the more traditional Pentecostal churches. According to this movement, the Reformation of the sixteenth century and the revivals after that were not enough. It was necessary to restore the church to its original obedience. And this was to be done under the leadership of "apostles" – people whom God had anointed for this task. This meant that the apostles and their followers should expect to be rejected by people and churches who do not have this vision. The apostles were, according to one of the leaders of the movement, "men who are true reformers . . . who with authority stand in the face of the power of religion and witchcraft within the church. They are those who break the spirit of Jezebel that supports the patterns and structures of power within the church."[10]

While using similar terminology, the numerous variations of this movement did not all agree among themselves. Their common theme, however, was that in the latter days God was raising new apostles for the "restoration, renewal, and restitution" of the church. These apostles were supposed to support each other. Some of them – the "vertical" apostles – would have a hierarchical function of supervision and guidance. Others – the "horizontal" apostles – were called to invite new members into the network. To be valid, a church or a ministry must be "under apostolic cover." Thus, those denominations, churches, ministry programs, or individuals who refused to be part of the movement and who therefore were not under apostolic cover were part of the old church – the Church of Jezebel – and were resisting the reformation that God was bringing about through the apostles.

In some branches of the apostolic networks, although not as much as in the Igreja Universal do Reino de Deus, there was also a measure of emphasis on

---

[10] Alianza Cristiana y Misionera, Foro Cristiano Evangélico Ekklesia Viva, http://www.foroekklesia.com/showthread.php?s=&threadid=7385&goto=nextnewest.

prosperity – and particularly a promise of success for ministers who placed themselves under apostolic cover. Thus, one of the leaders of the movement, when inviting pastors to place themselves under apostolic covering, boasted that before he became an apostle he used to "preach fifteen days in exchange for a bunch of bananas";[11] but not any more. Finally, these was also in the movement a triumphalistic and even theocratic emphasis, announcing that under the leadership of the apostolic networks, "the nations will come and worship, praise and serve the eternal God under the cover, submission and obedience to the body of Christ which is the church."[12]

The messianic tendencies that we have seen in movements such as La Luz del Mundo were also evident in a number of other similar movements. In 1942 in Puerto Rico, Pentecostal preacher Juana García began proclaiming that she represented "the fullness of the Spirit." Soon she became known as *la diosa Mita* (goddess Mita) – a title she accepted. With her, a new dispensation of the Spirit had begun – following the earlier dispensations of the Father in the Old Testament and then of the Son. Under her guidance, there was an apostolic college led by "Aaron," Mita's adopted son. The movement spread rapidly among the poor, particularly since it was also a system of support and sharing among them. Believers would give all their possessions and salaries to Mita, and this was invested so as to benefit the body of believers. Thus, the movement soon owned apartment buildings, laundries, bakeries, carpentry shops, and the like, where it employed its own members – who in turn put their income at the disposal of the movement. From Puerto Rico, the cult of Mita extended to the Dominican Republic and – to a much lesser measure – elsewhere. Mita died in 1970. Her mausoleum became a place of pilgrimage, and Aaron became the leader of the movement.

Along similar lines, Puerto Rican José Luis de Jesús Miranda, a former heroin addict who had served time in prison, founded the movement *Creciendo en Gracia* (Growing in Grace). With his headquarters in Miami, Miranda claimed that he was the second coming of Jesus Christ, and that therefore he could not die. His message was essentially one of absolute forgiveness. He would say, "There is no sin. It was taken out. My Father, who lives in me, said so." According to Miranda, not only the popes but also St. Peter deceived humankind with a lie that has lasted two thousand years, until he came to set the record straight. His disciples would praise him by explaining: "We were

---

[11] Roni Chávez, *Moviéndonos en lo Apostólico*, http://atalayasenaccion.net/estudios%20atalayas/Apostoles/MOVIENDONOS%20EN%20LO%20APOSTOLICO.doc.

[12] Centro Apostólico y Profético, *Bajo cobertura "apostolica* [sic] *y profética*," http://www.geoscopio.net.

angels with God that came to this earth to have a physical experience and he has taught us that we are perfect." Criticized for the size of his security corps – larger than those of many heads of state – he replied, "I will be the president of the biggest government the Earth has ever experienced."[13]

Needless to say, Miranda's teachings and claims were rejected by all other Christian bodies – Catholic as well as Protestant. Even so, he was said to have built an empire of several million dollars, and at the beginning of the twenty-first century Creciendo en Gracia had three hundred congregations throughout the world.

CONCLUSION

The impact of Pentecostalism and Charismatism on Latin American Christianity – even in those churches that do not consider themselves Pentecostal or Charismatic – is undeniable. Protestantism, which at the beginning of the twentieth century was a statistically negligible minority in most Latin American countries – the main exception being those countries where there had been large contingents of Protestant immigrants – by the end of that century had become an important presence in every country. Out of a total population in Latin America of 520 million, 170 million called themselves Pentecostals, Charismatics, or members of independent – usually Pentecostal – churches.

As has been shown in the preceding pages, Pentecostalism took many different forms. For that reason, it is difficult to characterize the movement as a whole. There are, however, some general statements one can make, if not about the entire movement, at least about significant sectors of it. The first such statement has to do with the development of Pentecostalism as a whole. Historian Carmelo Alvarez, who has worked among Pentecostals in Latin America for years, says that there are three main periods in the history of Latin American Pentecostalism: (1) 1909–1929. These years mark the beginnings, first within Latin America itself and very soon as the result also of missionaries from Pentecostal churches elsewhere. (2) 1930–1960. These were years of stabilization and organization, seeking to establish the character of the movement, developing systems of government and rules for them, and clarifying points of doctrine. (3) 1960–present. The time after 1960 was marked by explosive growth of the larger bodies and by the multiplication of independent churches and small denominations. It was also the time of the rise

---

[13] José Luis de Jesús Miranda, *Creciendo en Gracia*, http:/www.creciendoengracia.com.

of what Alvarez calls "heretical Pentecostal movements," as well as of a new emphasis on prosperity, success, and healing.

Second, in most cases Pentecostalism grew first among the urban poor then in small towns and rural areas. Finally, having reached its second and third generations, it began making inroads into the middle class. In 1968, sociologist Christian Lalive d'Epinay described Pentecostalism in Chile as "the haven of the masses." He saw that the movement was growing mostly among the disinherited and uprooted urban masses, and he pointed to its otherworldly emphasis as one of its main characteristics. Later, others have argued that non-Pentecostal Charismatism is the middle-class counterpart to Pentecostalism. By the end of the twentieth century, there were Pentecostal colleges, universities, and seminaries where a new middle class with Pentecostal roots was being educated.

Third, in spite of its otherwordly emphases, as Pentecostalism matured it became increasingly involved in social services and the development of cooperatives and other means to help the poor. Also, as their numbers grew, Pentecostals became more involved in politics – to the point that by 1982 a leader of the Pentecostal *Iglesia del Verbo* (Church of the Word), Efraín Ríos Montt, overthrew the government of Guatemala and ruled the country with an iron hand. In several countries, politicians had begun to seek their votes, and there was much discussion among the Pentecostal leadership as to what criteria Christians should follow when deciding how to cast their ballots.

Fourth, even though many Pentecostals insisted on the long-standing tradition of excluding women from positions of leadership, several denominations and independent churches moved far ahead of both Catholicism and traditional Protestantism in the roles they assigned to women. As we have seen, women played important roles in the founding of several denominations. The very principle, that the Spirit is free to choose those on whom the gifts are to be bestowed, did much to overcome prejudice against women in positions of leadership.

Fifth, it must be noted that some sociologists and historians of religion see a connection between Pentecostalism and traditional Latin American religiosity. Thus, the emphasis on spirit possession, and the manner in which this is manifested, is similar to ancient African practices and beliefs. The same is true of worship involving rhythmic movements of the body and repetitive phrases. In the appeal to religion and its practitioners for physical healing, and in the rites connected with this, some see much that is reminiscent of the ancient native healers. And the emphasis on prosperity and bargaining with God that is present in many fringe groups brings to mind the old Latin American Catholic tradition of making promises to the saints and bargaining with them. Finally, the traditional themes of ex-votos and retablos are often repeated in Pentecostal testimonios.

In the sixth place, there has been in Pentecostalism a strong propensity for groups and churches to divide. Very few denominations have avoided major schisms. Independent churches split when leaders arose who did not agree with the pastor's views – or whom the pastor simply saw as a threat. Thus, the total picture of Pentecostalism in Latin America included a few very large denominations as well as tens of thousands of independent churches and minor denominations.

In the seventh place, it is clear that the same lack of structures that led to divisions within Pentecostal churches also made it possible for movements to arise within Pentecostalism that the more established Pentecostal churches considered heretical or at least questionable – the goddess Mita, the Igreja Universal do Reino de Deus, La Luz del Mundo, the prosperity movement, apostolic networks, and many others.

Finally, there was often a very strong note of triumphalism among Pentecostals. Many spoke of the day Latin America would become "Christian" and seemed to take for granted that this would necessarily produce a better social order. Some even spoke in terms of establishing theocratic systems of government – which was one of the reasons why many Pentecostals in Guatemala welcomed and supported Ríos Montt, in spite of the many atrocities of his government.

In consequence of all this – and particularly of the explosive growth of the movement – at the beginning of the twenty-first century many were asking what would be the future shape of Christianity in Latin America. Would Pentecostalism become indeed the religion of the majority, as some Roman Catholic authorities feared? How would – and how should – the Catholic Church and the more traditional Protestant churches respond to the new situation? What changes were required of them? What would be their contribution to the future of the continent? What would be the future of Pentecostalism?

11

∾

By Way of Conclusion

The history of Christianity in Latin America – much as the history of Christianity in any other part of the world – defies simple categories, rigid periodization, or easy explanations. It is filled with seeming contradictions and perplexing developments, yet always has the energy and passion of any creation process. In this history, we can recognize transformations brought *by* Christianity to the Americas and others brought *to* Christianity by the Americas. We can see the changes within Christianity unfold as this region of the world struggled for its own identity. And we can witness the power of faith expressions emanating to the rest of the world from the crucible of the western hemisphere. But most of us cannot remain unaffected by Latin American Christianity.

As we come to the end of this rapid survey of the history of Christianity in Latin America, a *final overview* is in order, as well as a brief discussion of the *challenges* facing Latin American Christianity early in the twenty-first century and a brief word on the *impact* of this Christianity on the rest of the world.

FINAL OVERVIEW

As one looks back at the five hundred years of Latin American Christianity, one is struck first by its complexity. The form of Christianity that was brought to these lands from the Iberian Peninsula was in itself multilayered – from the simple faith of people going on pilgrimages to Santiago or appealing to the saints for crops and health, to the sophisticated debates at such places as the University of Salamanca, and all combined with a significant dose of nationalism. This Christianity was then preached to and imposed on a wide variety of indigenous peoples and their religions – some of them representing "great religious traditions" and some not. Then slaves were brought from Africa, and these slaves in turn brought their religious traditions with them. Later, Protestant immigrants and missionaries – and then the Pentecostal revival – added to the complexity of the picture. There were also influences from French positivism and from Kardecian Spiritism. These various religious layers produced different combinations – from the rigidly orthodox inquisitors and their supporters to those whose Catholic saints were in fact modified versions of ancient American and African deities, and including a wide variety of messianic movements.

Second, and as one more aspect of its complexity, Christianity in Latin America was often ambivalent on matters of justice, freedom, and the social order. This had much to do with the patronato real, which made the church leadership an arm of royal policies – policies that often conflicted with the convictions of some Christians. The result was what we have called the "two faces" of Christianity in Latin America. On one side were the conquistadors and those who helped them justify their atrocities with religious sanction. Against them stood Las Casas and many others who insisted that Christian faith required a different and more just behavior. When slaves were brought from Africa, these two faces appeared again – one in the slave traders, the slave holders, and most of their pastors, and the other in people such as Pedro Claver. At the time of the struggle for independence, while most of the religious hierarchy remained loyal to the crown, there were also a number of priests who played important roles in that struggle – and most of the leaders of the rebellion, while remaining faithful Catholics, also resisted and disobeyed the official directives of the church. Even with the coming of Pentecostalism, there were still two faces present. On the one hand, there were many in the movement who were led away from social consciousness and action; but on the other hand, there were also many Pentecostals – individuals as well as churches – whose contact with the impoverished led them to significant social service and action.

Third, throughout its history Latin American Catholicism has lacked sufficient clerical leadership. Already at the time of the conquest, missionaries reported baptizing hundreds of thousands, obviously with little or no pastoral guidance or supervision. Strictures against the ordination of Indians, Blacks, mulattoes, and mestizos did not help matters. The struggles for independence and the resulting tensions with loyalist bishops and with the Holy See itself worsened this situation and also undermined the authority of priests among the people.

Fourth, one result of this lack of priests was the development of a church that, at the popular level, was often led by laity. Since the mass could be celebrated only by a priest, lay-led alternative services, such as the public recitation of the rosary, became the most common form of worship for many. This further eroded the authority of the priesthood as well as decreased the number of young men willing to consider it as their vocation, which in turn tended to aggravate the lack of priests.

Fifth, the lack of priests and their waning authority made it possible for women to have significant roles of leadership, if not in the institutional church certainly in the religious life of the people. The story of Sor Juana Inés de la Cruz is significant in this regard, as she persisted in her intellectual pursuits in spite of the opposition of the leadership of the church. Santa Rosa of Lima and others eventually acknowledged as saints by the Catholic Church led their profound devotional lives in relative independence from the established monastic norms. It was at the grassroots, however, that the presence and impact of women were felt most strongly. The task of transmitting the faith from one generation to another has always fallen mostly to women; but in a church lacking male personnel for its traditional catechetical functions, this feminine contribution was both expanded and recognized. Within Protestantism – and particularly within Pentecostalism – while many denominations frowned on women in positions of leadership, others had women pastors and even women founders. Early in the twenty-first century, as the matter of the ordination of women was debated in the worldwide Roman Catholic Church, there were many women and men in Latin America who argued in favor of the ordination of women. (It is interesting to note, however, that while in other lands the most common argument was that women must have the same rights as men, in Latin America the most common argument was that the people have the right to ministry, and that if the Holy Spirit calls women to provide such ministry, the hierarchy has no authority to impede the Spirit. Perhaps this is the result of both the chronic lack of priests to serve the people and the emphasis on the Holy Spirit of Pentecostals .)

In the sixth place, there is no doubt that throughout most of its history Christianity in Latin America has been strongly dependent on the outside. During the period of colonial rule, and partly as a result of the Spanish patronato and the Portuguese padroado, Spain and Portugal provided all ecclesiastical leadership. Although a number of seminaries were founded quite early, these received most of their faculty from the Iberian Peninsula, and most of their students were either European-born or criollos. Additionally, the founding of convents, monasteries, dioceses, and parishes was regulated by colonial authorities. Although there was a printing press in Mexico quite early in the sixteenth century, throughout colonial history most theological and devotional books were imported from Europe. When Protestant missionaries arrived, with very few exceptions they founded churches that were patterned after the North American or European counterparts and that therefore were not able to support themselves. In Protestant seminaries most books were in English or German, or were translations from those languages. To a large degree, it was the Pentecostals who were first able to develop churches that were self-sustaining, self-governing, and self-propagating. And, in the field of theology, liberation theology was the first genuinely Latin American expression and interpretation of Christian faith.

Seventh, one must mention the vitality of Latin American Christianity. All the examples of diversity mentioned previously, from traditional expressions of the faith to the most bizarre messianic movements, are signs and results of that vitality. Once established on Latin American soil, Christianity could not be retained within the confines of its orthodox forms or its traditional institutional structures. People – natives, criollos, Blacks, Whites, men, women, children, mystics, reformers, heretics, Catholics, traditional Protestants, Pentecostals – expressed and lived their faith in their own particular ways. While this certainly produced confusion and conflict, it was also a sign of vitality that late in the twentieth century and early in the twenty-first manifested itself in such disparate ways as the development of liberation theology and Pentecostal worldwide missions.

Finally, a thread that runs throughout the entire history of Christianity in Latin America is the need for constant change. From its earliest days in the western hemisphere, the church has had to adapt to the realities it encountered in the Americas. There was no time at which the place of the church in society or the form of religious expression was static. From priests learning indigenous languages to parishioners speaking in tongues, from believers who were passive recipients of Christian teachings to those who were militant Catholics seeking to transform nations, from being a co-conqueror with the crowns of Iberia to being repressed by liberal national governments, and from being master to being servant, the church was and is constantly forced to find new ways to exist within the Americas.

CHALLENGES

The challenges before Latin American Christianity in the early years of the twenty-first century are many. Foremost is the question of the degree to which this Christianity will be able to harness its vitality so that it may have a positive impact on Latin American society. The tensions within Roman Catholicism – its perennial "two faces" – and the divisions within Protestantism hinder the influence of both on society at large. The remnants of the political polarization of the 1960s and 1970s must still be overcome. The Latin American Council of Churches still counts among its members only a fraction of all the Protestant churches in Latin America – and its relations with the Roman Catholic Church are tenuous and fragile. Thus, many Christian leaders in Latin America – Catholic as well as Protestant – see the ecumenical challenge as foremost while they seek a way into the future.

Second, some in the Catholic Church would say that the presence and growth of Pentecostalism is the greatest challenge they have to face. Indeed, many would say that Latin America is in the midst of a great religious struggle that will decide whether it will remain a Catholic region. In several countries, it would seem that the Catholic Church is fighting in a rear-guard action, trying to retain what remains of its former membership and influence. Obviously, this makes the ecumenical challenge even more difficult, because it results in a tendency for Pentecostals to see Catholicism as their main enemy or rival, and for Catholics to see Pentecostalism as theirs.

Third, there is the challenge of the resurgence of ancient native religions. Early in the twentieth century, it seemed that such religions had disappeared altogether, or that at best they subsisted only as undercurrents within popular Catholic piety. By the end of that century, however, it was apparent that several of those ancient religions were enjoying a revival as part of the struggle of native peoples to recover their identity. Increasing numbers of people of native descent began shedding the Christian veneer under which their ancient religions had survived. Now ancient Mayan ruins that had been considered tourist attractions are reinstituted as places of worship. Traditional rituals are being revived in the former Inca empire. Thus, challenges that had been dormant for five hundred years have now become apparent.

Fourth, and in connection with the third, there is the question of the degree to which Christianity should incorporate elements from those ancient native – and African – religions. This is a particularly acute challenge for some Protestant churches that are seeking to shed their identity as North American or European imports and to incorporate into their life and rituals elements from their own cultural traditions. What is the place of corn, fire, dance, or the sun in Christian worship? Can these be incorporated into worship without adulterating it? Early in the twenty-first century, there are churches – for instance, the Presbyterians in Guatemala – sharply divided over such issues.

Finally, and perhaps at the other extreme of the spectrum, there is the challenge of postmodernity. Postmodern influences are apparent throughout Latin America. Yet neither Latin America nor its various forms of Christianity were ever really modern. Thus the question arises, how will this Christianity make the leap from a nonmodern world to a postmodern one? Is not having been part of modernity a hindrance, or a help, as the church seeks to move into the postmodern age?

IMPACT

Ever since Europeans "discovered" the lands that are now Latin America, the traffic of people, goods, and ideas between these lands and the rest of the world has been constant. Although it certainly was in these lands that the impact of this traffic was strongest, the rest of the world was also affected. As we pointed out in the Introduction, the "discovery" changed the diet, the world-view, and even the economy of Europe. The new world and new populations hitherto unknown to Europeans provoked lively debate in ancient theological faculties such as that in the University of Salamanca. Shortly thereafter, as the vast lands of the western hemisphere provided opportunities for agriculture, which demanded labor, slaves began to be imported from Africa; and this had a profound impact on Africa itself. Britain, France, Portugal, and Spain fought many a battle on Latin American seas, all seeking to control trade with the region. The Latin American wars of independence were closely followed by all European powers – some supporting the rebels, and some opposing them, each according to its own interests. Europeans seeking land in times of economic hardship dreamt of settling on these shores – and thousands fulfilled those dreams. As the Protestant missionary movement gained impetus, Latin America was one of the lands to which many felt called. When the ecumenical movement was in its early stages, one of the points under discussion was whether Latin America, traditionally a Roman Catholic region, should be considered mission territory – and therefore whether Protestant missions to Latin America were legitimate. In most of these chapters of its history, Latin America played a passive role. It was discovered, colonized, evangelized, exploited, developed, and debated.

One of the most significant changes that took place in Latin American Christianity during the second half of the twentieth century was that it became a protagonist of its own history. Traditional Protestant churches became autonomous. National Pentecostal churches arose and outgrew traditional Protestantism. Roman Catholic bishops joined first in national conferences and then in the region-wide CELAM. Liberation theology sought to make the Gospel more relevant to the specific conditions of Latin America, frequently critiquing much of traditional theology.

There was, however, another change that was partly a result of the one just mentioned: for the first time in its history, Latin American Christianity became an active participant in world Christianity, making its presence felt in various parts of the world. What heretofore had been mostly a one-way street – missionaries, ideas, movements coming to Latin America from elsewhere – now began flowing also in the opposite direction. Therefore, we would be remiss were we not to offer at least an outline of the impact Latin American Christianity is having beyond its traditional geographic boundaries. In this context, we must take into account three elements that together illustrate that impact. First of all, we will deal with Latin American emigration and missions connected with it, and how this is changing the shape of Christianity elsewhere – particularly in North America. In the same context, we will point to some examples of individuals and movements from Latin America that have left their mark on Christianity elsewhere. This will lead us to discuss more particularly the impact of Latin American theology on worldwide Christian theology, and of Pentecostalism on the worldwide church. And, lastly, we will offer some concluding remarks about the history and present of Christianity in Latin America and its possible future significance.

Throughout most of history – and even in prehistoric times – the territory we now call Latin America has been a land of immigration. Indeed, most of the history retold in our previous chapters has to do with such immigration – first mostly from Spain, Portugal, Africa, and then from the United Kingdom, Germany, and other regions. It was in the twentieth century that Latin America became a land of emigration – mostly to North America, but also elsewhere.

The first large contingents of Latin Americans in the United States were not the result of immigration but rather of the annexation of territory by the United States. The war with Mexico left the United States in possession of vast lands that had formerly belonged to Mexico and where a significant Spanish-speaking population remained. For most Mexicans in these territories – particularly in California, Arizona, New Mexico, and Texas – the new border was not seen as an obstacle. People continued crossing back and forth in order to visit family, to find work, and some to settle in one country or the other. It was the Mexican Revolution that heralded a change in this state of affairs. Fleeing the uncertainties and the devastation of the revolutionary process, many Mexicans crossed the border in order to settle permanently in the United States. On its part, the United States was increasingly concerned, not so much over peaceful migration into its territories – which were still underpopulated – as over the danger that the chaos of the Mexican Revolution might spill into the American Southwest. This was particularly true after Francisco (Pancho) Villa crossed the border into New Mexico in 1916. At that point, American President Woodrow Wilson sent a military expedition to capture Villa – which it was not able to do. This marked the beginning of the militarization of the border. Since that time, emigration from Mexico into the United States continued at a variable pace. When the economic disparity between the two nations decreased, so did migration. When Mexico fell into times of great economic distress, immigration into the United States increased.

Those events point to the two main reasons for emigration from Latin America to the United States – and later to Canada and elsewhere. One reason was the economic disparity between Latin America and its neighboring lands. The other was the desire to flee political chaos, violence, and insecurity. It was not always easy to distinguish between the two, for quite often economic distress and inequities led to political instability, and the latter also led to economic downturns. In the United States, politicians and others emphasized one or the other of the two explanations according to their own agendas. For instance, during the 1980s, when proxy wars were fought in Central America between the United States and the Communist block, the American government admitted those fleeing from the leftist regime of Nicaragua as people seeking political asylum, while it dubbed those from right-leaning Guatemala and El Salvador "economic refugees" – and therefore not meriting asylum.

At any rate, during the second half of the twentieth century there was a constant flow of immigrants into the United States from Latin America. At first they came from Mexico; then also from Cuba, particularly after the revolution of 1959; and then from Central America. By 2005, the Bureau of the Census of the United States counted those of Latin American descent in the United States at 37.5 million – one out of every eight inhabitants. This did not include approximately four million in Puerto Rico, and an unknown number of undocumented immigrants who would normally avoid being counted by the census. Thus, there were estimates that the total Latino or Hispanic population under the jurisdiction of the United States was close to fifty million. Even on the basis of the official figures of the Bureau of the Census, this would make the United States the fourth largest Spanish-speaking nation in the western hemisphere – after Mexico, Argentina, and perhaps Colombia.

Although the figures were not quite as dramatic, Latin Americans had also emigrated to other nations. Foremost among these was Canada, whose open policy in granting political asylum to people fleeing from Central America led significant numbers of Salvadorans and Guatemalans to settle there. By 2005, the Latino population of Canada was estimated at more than half a million, or 1.8 percent of the total population. Latin American immigrants to Canada were most numerous in Toronto and Montreal. Besides Canada, there were significant numbers of Latin America in various countries in Western Europe, the Philippines, and Australia and New Zealand.

These migrations had an impact on the religious life of the countries where Latin Americans settled – above all in the United States. In the United States, at some point in the early twenty-first century, the membership of the Roman Catholic Church became more than half Hispanic or Latino. The Virgin of Guadalupe, until 1980 seldom seen in a North American Catholic church, was now venerated in churches as far north as Alaska and as far west as Hawaii. Similarly – although to a lesser degree – the Cuban Virgen de la Caridad and the Dominican Virgen de Altagracia were present in an ever increasing number of altars. In vast sections of Appalachia that had always been almost totally Protestant, now the largest church was the Roman Catholic. Priests in those areas who had always expected to serve a small number of parishioners now found themselves pastoring largely Hispanic congregations whose understanding of Roman Catholicism did not always agree with their own. Throughout the United States, the shortage of priests became more acute, and as a result the Catholic Church began importing priests from Latin America and Spain – although these did not suffice to keep pace with the fast rate of population growth. Several dioceses began programs that would bring young men from Latin America to the United States to be trained for the priesthood. Catholic seminaries and schools of theology became increasingly bilingual, as they sought to prepare priests to serve communities where many – particularly among the elderly – spoke only Spanish.

One of the most significant steps in the response of the Catholic Church in the United States to the Hispanic presence was the establishment in 1969 of a Division for the Spanish Speaking within the offices of the National Conference of Catholic Bishops – later to become the Secretariat for Hispanic Affairs, working within both the National Conference of Catholic Bishops and the United States Catholic Conference. One of the first steps of this new office was to seek the participation of the Latino Catholic grassroots in the process of planning Catholic work among them. This was done through a series of *Encuentros Nacionales Hispanos de Pastoral* (National Hispanic Encounters on Pastoral Practice). The first of these took place in 1972, and as the second Encuentro, in 1977, was being planned, it was clear that what many of the leaders of the movement were envisioning – and what in a way had already begun – was a radical change in the life of the Catholic Church in the United States. Following the lead of what was happening in Latin America with the base ecclesial communities, the preparatory documents for that meeting developed a methodology of grassroots consultations and affirmed the hope that this process "should serve to take the historic step from a mass Church to a Church of small ecclesial communities."[1] Progressively, however, it became clear that for this change to take place it would be necessary both to adapt the CEBs to the North American reality and to develop pastoral leadership that would understand the particularities of Latin American cultures and religious

---

[1] Secretariat for Hispanic Affairs, *Proceedings of the II Encuentro Nacional Hispano de Pastoral* (Washington, D.C.; NNCB, 1977), 25.

experience. This would mean important changes in the way priests and other leaders were trained. By 1983, the National Conference of Catholic Bishops was calling for a major overhaul in Catholic theological education. They declared:

> The scarcity of Hispanic priests, religious sisters, brothers, and permanent deacons is one of the most serious problems facing the Church in the United States. There are historical reasons, among them neglect, for the unfortunate lack of Hispanic vocations. In the past, too, a major reason for the failure of many Hispanic young people to persevere in pursuing vocations has been the presence in seminaries and convents of cultural expressions, traditions, language, family relationships, and religious experiences which conflicted with their own. Today, however, we are pleased to note that these conflicts are fewer and the situation is vastly improved. . . .
>
> We also encourage seminaries to provide courses in Spanish, Hispanic culture and religiosity, and Hispanic pastoral ministry for seminarians, priests, religious, permanent deacons, and all pastoral ministers.[2]

While this declaration stressed the need for more priests and for changes in their training, what in fact was taking place was that a Catholic Church was developing in which laity would have an increasing role. Already in 1972 the first Encuentro Nacional Hispano proposed that *Institutos de Pastoral* (Institutes of Pastoral Practice) be established throughout the country. These would be bilingual and bicultural, and their main purpose was to train Hispanic laity as "pastoral agents" of the Catholic Church, although these Institutos could also serve as a resource for the "retooling" of priests and other clerics whose formation had taken place before the great influx of Latin Americans. Furthermore, these Institutos de Pastoral, while serving people in their own communities, would also include "mobile formation teams" to offer their services to other dioceses. Soon there were such Institutos in Miami, Santa Fe, Chicago, New York, Los Angeles, Columbus, and San Antonio. They had hundreds of Latino and Latina students, while the number of Latinos in seminaries and schools of theology was minimal. Thus, by the end of the twentieth century, it was clear that the Hispanic presence in the United States would radically change – and had already changed – the face of Catholicism in the United States.

The changes in Protestantism, although different, were just as dramatic as within Catholicism. In city areas that had become mostly Hispanic, large church buildings originally erected to house an English-speaking congregation now were underused and falling into disrepair, while church judicatories

---

[2] National Conference of Catholic Bishops, *The Hispanic Presence: Challenge and Commitment* (Washington, D.C.: NCCB, 1983), 17.

sought ways to use them in order to serve the new population. Many among this population, though profoundly Christian, were unchurched. They were Roman Catholics who in their own lands had had tenuous connections with the church and in the United States had none – partly because the Catholic Church lacked sufficient leadership, partly because that leadership did not really understand the concerns and experiences of the new immigrants, and partly because for many their Catholic faith was closely tied to the land and conditions they had left behind. Others were already Protestant in their countries of origin and now requested that their denomination in the United States provide ministry for them. Given such circumstances, a number of Protestant denominations undertook ministry among Hispanics. Some of these ministries were quite successful. The Southern Baptist Convention of Texas, for instance, established a goal in the 1980s of having two thousand Hispanic churches by the year 2000; and they far surpassed that goal. Most traditional Protestant denominations began work among Hispanics. Some whose membership had been otherwise dwindling found that one of their few bright spots of numeric growth was in their Hispanic congregations. By the end of the twentieth century, most major Protestant denominations had developed responses such as a general plan for Hispanic ministries, an office to support such ministries, publications in Spanish, and programs for training people specifically for Hispanic ministries.

The influence of experiences in Latin America is clearly visible in many such plans. Thus, the United Methodist Plan for Hispanic Ministries, adopted and funded by the General Conference of that denomination in 1992, stresses the need to develop "faith communities," and then describes these communities in terms that are clearly patterned after the Latin American CEBs:

> The Plan envisions that congregations or community outreach ministries, led by teams of lay missioners and clergy, will form faith communities. These faith communities take the church to the people, meeting informally in homes and other nonchurch settings.
> Faith communities will:
>
> 1. Gather regularly to worship God, study the Scriptures, pray, and seek God's will for themselves in their setting.
> 2. Promote full congregational development by sharing their faith, inviting others to follow the Lord, and seeking ways to be involved in whatever forms of ministry and advocacy for justice the Lord requires in their communities.
> 3. Understand themselves as centers for evangelism, mission action, and mission training, both at the local level and globally.

4. Understand stewardship as crucial to Christian discipleship and be encouraged to contribute financially to their own support, as well as to the total mission of the church.
5. Be organically related to existing charges [the Methodist term for congregations and pastoral appointments] (Hispanic and/or non-Hispanic) until such a time as they may develop into congregations or join other similar groups to form a new congregation.
6. Reach people for whom no congregations are accessible, or who are not reachable using conventional methods, thus representing another way of "being the church."[3]

While this plan and many others within traditional Protestantism have had remarkable success, there is no doubt that they dwindle in comparison with the growth of Pentecostalism among Hispanics in both the United States and Canada. Some Pentecostal denominations do have plans for ministry among Hispanics. Some – such as the Assemblies of God and the Church of God, Cleveland – have Hispanic districts led by Hispanic superintendents or bishops. But most of the actual growth is spontaneous, having little to do with national denominational plans, and much with the work of thousands of members – lay and clerical – witnessing to their faith and creating new churches. As in Latin America, most of these churches are not planned by a denomination or any ecclesiastical judicatory. They simple emerge. Some are the result of a few families of believers gathering to form a church. Others are the product of the work of someone who felt called to ministry, went to a new area, and began gathering a congregation. And, as in Latin America, strange messianic movements are not lacking – quite often imported from Latin America, such as the Iglesia Universal do Reino de Deus (see Chapter 10).

This leads us to an important element in migration from Latin America that is often unseen. While it is true that many people leave their country seeking economic and personal safety, it is also true that there are among such emigrants others who are leaving their country as a response to a call to mission elsewhere. We have already mentioned the policy of several Roman Catholic dioceses in the United States of looking to Latin America for clerical personnel – sometimes bringing people who are already priests and sometimes simply bringing young men to prepare for the priesthood in the United States. Several traditional Protestant denominations have followed a similar policy, inviting pastors from Latin America to serve in Hispanic churches in the United States or Canada – and even Australia and the Philippines. Some

---

[3] The United Methodist Church, *National Plan for Hispanic Ministries*, Report to General Conference, 2004, 58.

invite Latin American leadership for short visits in which they work with non-Hispanic congregations, trying to communicate to them some of the experience and the zeal of their Latin American counterparts. However, in sending missionaries from Latin America to the rest of the world, it is once again some of the Pentecostal denominations that have taken the lead. Many of these go to another country simply to serve as pastors of existing Latino congregations. But others go in order to open new churches. We have already mentioned the wide missionary network of the Apostólicos. Similarly, most large Pentecostal denominations in Latin America have created an extensive network of missionaries and "sister churches." While most of this work has centered on North America, today there are Latin American Pentecostal missionaries throughout North America as well as in Europe, the South Pacific, and several countries in Africa and Asia.

Once again, one of the most remarkable events in the life of the Christian church at large in the late twentieth and early twenty-first centuries is that Latin American Christianity has ceased being a passive recipient of mission and direction, and has become an active participant in the life of the church throughout the world.

Latin American Christianity has also contributed to the rest of the church a number of significant leaders. Among Roman Catholics, Brazilian Dom Hélder Câmara is widely recognized as one of the outstanding Christian leaders of the twentieth century. The memory of Archbishop Oscar A. Romero is revered far beyond the confines of Latin America or the Catholic Church. Among Protestants, many individuals have become recognized leaders in world Christianity. Argentinian Methodist José Míguez Bonino and Cuban Presbyterian M. Ofelia Ortega, in their respective terms as presidents of the World Council of Churches, have left their imprint on that organization. In 1985, Uruguayan Methodist Emilio Castro was elected General Secretary of the World Council of Churches, a position that he filled with distinction until his retirement in 1992. C. René Padilla, from Ecuador, has been one of the outstanding leaders of the Lausanne movement – mentioned in Chapter 8. Several Latin American authors have contributed significantly to scholarship in various theological fields – notably José Severino Croatto and Elsa Tamez, both in biblical studies.

As an example of a movement of Christian inspiration, but not a church, born within Latin American Christianity and eventually having an impact beyond that region, one may mention Alfalit, founded in Costa Rica in 1961. A movement combining literacy with basic adult education, community services, and Christian witness, in a few years Alfalit was present in every country in Latin America. It then began working in the North American Southwest, and eventually expanded into Spanish- and Portuguese-speaking

Africa – Equatorial Guinea, Mozambique, and Angola – as well as into Spain and Portugal.

However, by far the two developments in Latin America that have been most discussed, emulated, and reviled elsewhere are liberation theology and Pentecostalism – discussed previously in Chapters 9 and 10, respectively.

During the last quarter of the twentieth century, Latin American liberation theology took center stage in theological debate throughout the world. It came at a time when similar issues of justice and liberation and their theological implications were being discussed elsewhere, and it soon was a major part-ner in a dialogue including black theology in the United States, postcolonial theology in Africa and parts of Asia, *Minjung* theology in Korea, and feminist theology in all of those contexts, as well as others. The Ecumenical Association of Third World Theologians (EATWOT), which held its first assembly in Dar-es Salaam, Tanzania, in 1976, became a channel for a worldwide conversation in which Latin American theologians had an important voice. Theology, which for centuries had been translated *into* Spanish and Portuguese, was now trans-lated *from* those languages. The most prestigious universities in Europe and North America began offering courses on Latin American liberation theology, and an ever-growing number of professors included books on liberation the-ology in their bibliographies. By the beginning of the twenty-first century, no one could claim to have a grasp of theology – or other theological fields, such as biblical studies or church history – without having some understanding of Latin American liberation theology.

Like liberation theology, Latin American Pentecostalism also had an enor-mous impact throughout the Christian world – an impact that went far beyond the immigrants, missionaries, and churches mentioned previously. The explo-sive growth of Latin American Pentecostalism led to renewed discussions on the doctrine of the Holy Spirit among all Christians – not only Pentecostal, but also Roman Catholic, Orthodox, and others. It also led to a world-wide interest in the reasons for Pentecostal growth in Latin America and what it might mean for churches elsewhere. In this sense, although the two are quite different, there is a point of contact between Pentecostalism and liberation theology: both point to the changing role of Latin America within worldwide Christianity as an active protagonist in theology, in evangelism, and in the entire life of the church. And the two have much to contribute to churches in other lands and continents.

Thus, the history of Latin American Christianity, which until recently may have been an appendix or a marginal note to the history of Christianity, has become an integral part of that history, to the point that if future generations of Christians in places such as the United States are to understand their own faith and its origins, they will have to take Latin America into account.

Some Suggestions for Further Reading

Since the history of Christianity in Latin America is embedded in the entire history of the area, some surveys of Latin American history may prove useful. Among these are Peter Bakewell's *A History of Latin America: c. 1450 to the Present*, 2nd edition, (Malden, MA: Blackwell Publishing, 2004); Hubert Herring's *A History of Latin American from the Beginnings to the Present* (New York: Knopf, 1955); and Benjamin Keen and Keith Haynes's *A History of Latin America*, 7th edition (Boston: Houghton Mifflin, 2004). As reference books we recommend the multivolume *Cambridge History of Latin America*, edited by Leslie Bethell (Cambridge: Cambridge University Press, 1984–1995), and *Cambridge Encyclopedia of Latin American and the Caribbean*, edited by Simon Collier et al. (Cambridge: Cambridge University Press, 1985).

More specifically, on Latin American Christianity, two general surveys are Enrique D. Dussel's *The Church in Latin America, 1492–1992* (Tunbridge Wells [England]: Oates & Burns, 1992) and *The Conflict between Church and State in Latin America*, edited by Frederick Pike (New York: Knopf, 1964). Many significant documents illustrating religious life in Latin America through the centuries can be found in H. McKennie Goodpasture's *Cross and Sword: An Eyewitness History of Christianity in Latin America* (Maryknoll, NY: Orbis Books, 1989).

For the church during the colonial period, see Richard Greenleaf's *The Roman Catholic Church in Colonial Latin America* (New York: Knopf, 1971), William B. Taylor's *Magistrates of the Sacred: Priests and Parishioners in Eighteenth-Century Mexico* (Stanford: Stanford University Press, 1996), and John Frederick Schwaller's *The Church in Colonial Latin America* (Wilmington, DE: Scholarly Resources Books, 2000).

The materials listed here may be consulted in addition to those found in "Sources Referenced" and each chapter's notes.

On post-colonial Christianity, see Jeffrey L. Klaiber's *The Church, Dictatorships, and Democracy in Latin America* (Maryknoll, NY: Orbis Books, 1998). Also see *On Earth as it is in Heaven: Religion in Modern Latin America*, edited by Virginia Garrard-Burnett (Wilmington, DE: Scholarly Resources, 2000). For a study that focuses on the Catholic Church in the twentieth century, see Anthony James Gil's *Rendering unto Caesar: The Catholic Church and the State in Latin America* (Chicago: University of Chicago Press, 1998).

A good introduction to the cultures and religions of the preconquest peoples of the Americas is Alvin M. Jospehy Jr.'s *America in 1492: The World of the Indian Peoples before the Arrival of Columbus* (New York: Knopf, 1992). The classical discussion of the Spanish treatment of these people is Lewis Hanke's *The Spanish Struggle for Justice in the Conquest of America* (Philadelphia: University of Pennsylvania Press, 1949). A more recent and thorough study of the Spanish interpretation of the New World and how it was used to justify the conquest is Luis N. Rivera's *A Violent Evangelism: The Political and Religious Conquest of the Americas* (Louisville, KY: Westminister/John Knox Press, 1992). Leonardo Boff and Virgil Elizondo's *1492–1992: The Voice of the Victims* (London: SCM Press, 1990) is a survey of the reaction of natives and other oppressed peoples. On the indigenous peoples of Brazil, see John Hemming's *Red Gold: The Conquest of the Brazilian Indians, 1500–1760* (Cambridge, MA: Harvard University Press, 1978). The permanence and continuing influence of pre-Columbian religion has been the subject of renewed research in recent decades. A good collection of studies on this and related topics is the book edited by Guillermo Cook, *Crosscurrents in Indigenous Spirituality: Interface of Maya, Catholic, and Protestant Worldviews* (Leiden: E. J. Brill, 1997).

The actual practice of religion in Spain during the early modern period has been thoroughly studied by William Christian Jr. Among his many writings is *Local Religions in Sixteenth-Century Spain* (Princeton, NJ: Princeton University Press, 1981). Other studies include Mark D. Meyerson and Edward D. English's *Christian, Muslims, and Jews in Medieval and Early Modern Spain* (Notre Dame, IN: University of Notre Dame Press, 1999) and Helen Rawlings's *Church, Religion, and Society in Early Modern Spain* (New York: Palgrave, 2002).

The African presence in Latin America has been the topic of much of Herbert Klein's work. See his *African Slavery in Latin America and the Caribbean* (New York: Oxford University Press, 1986). More recent studies include Margaret M. Olsen's *Slavery and Salvation in Colonial Cartagena de Indias* (Gainesville: University Press of Florida, 2004) and Darién J. Davis's *Slavery and Beyond: The African Impact on Latin America and the Caribbean* (Wilmington, DE: Scholarly Resources, 1995). The presence of African religions in Latin America is discussed in Patrick Bellegarde-Smith's *Fragments of Bone: Neo-African Religions in a New World* (Urbana: University of Illinois Press, 2005). Specifically on Santería, see Miguel A. de la Torre's *Santería: The Beliefs and Rituals of a Growing Religion in America* (Grand Rapids, MI: William B. Eerdmans, 2004).

There are numerous monographs on many of the figures discussed in this book. Outstanding among them is *Las Casas: In Search of the Poor of Jesus Christ* by Gustavo Gutiérrez (Maryknoll, NY: Obris Books, 1993). The works of Las Casas himself are also available in English. See, for example, *A Short Account of the Destruction of the Indies* (London: Penguin Books, 1992). A readable account of several other outstanding figures is Stephen Clissold's *The Saints of South America* (London: Charles Knight & Co. Ltd., 1972). For information on Peter Claver, see Angel Valtierra's *Peter Claver: Saint of the Slaves* (Westminister, MD: Newman Press, 1960). A good monograph on a notable eighteenth-century missionary is Jerbert Eugene Bolton's *Rim of Christendom: A Biography of Eusebio Francisco Kino, Pacific Coast Pioneer* (Tucson: University of Arizona Press, 1984). More controversial, in the next century, is Junípero Serra. The account by his contemporary Francisco Palóu, *Life of Fray Junípero Serra*, has been published in English (Washington, D.C.: Academy of American Franciscan History, 1955). George E. Tinker's *Missionary Conquest: The Gospel and Native American Cultural Genocide* (Minneapolis, MN: Fortress Press, 1993) is much more critical of Father Serra's work. In the twentieth century, Dom Hélder Câmara and Archbishop Oscar Romero merit particular attention. On the former, see José de Brouker's, *Dom Hélder Câmara: The Violence of a Peacemaker* (Maryknoll, NY: Orbis Books, 1970). On Archbishop Oscar Romero, see Jon Sobrino's *Archbishop Romero: Memories and Reflections* (Maryknoll, NY: Obris Books, 1990). Additionally, life stories of minor figures mentioned in our narrative help provide valuable insights into the spirituality of their times. Among these is Ursula de Jesús's story as translated and edited by Nancy E. van Deusen in *The Souls of Purgatory: The Spiritual Diary of a Seventeenth-Century Afro-Peruvian Mystic, Ursula de Jesús* (Albuquerque: University of New Mexico Press, 2004). On María de San José, see *A Wild Country Out in the Garden: The Spiritual Journal of a Colonial Mexican Nun*, edited by Kathleen Ann Myers and Amanda Powell (Bloomington: Indiana University Press, 1999). David Sowell recounts the story of Miguel Perdomo Neira in *The Tale of Healer Miguel Perdomo Neira: Medicine, Ideologies, and Power in the Nineteenth-Century Andes* (Wilmington, DE: Scholarly Resources Books, 2001).

Studies on the Inquisition provide a rare glimpse into religious practices and beliefs that society at large considered deviant. Among such examinations are Nora E. Jaffary's *False Mystics: Deviant Orthodoxy in Colonial Mexico*

(Lincoln: University of Nebraska Press, 2004) and the classic by Richard E. Greenleaf, *Zumárraga and the Mexican Inquisition, 1536–1543* (Washington, D.C.: Academy of American Franciscan History, 1961).

Women, some of whom were considered deviant, have become the topic of much historical research. On monastic women, for example, see Kathleen Ann Myers's *Neither Saints nor Sinners: Writing the Lives of Women in Spanish America* (Oxford: Oxford University Press, 2003) and Kathryn Burns's *Colonial Habits: Convents and the Spiritual Economy of Cuzco, Peru* (Durham, NC: Duke University Press, 1999). On the religious life of women in general, see Asunción Lavrin's *Religious Life of Mexican Women in the XVIII Century* (Cambridge, MA: Harvard University Press, 1962). More recent reflections on women and their role in church and society may be found in Elsa Tamez's *Through Her Eyes: Women's Theology from Latin America* (Maryknoll, NY: Orbis Books, 1989) and María Pilar Aquino's *Our Cry for Life: Feminist Theology from Latin America* (Maryknoll, NY: Orbis Books, 1993).

Among the many books on the impact of Vatican II on the church in Latin America, Joseph Gremillion's *The Church and Culture since Vatican II: The Experience of North and Latin America* (Notre Dame, IN: University of Notre Dame Press, 1985) may be particularly interesting for North American readers. The Medellin documents are available in English translation: Louis Colonnese, *The Church in the Present-Day Transformation of Latin America in the Light of the Council: Second General Conference of Latin American Bishops, Bogotá, 24 August, 26 August–6 September, Colombia, 1968*, in two volumes (Bogota: General Secretariat of CELAM, 1970–1973).

The book that is generally credited with giving impetus to Latin American liberation theology is Gustavo Gutiérrez's *The Theology of Liberation: History, Politics, and Salvation* (Maryknoll, NY: Orbis Books, 1973). A good introduction to the theme is Juan Luis Segundo's *The Liberation of Theology* (Maryknoll, NY: Orbis Books, 1976). A more critical discussion is J. Andrew Kirk's *Liberation Theology: An Evangelical View from the Third World* (Atlanta, GA: John Knox Press, 1979). For more bibliographical information on the subject, see Therrin C. Dahlin et al., *The Catholic Left in Latin America: A Comprehensive Bibliography* (Boston: G.K. Hall, 1981).

There is an extensive, though dated, bibliography on Latin American Protestantism: John H. Sinclair, *Protestantism in Latin America: A Bibliographical Guide* (South Pasadena, CA: William Carey Library, 1976). José Míguez Bonino's *Faces of Latin American Protestantism* (Grand Rapids, MI: William B. Eerdmans, 1997) offers a useful typology. See also Dow Kirkpatrick's *Faith Born in the Struggle for Life: A Re-Reading of Protestant Faith in Latin American Today* (Grand Rapids, MI: William B. Eerdmans, 1988) and Virginia

Garrard-Burnett's *Rethinking Protestantism in Latin America* (Philadelphia: Temple University Press, 1993).

Two late-twentieth-century books on the growth of Protestantism are David Stoll's *Is Latin America Turning Protestant?: The Politics of Evangelical Growth* (Berkeley: University of California Press, 1990) and David Martin's *Tongues of Fire: The Explosion of Protestantism in Latin America* (Oxford: Basil Blackwell, 1990).

Pentecostalism and its relationship to the social order had been much debated. Christian Lalive d'Epinay's *Haven of the Masses: A Study of the Pentecostal Movement in Chile* (London: Lutterworth Press, 1969) is highly critical. This is nuanced by Barbara Boudewijnse et al. in *More than Opium: An Anthropological Approach to Latin American and Caribbean Pentecostal Praxis* (Landham, MD: Scarecrow Press, 1998) and by Stephen D. Glazier in his *Perspectives on Pentecostalism: Case Studies from the Caribbean and Latin America* (Washington, D.C.: University Press of America, 1980).

On the significance of Pentecostalism for other churches, particularly those of the Reformed tradition, see Benjamin F. Gutiérrez and Dennis A. Smith's *In the Power of the Spirit: The Pentecostal Challenge to Historic Churches in Latin America* (Louisville, KY: Presbyterian Church [USA], Worldwide Ministries Division, 1996).

The above suggestions are limited to materials in English. Readers who are familiar with Spanish and Portuguese will find other valuable resources. Most significant is the work of CEHILA (Comisión para el Estudio de la Historia de la Iglesia en América Latina y el Caribe), founded in 1973 under the inspiration of historian Enrique Dussel. While mostly Roman Catholic in membership, CEHILA also includes Protestant historians and is concerned with the entire history of Christianity in Latin America. It has published dozens of books and monographs, which advance our understanding of a number of areas. Two extremely useful and detailed, but dated, volumes on the history of the Catholic Church are León Lopetegui, S.J., and Félix Zubillaga, S.J., *Historia de la Iglesia en la América española desde el descubrimiento hasta comienzos del siglo XIX: México, América Central. Antillas* (Madrid: Biblioteca de Autores Cristianos, 1955) and Antonio de Egaña, S.J., *Historia de la Iglesia en la América española desde el descubrimiento hasta comienzos del siglo XIX: Hemisferio sur* (Madrid: Biblioteca de Autores Cristianos, 1956).

Sources Referenced

CHAPTER 1: FOUNDATIONS

Christian, Jr., William A. *Local Religion in Sixteenth-Century Spain.* Princeton, NJ: Princeton University Press, 1981.

Clendinnen, Inga. *Ambivalent Conquests: Maya and Spaniard in Yucatan, 1517–1570.* Cambridge: Cambridge University Press, 1987.

Elliott, J. H. *Imperial Spain: 1469–1716.* New York: St. Martin's Press, 1963.

León-Portilla, Miguel. "Those Made Worthy by Divine Sacrifice: The Faith of Ancient Mexico." In *South and Meso-American Native Spirituality: From the Cult of the Feathered Serpent to Theology of Liberation,* edited by Gary H. Gossen in collaboration with Miguel León-Portilla. New York: Crossroads Publishing Company, 1993.

Marzal, Manuel M. "Transplanted Spanish Catholicism." In *South and Meso-American Native Spirituality: From the Cult of the Feathered Serpent to Theology of Liberation,* edited by Gary H. Gossen in collaboration with Miguel León-Portilla. New York: Crossroads Publishing Company, 1993.

Redfield, Robert. "The Social Organization of Tradition." In *Peasant Society: A Reader,* edited by Jack M. Potter, May N. Díaz, and George M. Foster. Boston: Little, Brown and Co., 1967.

CHAPTER 2: THE ARRIVAL OF CHRISTIANITY

Bakewell, Peter. *A History of Latin America,* 2nd ed. Oxford: Blackwell Publishing, 2004.

Burns, Bradford, ed. *A Documentary History of Brazil.* New York: Alfred A. Knopf, 1966.

Hanke, Lewis. *The Spanish Struggle for Justice in the Conquest of America.* Philadelphia: University of Pennsylvania, 1949.

MacCormack, Sabine. *Religion in the Andes: Vision and Imagination in Early Colonial Peru.* Princeton, NJ: Princeton University Press, 1991.

Pagden, Anthony. *The Fall of Natural Man: The American Indian and the Origins of Comparative Ethnology.* Cambridge: Cambridge University Press, 1982.

Taylor, William B. "Two Shrines of the Cristo Renovado: Religion and Peasant Politics in Late Colonial Mexico." *American Historical Review* 110, no. 4 (October 2005): 945–974.

Villa-Flores, Javier. "'To Lose One's Soul': Blasphemy and Slavery in New Spain, 1596–1669." *Hispanic American Historical Review* 82, no. 3 (2002): 435–468.

CHAPTER 3: THE SHAPING OF THE FAITH

Andrien, Kenneth J. *Andean Worlds: Indigenous History, Culture, and Consciousness under Spanish Rule, 1532–1825*. Albuquerque: University of New Mexico Press, 2001.

Burns, Kathryn. *Colonial Habits: Convents and the Spiritual Economy of Cuzco, Peru*. Durham, NC: Duke University Press, 1999.

Clissold, Stephen. *The Saints of South America*. London: Charles Knight and Co. Limited, 1972.

Cushner, Nicholas P. *Farm and Factory: The Jesuits and the Development of Agrarian Capitalism in Colonial Quito, 1600–1767*. Albany: State University of New York Press, 1982.

Ganster, Paul. "Churchmen." In *Cities and Society in Colonial Latin America*, edited by Louisa Schell Hoberman and Susan Migden Socolow. Albuquerque: University of New Mexico Press, 1986.

Holler, Jacqueline. *Escogidas Plantas: Nuns and Beatas in Mexico City, 1531–1601*. Washington, D.C.: American Historical Association/Columbia University Press, Gutenberg-e, 1999.

————. "The Spiritual and Physical Ecstasies of a Sixteenth-Century *Beata*: Marina de San Miguel Confesses before the Mexican Inquisition." In *Colonial Lives: Documents on Latin American History, 1550–1850*, edited by Richard Boyer and Geoffrey Spurling. New York: Oxford University Press, 2000.

Hordes, Stanley. "The Inquisition as Economic and Political Agent: The Campaign of the Mexican Holy Office against the Crypto-Jews in the Mid-Seventeenth Century." *The Americas* 39, no. 1 (July 1882): 23–38.

Lockhart, James. *The Nahuas after the Conquest: A Social and Cultural History of the Indians of Central Mexico, Sixteenth through Eighteenth Centuries*. Stanford: Stanford University Press, 1992.

MacCormack, Sabine. *Religion in the Andes: Vision and Imagination in Early Colonial Peru*. Princeton, NJ: Princeton University Press, 1991.

Marrero, Leví. *Cuba: Economía y sociedad*. Vol. 5, *El Siglo XVII (III)*. Madrid: Editorial Playor, S.A., 1976.

Martín, Luis. *Daughters of the Conquistadores: Women of the Viceroyalty of Peru*. Dallas, TX: Southern Methodist University Press, 1983.

Myers, Kathleen Ann. *Neither Saints nor Sinners: Writing the Lives of Women in Spanish America*. Oxford: Oxford University Press, 2003.

Myscofski, Carole A. "The Magic of Brazil: Practice and Prohibition in the Early Colonial Period, 1590–1620." *History of Religions* 40, no. 2 (November 2000): 153–176.

Schwaller, John F. *The Church in Colonial Latin America*. Wilmington, DE: Scholarly Resources, 2000.

Silverblatt, Irene. "New Christians and New World Fears in Seventeenth-Century Peru." *Comparative Studies in Society and History* 42, no. 3 (July 2000): 524–546.

van Deusen, Nancy. *The Souls of Purgatory: The Spiritual Diary of a Seventeenth-Century Afro-Peruvian Mystic, Ursula de Jesús*. Albuquerque: University of New Mexico Press, 2004.

CHAPTER 4: REFORM MOVEMENTS

Alcaide, Elisa Luque. "Reformist Currents in the Spanish-American Councils of the Eighteenth Century." *The Catholic Historical Review* 91, no. 4 (October 2005): 743–760.

Arrom, Silvia Marina. *Containing the Poor: The Mexico City Poor House, 1774–1871*. Durham, NC: Duke University Press, 2000.

Bakewell, Peter. *A History of Latin America*, 2nd ed. Oxford: Blackwell Publishing, 2004.

Brown, Jonathan C. *Latin America: A Social History of the Colonial Period*. Belmont, CA: Wadsworth/Thomson, 2000.

Clune, John James. "A Cuban Convent in the Age of Enlightened Reform: The Observant Franciscan Community of Santa Clara of Havana, 1768–1808." *The Americas* 57, no. 3 (January 2001): 309–327.

Karasch, Mary. "Zumbi of Palmares: Challenging the Portuguese Colonial Order." In *The Human Tradition in Colonial Latin America*, edited by Kenneth J. Andrien. Wilmington, DE: Scholarly Resources, 2002.

Kuznesof, Elizabeth Anne. "Slavery and Childhood in Brazil (1550–1888)." In *Raising an Empire: Children in Early Modern Iberia and Colonial Latin America*, edited by Ondina E. González and Bianca Premo. Albuquerque: University of New Mexico Press, 2007.

Lynch, John. *Bourbon Spain, 1700–1808*. Oxford: Blackwell Publishers, 1989.

Mörner, Magnus. "The Expulsion of the Jesuits from Spain and Spanish America in 1767 in Light of Eighteenth-Century Regalism." *The Americas* 23, no. 2 (October 1966): 156–164.

Seed, Patricia. *To Love, Honor, and Obey in Colonial Mexico: Conflicts over Marriage Choice, 1574–1821*. Stanford: Stanford University Press, 1988.

Socolow, Susan M. "Acceptable Partners: Marriage Choice in Colonial Argentina, 1778–1810." In *Sexuality and Marriage in Colonial Latin America*, edited by Asunción Lavrin. Lincoln: University of Nebraska Press, 1989.

Taylor, William B. *Magistrates of the Sacred: Priests and Parishioners in Eighteenth-Century Mexico*. Stanford: Stanford University Press, 1996.

CHAPTER 5: THE CHURCH IN TURMOIL

Agassiz, Louis, and Elizabeth Cabot Cary Agassiz. *A Journey in Brazil*. Boston: Ticknor and Fields, 1867.

Butler, Matthew. "Keeping the Faith in Revolutionary Mexico: Clerical and Lay Resistance to Religious Persecution, East Michoacán, 1926–1929." *The Americas* 59, no. 1 (July 2002): 9–32.

Calderón de la Barca, Frances. *Life in Mexico during a Residence of Two Years in that Country*. Boston: Little, Brown and Co., 1843.

Cooney, Jerry W. "The Destruction of the Religious Orders in Paraguay, 1810–1824." *The Americas* 36, no. 2 (October 1979): 177–198.

Hahner, June E. *Women Through Women's Eyes: Latin American Women in Nineteenth-Century Travel Accounts.* Wilmington, DE: Scholarly Resources, 1998.

Knowlton, Robert. "Expropriation of Church Property in Nineteenth-Century Mexico and Colombia: A Comparison." *The Americas* 25, no. 4 (April 1969): 387–401.

Lavrin, Asunción. "Mexican Nunneries from 1835 to 1860: Their Administrative Policies and Relations with the State." *The Americas* 28, no. 3 (January 1972): 288–310.

Lynch, John. *Argentine Caudillo: Juan Manuel de Rosas.* Wilmington, DE: Scholarly Resources, 2001.

Macklin, Barbara June, and N. Ross Crumrine. "Three North Mexican Folk Saint Movements." *Comparative Studies in Society and History* 15, no. 1 (January 1973): 89–105.

Mead, Karen. "Gender, Welfare and the Catholic Church in Argentina: Conferencias de Señoras de San Vicente de Paúl, 1890–1916." *The Americas* 58, no. 1 (July 2001): 91–119.

Nava, Alex. "Teresa Urrea: Mexican Mystic, Healer, and Apocalyptic Revolutionary." *Journal of the American Academy of Religion* 73, no. 2 (June 2005): 497–519.

Román, Reinaldo L. "Spiritists versus Spirit-mongers: Julia Vázquez and the Struggle for Progress in 1920s Puerto Rico." *Centro Journal* 14, no. 2 (Fall 2002): 27–43.

Sowell, David. *The Tale of Healer Miguel Perdomo Neira: Medicine, Ideologies, and Power in the Nineteenth-Century Andes.* Wilmington, DE: Scholarly Resources, 2001.

Toussaint-Samson, Adèle. *A Parisian in Brazil.* Trans. Emma Toussaint. Boston: James H. Earle, 1891.

Winn, Peter. *Americas: The Changing Faces of Latin America and the Caribbean.* 3rd ed. Berkeley: University of California Press, 2006.

Yeager, Gertrude. "Female Apostolates and Modernization in Mid-Nineteenth Century Chile." *The Americas* 55, no. 3 (January 1999): 425–458.

CHAPTER 6: THE CHURCH'S NEW PLACE

Brown, Diana De G., and Mario Bick. "Religion, Class, and Context: Continuities and Discontinuities in Brazilian Umbanda." *American Ethnologist* 14, no. 1 (February 1987): 73–93.

Hortal, Jesús. "Instituições eclesiásticas e evangelização no Brasil." In *Missão da igreja no Brasil.* São Paulo: Edições Loyola, 1973.

Isasi-Díaz, Ada María. "Lo Cotidiano: A Key Element of Mujerista Theology." *Journal of Hispanic/Latino Theology* 10, no. 2 (August 2002): 5–17.

Klaiber, Jeffrey L. "The Catholic Lay Movement in Peru: 1867–1959." *The Americas* 40, no. 2 (October 1983): 149–170.

Levine, Robert M., and José Carlos Sebe Bom Meihy. *The Life and Death of Carolina Maria de Jesus.* Albuquerque: University of New Mexico Press, 1995.

Mallimaci, Fortunato. "La Iglesia en los regímenes populistas (1930–1959)." In *Resistencia y esperanza: Historia del pueblo cristiano en América Latina y el Caribe,* edited by Enrique Dussel. San Jose [Costa Rica]: DEI, 1995.

Pineda, Ana María. "Imágenes de Dios en el camino: Retablos, Ex-votos, Milagritos, and Murals." *Theological Studies* 65, no. 2 (June 2004): 364–379.

Portuondo Zúñiga, Olga. *La Virgen de la Caridad del Cobre: Símbolo de cubanía.* Santiago de Cuba: Editorial Oriente, 1995.

Prien, Hans-Jürgen. *La historia del cristianismo in América Latina.* Salamanca: Ediciones Sígueme, 1985.

Schoultz, Lars. "Reform and Reaction in the Colombian Catholic Church." *The Americas* 30, no. 2 (October 1973): 229–250.

Sigmund, Paul E. "Revolution, Counterrevolution, and the Catholic Church in Chile." *Annals of the American Academy of Political and Social Science* 483 (January 1985): 25–35.

Williams, Margaret Todaro. "Integralism and the Brazilian Catholic Church." *The Hispanic American Historical Review* 54, no. 3 (August 1974): 431–452.

CHAPTER 7: PROTESTANT IMMIGRATION

Alberdi, Juan Bautista. *Bases y puntos de partida para la organización política de la República Argentina.* Buenos Aires: Ediciones Estrada, 1943.

CHAPTER 9: CATHOLICISM AFTER VATICAN II

Aquino, María Pilar. *Nuestro clamor por la vida: Teología latinoamericana desde la perspectiva de la mujer.* San Jose [Costa Rica]: Editorial DEI, 1992. Translated by Dinah Livingstone under the title *Our Cry for Life: Feminist Theology from Latin America* (Maryknoll, NY: Orbis Books, 1993).

Boff, Leonardo. *Iglesia, carisma e poder: Ensayos de eclesiología militante.* Bogota: Indo-American Press Service, 1982. Translated by John Dierksmeyer under the title *Church, Charisma and Power: Liberation Theology and the Institutional Church* (New York: Crossroads Publishing Co., 1985).

Cardenal, Ernesto. *El evangelio en Solentiname.* Salamanca: Ediciones Sígueme, 1975–1977. Translated by Donald D. Walsh under the title *Gospel in Solentiname* (Maryknoll, NY: Orbis Books, 1976–1978).

Dussel, Enrique D. *Historia de la iglesia en América Latina.* 2nd ed. Barcelona: Editorial Nova Terra, 1972.

Gutiérrez, Gustavo. *En busca de los pobres de Jesucristo.* Lima: Instituto Bartolomé de las Casas-Rimac, 1992. Translated by Robert R. Barr under the title *Las Casas: In Search of the Poor of Jesus Christ* (Maryknoll, NY: Orbis Books, 1993).

_____. *Teología de la liberación: Perspectivas.* Lima: CEP, 1971. Translated by Sister Caridad Inda and John Eagleson under the title *Theology of Liberation: History, Politics, and Salvation* (Maryknoll, NY: Orbis Press, 1973).

Hennelly, Alfred T., ed. *Santo Domingo and Beyond: Documents and Commentaries from the Fourth General Conference of Latin American Bishops.* Maryknoll, NY: Orbis Books, 1993.

Lewis, Oscar. *The Children of Sánchez: Autobiography of a Mexican Family.* New York: Random House, 1961.

_____. *La Vida: A Puerto Rican Family in the Culture of Poverty–San Juan and New York.* New York: Random House, 1966.

Prien, Hans-Jürgen. *La historia del cristianismo in América Latina.* Salamanca: Ediciones Sígueme, 1985.

Sacred Congregation for the Doctrine of the Faith. *Instruction on Christian Freedom and Liberation: "The Truth Makes Us Free."* Boston: St. Paul Editions, 1986.

Segundo, Juan Luis. *Teología abierta para el laico adulto.* 5 vols. Buenos Aires: Ediciones C. Lohlé, 1968–1972. Translated by John Drury under the title *A Theology for Artisans of a New Humanity* (Maryknoll, NY: Orbis, 1973–1974).

Sobrino, Jon. *Cristología desde América Latina: Esbozo a partir del seguimiento del Jesús histórico.* Mexico City: Ediciones CRT, 1977. Translated by John Drury under the title *Christology at the Crossroads: A Latin American Approach* (Maryknoll: Orbis Books, 1978).

CHAPTER 10: PENTECOSTALISM AND AUTOCHTHONOUS MOVEMENTS

Álvarez, Carmelo E., "Panorama histórico dos pentecostalismos latino-americanos e caribenhos." In *Na força do espírito: Os pentecostais na América-Latina: Um desafio às igrejas históricas,* edited by Benjamim F. Guitérrez and Leonildo Silveira Campos. São Paulo: Asociación de Iglesias Presbiterianas y Reformadas de América Latina, 1996.

Lalive d'Epinay, Christian. *El refugio de las masas: Estudio sociológico del protestantismo chileno.* Santiago [Chile]: Editorial del Pacífico, 1968.

Index